# Elkhart County

## Interim Report

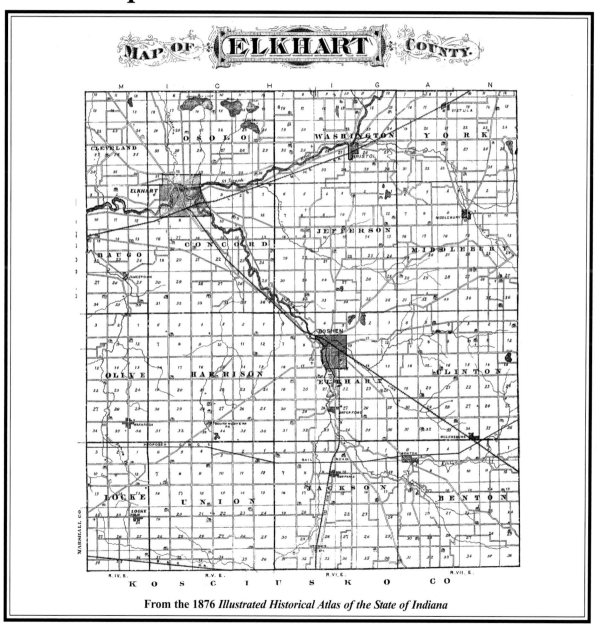

From the 1876 *Illustrated Historical Atlas of the State of Indiana*

This interim report is designed to be utilized as a working document by government agencies, local organizations, and private citizens as the basis for a wide variety of projects.

2nd Edition, Published September 2005

# Contents

# Contents

# Introduction

# Methodology

# History and Architecture

# Catalog

# Conclusion

# Bibliography

# Index & Glossary

---

**Opposite: The 1840 woolen mill at Baintertown was demolished in 1923.** *Photo courtesy of the Elkhart County Historical Museum*

---

**Cover: Horses and buggies await passengers in front of the Bristol School, c.1905. The building now houses the Elkhart County Historical Museum (06026).** *Photo courtesy of the Elkhart County Historical Museum*

Published by:

**HISTORIC LANDMARKS FOUNDATION OF INDIANA**

# Credits

### *Survey Coordinator and Architectural Historian*

Shannon Hill

### *Survey Data Coordinators*

Melanie Chastain and Jennifer Hoffman-Stonebraker

### *Field Surveyors*

Brian Beadles, Senior Surveyor; Scott Brown; Amber Chellis; and Jay Garvey

### *Layout and Typesetting*

Shannon Hill and Candy Hudziak

### *Editorial Assistant*

Candy Hudziak

### *Publication Maps*

Nancy Connor

INDIANA DEPARTMENT OF NATURAL RESOURCES

HISTORIC PRESERVATION AND ARCHAEOLOGY

# Acknowledgments

## *Indiana Department of Natural Resources*

Kyle J. Hupfer, Director,
Department of Natural Resources and
State Historic Preservation Officer

Jon C. Smith, Director,
Division of Historic Preservation and Archaeology;
Deputy State Historic Preservation Officer

Frank D. Hurdis, Jr.,
Chief of Registration and Survey,
Division of Historic Preservation and Archaeology

Steven D. Kennedy,
Chief of Grants and Administration,
Division of Historic Preservation and Archaeology

## *Historic Landmarks Foundation of Indiana*

Suzanne Stanis,
Director of Heritage Education and Information

Todd Zeiger, Northern Regional Director

# Special Thanks

In addition to those individuals and organizations directly involved in the survey and its publication, many Elkhart County residents contributed their time, knowledge, and memories to this project. Among those especially helpful were: Ervin Beck, Frank Fisher, Tina Mellott, Tammy O'Rourke, Martha M. Pickrell, and Eric Trotter.

Historical photos were provided courtesy of:
The Elkhart County Historical Museum
*Images of America, Elkhart, Indiana* and *Images of America, Around Nappanee, Hometowns of the Heritage Trail,* by Amy (Lant) Wenger
Tina Mellott
*Waterford from Then to Now* by Lowell Bechtel

Line drawings were provided courtesy of the Indiana Department of Natural Resources, Division of Historic Preservation and Archaeology.

Priority Press was responsible for the printing of this interim report.

Base maps were prepared in ArcView GIS from TIGER data provided by the United States Bureau of the Census.

# In Appreciation

This project was funded in part by a U.S. Department of the Interior, National Park Service Historic Preservation Fund grant administered by the Indiana Department of Natural Resources, Division of Historic Preservation and Archaeology.

Historic Landmarks Foundation of Indiana wishes to thank the following, whose support and sponsorship made this project possible:

Amish Acres, Elkhart County Community Foundation, Elkhart County Historical Museum, Jimtown Historical Society, and Paul Thomas

**Opposite: The Elkhart County Courthouse in Goshen, c.1913. *Photo courtesy of the Elkhart County Historical Museum***

# Introduction

COURT HOUSE, GOSHEN, IND.

# History

The Indiana Division of Historic Preservation and Archaeology (DHPA) has conducted the Indiana Historic Sites and Structures Inventory as a continuing program since 1975. Historic Landmarks Foundation of Indiana (HLFI) assisted in developing the program and has surveyed 74 of the 80 counties surveyed to date in cooperation with the DHPA.

The major impetus for a comprehensive inventory of Indiana's cultural resources came from the National Historic Preservation Act of 1966. The Act declared it the role of the federal government to foster the preservation of our cultural resources in partnership with state and local governments and the private sector. In order to implement this policy, the Act created the National Register of Historic Places, comprised of buildings, sites, structures, objects, and districts significant in American history, architecture, archaeology, engineering, and culture (see Fig. 2, p. 10 for more information). It also established a partnership between the federal government and the states, whereby each state developed a state historic preservation program to be approved by the U.S. Secretary of the Interior. To gain approval, the governor of the state must appoint a State Historic Preservation Officer (SHPO) and a State Review Board. One of the responsibilities of the SHPO is to conduct a comprehensive statewide survey of historic properties and maintain inventories of such properties for the purpose of locating, identifying, and evaluating cultural resources. Another responsibility is to ensure that historic properties are taken into consideration in planning and development through the environmental review process, known as Section 106.

Opposite: Horse-drawn carriages and pedestrians cross the Main Street Bridge in Elkhart, c.1885. *Photo courtesy of the Elkhart County Historical Museum*

# Uses of the Survey

Upon completion of any county inventory, all original survey forms, maps, and photographs are filed with the DHPA. The DHPA uses the inventory to administer state and federal programs for historic preservation, particularly the environmental review process. By examining the inventory data, DHPA staff can determine whether any historically significant properties fall within the area to be affected by a proposed project, and take steps to mitigate that impact.

The DHPA also uses the inventory in the nomination process for the National Register of Historic Places. The survey forms indicate which properties are likely to be eligible for the National Register and provide information useful in preparing nominations. When owners or other interested citizens prepare National Register applications, the DHPA uses the survey data to evaluate the property's significance relative to others that have also been recorded in the inventory and to check the completeness of the information provided.

The survey data is also used by other governmental agencies and organizations involved in project planning and development to determine if historic properties will be affected by their projects. The inventory and its summary report also boost private citizens' awareness of the cultural heritage present in their communities. Finally, the inventory provides a permanent historical record of a county's resources at a particular point in time.

Ultimately, all counties in Indiana will be surveyed to locate, identify, and evaluate cultural resources. Like historic sites and structures, archaeological sites are also being surveyed under a similar program. Together, the two programs will provide an overall view of what cultural resources are present in the state. The survey will not end with the last county, however. The DHPA will continuously supplement and update existing data as the resources grow older and change and as later structures acquire significance with time.

# Elkhart County Inventory and Interim Report

Using monies from the U.S. Department of the Interior, National Park Service, the Indiana Department of Natural Resources, Division of Historic Preservation and Archaeology, awarded a grant for the survey of Elkhart County to HLFI. HLFI gratefully acknowledges its local sponsors for their support.

Initial work on the survey began in 2003. As a result of the survey, which covered 464 square miles, the surveyors entered a total of 3,671 sites and structures into the final inventory. The original inventory forms are on file at the Division of Historic Preservation and Archaeology, 402 W. Washington Street, Room W274, Indianapolis, Ind. 46204.

Approximately 30% of the structures documented in the 1978 *Elkhart County Interim Report* do not appear in this second edition, either because they no longer exist or are changed in such a way as to be non-contributing. Conversely, roughly 90% of the entries in this second edition are new, having gained historical significance in the past three decades.

This report reflects information available at a specific point in time. DHPA calls these reports "interim" because it expects that further research will result in additions and corrections to the inventory. Those with corrections or additional information to contribute should contact the DHPA at the above address.

The evaluations and ratings expressed in this interim report represent the opinions of the surveyors and consultants involved in this survey project. The Indiana Department of Natural Resources, the Indiana State Review Board and the U.S. Department of the Interior make final decisions on the eligibility of properties for the Indiana Register of Historic Sites and Structures and the National Register of Historic Places.

# Methodology

# Selection of Counties

The Division of Historic Preservation and Archaeology takes many criteria into consideration when deciding which counties will be surveyed. It gives preference to counties in areas that have seen little or no survey activity and about which little is known. If it is known that development, particularly state- or federally-assisted activities, will soon affect a particular region, then a county there will receive priority.

The DHPA also gives special consideration to counties that are thought to have a greater-than-average number of historic resources, particularly if they are threatened. The DHPA annually assesses survey priorities, which the State Review Board changes if necessary.

# Preliminary Research

Before field documentation began in Elkhart County, preliminary research and interviews with local historians provided the surveyors with a basic orientation to the county's development. Early maps and historical accounts revealed dates of settlement, early major industries, historical transportation routes, agricultural evolution, and original town boundaries. Evaluation of this information indicated areas of the county that might contain concentrations of historic sites and structures. Surveyors drove all county roads to obtain a general assessment of existing cultural resources. They noted any building types or styles unique to the area and conducted additional research using public records, county histories, newspapers and other historical publications. They also consulted historical photographs.

# Identification and Inventory

In inventorying Elkhart County, surveyors looked for buildings, bridges, markers, outbuildings, and anything that might meet the criteria of the National Register of Historic Places (Fig. 2, p. 10). In general, they examined most structures built in or before 1963. They excluded buildings constructed after 1963 unless they were within a historic district or had outstanding architectural or historical importance. Alterations or additions obliterating the historical and architectural integrity of a building may have kept it from being included in the inventory. Buildings were not, however, excluded solely on the basis of their physical condition if their historic integrity remained intact.

Surveyors used the Indiana Historic Sites and Structures Inventory form (Fig. 1, p. 9) to record information on each structure, often speaking to the current occupant. They also took black and white photographs.

Surveyors inventoried most properties as individual entries. In instances where several structures were architecturally or historically related, surveyors recorded them together on a single form. Thus a farmhouse and its barns, or a house and its landscaped grounds, were recorded as a single entry.

In cities and towns with high densities of significant structures, surveyors defined boundaries and inventoried some areas as historic districts. Surveyors determined general boundaries by historic and/or geographic factors as well as the historic and architectural cohesiveness of the area. The DHPA considers these boundaries advisory, however, until it receives more detailed research and an applicant prepares actual nomination forms for the National Register.

Surveyors collected information on each building within a historic district's working boundaries, including those evaluated as non-contributing, on a street-by-street basis. They compiled additional research with the assistance of experts in local history, and prepared short narratives on the historical and architectural development of these areas. After the surveyors completed and verified the field work, they assigned ratings to each site.

# Criteria and Evaluation

Professional architectural historians at HLFI and DHPA evaluated the significance of each inventory entry by measuring it against the National Register criteria for evaluation (Fig. 2, p. 10). They assessed properties in terms of their historical significance, architectural merit, environment and integrity before assigning one of the rating categories (O, N, C, or NC, explained on p. 9-10).

To explain the significance of the historic sites and why they appear in the inventory, surveyors chose from a list of 29 historical themes or areas of significance that establish a context for evaluating the resources (see Fig. 1, p. 9). Surveyors checked one or more areas of significance for each resource with the exception of entries in historic districts, in which case surveyors evaluated the significance of the entire district.

# Ratings

In assessing integrity, surveyors attempted to determine how much of the original architectural fabric remained. They may have lowered a property's rating if it experienced extensive alterations, such as the application of artificial siding, removal of trim or porches, later additions, changes to windows, or structural modifications. The relocation of a building from its original site often lowered its rating. After consideration of these factors, DHPA and HLFI assigned one of the following ratings to each property.

## Outstanding (O)

The "O" rating means that the property has enough historic or architectural significance that it is already listed, or may be eligible for listing, in the National Register of Historic Places. "Outstanding" resources can be of local, state, or national importance.

## Notable (N)

The "N" rating means that the property did not quite merit an "outstanding" rating but still is above average in its importance. Further research may reveal that the property is eligible for National Register listing.

## Contributing (C)

A "C" rating means that the property met the basic inventory criterion of being pre-1964, but that it is not important enough to stand on its own as individually "outstanding" or "notable." Such resources are important to the density or continuity of an area's historic fabric. "Contributing" properties may appear in the National Register if they are part of a historic district but do not usually qualify individually.

---

1. Rating  □ O  □ N  □ C    □ n/c
2. County
3. Survey No.
4. Historic Name
5. Township
Preliminary No.
6. Address
7. City
8. Quad Name

INDIANA HISTORIC SITES AND STRUCTURES INVENTORY    State of Indiana Department of Natural Resources    State Form 16822 (R 2/2-99)

Mount Contact Prints Here

9. Common Name
10. Visible  □ Yes □ No
11. Endangered  □ Yes □ No    Explain
12. Ownership  □ Public □ Private    Owner's Address (if different)
13. Use  Present  Past
  □ □ Residence
  □ □ Commercial
  □ □ Vacant
14. Category
  □ building
  □ district
  □ site
  □ structure
  □ object
  □ landscape
15. Surveys / Legal Protections
  □ National Register
  □ State Register
  □ Hoosier Homestead
  □ National Historic Landmark
  □ Local Designation
  □ Protective Covenants
  □ Other...
16. Location Notes/Legal Description
17. Condition
  □ Excellent
  □ Good
  □ Fair
  □ Deteriorated
  □ Ruins
18. Integrity
  □ Unaltered
  □ Slightly Altered
  □ Severely Altered
  □ Moved
  Date Moved
19. Time Period(s)
20. Type/Style(s)
21. Architect/Builder

22. SPECIFY ALTERATIONS
Removals    Replacement □ Windows □ Roof □ Other...    Additions □ Siding □ Wings □ Other...    Other

23. DESCRIPTION
Stories □ 1 □ 1½ □ 2 □ 2½ □ Other...    # Bays    Foundation
Plan □ Rectangular □ T □ U □ Polygonal    Depth □ Single-pile □ Irregular/massed
  □ L □ X □ irreg. □ Other    □ Double-pile □ Other...
Walls
Roof □ Side-gable □ Front-gable □ Cross-gable □ Hip □ Pyramidal □ Mansard □ Other...
Roof material    Roof features
Porches □ 1. Front □ 2. Side □ 3. Rear
Openings (type, position, trim)
Interior
24. SITE PLAN    N
25. # Contrib. Res.
26. # Non- contrib. Res.
27. Environment

Outbuildings
□ Bank/basement barn  □ Corn crib  □ Granary  □ Machine shed  □ Schweitzer barn  □ Summer kitchen  □ Workshop
□ Blacksmith shop  □ Dairy barn  □ Grain bin  □ Midwest 3-portal barn  □ Shed  □ Tool shed  □ Other...
□ Brooder house  □ Drive-thru corncrib  □ Hog house  □ Milk house  □ Silo  □ Transverse-frame barn
□ Carriage house  □ English barn  □ Iron fence  □ Privy  □ Smokehouse  □ Wash house
□ Chicken house  □ Garage  □ Livestock barn  □ Pumphouse  □ Spring house  □ Windmill
□ Cold cellar  □ Gate  □ Log crib barn  □ Round/polygonal barn  □ Stable  □ Wood shed

28. Areas of Significance:
□ Agriculture
□ Architecture
□ Art
□ Commerce
□ Communications
□ Community Planning
□ Conservation
□ Economics
□ Education
□ Engineering
□ Entertainment/Recreation
□ Ethnic Heritage
□ Exploration/Settlement
□ Health/Medicine
□ Industry
□ Invention
□ Landscape Architecture
□ Law
□ Literature
□ Maritime History
□ Military
□ Performing Arts
□ Philosophy
□ Politics
□ Religion
□ Science
□ Social History
□ Transportation
other ____

Outbuildings
29. Historic Context(s)/Statement of Significance/Additional Description:

ATTACH NEGATIVE
ENVELOPE HERE

30. FOR STATE OFFICE USE ONLY
NR ____
SR ____
E ____
NE ____
31. UTM    1,6

□ SEE CONTINUATION SHEET
32. Information Sources
33. Surveyor    Affiliation □ HLFI □ ARCH □ Other...    Date
34. Revised by    Affiliation    Date
35. Revised by    Affiliation    Date

Fig. 1

## Non-Contributing (NC)

Properties rated "NC" are not included in the inventory unless they are located within a historic district. Such properties are usually built after 1963, are older structures that have undergone alterations and lost historic character, or are otherwise incompatible with their historical surroundings. These properties are not eligible for the National Register.

Of the 3,671 entries included in the *Elkhart County Interim Report*, DHPA and HLFI rated 159 "outstanding" and 584 "notable." Again, readers should view these ratings as advisory recommendations based on the information available to the surveyor at the time of the survey. Change in location, sensitive restoration, additional research, extensive physical damage, or inappropriate remodeling could affect the entry's significance and rating at a later date.

Fig. 2

# National Register Criteria for Evaluation

The following criteria are the National Register standards for evaluating the significance of properties. The National Park Service designed these criteria to guide states, federal agencies, the Secretary of the Interior, and others in evaluating potential entries. The quality of significance in American history, architecture, archaeology, engineering, and culture is present in districts, sites, buildings, structures, and objects that possess integrity of location, design, setting, materials, workmanship, feeling, and association, and:

A. that are associated with events that have made a significant contribution to the broad patterns of our history; or

B. that are associated with the lives of persons significant in our past; or

C. that embody the distinctive characteristics of a type, period, or method of construction, or that represent the work of a master, or that possess high artistic values, or that represent a significant and distinguishable entity whose components may lack individual distinction; or

D. that have yielded, or may be likely to yield, information important in prehistory or history.

## Criteria Considerations

Ordinarily, cemeteries, birthplaces, or graves of historical figures, properties owned by religious institutions or used for religious purposes, structures that have been moved from their original locations, reconstructed historical buildings, properties primarily commemorative in nature, and properties that have achieved significance within the past 50 years shall not be considered eligible for the National Register. However, such properties will qualify if they are integral parts of districts that do meet the criteria or if they fall within the following categories:

A. a religious property deriving primary significance from architectural or artistic distinction or historical importance; or

B. a building or structure removed from its original location but that is significant primarily for architectural value, or is the surviving structure most importantly associated with an historic person or event; or

C. a birthplace or grave of an historical figure of outstanding importance if there is no other appropriate site or building directly associated with his productive life; or

D. a cemetery that derives its primary significance from graves of transcendent importance, from age, from distinctive design features, or from association with historic events; or

E. a reconstructed building when accurately executed in a suitable environment and presented in a dignified manner as part of a restoration master plan, and when no other building or structure with the same association has survived; or

F. a property primarily commemorative in intent if design, age, tradition, or symbolic value has invested it with its own historical significance; or

G. a property achieving significance within the past 50 years if it is of exceptional importance.

# Mapping and Numbering

## Mapping

HLFI recorded all inventory entries on United States Geological Survey (USGS) 7.5 Minute Series topographical maps. The United States Department of the Interior also uses this quadrangle map series for the National Register program. Each USGS map has its own name and assigned three-digit number that is included in the survey number (see Fig. 3, p. 11, for the USGS map overlay for Elkhart County). Surveyors record the map coordinates of each entry on the inventory forms so that people can precisely locate the property on any copy of the USGS map.

A graphic artist created the smaller maps used in this publication based on TIGER data from the U.S. Bureau of the Census, adding street names and locating entries with a site dot and three-digit number. For districts or scattered sites within a community, she created more detailed maps to indicate the location of historic resources within the area.

## Inventory Number

HLFI assigns a site number to each inventory entry for filing purposes. Three orders of site location information have been incorporated into the 11-digit numbers, as seen in the example below.

| COUNTY | QUAD MAP | SITE |
|--------|----------|------|
| 039 | 656 | 60029 |

**County Number:** The first block of three digits identifies the county. The National Park Service assigned this number to identify the county for National Register nominations. The number for Elkhart County is 039.

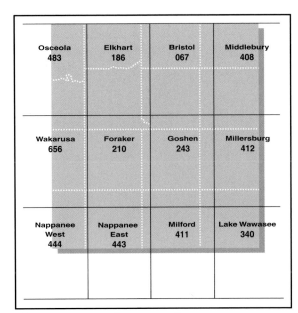

**Fig. 3 USGS Quad map overlay**

**Quad Map Number:** The second block of three digits identifies the USGS quadrangle map on which the resource is located. Based on Fig. 3, the 656 in the example refers to the Wakarusa quadrangle map.

**Site Number:** The last block of five digits forms a discrete site number. The first two digits refer to the site's township and the final three digits are its actual number.

DHPA assigns township numbers in increments of five (see Fig. 4). For example, York Township, the northeastern-most township, begins with site 00001. Washington, the next township, is 05000, Osolo is 10000, and so on. The site number 60029 refers to the 29th site in Olive Township.

Surveyors number areas of scattered sites or historic districts according to the township in which they are located. Since DHPA numbers townships in multiples of five, the scattered sites and districts take the next number up from the township

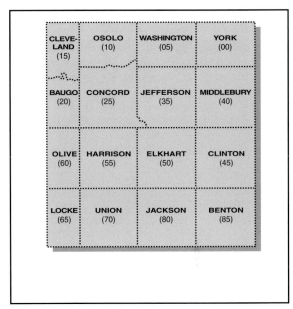

**Fig. 4 Elkhart County township numbering**

number, to a maximum of four. For example, the city of Elkhart has seven historic districts and its own area of scattered sites. Since Elkhart is located in Concord Township (whose first two digits are 25), the first district takes the number 26, the second takes the number 27, and so on. The scattered sites take the number 33. DHPA always lists the courthouse square or commercial historic district first, followed by residential or industrial districts, then the scattered sites.

## Elkhart County Road Numbering and Address System

North-south roads have odd numbers progressing from County Road 1 near the west boundary of the county to County Road 43 near the east boundary. East-west roads have even numbers progressing from County Road 2 near the north boundary of the county to County Road 56 near the southern boundary.

**11**

# History and Architecture

# Elkhart County History

Elkhart County, comprised of 16 townships, is bordered on the north by the state of Michigan, to the east by LaGrange and Noble counties, to the south by Kosciusko County, and to the west by Marshall and St. Joseph counties. Elkhart County is part of the St. Joseph River valley. The St. Joseph River flows in a southeasterly direction in the northern part of the county, eventually reaching Lake Michigan. The Elkhart River flows into the county in its southern townships and joins the St. Joseph River in Elkhart. Much of the county was heavily forested except for three large prairies: Elkhart Prairie located southeast of Goshen, Two Mile Plain (or Two Mile Prairie) situated east of Elkhart, and Pleasant Plain south of Elkhart.

The first identified inhabitants of Elkhart County were Miami Indians. Potawatomi Indians arrived in the area later in the early 1700s, establishing several villages along the rivers. They traded with European explorers and missionaries who traveled on the St. Joseph River.

Local legend asserts that the name "Elkhart" derives from native inhabitants' observation that the island at the confluence of the St. Joseph and Elkhart rivers resembled an elk's heart. Scholars disagree on the accuracy of that legend, but the island itself, originally known as Park Island and later Island Park, was donated to Elkhart by James Rufus Beardsley in 1887.

In 1812, General Anthony Wayne sent Colonel John Jackson with troops from Fort Wayne to the area in an effort to drive out the Potawatomi and Miami Indians who were viewed as a hindrance to the settlement of northeastern Indiana. Jackson and his troops burned a Potawatomi Indian village known as Aubenaubee in what is now Jackson Township. In 1829, Jackson permanently settled in the county and became a prominent resident. Most of the remaining Potawatomi Indians left Elkhart County for western reservations by 1840, and most of the remaining Miami Indians left shortly thereafter. As early as 1815, a French trader had settled in what is the area. Most white settlers began arriving in the late 1820s, like Joseph Noffsinger, who lived along the St. Joseph River as early as 1821 in what became the city of Elkhart. A post office was established on the Elkhart Prairie in 1829 with Jackson serving as the first postmaster.

The state legislature organized Elkhart County in 1830 with two townships. Concord Township was eventually divided into the townships of Cleveland, Osolo, Washington, Baugo, Concord, and Jefferson. Elkhart Township was divided into the townships of York, Middlebury, Olive, Harrison, Elkhart, Clinton, Locke, Union, Jackson, and Benton. Some residents wanted the county seat located near the confluence of the St. Joseph and Elkhart Rivers in what became the city of Elkhart, while others wanted it near the center of the county in what is now the city of Goshen. They settled on a location between the two in today's Concord Township, but both sides petitioned the state legislature to relocate the county seat. The state legislature granted a petition deeding a three-mile wide portion of western Elkhart County to St. Joseph County, resulting in the half-sized townships on Elkhart County's western edge. In 1831, the state legislature moved Elkhart County's seat to centrally-located Goshen.

Forests were cut creating farmland, while the county's streams and rivers provided water power for early flour, grist, and saw mills. The first road in the county was the Logansport and White Pigeon Road established by the state

**Workers pose with an early high stack switch engine, c.1910.** *Photo courtesy of the Elkhart County Historical Museum*

legislature in 1830. It ran north, roughly following what is now State Road 15 to Goshen, County Road 22 to Middlebury, and State Road 13 to White Pigeon, Michigan. Many early settlers came to the county from Ohio and Pennsylvania on the Fort Wayne Road, which was completed in 1833. The 76-mile road that connected Fort Wayne to South Bend later became the Lincoln Highway and is now U.S. 33. Another early route, the Vistula Road that connected South Bend to Vistula (Toledo), Ohio, has become State Road 120.

In 1852 two railroad lines crossed through Elkhart County, and very quickly the area became laden with tracks. The Michigan Southern Railroad built a line connecting Elkhart to Monroe, Michigan, while the Northern Indiana Railroad constructed a line linking La Porte to Elkhart. The next railroad line built was in 1870 by the Warsaw, Goshen, and White Pigeon Railroad that connected Warsaw to Goshen, and eventually extended into Michigan. In 1888 the Canada and St. Louis Railway laid tracks linking Goshen to Sturgis, Michigan. The Wabash Railroad constructed a line through Elkhart County in 1892 linking Wakarusa, Foraker, New Paris, Benton, and Millersburg.

Herbert E. Bucklen, an Elkhart patent medicine manufacturer, built the Elkhart and Western Railroad in 1893. It connected the Lake Shore and Michigan Southern Railroad in Elkhart with Mishawaka in St. Joseph County. In 1898, Bucklen sold his railroad to the Lake Shore and Michigan Southern Railroad. Bucklen went on to establish and finance the St. Joseph Valley Railway, an interurban line that connected Elkhart with Columbia, Ohio. Service ended in 1918 due to financial problems partly resulting from Bucklen's death the year before.

Many cities and towns within the county owe their development to the advent of the railroad. Nappanee sprang up after the Baltimore and Ohio Railroad created a stop there. Shortly thereafter, the town grew exponentially. Industries like the Globe Iron Works begun by C.D. Volkmann, and Joseph Strohm's planing and sawmill were the first businesses in Nappanee. Later the Coppes brothers purchased Strohm's mill, as well as established the Nappanee Furniture Company in 1902. Another notable business was George Freese's poultry and dairy plant, which processed 6,000-10,000 pounds of butter every day.

Other towns in Elkhart County owe their initial growth to proximity to water, which was later augmented by the railroads. Bristol, located along the Lake Shore & Michigan Southern Railroad (later the New York Central), also lies along the southern bank of the St. Joseph River. This location made it attractive to early settlers in the 1830s, who appreciated the area's fertile farmland. Bristol's growth was furthered by construction of a dam in 1841 and a number of mills. For these reasons, early Bristol experienced more business activity than the county seat and Elkhart.

Goshen mirrored Bristol's development when it too, restructured its waterway to encourage business growth. In 1868 Goshen built a hydraulic canal to allow larger boats access to the town, and a series of mills opened along the waterway in response. These included a linseed oil mill, woolen mill, saw and planing mill, and flour and grist mills, among others. Industries also took advantage of the new canal, and an iron foundry and several furniture factories opened.

Finally, the city of Elkhart's early economic development is directly linked to its position at the confluence of the Elkhart and St. Joseph rivers. Its trade greatly increased in 1844 with the arrival of river steamboats that could store greater amounts of goods on board. Elkhart became a true river town as a result, with docks and wharves servicing water-borne trade. In the 1870s, Elkhart's economic growth boomed once more when the Lake Shore & Michigan Southern chose the city as its terminus station. A host of railroad-related facilities came to Elkhart, including locomotive service shops, foundries, and mechanic stations.

The combination of fertile farmland, two major rivers transversing the area, and numerous railroad lines created bountiful opportunities for development throughout Elkhart County's history.

**33068  Construction of the St. Joseph River Dam in Elkhart, c.1912.** *Photo courtesy of the Elkhart County Historical Museum*

# Designated/Documented Properties

## National Register of Historic Places

**Ruthmere/Albert R. Beardsley House, 1908-1910**
302 East Beardlsey Avenue, Elkhart (28014)

**Dr. Havilah Beardsley House, 1848/1875**
102 West Beardsley Avenue, Elkhart (28012)

**Emmanuel C. Bickel House, c.1870**
614 Bower Street, Elkhart (33145)

**Bonneyville Mill, c.1837**
53373 CR 131, 2.5 miles east of Bristol (00020)

**Frank and Katharine Coppes House, c.1887**
302 East Market Street, Nappanee (72092)

**Downtown Nappanee Historic District, 1874-1939**
Main and Market streets, Nappanee (71001-043)

**Elkhart County Courthouse, 1870**
Courthouse Square, Goshen (51024)

**Elkhart Downtown Commercial Historic District, 1868-1930**
Roughly bounded by East Jackson and Second streets, Waterfall Drive, and Tyler Avenue, Elkhart (26001-098)

**Solomon Fowler Mansion, 1868-c.1930**
1105 W Vistula Street, Bristol (06032)

**Goshen Carnegie Public Library, 1901**
202 South 5th Street, Goshen (51554)

**Goshen Historic District, 1831-1930**
Bounded by Pike, railroad tracks, Cottage, Plymouth, Main, Purl, the Canal, and Second streets, Goshen (51001-858)

**Green Block, 1895**
109-115 East Lexington, Elkhart (26013)

**Lerner Theatre (Elco Theatre), 1924**
401 South Main Street, Elkhart (26078)

**Arthur Miller House, 1922**
253 East Market Street, Nappanee (72106)

**Mark L. and Harriett E. Monteith House, 1910**
871 East Beardsley Avenue (33038)

**Nappanee Eastside Historic District, 1880-1940**
Roughly bounded by Market, Main, John, and Summit streets (72001-198)

**Nappanee West Park and Pavilion, 1923**
Nappanee and Van Buren streets, Nappanee (73008)

**Joseph and Sarah Puterbaugh Farm, 1850**
59123 CR 9, Elkhart (25049)

**Joseph J. Rohrer Farm, 1854-1900**
24394 CR 40, Goshen vicinity (55055)

**St. John of the Cross Episcopal Church, 1847, Rectory, 1830, and Cemetery**
601 and 611 East Vistula Road, Bristol (06014)

**St. John's Lutheran Church, 1853**
Northeast corner of CR 15 and 32, Goshen vicinity (55019)

**Stahly-Nissley-Kuhns Farm, 1874-1939**
1600 West Market Street, Nappanee (74005)

**State Street-Division Street Historic District, c.1868-1930**
Roughly both sides of State and Division between Main and Monroe, Elkhart (31001-133)

**Washington Township School, 1903, 1923, 1925**
304 West Vistula Street, Bristol (06026)

**William N. Violett House, c.1854**
3004 South Main Street, Goshen (53244)

**Young Women's Christian Association, 1919**
120 West Lexington Avenue, Elkhart (26009)

## Indiana Register of Historic Sites and Structures

**Elkhart River Race Industrial District**
Roughly bounded by East Jackson Boulevard, Clark Street, Elkhart Avenue, and Elkhart River
DEMOLISHED

**Phelps House/Knickerbocker Weddings, c.1875**
525 West Lexington, Elkhart (33206)

## HABS/HAER (page 222)

**Commercial Building, c.1880**
105 South Main Street, Elkhart  DEMOLISHED

**Commercial Building, c.1880**
107 South Main Street, Elkhart  DEMOLISHED

**Commercial Building, c.1880**
111 West Jackson Street, Elkhart  DEMOLISHED

**Commercial Building, c.1880**
113-115 West Jackson Street, Elkhart  DEMOLISHED

**County Line Bridge/Ash Road Bridge, 1929-1930**
Spanning St. Joseph River at State Road 219, Osceola vicinity (15051)

**Concord Township District No. 10 School, c.1890**
Hammond Avenue, Elkhart (33378)

# Historical Themes in Elkhart County

This inventory contains 3,671 listings for historic resources including sites, buildings, landscape features, and structures. Surveyors evaluated each resource according to the 29 areas of significance that appear on the survey form (see p. 9). In Elkhart County, seven areas of significance emerged as dominant themes: transportation, architecture (both high-style and vernacular), agriculture, commerce, industry, religion, and education.

This report presents these themes in order of historical development. Transportation, which is usually the earliest element to appear during an area's settlement period, appears first, followed by a discussion of the county's vernacular architecture and agricultural development. Subsequent themes describe major institutions that appeared as the county was settled. The report develops each theme, placing Elkhart County resources within the historical context of local, state, and national trends.

## Transportation

The evolution of transportation is a key component in any region's historical development. The earliest routes followed Indian trails or waterways to gain access to uninhabited lands. As an area was settled, crude roads, often following the routes of the old Indian trails, were cut out of the wilderness. Turnpikes or toll roads soon appeared, serving private interests.

The Land Ordinance Act of 1785 greatly affected transportation in Indiana. The Act called for land surveys to be made according to a square grid, and roads generally followed the section lines of the grid. The grid system is more evident in northern Indiana because of its even terrain. In southern Indiana, where the earliest transportation routes developed, the irregular terrain did not lend itself as readily to the grid system.

After achieving statehood in 1816, Indiana devoted its formative years to infrastructure improvements. Workers completed the Michigan Road, which linked Madison with Michigan City in 1826. The National Road, which linked Cumberland, Md., to Vandalia, Ill., reached Richmond, Ind., in 1828 and arrived in Terre Haute by 1832. The government-funded roadway opened the frontiers of Ohio, Indiana and Illinois to settlement.

Indiana's 1836 Internal Improvement Bill provided for the construction of a network of canals. The legislation eventually bankrupted the state, but not before completion of the Indiana stretch of the Wabash and Erie Canal, linking Evansville to Lake Erie. However, even as the canals reached completion, they were already becoming obsolete. The state's first railroad line was completed from Madison to Indianapolis in 1847, ushering in a century that would be dominated by the railroad.

Many historic resources associated with Elkhart County's numerous forms of transportation remain. The impact of the railroad on both the urban and rural areas of Elkhart County was substantial. Rail lines through the county provided outlets for the area's farmers to the larger markets in Indianapolis and Chicago. By the close of the 19th century, many towns could trace their beginnings to the construction of the rail lines, including Elkhart and Goshen. One of the most visible resources associated with the railroad is, of course, the depot (33294, 33295). Railroad bridges, though less distinctive, are more commonly found.

An outgrowth of the railroad was the development in many cities of interurban railroad systems. A rival to the soot-spewing steam engines, electric railroad engines began to make their appearance in the closing years of the 19th century. Initially developed as street railways in urban centers, the electric railroads provided clean and quiet, if not always reliable, transportation. Improvements in technology allowed for larger cars that could go longer distances. The interurban railway dates from 1888, when Lafayette had the first city-wide electric intraurban line, to 1893, when the tracks moved beyond the limits of the city of Brazil, eventually reaching as far as Knightstown.

Steel rails laid down by small companies tied cities and towns together. Consolidation of these lines led to larger, more efficient lines connecting more distant parts of the state. Large networks of lines owned by companies such as the Union Traction Company; the Terre Haute, Indianapolis and Eastern Traction Company; the Fort Wayne and Northern Traction Company; and the Chicago, South Shore and South Bend Railroad soon tied most of Indiana's major towns and cities together. By 1920, one could travel from any part of the state to the Union Traction terminal in Indianapolis.

Increased pressure from newer, more efficient railroad engines and the automobile signaled the end of the electric interurban system. One by

**33294 The Lake Shore & Michigan Southern Railroad Passenger Depot in Elkhart was built in the Romanesque Revival style in 1900.**

one, the tracks closed during the Depression, and after World War II, the trains became a thing of the past. Only the South Shore Line from South Bend to Chicago was left to serve the northern populace. It still runs, carrying commuters across the industrial region of Northwest Indiana.

Just as the railroad replaced the canals as a major mode of transportation during the 19th century, the advent of the automobile during the early 20th century would forever change the face of Indiana. Elkhart County's road system improved greatly. Roads went from narrow dirt paths to gravel and macadam on more heavily traveled routes. These improvements and expansion of the road system affected the country's economic and social systems. With the establishment of the State Highway Commission in 1919, the state began construction of a 3,200-mile network of roads, linking county seats and communities with populations of more than 5,000 and connecting Indiana with adjoining states. The Lincoln Highway, the nation's first coast-to-coast route, ran east-west through northern Indiana.

With these developments came the replacement of wooden bridges, first with the more durable and stronger metal-truss bridges and later with concrete. New bridges are replacing early metal-truss and concrete bridges at an alarming rate; Elkhart County retains some metal bridges, including examples of Pratt (53198) and Warren (53022) truss systems.

53198 The 1909 Murray Street Bridge in Goshen is an example of a Pratt pony truss bridge, constructed by the Elkhart Bridge & Iron Company. Though no longer used by motorized traffic, the bridge is open to pedestrians.

Just as important to auto travel as roads and bridges are facilities to maintain the automobile and its passengers. Gas stations, service garages, roadside diners, and tourist cabins sprang up along Indiana's roads to serve the motoring public. Elkhart County boasts several examples of the small house-with-canopy-style gas station (51151, 51432).

Because early automobiles were usually not completely enclosed, they were particularly vulnerable to the weather. Some owners kept their cars in large public garages, while others used existing barns or carriage houses. Soon, the private garage or "automobile house" began to appear. At first, homeowners built garages away from the house due to the fear of fire from gasoline, which drivers often stored in large tanks in or near the garage. With the proliferation of gas stations in the 1920s, it was no longer necessary to store gasoline at home, and the garage moved closer to the house, eventually becoming part of the house as attached garages gained popularity.

## *Vernacular Architecture*

Many houses in both the rural and urban areas of our country fall into easily identifiable forms or house types. These house types had their origins in Europe, came to North America with the colonists, and subsequently moved westward with the settling of the frontier. Often, builders adapted these traditional house types to a particular locale and combined them with popular trends in architecture to produce what is referred to as vernacular architecture.

The people who settled in Indiana came from widely diverse backgrounds, bringing with them a variety of building traditions. Because the earliest Indiana settlers generally came north from the Ohio River, many originated from southern states such as Kentucky, Virginia, and North Carolina. It is no wonder then that housing types popular in the south appear in abundance in the southern one-third of the state. Across the

northern section of Indiana, settlers from the New England states as well as various ethnic groups brought building types familiar to them. As the state became increasingly homogeneous, these regional housing types grew in popularity and eventually spread throughout Indiana.

The following are some of the vernacular building types found in Elkhart County.

## Log-Construction/Single Pen

The earliest permanent buildings constructed after the European settlement of the frontier were of hewn-log construction. While not of a particular architectural style, hewn-log buildings and especially log houses are of diverse origin. Generally, they combine various building and house types of British tradition with horizontal hewn-log construction techniques. The precise origins, if such exist, of hewn-log construction as manifested in Indiana are not known. Similar, though not identical, construction techniques appear in the heavily forested regions of northern and central Europe and in Scandinavia. Some theorists attribute the dissemination of horizontal log construction in America to German and Scandinavian immigrants, though this is not certain. In any case, hewn-log construction flourished in the hardwood forests of the American frontier. Americans adopted the log building, usually referred to as a "cabin," as a favorite symbol, if not an icon, which represents the self-reliant and honest virtues of the frontier.

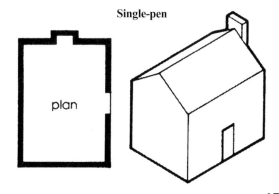

**54006 The William Layton Baker Log House in Waterford dates to c.1834.**

Today, the apparent simplicity of log buildings often belies the sophistication of the flush corner notching systems by which builders joined the logs as well as the high level of craftsmanship invested in the hewing of logs. Please note that hewn-log buildings differ from the so-called log cabins, which were of round-log construction and were in most cases crude, temporary buildings that have not survived to the present.

Usually, settlers replaced their hewn-log buildings with larger buildings of frame or brick construction and quite often relegated them to less prominent locations where they served as outbuildings or became abandoned. In other cases, log buildings were incorporated into newer structures so that their form and construction are virtually unrecognizable. Most log buildings date to the early years of European settlement. However, construction of hewn-log buildings was not uncommon throughout the first half of the 19th century and even later in some places.

The single-pen house was normally a one-room rectangular-plan structure with a sleeping loft above. The gable-end chimney, built of fieldstone, could be either on the interior or exterior of the structure. The windows were small, and because of the scarcity and impracticality of glass on the frontier, were covered with oilcloth or wooden shutters. Elkhart

County retains several single-pen log houses (15045, 54006, 55010).

## Double-Pen

One of the most common methods of expanding the single-pen log house, a frequent occurrence as settlers' spatial needs increased, was simply to add another similar or identical pen to one of the gable ends of the existing pen. In many such cases, builders left the gable-end wall, now the shared interior wall of the two pens, intact. With the pens thus not being connected by a passage through the interior wall, an exterior door for each pen was needed. This resulted in the double-pen house (55057, 70052).

One variant of the double-pen house is the **saddlebag**, which is distinguished by its central chimney. In its original form, the saddlebag was a single-pen house to which a second pen had been added on the far side of the chimney. Often, the two pens were separated by the width of the chimney, forming a space that was usually covered with siding. Doors next to the chimney connected the two pens.

Though the two front doors on double-pen and saddlebag houses were most common in log construction, the double-pen form also appears in houses not built of logs. Stone, brick, and frame houses may also have two doors on the facade. Some historians explain this as the continuation of the Upland South building tradition, but this theory does not explain why

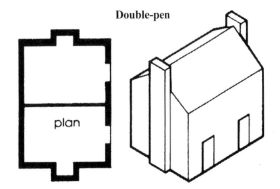

**Double-pen**

plan

**70052 The Solomon Stump House in Union Township is an unusual example of a double-pen house because it has two stories.**

double-entry houses occur in areas far removed from southern influences.

A more likely theory is that the double-entry house developed from the tradition of keeping private, family space separate from that used for formal entertaining. Visitors would use the "formal" door that led directly into the formal parlor, while family would use the other door that gave access to the more comfortable (and probably less well-furnished) family space. Families with many children would also find two doors more convenient than one. Occasionally, one will find that one of the two doors is more ornate or of more expensive construction, which suggests the idea of "public" space. If this theory is correct, many of the double-entry houses are more closely related to the hall-and-parlor than to the double-pen type. Since field surveyors were not always able to determine the internal arrangement of rooms, most double-entry houses are classified as "double-pen" for the purpose of this survey.

## Hall-and-Parlor

The hall-and-parlor house, like the double-pen house, is composed of two rooms arranged side by side, though with only one exterior door. The hall-and-parlor house, as it exists in Elkhart County, is related to the medieval English house type of the same name. In this case, the hall is

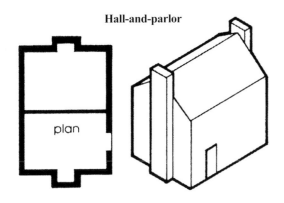

**Hall-and-parlor**

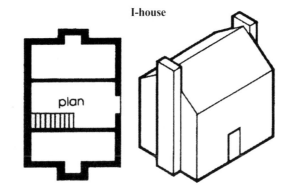

**I-house**

not a passageway but a large, multi-purpose room, while the parlor is the more private of the two rooms and is often smaller. Door placement is usually off-center. In the earlier examples, chimneys were located at one or both gable ends; later examples have interior chimneys. Like the double-pen houses and other linear-plan house types, the hall-and-parlor usually had a rear extension forming an L- or T-plan, and in many cases, these extensions, along with the front portion of the house, are original. Examples of the hall-and-parlor house remain throughout Elkhart County (55056, 65003, 70073).

55056 The 1836 Beitler/Wenger/Nunemaker Log House in Harrison Township displays a hall-and-parlor plan.

## I-House

The natural progression of housing types from the simple one-and-one-half-story hall-and-parlor

house to a full two-story structure culminated with the development of the I-house. Like the hall-and-parlor house, the I-house evolved from the English one-room house with an end chimney. The addition of a second story onto the basic floor plan of the hall-and-parlor or central-passage house reflected the growing prosperity of an agrarian economy. Therefore, it is little wonder that the I-house was the predominant housing type in rural areas.

Geographically, the I-house can be found from the Middle Atlantic region, south to Maryland and Virginia, and then west. First identified as a distinct building type during the 1930s, the I-house was most pervasive in Indiana, Illinois, and Iowa, hence the name I-house. Its basic

25070 This c.1850 3-bay I-house in Concord Township has well-scaled Greek Revival details.

form made it easily adaptable to a variety of architectural styles so that the I-house persisted from the late-18th to the early-20th centuries. Despite the diversity of floor plans utilized in the I-house, its basic form is constant. The house is two stories, one room deep, and at least two rooms wide. Typically, the facade is symmetrical with a central entry in a three- or a five-bay configuration. Sometimes, a four-bay I-house will feature two entries. Besides these shared characteristics, the I-house took a variety of forms. Building materials included brick, clapboard, or stone. Placement of chimneys varied; they might be found at each gable end flush with the wall, on the house's exterior, or paired at the center of the structure. Demands for additional space necessitated the building of ells or wings at the rear of the house as well as the addition of porches. However, despite these modifications, the basic form of the I-house remained unchanged. Because of its simplicity of form, builders could freely apply decorative details representing diverse architectural styles. As a result, Greek Revival details such as corner posts and cornice returns, or Italianate-style brackets and elaborate porches, were common additions to the I-house. These reactions to popular architectural styles bridged the gap between rural, folk-derived building types and the academic, architect-designed structures of urban areas.

A variety of I-houses remain in Elkhart County, including three-bay (25070), five-bay (20020) and stacked (35009) examples.

## Saltbox

The saltbox house is discernible by its uneven roof line (the rear slope is longer than the front slope), differing from the preceding house types in that its rooms are not arranged in a strictly linear fashion but rather in a massed form (i.e. the main body of the saltbox house is two rooms deep). The distinctive roof line developed as a means of dealing with severe New England

**19**

**25012** This double-entry saltbox log house is located in Concord Township and dates to c.1840. In 1975, the structure was dismantled and moved from a location ten miles south of its current site.

winters. The front of the house with its shorter roof slope and greater facade area faced south to receive heat and light from the sun, while the long rear slope of the roof facing north collected an insulating blanket of snow (25012).

As with many of the vernacular house types, builders forgot the original function of the saltbox's uneven roof as it became an established house type. In some cases, saltbox houses resulted from additions along the rear of linear-plan houses.

## Double-pile

Another massed-plan type, the double-pile house, is rectangular in plan, two or two-and-one-half-stories in height, two rooms wide, and two rooms deep with a central passage running

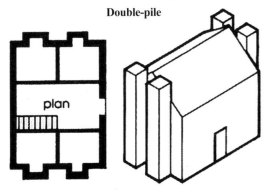

Double-pile

**00001** This 1873 double-pile house in York Township is unusual with its board and batten siding and half-size windows on the front facade.

from front to rear. Builders frequently employed this form of house during the 18th century in the United States, and it is often referred to as a "Georgian" plan house, though, as we see in Elkhart County, builders continued to build the double-pile house throughout the 19th century, transcending stylistic classification (00001, 35039, 55055).

One variant of the double-pile house has two front entries (05008, 15006, 33417). Architectural historians sometimes call these "Pennsylvania farmhouses," but local historians call them "double-entry, double-pile" houses because they often lack the gable-end windows and masonry construction found in true Pennsylvania farmhouses.

## Gable-front

Architectural historians distinguish gable-front houses by their front-facing, gabled roof above the façade possessing the main entrance (51480, 74006, 80019). These are found in all parts of the county dating from the mid-19th to well into the 20th century.

The gable-front house is rectangular in plan and most commonly one-and-one-half stories in height. Gable-front houses developed into a

Gable-front

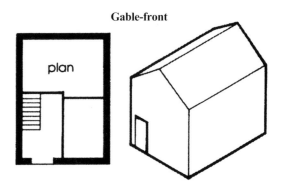

popular house type during the Greek Revival era, when architects designed American buildings to be reminiscent of Greek temples. They achieved the effect of a classical pediment by placing the principal facade beneath a gable end, which forms a triangle. Architectural historians call gable-fronts "temple-front" houses when they are fully attired in Greek Revival dress. While the temple-front variety was common in New England and upstate New York, Midwestern

**51480** This gable-front house in the Goshen Historic District dates to c.1890 and features original clapboard siding and wood windows, a decorative cornice, and front porch with square columns.

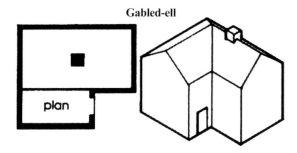

**Gabled-ell**

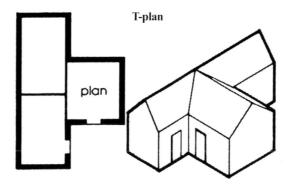

**T-plan**

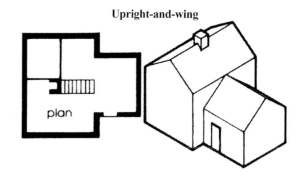

**Upright-and-wing**

examples appear mainly in northern Indiana and southern Michigan.

Rural areas as well as towns boast gable-front houses. The type's suitability to narrow-fronted lots in expanding urban areas made it a popular house type, as did its adaptability to a variety of styles, including Greek Revival, Italianate, Queen Anne, and Craftsman.

Several sub-types of the gable-front house appear with great frequency in Elkhart County and warrant mention. The **gabled-ell** is a gable-front house with a side extension, which forms an L-shaped plan. Gabled-ell houses can be one, one-and-one-half, or two stories in height, and in all cases, the ell (or side extension) is the same height as the gable-front portion of the house (33145, 40018, 40024).

**33145 This gabled-ell house in Elkhart features some elements of the Italianate style, such as its tall, narrow windows and a decorative wrap-around porch.**

**51264 This T-plan house is in the Goshen Historic District.**

Similarly, a gable-front house having a perpendicular front projection that forms a T is referred to as a **T-plan** house. These are also found in a variety of heights, with both front and rear portions of the same height (50033, 50042, 51097). A T-plan house whose wing extends to the side instead of the front is known as a "**lazy T**." Most of these T-plan houses are one or one-and-one-half stories tall (20001, 33130, 80045), while the similar "**upright-and-wing**" house has a two-story main portion and a shorter wing (10012, 10038, 15045).

**10012 This 1854 upright-and-wing house in Osolo Township features Greek Revival details.**

An interesting variation of the gable-front house occurs in Elkhart County: the **cross-gable square** house usually dates from 1860 to 1885 and has a square footprint with a large gable on each side (30056, 41067, 72090).

## Pyramidal-Roof Cottage

Identifiable by its roof shape, the pyramidal-roof house is a one-story building commonly of frame construction. Its square plan allows for a simple, informal massing of rooms. The exterior of the pyramidal-roof house is generally plain, though additions such as ells, porches, corner towers and applied ornamentation lend variety to some examples. Door and window placement varies according to the interior arrangement of rooms.

**Pyramidal-roof cottage**

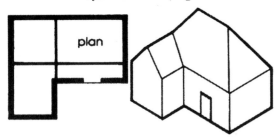

Chimneys, centrally located within the house, usually appear at the apex of the steeply pitched roof (33321).

The origins of the pyramidal-roof house are not clear. It appeared in the late 19th century and remained popular into the early decades of the 20th century. Some pyramidal-roof houses in the lower Mississippi Valley may have developed out of French colonial house types; however, in the Ohio River Valley, the folk origin of the pyramidal-roof is less certain. What is clear is that it was a popular house type in many industrial areas, where it was often mass-produced as inexpensive workers' housing.

**33321** Though not originally a residence, the McQuiston School in Elkhart is a good example of the pyramidal-roof type.

## Bungalow

Shortly after the turn of the century, the bungalow type emerged. By the 1930s, it had become the dominant house form in American

**32013** This house in Elkhart's Morehouse Historic District is a fine example of a California bungalow with its front-gable roof and gabled porch.

domestic architecture. The term "bungalow" comes from India, where it refers to a low house surrounded by galleries or porches. The American bungalow originated in California and spread nationwide largely through the work of Charles and Henry Greene and by way of pattern books and architectural magazines. The inexpensive, fashionable, and generally modest scaled bungalow was particularly suitable to the burgeoning middle class in America's urban and suburban areas. Rooted in the Arts and Crafts movement, which stressed the importance of "honest" materials and construction, the bungalow type featured simplicity of detail and massing, roofs with exposed rafters and knee

**46009** The Clark A. Rink House in Millersburg is an excellent example of an Arts and Crafts-influenced dormer-front bungalow.

**33110** This house in Elkhart is a nice example of a western bungalow with its hipped roof and hipped dormers on each roof slope.

braces, and facade surfaces of stucco, wood or rubble stone. Porches, normally under an extension of the main roof, were essential components of the bungalow.

Bungalows are typically small buildings, one or one-and-one-half stories tall. However, they were so popular that architects incorporated many elements of the bungalow style, such as knee braces, ribbon windows, large porches, and overhanging eaves, into larger buildings. Architectural historians often categorize these bungalow-style architectural and decorative elements as Craftsman.

Bungalows usually appear in three basic types: the **California bungalow**, which has a gable front, with a gable-front or hipped porch (32013, 33037, 53197); the **dormer-front bungalow**, which has a facade dominated by a single central dormer (29034, 32068, 46009); and the **western bungalow**, which has a hipped roof, often with dormers (33013, 33110, 34006). In its later stages, the bungalow form often appeared with Colonial Revival details or no stylistic details at all.

## American Foursquare

Similar to bungalows in style and widespread popularity is the American foursquare house. Like the bungalow, its relative simplicity and

28011 The Chamberlain/Bucklen House in Elkhart's Beardsley Avenue Historic District is a high-style example of the vernacular American foursquare form.

62019 This modest house in Wakarusa is a well-preserved example of the minimal traditional form.

00023 The Ward Kessler House in York Township is an example of an early traditional ranch house. Kessler worked for a window company and used different types of windows throughout the home.

practicality made it enormously popular. Sometimes classified as **vernacular Prairie**, **cornbelt cube**, or **Midwest box**, the standard two-story American foursquare house has a low-pitch, hipped roof with hipped attic dormers; wide, enclosed eaves; and a one-story porch spanning the width of the front facade. American foursquares are frequently seen with Craftsman elements such as tile roofs, knee braces, and ribbon windows; some have no decoration at all, while others may have Colonial Revival details on entries, windows, and porches.

Builders prefabricated many American foursquares and bungalows and marketed them through catalogs. Elkhart County has many American foursquares (28011, 51299, 51767).

## Minimal Traditional

Appearing in the 1930s through the 1950s, minimal traditional houses may appear similar to older vernacular types. Usually side-gabled, the roof often has a front-facing cross-gable. The porch is usually very small, and may be integral to the house or have its own separate roof (55050, 62019, 70006). Even less ornate are **Depression** houses. Small, one or one-and-one-half-story homes, they are characterized by square massing, a lack of ornament, and metal-framed windows.

## Postwar Houses

The Second World War halted all non-essential building; this, coupled with the pre-war slowdown in house construction due to the Depression, caused a huge demand for single family housing after the war. Returning servicemen, armed with the GI Bill of Rights and wanting to start families, began pursuing the "American Dream": a family, job, and home of their own.

The housing of the postwar era showed a dramatic change in style and taste from even those houses built just before the war. Gone entirely were the European-influenced period revival styles; the Colonial Revival endured due to its broad appeal, but began to lose its distinctiveness. New forms and trends began to make inroads into the popular tastes. Cheap transportation, new construction methods, and the availability of land all impacted the types of houses built in the years between 1946 and 1959. Chief among the new, popular houses was the ranch. An outgrowth of a style rooted in California and other western states, the ranch flourished in the land-rich suburban housing boom.

Three distinct subtypes based on the footprint or massing of ranch houses may be found in Indiana. Within the subtypes, builders could add

different stylistic elements, changing the appearance externally. In the 1930s, West Coast architects adapted the one-story **traditional ranch,** characterized by its linear plan and defined organization of living space. Its footprint varies, with L- and U-shape plans being most common. Roofs of traditional ranches are usually low-pitched and hipped with wide, boxed eaves. Native stone, brick, or a combination of the two are the most typical wall materials. Though usually hidden, garages are an integral part of the plan (00023, 72056, 81064).

The **massed ranch** subtype, as its name suggests, has a massed rather than a linear plan. It shares some characteristics with traditional ranches, including a low-pitched, hipped roof (often with multiple planes) and wide, boxed eaves. What sets it apart is the width and depth of its footprint, which has less frontage to the street and extends deeper into the lot upon which it is built. The massed ranch typically features an attached garage, but it is not integral to the plan (05026, 20023, 72139).

As the ranch began to grow in popularity, attention to detail, by necessity, began to wane.

05026 This house in Washington Township is an example of a massed ranch, having a deep footprint.

**51247** This minimal ranch house in Goshen features an outward slanting picture window.

The mass construction practices perfected during the war and the rapid expansion of the suburbs led to an explosion of the ranch house's popularity. The **minimal ranch** house was an outgrowth of this popularity. Architects designed these inexpensive homes as scaled-down versions of the traditional ranch. Characteristics of minimal ranches include side-gabled roofs, a strict linear plan and footprint, and minimal use of masonry. Many of these homes lacked garages, though builders might attach a carport to a gable-end (10035, 51246, 51247).

## *Agriculture*

Traditionally, a close tie exists between agriculture and Indiana's heritage. Since the pioneer days, the raising of crops and livestock has played an important role in the state's economic, social and educational systems. With the passage of the Land Ordinance Act of 1785, the U.S. government established guidelines for the sale of land in the Northwest Territories. The Act provided for the now-familiar rectangular survey system of one-mile squares. This system also provided for a more organized means of land transfers and decreased the possibility of boundary disputes. Settlers could purchase parcels of land in offices established throughout the state. Indiana's earliest agricultural activity centered around southern Indiana. The area's uneven terrain and undeveloped transportation system limited these early farms to subsistence levels, but corn and livestock provided food for

the settler and were used as a means of exchange.

As transportation routes developed in northern Indiana, its open prairie and rich soil invited more and more settlers. Agriculture emerged as an important component of the state's economy and farmers diversified their crops. By the 1850s, advances in transportation and technology were producing dramatic changes in agriculture, expanding it beyond the subsistence level. The Morrill Act in 1862, which provided for the establishment of colleges of agriculture and mechanical arts, encouraged this agricultural expansion. Twelve years later, Purdue University opened in West Lafayette. The University offered courses in agriculture and provided extension services for the state's farmers. Local organizations such as the Grange formed to promote social, cultural, and educational programs in rural areas. Grange buildings, farmers' clubs and grain elevators are part of the state's agricultural heritage not associated with individual farms, and many people overlook their importance.

Distant markets became more accessible to farmers via the new railroads, boosting their productivity. Moreover, improved agricultural implements and machinery increased the amount of crops grown and harvested. The resulting agricultural expansion touched other areas of Hoosier life as well. The farmer could now afford to build larger, more elaborate houses and outbuildings. Rural communities and their small businesses prospered, as did the railroads. As agriculture became more sophisticated, it slowly evolved from being a way of life to being a business. More sophisticated farm machinery decreased the amount of labor needed and increased the size of farms. However, a slowly urbanizing society eroded agriculture's dominance of rural life and its economy.

The following are the most common agricultural buildings in Elkhart County:

## Grain Elevators

Integral to the familiar rural landscape is the prairie skyscraper—the grain elevator. Dominating the skyline of many small towns, sometimes even overshadowing the county courthouse, the grain elevator stands in silent testimony to one of the greatest industries in the world—grain farming. Following the axiom "form follows function," grain elevators, with their hodgepodge appearance, do not often appear to the casual observer as notable examples of architectural beauty. However, close

**46018** The Lyon & Greenleaf Grain Elevator in Millersburg was built in 1920.

examination finds them to be quite stylish in their simplicity of form, honesty in material, and straightforward functionality (46018, 73070).

As long as farmers have had the ability to produce grain beyond the needs of themselves and their immediate locale, grain elevators have proven a necessity. Typically, there are two classifications of elevators: country or rural elevators that serve a small section of farmland and terminal or urban elevators that serve regions of land. Farmers brought grain to the rural elevator by truck, wagon, or rail. Workers then weighed, sorted, and shipped the grain to the larger terminal elevator, where it could be distributed locally, nationally, or internationally.

Small towns built on feeder tracks of major rail lines often boast elevators constructed of wood or concrete. Whether of crib construction akin to a log cabin or of stud construction similar to a frame house, wood frame elevators are typically sheathed in non-combustible materials such as asbestos shingles or corrugated sheet metal to reduce the danger of fire. Farmers were still building wood frame elevators well into the 20th century, though not as commonly as before 1900. Poured concrete was a safer, sturdier material to use, but it was not until the advent of slipform technology—in which short molds are filled with concrete, then "slipped" up to the next level—that constructing elevators of concrete became cost effective.

By 1915, most farmers built their new elevators of concrete. Concrete elevators were sturdier, had a greater capacity than the framed structures and, most importantly, were fireproof. Sometimes they retained a rectangular footprint like the frame examples, and sometimes they were built with more efficient round bins.

Explosion and fire have been the bane of grain elevators since their inception. Consolidation and abandonment are the current enemies. The closing of spur lines and consolidation of shipping signaled the end for many rural elevators. Some may find a niche in the community as retail outlets for agricultural

products or storage facilities. Others shut down operations, unable to compete in today's economy. Whether left empty or still used, they acknowledge the historic importance of the farmer, the railroad, and technology in American history.

Indiana's "golden age" of agriculture extended into the 20th century. By 1900, agriculture so dominated the state's economy that the top four industries in Indiana were agriculture related. However, with the rise of other industries, the evolution of an urban society and changes in transportation, agriculture's dominance of the Hoosier lifestyle lessened. Despite this downturn in the agrarian economy, agriculture remains a vital part of Indiana's traditions.

# Barns

The barn is the most prominent and recognizable structure within the farm complex. Farmers constructed early barns according to traditional building methods, both in form and craftsmanship. Heavy hand-hewn timbers are characteristic of these traditional barns. Toward the end of the 19th century, traditional barn types gave way to barns whose designs were promoted by agricultural journals, land-grant college programs, and later by the United States Department of Agriculture. Following the Great Depression and World War II, barn building techniques changed drastically, and the construction of pole barns and prefabricated structures almost entirely superseded traditional methods of barn construction.

## *English Barn*

English settlers brought the English barn to the New England and Chesapeake Bay area. It became the dominant barn type there and traveled to the Midwest with few modifications.

English barns are timber-framed and rectangular in plan. They differ from transverse-frame barns in that their major entry is not on the gable end

40024  English barns have sliding doors located on the structure's long side. This example is on a farm in Middlebury Township.

but on the barn's long side. The entry is usually centered and consists of double doors. The English barn is commonly separated into three bays. Farmers used the center space as a threshing area and sections to either side as grain and hay storage. They clad English barns in vertical siding and gave them few windows.

Elkhart County retains many examples of the English barn (15045, 25060, 40024).

## *Basement/Bank Barn*

The basement, or bank, barn consists of an English barn raised on a stone, concrete, or brick foundation. In addition to the centered door on the barn's long side, small doors on each gable

35041  This basement/bank barn is located on the George P. Rowell, Sr. Farm in Jefferson Township.

end provide access to the basement. Typically, an earthen wagon ramp provides access to the upper floor. Farmers could also build the barn into a hillside, with the top of the hill providing upper-floor access. They used the lower level of the basement barn to house livestock and the upper level for crop storage and as a threshing floor.

Elkhart County has many examples of basement/bank barns (15019, 25070, 35041).

### Sweitzer Barn

The Sweitzer barn first appeared in America in southeastern Pennsylvania. A variation of the German bank barn, it gradually extended west through Ohio and into Indiana and Illinois. It is a common barn type in northern Indiana and is found elsewhere in the state in isolated areas with a strong Swiss-German heritage.

Sweitzer barns consist of two-and-a-half stories. The first floor that was used to stable animals is partially excavated and normally built into the side of a hill. That siting provides for warmth in the winter and a cool environment during the summer. The second floor is accessed by central double doors on the upslope side, similar to basement barns. Doors are also located opposite the main doors to provide a draft for threshing.

The Sweitzer barn's single most identifiable feature is its forebay that extends over the lower level. The

25001  This impressive Sweitzer barn is part of Pine Creek Acres in Concord Township.

overhang provides protection for the animals as well as a means for feed to be dropped from the upper level to the lower level.  The forebay is the only feature that distinguishes the Sweitzer barn from a basement/bank barn (25001, 25049, 35029).

### Transverse-frame Barn

The transverse-frame barn is the culmination of a barn type that evolved from a basic single-crib log structure. The single-crib barn was simply one square or rectangular crib with a gable roof. It was commonly of log construction and used for grain storage and the stabling of animals. As farmers required additional space, the double-crib and four-crib barns evolved. Both these barn types used the single-crib barn as the basic unit and simply added additional cribs in two distinct configurations.

Similar to the English barn, the double-crib barn consisted of two cribs separated by a breezeway and sharing a gable roof. The four-crib barn had cribs at each corner with a common roof and intersecting aisles that formed a cross.

The transverse-frame barn evolved from the four-crib barn. The cross aisle was closed off and stalls or cribs were built along the wall. Farmers placed entrances to the transverse-frame barn at either end so that they could drive wagons through the structure. Rows of storage cribs or

35030  Transverse-frame barns have a sliding door located on the gable-end. This example is in Jefferson Township.

stables lined each side of the barn. Unlike crib barns, transverse-frame barns were primarily of frame construction (35030, 55015).

### Round/Octagonal Barn

Round and octagonal barns are a unique part of our architectural heritage. Most date from the early 20th century, a time of rising prosperity and innovation in American agriculture. Numerous agricultural and builder's journals disseminated designs for labor- and material-saving round barns.

Both enthusiasm and derision greeted the appearance of round or octagonal barns, which were regarded as something of a fad. The deepening agricultural depression of the 1920s and subsequent changes in agricultural technology and economy curtailed their construction. Today, one round barn remains in Elkhart County (74007).

74007  The 1911 Frank Aker Round Barn was moved from the Goshen-Plymouth Trail south of Bremen  to Amish Acres where it was converted into a theater.

### Non-Traditional Barns

Toward the end of the 19th century, forces other than tradition influenced barn building. The use of cut-to-size dimensional lumber rather than heavy timber in barn construction resulted in lighter framing systems that, in turn, allowed for large, unobstructed lofts sheltered by gambrel or

00029 This rainbow-roof dairy barn in York Township was built in 1955, replacing an earlier barn that had been depicted in the 1874 *Elkhart County Illustrated Atlas*.

round-arched roofs. Research at agricultural experiment stations also had a great impact on barn designs through the promotion of efficiency and sanitation as well as new construction techniques. Many of the dairy and livestock barns built in the early 20th century resulted from these designs. The typical 20th-century livestock barn has a gambrel roof and doors on either the side or the end of the building (00029, 10005, 15003).

## Silos

Silos became popular around the turn of the 19th century as a means of storing green crops, or silage, to feed cattle over the winter (00013, 25001, 35032). Builders constructed the first silos of wood, often in a square shape. At first, the square silos were sometimes built into a corner of the barn, but this reduced the available area for livestock or hay storage. Square silos were also not as practical as round ones because the silage did not pack down into the corners well, which allowed air to get in and rot the mixture.

In the 1920s, concrete and glazed tile silos came into widespread use. Tile was not as popular as concrete because it was fragile, and the curved tiles determined the size of the silo. Concrete was easy to use; builders could pour it in rings or assemble it in vertical staves. Metal was also a popular silo material. After World War II, the familiar blue Harvestore silos began to dot the

35032 This concrete silo is attached to a livestock barn on the Benjamin Ziglar Farm in Jefferson Township.

landscape. Today, wooden silos are very rare in Indiana.

## Outbuildings

Historically, several types of outbuildings supported the operations of a farm. Generally smaller than the house and barn, they were usually devoted to one specific function.

The historic farmstead contained a variety of ancillary buildings used in the preparation and storage of food for human consumption. **Smokehouses** for curing meat are often identified by the coating of soot and creosote that has built up on the inside of the door (40018); **milk houses** to keep dairy products cool; **root cellars** for winter storage of apples, potatoes, and onions; and insulated **warm houses** for the storage of canned goods year round exist on numerous farms. These basic structures were usually rectangular in plan and could be of frame, brick, or block construction. Glazed tile was a popular and sanitary construction material in the 1920s through 1940s.

Many farmsteads retain **summer kitchens**, which removed unwanted heat, odors, and fire risks from the main house. These buildings could either be freestanding (40029) or attached to the rear of the house by a covered breezeway.

Another building, the **privy**, was perhaps the humblest of buildings on the farmstead, yet one of the most important. During the 1930s, the Works Progress Administration (WPA) built and distributed plans for "sanitary" privies to replace inadequate structures. Many of the privies remaining on farms today are built to WPA specifications, which are very similar to facilities found in national parks and campgrounds. Ubiquitous until quite recently, privies, like many of the outbuildings associated with the historic farmstead, are increasingly scarce.

Other outbuildings that hold agricultural produce include structures such as **granaries** and **corn cribs**. Corn needs the circulation of air around it, so it is stored in wire mesh or slatted wood cribs (25060, 35032). Grain needs to be protected from moisture and vermin, so it is usually stored in more airtight structures that are often raised above the ground on piers. At this time, architectural historians do not consider the round metal grain bins seen on many modern farms historic.

Hog pens, hen houses, and brooder houses are a few of the special types of structures that shelter animals. **Hen or chicken houses** are usually long, low, rectangular buildings with many windows. **Brooder houses** are frequently round or octagonal to prevent baby chicks from getting stuck in corners. Farmers often scattered **hog**

40018 This smokehouse is located on a farm in Middlebury Township.

25060  This drive-thru corncrib is located on a farm in Concord Township.

**houses** within or around the perimeter of a fenced enclosure, constructing them out of wood or half of a corrugated metal culvert.

# *High-Style Architecture*

For the most part, architectural styles in Indiana, especially in the areas outside the urban centers, were expressed in a popular rather than a pure academic fashion. They reached the state first not through trained architects but by way of carpenters' guides and builders' manuals. In the pre-railroad era, builders applied stylistic motifs derived from these books to otherwise vernacular building forms. After the arrival of the railroads, the range of stylistic possibilities broadened as new building products and technologies became available and as communication in general improved. Also, the post-Civil War era witnessed the rise of the architectural profession in America, which resulted in an increase in the number of "high-style" buildings.

The following are some of the most common architectural styles in Indiana:

## Federal

The first architectural style to appear in Elkhart County was the Federal style, popular during the first four decades of the 19th century, which coincided with the first wave of settlement. It is essentially an extension of the late Georgian style and is sometimes referred to as the Adam style for Scottish architect and designer Robert Adam (1728-92). Adam's work had a tremendous impact on British architecture during the late 18th century and on American architecture in the years between the War for Independence and the War of 1812. The continued reliance upon Britain as a cultural model is reflected in Federal architecture, which takes its name from the Federalists, a conservative American political party during the nation's early years. Federalists favored maintaining close ties with Britain during the late 18th and early 19th centuries. The style remained popular long after America's relations with Britain had soured, especially in areas of westward expansion.

The Federal house is characterized by sparse ornamentation, such as narrow cornice moldings and simple door surrounds, if any. Windows tend to be large, evenly spaced, and multi-paned. Doors have transoms, sometimes of a semi-elliptical shape in the more refined homes. Chimneys are located at the narrow ends of the building and the roof usually is low-pitched and side-gabled. Elkhart County retains several examples of the Federal style (50041, 65035).

50041  This stacked I-house in Elkhart Township has federal-style details, including its flat window lintels and sills and heavy cornice line.

## Greek Revival

The next style to appear, Greek Revival, was the first and most popular of several romantic revivals that dominated 19th-century American architecture. After the War of 1812, Americans desired to sever their strong cultural bonds with Britain. As a result, the American people sought an architectural style that reflected their increasingly democratic values and aspirations, and for this they turned to the architecture of ancient Greece.

Several important factors account for the Greek "mania," which swept across America in the early 19th century. Archeological discoveries in Greece, and later the Greek War for Independence (1821-30), aroused much interest and sympathy among Americans. Also, the Greek Revival style, remotely patterned after the temples of ancient Greece, was a bolder and more vigorous style than the refined and delicate Federal style and thus better suited to the American landscape and mentality.

It is no accident that the style's popularity was at its height during a period of increased male suffrage and general political liberalization.

41037  This Greek Revival house in Middlebury was moved from its original location on South Main Street.

Americans viewed themselves as successors to Athenian Democracy, and by the time the Greek Revival had run its course, it appeared in all settled areas of the United States, applied to buildings of virtually every function.

The chief features of the style are the often minimal references to ancient Greek temples found in such elements as wide entablature moldings, cornice returns, doors with paneled jambs, and classical surrounds. Less common, though present in many high-style examples, are classical porticos.

As typical with the Federal style, most of the county's examples of the Greek Revival style are vernacular house types with applied architectural details referring to the style (10012, 35032, 41037).

## Gothic Revival

Even more romantic than the Greek Revival is the Gothic Revival, popular in Indiana domestic architecture from the 1840s through the 1860s and in ecclesiastical architecture from the 1840s well into the 20th century (33165, 41008, 45015). For this style, much of the inspiration came from Britain, though the American expression is quite different and came a generation or more later. Increased industrialization, evidence of political corruption, and various other anxiety-producing factors of the mid-19th century evoked a yearning for a simpler and purer way of life. This was reflected in all areas of culture—painting, music, and most notably, literature. For instance, the writings of Scottish novelist Sir Walter Scott, which portrayed the medieval era in glowing terms, were enormously popular. Architecture also responded to the romantic sentiments of the mid-19th century by incorporating Gothic forms based on models from the 12th through the 15th centuries into building designs.

Most people connect the Gothic style with religious architecture; it is an emotional, upward-soaring style usually associated with the great

**33165 St. John's Episcopal Church in Elkhart is a fine example of the Gothic Revival style applied to ecclesiastical architecture.**

stone cathedrals of Western Europe. American builders, using native materials such as wood and brick (stone was reserved for elaborate buildings), translated elements of the Gothic style into a purely American expression, which was at its most charming in domestic architecture.

The most characteristic element of the Gothic style is the pointed arch. Used by medieval builders to span widths and scale heights of ever greater dimensions, the pointed arch in the hands of American builders became a primarily decorative device, faintly echoing its structural origins. Another converted component of the Gothic style is the ornate tracery that American builders executed in wood with the aid of the newly invented steam-powered scroll saw. This tracery was applied to the eaves at gable ends and appeared in ornate porches. Steep-pitched gable roofs, often with finials at the apex, expressed the Gothic verticality and caused the Gothic Revival to be dubbed the "pointed style" in the 19th century. Eared drip moldings were placed above doors and windows, and some Gothic Revival buildings had parapets resembling medieval fortresses. The preferred facade material was board-and-batten siding, which reinforced the verticality (05036). Brick and clapboard were also common.

The Gothic Revival style remained popular in ecclesiastical and funerary structures until approximately 1930. Gothic churches, tombstones, and mausoleums appeared at various levels of sophistication, and by the 20th century, there was a greater concern for accuracy in the display of Gothic elements.

## Italianate

The Italianate style appeared in Elkhart County a few years after the Gothic Revival, gaining widespread acceptance in both rural and urban areas and in commercial and domestic architecture. Its extraordinary popularity lasted as late as the 1890s, particularly in commercial buildings. Based on the domestic architecture of the Italian Renaissance, the Italianate style tended to emphasize the picturesque qualities of rural Italian villas, though, as in the preceding styles, the American expression was quite distinct from its historical inspiration.

Important features of the domestic Italianate style are the wide, projecting eaves with ornate

**06032  The Solomon Fowler House in Bristol is listed in the National Register of Historic Places. Prominent Italianate features include paired decorative brackets beneath overhanging eaves, round-arch windows and an impressive entry.**

brackets and tall, narrow windows with round or segmental-arch heads. The roof is often hipped and has a low pitch (06032, 25049, 35037). Italianate ornamentation was often applied to I-houses; other common house types are the four-over-four variety, sometimes called **Italianate cube** (15021, 33007, 51515), and the L-plan house, sometimes with a tower. More elaborate Italianate houses may have a belvedere, ornate

**15021  This Italianate cube house in Cleveland Township retains its square cupola.**

window-hood moldings, and quoins at the corners. Builders equipped most homes with ornate wooden porches. They used both brick and frame construction, with the less expensive balloon-frame construction prevailing after the economic panic of 1873.

The Italianate style was also immensely popular in late-19th-century commercial buildings (06019, 33103, 41021). These were rectangular commercial blocks, two or three stories in height, with flat roofs and large storefront windows. Cast-iron vertical members supported the storefront windows. Italianate detail appeared in the often elaborate cornices, round or segmental-head upper-story windows and moldings, and sometimes in additional ornamentation such as ashlar block veneer and quoins. While cornice detail and window-hood moldings were first executed in wood and stone, they were later manufactured in prefabricated stamped metal. This allowed for lavish ornamentation at an economical price. Metal cornices and window hoods appear on some Italianate homes as well.

The Italianate style was quite popular in Elkhart County, coinciding with the growth of the railroad and the ensuing prosperity.

## Second Empire

During the 1860s and 70s, a new style enjoyed brief and intense popularity. American architects modeled the Second Empire style, sometimes called the French Mansard style, after contemporary French architecture. During Louis Napoleon's reign over France's Second Empire (1851-1870), French architects revived the mansard roof, a 17th century design associated with the work of architect François Mansart. The French Second Empire was a period of highly-charged nationalism and to the French people, the mansard roof was a distinctly French innovation whose 19th century revival evoked the glories of their country's late-Renaissance era. To Americans who increasingly looked to Paris for the latest in fashion, the Second Empire style

**29021 This Second Empire house is in Elkhart's Riverside/Prospect Historic District.**

was a strikingly modern and sumptuous form of architecture.

The mansard roof, the Second Empire style's major defining element, is a dual-pitched, hipped roof. Its lower slope is steep with a concave, convex, or straight surface, while the upper slope has a low pitch and is often concealed. In addition, the Second Empire style is characterized by lavish ornamentation and boldness of form. Second Empire homes and public buildings are generally imposing structures, often boasting towers. Roof ridges might be topped with cast iron crestings, while decorative eave brackets support overhanging eaves. Quoins accent corners while window and door openings are embellished with highly-decorative surrounds. The style was well suited to the flamboyant post-Civil War and post-railroad era when ostentation and excessiveness of taste were not discouraged.

Elkhart County retains several examples of the Second Empire style (29021, 41051, 51760).

## Romanesque Revival

Architects used the Romanesque Revival style, appearing in various phases from the 1880s through the first decade of the 20th century, less in houses than in large public and commercial buildings. The Romanesque Revival style looked to the 10th through 13th centuries when builders in Europe rediscovered ancient Roman forms. The most prominent elements of the Romanesque style and its 19th-century counterpart are the round arch and the heavy masonry facades. Romanesque Revival buildings tend to have massive hipped roofs, many with wall gables and conical or pyramidal-roof towers or belfries. They are generally ponderous and fortress-like, conveying an impression of defiance (06015, 32099, 33167).

The most influential proponent of the style, Henry Hobson Richardson (1838-1886), developed his own Romanesque vocabulary, which became known as the **Richardsonian Romanesque** style. Architects of large public buildings to which the style was well suited often imitated it, though not always successfully. In Indiana, several courthouses, churches and schools approximate the Richardsonian Romanesque style.

**06015  The Romanesque Revival style is evident in the Bristol Town Hall's round-arch entry.**

## Stick

Stick style houses feature exterior walls of wood clapboard or shingles. Decorative boards raised above the wall surface and placed vertically, horizontally, or diagonally give the style its name. The style arose from ideals popularized by Andrew Jackson Downing in his successful pattern books of the mid-1800s. Medieval half-timbered houses provided the style its inspiration, as the stickwork mimics the varied surface patterns of the past. The style was most popular from 1860 to 1890, as architects and

**62056  The Wakarusa Depot is an example of the Stick style with its varied siding and eave decorations.**

carpenters applied Stick ornamentation to houses and other buildings.

Other decorative elements of the Stick style include trusses under gable eaves, exposed rafter tails, and braces on porch supports. Stick style houses are relatively rare when compared to other styles of the period, such as the Italianate and Romanesque Revival styles. Many architectural historians consider Stick style to be transitional, linking the Gothic Revival and Queen Anne styles. The Stick style's emphasis on using wall surfaces as decoration was an idea embraced by the subsequent Queen Anne style.

## Queen Anne

The Queen Anne style was popular in Elkhart County during the 1880s and 1890s. The style originated in England in the 1860s and was an informal blend of 18th-century English architecture and earlier medieval motifs. As the Queen Anne style spread across the United States, it lost much of its 18th-century character and acquired a vague resemblance to late medieval English architecture. An American contribution to the style was the profusion of readily available wooden ornamentation and the

**51557  The Dale-Zook House in the Goshen Historic District was built in the Queen Anne style in 1890. Wilbur Peat featured the house in his 1962 book, *Indiana Houses of the Nineteenth Century*.**

substitution of wooden facade shingles for clay tiles found in the English counterparts.

The style typically featured asymmetrical massing, irregular fenestration, diversity of wall treatments and projecting bays, and a feeling of

**41074  The J.F. Nusbaum House in Middlebury was built in 1894 in the Free Classic style and features a pseudo-Palladian window on the side gable.**

intentional informality (33423, 51336, 51557). These buildings were statements of individuality and uniqueness in an increasingly regulated and mass-produced world. Builders used the style chiefly in domestic architecture, though occasionally in commercial architecture, and it is often synonymous with the popular conception of late-Victorian architecture in America.

A later variation of the Queen Anne style is referred to here as the **Free Classic** style. This sub-type typically appeared during the first decade of the 20th century as the Queen Anne style's popularity was waning. The Free Classic style has a more formal feel and applies classical features to the asymmetrical massing of the Queen Anne house. Distinctive features may include a Palladian window in the front gable, a porch with classical columns, and a pediment over the entry (41074, 51545, 51584).

## Neoclassical/Classical Revival

By the turn of the 20th century, the Neoclassical style emerged as a dominant force in American architecture. In the Neoclassical style, there was concern for historical correctness of detail but not of overall execution or scale. Neoclassical buildings tend to be meticulously detailed and of massive scale, which sets them quite apart from Greek Revival buildings with casually interpreted classical ornamentation and modest scale. Architectural Neoclassicism prevailed into the 1930s, most notably in large public and commercial buildings including skyscrapers. Characteristics of the style include the use of classical elements such as columned porticos, pilasters, keystones, pedimented openings, and dentils along the cornice (26023, 30020, 33024).

26023 Designed by local architect E.H. Turnock in the Neoclassical style, the F.K.A. Masonic Temple is in Elkhart's Downtown Commercial Historic District.

## Colonial Revival

Around the turn of the 20th century, the Colonial Revival style gained prominence, and it retained much popularity throughout the 20th century. Several factors accounted for this: the American centennial in 1876, which stimulated an unprecedented interest in American heritage in general and in colonial American architecture in particular; the growing tendency in the late 19th century among America's trend-setting architects to build period houses in a variety of eclectic styles, which often incorporated colonial elements; and the 1893 Chicago Columbian Exposition, which emphasized accuracy and correctness in the use of historical styles and established Neoclassical and Colonial Revival as the dominant styles in American architecture.

Historical accuracy in the Colonial Revival style was confined more to specific elements than to

28010 This Colonial Revival House in the Beardsley Avenue Historic District features a slate roof with three protruding dormer windows.

the building as a whole. For instance, a Colonial Revival house is usually of much larger scale than its 17th- or 18th- century prototype, and it may bear the influence of more than one phase of the colonial period. Elements of the style include dentils, heavy cornices, entrances with fanlights and sidelights, pedimented dormer windows, keystones, and quoins (28010, 46001, 51786). A variation on the style that features gambrel roofs is called **Dutch Colonial Revival**.

The **Cape Cod** house has its roots in the Massachusetts area from which it takes its name. Originally built by colonists as simple shelter against the unforgiving New England elements,

10005 This c.1940 Cape Cod house is located on a farm in Osolo Township.

this small house type became popular in the 1930s and endures to this day. A simple house, it was inexpensive to build. Cape Cods are one or one-and-one-half stories, side gabled with an expansive roof and central chimney, with little or no eave overhang. Builders typically clad Cape Cods in clapboard or wood shingle siding (10005, 50004, 51199).

## Prairie

Influenced by the Arts and Crafts movement, Chicago architect Frank Lloyd Wright created a completely original American style at the turn of the twentieth century. Dubbed "Prairie" in honor of the Midwest farmlands that served as his inspiration, Wright's style flourished throughout the country, popularized in pattern books. Architects designed all types of buildings in the Prairie style, but it was most common to residential construction.

Characterized by low-pitched, hipped roofs having wide, overhanging eaves, Prairie style houses are two-stories in height and have large porches supported by square piers. Ribbon windows and other decorative elements emphasize the horizontal. Intended to blend into the environment, their overall massing is wide and low to the ground. They most often have

brick exteriors, but stucco, wood, and stone were also used (27021, 29007, 33001). Vernacular examples of the Prairie style resemble American foursquares. The two share many similar characteristics; however, true Prairie style structures are architect-designed and asymmetrical in form, while foursquares tend to be symmetrical. The Prairie style faded in popularity after World War I.

## Craftsman

In reaction to the ostentatious Queen Anne and Classical Revival styles that were so prevalent at the dawn of the 20th century, the Craftsman style decried ornamentation and pretension. Rooted in the American Arts and Crafts movement as espoused by Gustav Stickley, the Craftsman style utilized natural materials and handmade, rather than mass-produced, goods. It emphasized honesty of design, meaning that whenever possible the designer left construction methods exposed rather than hidden. Low rooflines with exposed rafters and wide eaves supported by knee braces are typical (30017, 31031, 51221). Stone or brick foundations support walls clad in

a variety of natural materials. Intended to blend in with the natural landscape, the Craftsman house exhibits muted earth-tone colors. Bands of multi-pane windows, often asymmetrically placed, lighted the interior. As the style gained popularity before and after World War I, its stylistic elements were applied to various types of houses, such as bungalows and American foursquares. Ironically, by the end of its popularity, the Craftsman style had become little more than surface ornamentation, the very trend that it had been created to protest.

## Eclectic Period Revivals

A variety of eclectic styles became popular around the turn of the century and, as in the Neoclassical style, the buildings feature a somewhat free application of carefully studied detail. The diverse styles of these buildings usually bear apt titles such as **Mediterranean Revival**, **Italian Renaissance Revival**, etc. (27040, 27090, 33054). That period houses reached a high point of popularity during the 1920s has been attributed in part to servicemen who, upon returning from World War I, wished to pattern their homes after the picturesque buildings they had seen in Europe.

**29007  The Prairie style was extremely popular in Elkhart County. This example is in Elkhart's Riverside/Prospect Historic District.**

**51221  This Craftsman-style house in the Goshen Historic District features overhanging eaves with exposed rafter tails, original windows with flared wood surrounds, and a front porch with tapered columns.**

**53187  This English Cottage in Goshen retains original wood shake siding on dormers and original six-over-one double-hung sash and historic 8-pane casement windows.**

27040 **This impressive Mediterranean Revival house is in Elkhart's East Jackson/St. Joe Manor Historic District.**

The **English Cottage** style exhibits very steep gable roofs, picturesque chimneys, and facades of stone veneer or simulated half-timbering (53187, 62049, 72010). The **Pueblo** or **Mission Revival** styles often have stucco facades and tile roofs. The **Tudor Revival** style (05030, 33200, 51165), or **Tudor Gothic** (33257), distinguishable by its Tudor arch, found wide use in early-20th-century religious architecture and was used so regularly in educational buildings that it is sometimes referred to as **Collegiate Gothic**. The eclectic styles achieved their highest expression in the often lavish period houses built before the Great Depression but were also applied to a variety of building types other than residential. For instance, many early gas stations were built in the English Cottage style.

## Art Deco

Art Deco flourished between the World Wars. Art Deco, as its name suggests, was based on French decorative arts, which were highly stylized and

41073 **The 1939 Middlebury Township School is an example of the Art Deco style with its emphasis on the vertical.**

ultra modern in the 1920s. It was widely used in public and commercial buildings, theaters, and skyscrapers, but rarely in domestic architecture other than apartment buildings. Features of the Art Deco style are its emphasis on verticality and the use of angular, geometric ornaments such as zigzags, chevrons and other stylized decoration of slightly Egyptian or Persian flavor (41073, 51395, 82002).

## Art Moderne

Art Moderne developed during the 1930s and continued in ever-simplified forms through the 1950s. Art Moderne, as opposed to Art Deco, emphasized the horizontal line, often with rounded corners and streamlined decorations. Builders constructed a few residences in the Art Moderne style, but the style was more prevalent in commercial buildings, particularly gas stations (15004, 33069, 51500).

15004 **The Walter Ford House in Cleveland Township was built in 1945-46 by the current owner's grandfather. The house's low profile and wall treatments emphasize the horizontal.**

## Contemporary

Gaining popularity in the 1950s, contemporary houses ignored the look of the past and were purely modern in inspiration. Often architect-designed, contemporary houses may have flat, gabled or shed roofs. They often incorporate wood, brick, and stone into the facades. Contemporary houses with flat-roofs evolved from the **International** style of architecture and are sometimes classified as International style in this survey (10036, 33008, 33021). The gabled forms often have wide eave overhangs and

exposed rafters like Prairie-style homes. Contemporary houses with shed roofs originated in the early 1960s and persist to the present and may exhibit multi-directional sheds, sometimes combined with gables. Contemporary houses are not bound to a particular shape but may have linear, massed, or irregular plans. They have no decorative detailing, instead making use of the textures of materials and landscaping for their ornament.

33008 **This International style house in Elkhart was built in 1958 and features a completely flat roof and prominent carport.**

## *Industry*

The earliest industries to appear in Indiana relied almost exclusively upon the agricultural economy and accessibility to raw materials. Settlers built water-powered gristmills and sawmills along streams and rivers, encouraging development. These were small, multifunctional operations with only one or two workers. The mills not only served as a place of business but were also used as post offices, polling places, and meeting places. Craftsmen plied their specialized trades in home industries. Coopers, wheelwrights, and blacksmiths were common tradesmen up until the advent of mass-production techniques.

Gristmills were often at the center of early settlements. Corn, the staple of pioneer life, was milled into flour for food and as a means of exchange. Distilleries, another common early industry, also used corn. Sawmills took advantage of southern Indiana's seemingly inexhaustible supply of timber, so that lumber

People pose in front of the Woolen Mill in Baintertown, c.1890. *Photo courtesy of the Elkhart County Historical Museum*

soon emerged as one of the state's largest industries, especially in Elkhart County.

With few overland routes available, the Ohio River developed as the major means of transportation in southern Indiana during the early and mid-19th century. The river provided access to markets for manufactured goods as well as to raw materials. River towns such as Madison and Jeffersonville developed as major manufacturing communities. Madison was at one time the nation's largest pork-packing center. Jeffersonville gained national renown for the hundreds of steamboats built in its shipyards.

With the advent of the railroad during the 1850s, the scope of Indiana's industrial base widened dramatically, although most industry was still found in southern Indiana. While milling and lumbering retained their dominance, the railroad contributed to the emergence of other industries. Workers mined coal from fields in southwestern Indiana to meet the increased demand for energy.

As the railroad network developed, industry slowly became more sophisticated. Increased availability of raw material, access to distant markets, and the demand for manufactured

goods as a result of the Civil War spurred Indiana's industrial growth. The state's industrial centers slowly shifted north toward Indianapolis. By the 1880s, many of the state's largest industries made homes in the capital city and in emerging industrial cities such as South Bend and Fort Wayne.

Specialized factories soon appeared, employing sometimes hundreds of workers. Coal, natural gas, and steam replaced water power. Production shifted from the manufacturing of agriculture-based goods to durable goods that were easy to ship to distant markets. The discovery of natural gas in north-central Indiana accelerated the state's industrial growth near the end of the 19th century.

With the advent of the internal combustion engine, industry became more efficient and diversified. The arrival of the automobile introduced a new focus in manufacturing, and the auto industry took on a dominant role in the economy of Indiana.

Around the turn of the century, some buggy manufacturing companies in the county restructured their businesses to begin testing, designing, and producing some of the county's earliest automobiles. By the 1920s, manufacturing had surpassed agriculture as the state's largest industry. Factories were larger, more sophisticated, and operated more efficiently because of the internal combustion engine.

53139  Reuben Whitmer established the Goshen Sash & Door Company in 1869; until recently, it was the oldest continuously operated industry in Goshen.

## Religion

Religious congregations were often one of the first institutions established in newly settled areas. Initially there were no formal churches in which to worship, so settlers gathered in private homes for services. Itinerant preachers or circuit riders sent from established churches in neighboring areas usually conducted these services. As a region developed, congregations became more organized and formal church buildings were constructed. Typically, early church buildings were crude log structures, replaced gradually by simple frame buildings as the congregations grew. Often these structures were the only public buildings located outside villages, resulting in their use for a variety of functions. Rural communities sometimes used churches as schools and public meeting places. In many cases, several different congregations shared one building. Eventually, as a congregation grew larger and wealthier, it replaced its church building with a more elaborate structure.

French Catholic missionaries in southern Indiana established the state's earliest churches. The Baptists and Methodists soon followed and developed into Indiana's two dominant religious

45015  The 1878 St. John's Evangelical Lutheran church in Clinton Township is a well-preserved example of a rural, gable-front church.

groups. Both denominations were well established in the South, where many of Indiana's earliest settlers originated. The Methodists and the Baptists provided lay preachers, while other religious groups depended on churches in the East to send trained clergy. Until the 1860s, Presbyterian and Catholic churches, among others, considered Indiana a missionary field. Members of the Friends denomination also heavily settled parts of Indiana.

Sparse population, poor transportation, and lack of clergy severely limited the attendance of religious services. Simple rural churches of log or frame construction dotted the countryside. Often, burial grounds accompanied these rustic

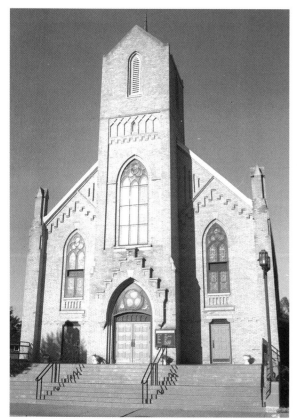

33302 The 1886 St. Vincent DePaul Catholic Church in Elkhart is an example of the Gothic Revival style.

55012 The Stutsman Cemetery in Harrison Township has family burials dating between c.1849 and c.1936.

buildings. However, as the railroad reached more Indiana communities, larger congregations formed, especially in towns and cities. They built bigger, more expensive churches to replace the modest frame buildings of only a few years before. The rise of the state's urban areas during the early 20th century hastened the growth of organized religion in Indiana, as congregations supported increasingly larger churches.

However, the gradual migration from a rural to an urban populace, the merging or decline of rural congregations, and the cost of maintaining church buildings have had a negative impact on religious structures in recent years. As the number of abandoned or neglected buildings increases, the challenge of preserving and reusing these churches becomes more imperative. Despite a decrease in the number of church buildings in recent years, especially in rural areas, religion remains an important part of the state's heritage.

Elkhart County's religious history is well represented by its collection of rural and urban churches. Typically, the faithful built simple rural churches in the gable-front form of many New England churches (45015). As towns boasted larger congregations, they built larger and more impressive churches (33302).

An important part of the built environment frequently overlooked is the numerous cemeteries found throughout Elkhart County (15007, 20016, 33261). Often, cemeteries are

historically connected with church buildings. As congregations died out or consolidated, burial grounds were often all that remained. Other rural cemeteries might be family plots, the final resting place of hard-working settlers, their families, and neighbors, such as the Stutsman Cemetery, established c.1849 (55012).

In many cases, cemeteries provide us with the only record of a person's or a family's presence in a time and place. The earliest markers were slabs of sandstone or marble that bore inscriptions and occasionally bas-relief, followed by classically inspired shafts, urns, or obelisks that corresponded to the Greek Revival period in architecture. Later, Gothic markers appeared, using the pointed arch motif. For a few decades in the late 19th century, cast "white bronze" monuments were popular and affordable alternatives to expensive stone monuments. Like the stamped metal cornices common among Italianate buildings, the cast monuments provided many rural areas with a sense of inexpensive opulence.

This survey has attempted to locate cemeteries within Elkhart County but does not include pre-contact, Native American burial grounds. Laws protect the locations of those burial grounds to prevent looting.

## Education

In addition to religious congregations, settlers usually established educational institutions in frontier areas. Familiar one-room schoolhouses dotted the landscape. They were typically subscription schools, in which residents banded together and hired a teacher of suitable training. Like church buildings, schools were multi-functional, serving as meeting places, polling places, and in some instances, churches. As the idea of public education gained support, subscription schools slowly gave way to the opening of tax-supported township schools.

55026 The Harrison Township District No. 5 School is a well-preserved example of a late district school. Today it is used as a meeting house.

The Land Ordinance Act of 1785 greatly affected Indiana's educational system. Provisions in the Act allowed the leasing of public lands to support local schools and set aside one section of each 36-mile-square township for a school. However, localities did not always adhere to this system and abuses occurred. In many areas, subscription schools and private academies prevailed until the 1850s, when a free public school system began in Indiana. The state authorized the levying of taxes for school construction, established standards for teachers, and provided money for school libraries. It was during the late 19th century that the familiar brick one- and two-room schoolhouses proliferated. Officials built township schools within several miles of each other so that students could walk to them. The one-room schoolhouse persisted throughout the 19th century into the early 20th century until school consolidation began.

Consolidation of district schools into township schools began in the years before World War I. Better roads and motor transportation led to the creation of centralized, all-grade schools; one by one, the single-room schools were closed, abandoned, or converted into homes, barns, or sheds. The larger township schools, often located in the center of the township or in the closest town, began consolidating in the 1960s. Some of the older township schools then served as elementary schools, but most closed their doors forever.

Consolidation of rural schools presented both positive and negative results. Larger schools allowed for more teachers, better facilities, and more students. With the coming of paved roads and school buses, the school no longer had to be within walking distance. Despite the advantages of consolidation, proponents of the neighborhood school saw its closing as contributing to the exodus of young people from the farm as well as a decline in community spirit. Between the years of 1890 and 1900, more than half of the state's 8,000 one-room schools were abandoned. Officials replaced these schools with larger grade and high schools, usually located in the township's largest community. Like the advent of public schools decades before, school consolidation produced dramatic changes in the educational system. School consolidation continued during the 20th century, resulting in the loss of many historic schools.

Elkhart County's collection of schools reflects the history of educational trends (32001, 33263, 55026).

## Commerce

The areas of commerce and transportation are interrelated; without access to waterways, roads, and railroads, the exchange of goods and services is not possible. That is why an area's earliest commercial activity usually occurred along rivers or Indian trails.

French fur traders established early trading posts at places like Lafayette, Fort Wayne, and Vincennes. Mills were usually the first businesses to appear in a frontier area, providing a variety of services to the surrounding population. Gristmills produced flour for settlers to use as food and as a medium of exchange before the widespread use of hard currency. Often, the mill was multi-functional, serving as a general store, a post office, and a school.

As settlers poured into the state, the Ohio River took on an important role in Indiana's commercial development. Southern Indiana river ports such as Madison, Jeffersonville, and Evansville became major economic centers. As the state's transportation system developed with the construction of canals and roads, economic growth slowly shifted to central and northern Indiana. The opening of the state's first railroad in 1847 ushered in a period of dramatic changes in the area of commerce. The development of towns along rail lines had a profound impact on commerce, moving it from a subsistence level based on bartering to a more complex activity. Until the advent of the automobile, most business took place in small-town, family-owned specialty stores.

The railroad enabled merchants to offer a wider selection of goods at a cheaper cost. Advances in building technology coupled with product diversification resulted in the development of the familiar late-19th-century commercial building. The introduction of cast iron and advances in the manufacturing of glass enabled the storefront to offer a larger display area. A decorative wood panel on the bottom and a transom with small panes of prism glass on top usually framed the display window. The building's second floor often served as residential space for the business owner and had windows with decorative

Employees stand in front of the Barger Brothers Box Company, c.1910. *Photo courtesy of the Elkhart County Historical Museum*

pressed-metal hoods. An ornate pressed-metal cornice, sometimes with the merchant's name cast into it, might top the building. This type of commercial building dominated the Main Streets of railroad-era towns across Indiana, and its popularity persisted into the early 20th century.

The automobile was responsible for dramatic changes in small-town-based economy and slowly changed the state's commercial focus. By 1930, a large percentage of Indiana's rural population owned automobiles and were able to drive to larger towns to conduct their business. The Great Depression, which brought a number of bank and business failures and a population shift from rural to urban areas, hit small communities hard. The growth of suburbs after World War II further contributed to a decentralization of the business district and a decline in downtown commercial districts. Clusters of commercial buildings soon appeared along streetcar routes or in suburban areas. Residents no longer conducted business exclusively in downtown areas. As suburbs developed their own commercial areas, people did not need to travel into town to shop. During the mid- to late-20th century, strip shopping centers and the development of the suburban mall further drained business away from the downtown.

Recently, attempts to reverse this trend have met with positive results, and a renewed interest in the small town business district is evident. Since the establishment of the Indiana Main Street Program in 1986, small-town business districts have re-emerged as an important part of a community's commercial activity. In Elkhart County, Bristol, Elkhart, Goshen, Nappanee, and Wakarusa are members of Indiana Main Street.

The survey classifies commercial buildings by their styles and/or vernacular types. The most common vernacular types in Indiana follow:

## 1- or 2-part Commercial Block

The simplest commercial buildings may often be described as 1- or 2-part commercial blocks. These masonry commercial structures have little or no decorative detailing and are usually one or two stories tall, as indicated by the numeral preceding "part." The boxy buildings usually have large glass display windows and flat roofs (26053, 46008, 75004).

46008  The Knights of Pythias Building in Millersburg is a good example of a common 2-part commercial block. This building was built in 1910, one year after a fire destroyed much of Millersburg's business area.

## Parapet-front

Parapet-front commercial buildings have a principal façade wall that extends vertically beyond the roof line. That extension is called a "parapet." Parapets can be simple rectangular extensions, stepped, or elaborately designed in the Spanish Mission style. Often, the building's name or date is placed on the parapet (53126).

53126  The Thomas-Albright Company in Goshen was established in 1878 and made hydraulic presses. This parapet-front structure was built c.1911.

## 19th or 20th Century Functional

If a building does not fall into a style or one of the above vernacular-type categories, the survey classifies it as "Functional" according to the century in which it was built. These are generally utilitarian buildings like warehouses, factories, or garages that have little or no decorative features (31128, 33098, 51102).

51102  The 1898 Tailgates Building in Goshen along the canal is an example of a 19th century functional structure because its design was primarily utilitarian.

# Current Map of Elkhart County

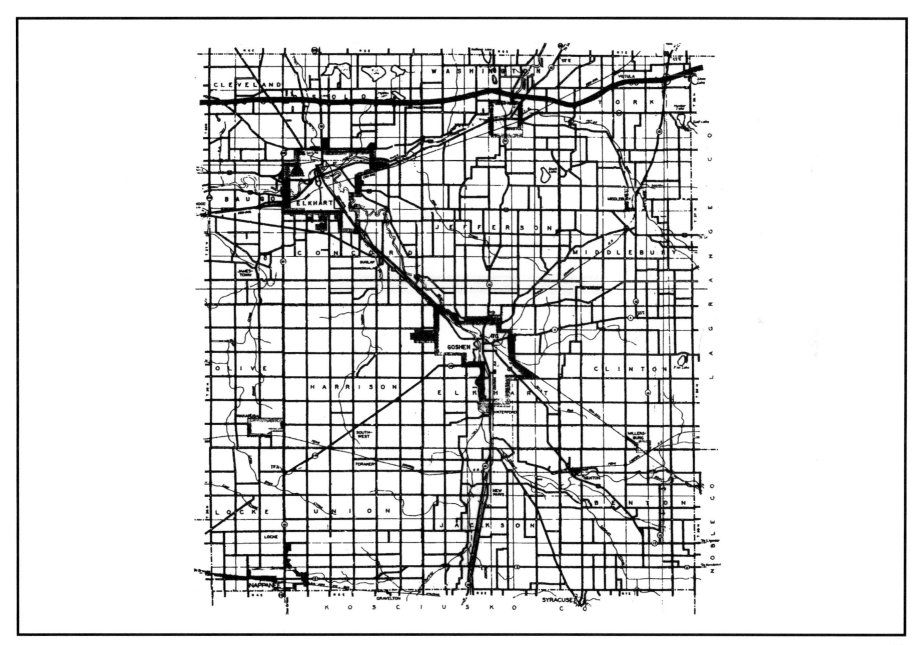

# Catalog

# How to Read the Catalog

Each section of this catalog begins with the name of the township, community, or historic district, with its range of site numbers printed in parentheses. A map showing the location of the sites follows. For historic districts, towns, and townships, a short descriptive narrative also appears. The actual list of sites included in the inventory follows in numerical order. Each entry provides the following information:

## *Number*

The last three digits of the property's individual site number precede each catalog entry. This three-digit number is also used on the accompanying map to show the site's location.

## *Rating*

The next column of information contains the rating for each inventory entry (O, N, C, or NC). See the section on p. 8, "Criteria and Evaluation," for a full explanation of the rating system.

## *Description*

### Name

When original property owners' names were available, the report couples them with the type of resource, e.g. "Smith Farm." It lists institutional properties according to their original names when these are available, such as "Methodist Episcopal Church." If the historic name is unknown, a general name has been used, such as "House," "Commercial Building," or "Farm."

### Address

The property's address follows the name. If the street number was not available to the surveyor, the abbreviation "NA" has been used in historic districts.

### Form and Style

The report identifies structures by form, style, or a combination of both. A building's form is usually based on folk or vernacular traditions, while its style derives from trends found in architect-designed buildings. In most cases, buildings combine vernacular forms with embellishments derived from architectural styles. For example, when a house is identified as "I-house/Greek Revival," the building's form (I-house) and its style (Greek Revival) are indicated. For sites with more than one structure (farm complexes, for example), both the house and prominent outbuildings are noted. A "1½" preceding the form means that the house is a one-and-one-half-story variant of a normally one- or two-story house type.

### Date

An exact date appears when verifiable information exists. Most inventory entries, however, have an approximate date given with the "circa" (c.) notation.

### Architect/Builder

The architect or builder, if known, follows the date.

### Significance

The report attempts to indicate the category of significance for each entry (except in historic districts). See the section on "Criteria and Evaluation" (p. 8) for a discussion of the categories of significance. A notation indicates if an entry is listed in the National Register of Historic Places (NR), or recorded by the Historic American Buildings Survey (HABS) or the Historic American Engineering Record (HAER).

### USGS Map Number

Except in historic districts, the code number of the USGS quadrangle map on which the entry is located has been noted in parentheses. Figure 3 (p. 11) shows the USGS quad map overlay for Elkhart County.

## *Historic Districts*

Historic district entries follow the format given above except for three differences. The report organizes each historic district by street, listing east-west streets first, one side at a time, starting with the northernmost streets in the district and moving south. North-south streets follow, beginning with the westernmost streets and moving east.

The report does not list categories of significance for each entry in a district since the accompanying narrative describes the significance of the district as a whole.

The third difference in historic district listings is that the USGS map number does not appear after each entry but instead is given at the beginning of the narrative description of the district.

**Opposite: The 1893 Lake Shore & Michigan Southern Railroad Depot was torn down in 1900 and replaced by the present depot at Tyler and 2nd streets in Elkhart.**
*Photo courtesy of the Elkhart County Historical Museum*

# York Township (00001-032)

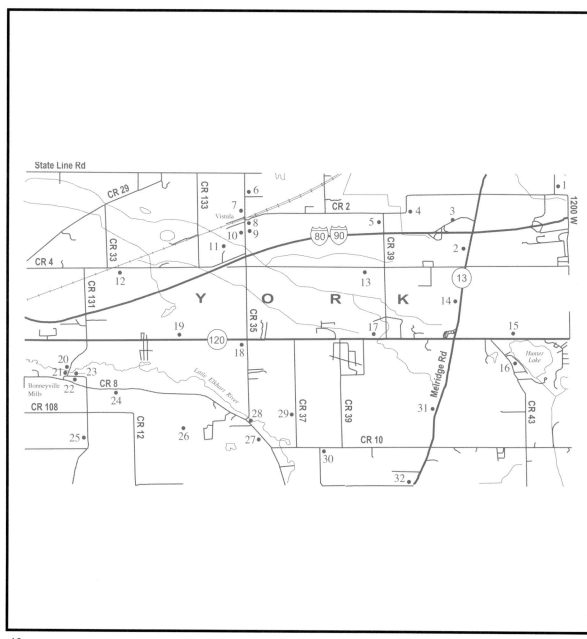

State Line Rd
CR 29
CR 133
Vistula
CR 33
CR 4
CR 131
Y  O  R  K
CR 35
CR 8
Bonneyville Mills
CR 108
CR 12
Little Elkhart River
Hunter Lake
Melridge Rd
CR 37
CR 39
CR 43
CR 10
CR 2
CR 39
1200 W
80 90
120
13

Located in the northeastern corner of Elkhart County, York Township is bordered to the north by the state of Michigan and to the east by LaGrange County. Hunter Lake and the western portion of East Lake are located in the township and the Little Elkhart River flows in a northwestwardly direction through the township. The Lake Shore and Michigan Southern Railroad passes through Vistula, the township's largest town.

William T. Hunter came to the heavily forested area in 1833 and settled along the Little Elkhart River. Others followed the next year, generally settling along Vistula Road, now State Road 120. Among the settlers from the state of New York was John Van Frank, who successfully petitioned to have York Township established from part of Middlebury Township in 1837. That year, the first school was built and Samuel Eby, buried in the Vistula Christian Church Cemetery (00006), established a distillery. Fruit such as plums, strawberries, and grapes, were once prominent crops in the hilly western portion of the township.

Edward Bonney came to the county in 1834 and built the Bonneyville Mill with Nathan Whipple on the Little Elkhart River in 1837 (00020). Bonney intended the mill to become the center of a town, but this never transpired. Bonney became a Civil War veteran and is buried in the Bonneyville Cemetery (00024). In 1923, the Indiana Historical Society declared the Bonneyville Mill to be the oldest continuously operating mill in the state. An additional water wheel and electric generator were installed at the mill in 1931 to provide power to nearby farms.

During the construction of the Michigan Southern Railroad through York Township (subsequently the Lake Shore and Michigan Southern Railroad) in about 1851, several citizens from Middlebury successfully appealed for the railroad to establish a stop at what became the town of Vistula. Originally known as Middlebury Station, it became an important shipping point for Middlebury products that previously had to be exported from Bristol or Goshen. Station agent and postmaster William Caldwell officially renamed Middlebury Station "Vistula" when a post office was established there in 1865. Named after nearby Vistula Road, the town was laid out that year on both sides of the railroad, east of County Road 31. Additional lots were laid out on the eastern side of County Road 31 where the Vistula School (00009) was built.

## YORK TOWNSHIP SCATTERED SITES (00001-032)

**No. Rtg. Description**

**001 O Farm;** 50926 CR 43; 1 ½ double-pile; 1873; Outbuilding: English barn; *Agriculture, Architecture* (408)

**002 C Farm;** SR 13; Dormer-front bungalow; c.1910; Outbuildings: corn crib, English barn, garage, privy, stable, transverse-frame barn; *Agriculture, Architecture* (408)

**003 C Indiana Toll Road Plaza 107;** I 80/90 & SR 13; 20th century functional; 1956; *Architecture, Transportation* (408)

**004 C Farm;** 11748 CR 2; T-plan; c.1880; Outbuildings: English barn, privy, silo, tool shed; *Agriculture, Architecture* (408)

**005 C House;** 51411 CR 39; Gabled-ell; c.1860; Outbuildings: garage, shed; *Architecture* (408)

**006 N Vistula Christian Church Cemetery;** CR 35; c.1850-present; *Military, Religion* (408)

**007 C Disciple Church/Vistula Christian Church;** 51223 CR 35; Gable-front; 1875; Outbuilding: bell; *Architecture, Religion* (408)

**008 C Vistula Hotel;** 51340 CR 35; Lazy-T; c.1860; Outbuildings: garage, shed, workshop; *Architecture, Commerce* (408)

**009 C Vistula School;** 51448 CR 35; T-plan; 1900; *Architecture, Education* (408)

**010 C House;** 51479 CR 35; Second Empire; 1897; *Architecture* (408)

00008 William Barker built and operated the c.1860 Vistula Hotel.

**011 C Farm;** 13709 CR 4; Lazy-T; c.1870; Outbuildings: chicken house, English barn, garage, workshop; *Agriculture, Architecture* (408)

**012 C Farm;** 14834 CR 4; Lazy-T; c.1880; Outbuildings: English barn, machine shed, milk house, shed, stable; *Agriculture, Architecture* (067)

**013 N House;** 12220 CR 4; I-house; c.1840; Outbuilding: silo; *Agriculture, Architecture* (408)

**014 C Ivins-Osborn Cemetery;** SR 13; c.1839-present; *Exploration/Settlement, Religion* (408)

**015 C House;** 10583 SR 120; Midwest cube; c.1900; *Architecture* (408)

**016 C House;** 53372 CR 43; I-house; c.1860; Outbuilding: privy; *Architecture* (408)

00013 This simple one-and-one-half story I-house dates to c.1840.

00020 The Bonneyville Mill is the state's oldest continuously operating grist mill, dating to c.1837. Now part of the Bonneyville Mill County Park, the mill is open to the public during warm months and still produces stone-ground flour.

**017 C Farm;** 12141 SR 120; Upright-and-wing; c.1850; Outbuildings: privy, pumphouse, grain shed; *Agriculture, Architecture* (408)

**018 C York Center School;** 53017 CR 35; Side-gable; 1904; Outbuilding: garage; *Architecture, Education* (408)

**019 C Farm;** 14177 SR 120; Gable-front; c.1880; Outbuildings: English barn, granary, shed; *Agriculture, Architecture* (408)

**020 O Bonneyville Mill;** 53373 CR 131; 19th century functional; c.1837 (Edward Bonney, builder); *Agriculture, Architecture, Industry* (067) **NR**

A view of the Bonneyville Mill and a Pratt truss bridge that once spanned the Little Elkhart River, c.1910. *Photo courtesy of the Elkhart County Historical Museum.*

00022 The group, One Room Schoolhouse, Inc., dismantled the Marsh-Union School in 2001 and reconstructed it at its current site in 2003. The 1887 school was originally located at CR 17 & CR 34 where it operated as a school until 1912.

021  N   House; 53411 CR 131; Lazy-T; c.1890; Outbuildings: chicken house, Interurban waiting room, windmill, workshop; *Architecture, Transportation* (067)

022  C   **Marsh-Union School/York Township District No. 12 School;** CR 131; Gable-front; 1887/2003; *Architecture, Education* (067)

00025 This abandoned I-house has bold Greek Revival ornament and clerestory windows.

00026 The 1862 Jacob Dillman House was originally located on the George Hay Farm in Goshen and is an example of "piece-on-piece" construction having small logs that serve as both structure and wall fill. It was moved to its current site in 1986.

023  N   **Ward Kessler House;** 15303 CR 131; Traditional ranch; c.1941; Outbuildings: cupola, gate, stable; *Architecture* (607)

024  C   **Bonneyville Cemetery;** CR 8; c.1840-present; *Exploration/Settlement, Religion* (067)

025  C   **Farm;** 54331 CR 131; Dormer-front bungalow/Craftsman; c.1920; Outbuildings: English barn, grain bin, house, privy, shed, silo; *Agriculture, Architecture* (607)

026  C   **Jacob Dillman Log House;** 13698 CR 8; Side-gabled/double-pile; 1862 (Jacob Dillman, builder); *Architecture* (408)

027  C   **Farm;** 54387 CR 8; American foursquare; 1930; Outbuildings: bank/basement barn, garage; *Agriculture, Architecture* (408)

028  C   **Pleasant Valley Church of the Brethren and Cemetery;** CR 8; Gable-front; 1867; Cemetery: c.1867-present; *Architecture, Religion* (408)

029  N   **Farm;** 53969 CR 37; Greek Revival/New England 1 ½ cottage; 1852; Outbuildings: chicken house, corn crib, dairy barn, garage, grain bin, hog houses, machine shed, milk house; *Agriculture, Architecture* (408)

00029 This 1852 New England one-and-a-half-cottage has Greek Revival details and clerestory windows.

030  C   **Nihart School/York Township School District No. 7;** CR 10; Italianate; c.1890; *Architecture, Education* (408)

031  C   **Farm;** 53955 SR 13; T-plan; c.1890; Outbuildings: corn crib, garage, machine shed, workshop; *Agriculture, Architecture, Politics* (408)

032  C   **Farm;** 11751 CR 12; T-plan; c.1910; Outbuildings: corn crib, drive-thru corn crib, English barn, grain bin, milk house, stable; *Agriculture, Architecture* (408)

People stand in the ruins of a devastating fire that swept through Vistula in 1909. *Photo courtesy of the Elkhart County Historical Museum*

# Washington Township (05001-038)

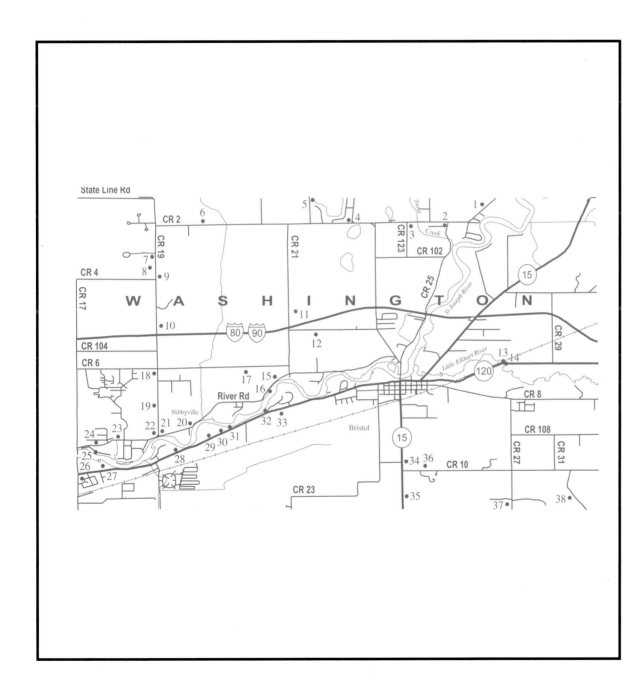

Washington Township lies in the north-central part of Elkhart County and borders the state of Michigan to the north. It was originally part of Middlebury Township until 1835 when it was divided from it. Named in honor of the first president, George Washington, it was further divided in 1836, creating Jefferson Township.

The first residents in the township were James Nicholson and his family who settled in the present location of Bristol in 1829. Within a year, the families of Peter Marmen, Aaron Brown, Reuben Bronson and James Cathcart arrived in the area. Bronson, Cathcart, and others grew fruits and developed an area known as the 'Bristol Fruit Hills.' The Fruit Hills became the largest area of vineyards in the state. Additionally, farmers grew strawberries, grapes, apples, peaches, and plums there.

The town of Bristol lies along the southern bank of the St. Joseph River near the confluence of the Little Elkhart River. Samuel P. Judson, Lewis M. Alverson, and Hiram Doolittle laid out and platted the town in 1834. The St. Joseph River was dammed in Bristol in 1841 to build flour, saw, and later, woolen mills. In 1861, the Little Elkhart River was also dammed and flour and saw mills were constructed. In 1868, the Bristol Hydraulic Company formed and built a more substantial dam on the St. Joseph River to operate a flour mill and furniture factory. These activities were short lived, however, as fires and lawsuits forced the Hydraulic Company to abandon its operations.

The first church in the township was built in Bristol between 1843 and 1847. The slightly altered church building still stands as St. John of the Cross Episcopal Church (06014).

The first schoolhouse in the township was built in 1838. Another building replaced it in 1858 and was expanded in 1892-93 to house twelve grades. In

1903, the township consolidated its one-room schools and a larger, brick schoolhouse was built (06026). Enrollment grew steadily and the building was enlarged in 1923 and 1925 to include more classrooms and a gymnasium. The building closed as a school in 1966. Today, Bristol has a modern elementary school and high school students are bussed into Elkhart. However, several one-room schoolhouses still exist (05007, 05019) as reminders of the past.

In the 1950s, Interstate 80/90, known as the Indiana Toll Road, was built through the township, bypassing Bristol to the north. Two exits provide easy access for residents and travelers to the area.

## WASHINGTON TOWNSHIP SCATTERED SITES (05001-038)

**No. Rtg. Description**

**001 C Farm;** 50763 CR 25; Upright-and-wing; c.1870; Outbuildings: cold cellar, corn crib, drive-thru corn crib, English barn, silo; *Agriculture, Architecture* (067)

**002 C Farm;** 51023 CR 25; Lazy-T; c.1870; Outbuilding: transverse-frame barn; *Agriculture, Architecture* (067)

**003 C Trout Creek Cemetery;** CR 2 & CR 123; c.1854-present; *Religion* (067)

**004 C House;** 50991 CR 23; Upright-and-wing; c.1870; *Architecture* (067)

**005 C House;** 50654 Teall Rd.; Dormer-front bungalow/Craftsman; c.1930; Outbuilding: garage; *Architecture* (067)

**006 C Teall Farm;** 20409 CR 2; New England 1 ½ cottage; c.1900; Outbuildings: corn crib, English barn, pumphouse; *Agriculture, Architecture* (067)

**007 N Washington Township District No. 6 School;** 51528 CR 19; Gable-front; 1879; *Architecture, Education* (067)

**008 N Rau-Halstead House;** 51591 CR 19; Double-entry, double-pile/Greek Revival; c.1850; *Architecture* (067)

**009 C House;** CR 19; Gable-front; c.1880; *Architecture* (067)

05007 The 1879 Washington Township District No. 6 School has been converted into a residence.

**010 C Farm;** 52298 CR 19; Lazy-T; c.1890; Outbuildings: English barn, silo, transverse-frame barn; *Agriculture, Architecture* (067)

**011 C Jonathan Rover House;** 52284 CR 21; Double-pile/Greek Revival; c.1850; *Architecture* (067)

**012 C Farm;** 19248; CR 104; Dormer-front bungalow; c.1930; *Agriculture, Architecture* (067)

**013 C Railroad Bridge;** Over Little Elkhart River; Plate-girder; c.1920; *Engineering, Transportation* (067)

**014 C Bridge;** SR 120 over Little Elkhart River; 1927; *Engineering, Transportation* (067)

**015 C Farm;** 19467 CR 8; Upright-and-wing/Greek Revival; 1878; Outbuilding: bank/basement barn; *Agriculture, Architecture* (067)

**016 C House;** 19788 CR 8; Massed ranch; c.1950; *Architecture* (067)

**017 C Proctor Cemetery;** CR 6; c.1836-c.1912; *Exploration/Settlement, Religion* (067)

**018 O Zion Lutheran Church & Cemetery;** 53176 CR 19; Gothic Revival; 1857/1949; Cemetery: c.1858-present; *Architecture, Exploration/Settlement, Religion* (067)

**019 N Washington Township School District No. 5;** Gable-front; 1885; *Architecture, Education* (067)

**020 C G.B. Garman Farm;** 20833 CR 8; Upright-and-wing; c.1880; Outbuildings: corn crib, Sweitzer barn; *Agriculture, Architecture* (067)

05008 The Rau-Halstead House is a double-entry double-pile with Greek Revival details dating to c.1850.

**021 C Long Farm;** 53830 CR 19; Lazy-T; c.1860; Outbuilding: Sweitzer barn; *Agriculture, Architecture* (067)

**022 C House;** CR 8; T-plan; c.1880; Outbuilding: iron fence; *Architecture* (067)

**023 C Barn;** CR 8; Sweitzer barn; c.1890; *Agriculture, Architecture* (186)

**024 C Farm;** 21776 CR 8; Dormer-front bungalow/Craftsman; c.1880/c.1920; Outbuildings: drive-thru corn crib, English barn, machine shed, shed; *Agriculture, Architecture* (186)

**025 C House;** CR 10 E; Cape Cod; c.1945; *Architecture* (186)

05018 The Zion Lutheran Church congregation dates to 1857 and its building exhibits Gothic Revival details.

05019 The 1885 Washington Township District No. 5 School has been converted to a residence.

026 C **House;** 54558 CR 17; Massed ranch; c.1950; *Architecture* (186)

027 N **House;** 21593 SR 120; Side-gable bungalow/Craftsman; c.1935; *Architecture* (186)

028 N **House;** SR 120; Colonial Revival; c.1915; Outbuilding: garage; *Architecture* (067)

029 C **House;** SR 120; Minimal traditional; c.1945; *Architecture* (067)

030 N **House;** 20211 SR 120; Tudor Revival; c.1930; Outbuilding: garage; *Architecture* (067)

031 C **House;** 20145 SR 120; Colonial Revival; c.1930; *Architecture* (067)

032 C **House;** SR 120; Depression modern; c.1930; *Architecture* (067)

05027 This side-gable bungalow exhibits Craftsman-style details, including knee braces beneath the eaves and original board and batten siding.

05028 This Colonial Revival house features wide clapboard siding and double-hung sash windows.

033 C **House;** 19568 SR 120; Side-gable bungalow/Craftsman; c.1920; *Architecture* (067)

034 C **House;** 54430 SR 15; T-plan; c.1880; *Architecture* (067)

035 C **House;** 54910 SR 15; Upright-and-wing; c.1890; Outbuilding: pumphouse; *Architecture* (067)

036 N **Beardsley House;** 17929 CR 10; Gothic Revival; c.1835; *Architecture* (067)

05030 This Tudor Revival house features stuccoed and half-timbered walls, double-hung sash windows, and a oriel window.

05036 The Beardsley House is a high-style example of the Gothic Revival and is featured in the book *99 Historic Homes of Indiana*. The oldest portion of the house dates to c.1835.

037 C **J.S. Leatherman Farm;** 54977 CR 27; Gable-front bungalow; c.1925; Outbuildings: English barn, shed; *Agriculture, Architecture* (067)

038 C **Farm;** CR 31; Hall-and-parlor; c.1860; Outbuildings: spring house, transverse frame barns; *Agriculture, Architecture* (067)

The Trout Creek Church, c.1900. The church was located on CR 2, two miles north of Bristol. *Photo courtesy of the Elkhart County Historical Museum*

# Bristol Scattered Sites (06001-043)

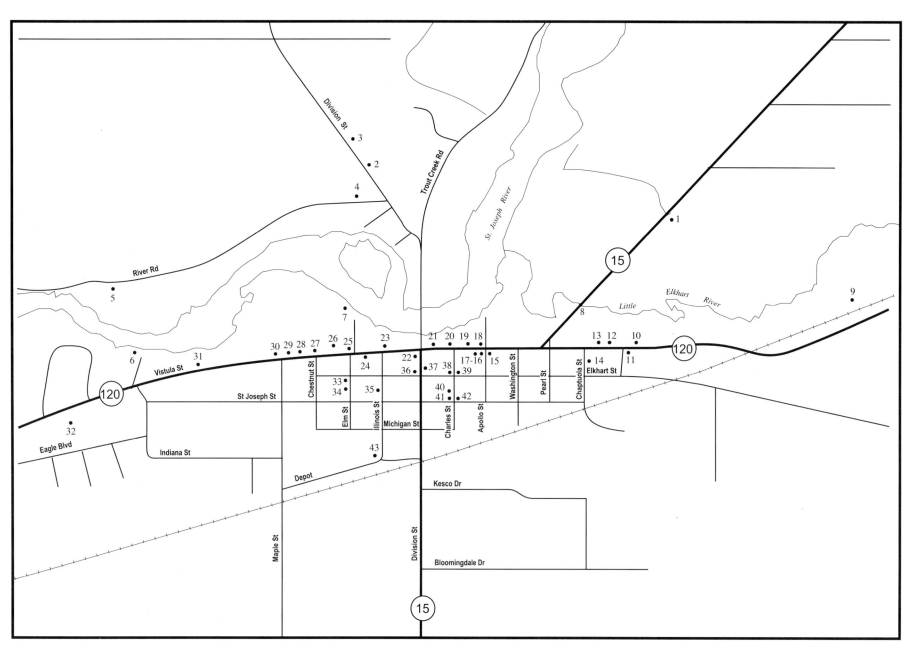

Centrally located in Washington Township, the town of Bristol lies along the southern bank of the St. Joseph River near the confluence of the Little Elkhart River. Today's Bristol encompasses two early settlements. Samuel Judson, Lewis Alverson, and Hiram Doolittle platted the eastern half of Bristol in 1834 and named it after a town in England. Dr. H. H. Fowler platted its western half around the same time, naming it Sydneyham after the town in England where his family lived. As the two settlements grew, they eventually merged taking the name of Bristol.

Early commerce and activity in Bristol centered on the St. Joseph and Little Elkhart Rivers. Lewis and Edward Hanchett and Thomas Wheeler dammed the St. Joseph River in 1841. Flour, wool, and saw mills operated along the river at that time. In 1861, John Boyer and Simon Bickell dammed the Little Elkhart River and built flour and saw mills. In 1868, the Bristol Hydraulic Company built a larger dam on the St. Joseph River and operated a flour mill and furniture factory. Unfortunately, the size and location of the hydraulic company's dam rendered the other dams and mills in the area ineffective. Bitter feelings arose among some businessmen and suspected arsons plagued the hydraulic company's buildings. Lawsuits from those who ran mills on the other area dams curbed efforts to rebuild the hydraulic company's enterprises and eventually its dam was abandoned and destroyed. According to some accounts, the failure of the Bristol Hydraulic Company limited the future commercial development and growth of Bristol. The arrival of the railroad in Bristol did little to boost its economy because nearby Elkhart absorbed the majority of the railroad's commerce.

The first church built in the area still stands in Bristol. Listed in the National Register of Historic Places, St. John's Episcopal Church was constructed in 1847 and expanded by the addition of a large meeting room (06014).

Educational facilities in Bristol have grown from simple, one-room schools to more modern facilities. In 1903, the county's first consolidated school was built in Bristol. The large, brick school was later enlarged as enrollment grew (06026). In 1957, elementary students moved from the old school to a new building and high school students were bussed to Elkhart. The old school building now houses the Elkhart County Historical Museum and is listed in the National Register.

## BRISTOL SCATTERED SITES (06001-043)

| No. | Rtg. | Description |
|-----|------|-------------|
| 001 | C | **House;** 706 Mottville Rd.; Gable-front; c.1915; *Architecture* (067) |
| 002 | C | **House;** 806 N Division St.; Side-gable bungalow; c.1930; *Architecture* (067) |
| 003 | C | **House;** 908 N Division St.; Midwest box; c.1930; *Architecture* (067) |
| 004 | C | **House;** 206 CR 8; American foursquare; c.1920; *Architecture* (067) |
| 005 | C | **Barn;** CR 8; Bank/basement barn; c.1925; *Agriculture, Architecture* (067) |
| 006 | N | **House;** 900 W Vistula St.; Tudor Revival; c.1925; *Architecture* (067) |
| 007 | C | **Cathcart Cemetery;** 210 W Vistula St.; c.1835-c.1881; *Exploration/Settlement, Religion* (067) |
| 008 | C | **Bridge;** SR 15 over Little Elkhart River; 1941; *Engineering, Transportation* (067) |
| 009 | C | **Oak Ridge Cemetery;** SR 120; c.1838-present; *Exploration/Settlement, Religion* (067) |

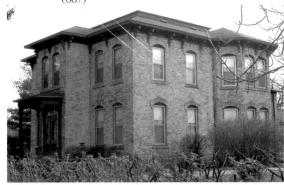

**06011** The 1873 George Milburn House is an excellent example of the Italianate style with its decorative brackets beneath overhanging eaves, tall, rounded windows, and hipped roof.

**06014** The Saint John of the Cross Episcopal Church dates to 1847 and is an excellent example of the Gothic Revival style. It features clapboard siding, original pointed-arch stained glass windows, and a centered bell tower.

| | | |
|-----|------|-------------|
| 010 | C | **House;** 802 E Vistula St.; Prairie; c.1925; *Architecture* (067) |
| 011 | N | **George Milburn House;** 707 E Vistula St.; Italianate; 1873; *Architecture* (067) |
| 012 | C | **House;** 610 E Vistula St.; American foursquare; c.1925; *Architecture* (067) |
| 013 | C | **Knights of Pythias Lodge;** 608 E Vistula St.; Gable-front; c.1920; *Architecture, Social History* (067) |
| 014 | O | **Saint John of the Cross Episcopal Church, Rectory, and Cemetery;** 601-611 E Vistula St.; Gothic Revival; 1847; Rectory: 1830; Cemetery: c.1847-present; *Architecture, Exploration/Settlement, Religion* (067) **NR** |
| 015 | N | **Bristol Town Hall;** 301-303 E Vistula St.; Romanesque Revival; c.1900; *Architecture* (067) |
| 016 | C | **House;** 223 E Vistula St.; Gable-front/Greek Revival; c.1844; *Architecture* (067) |

**017 C** **Commercial Building;** 207 E Vistula St.; Second Empire; 1883; *Architecture, Commerce, Health/Medicine* (067)

**018 C** **Commercial Building;** 220 E Vistula St.; Parapet-front; c.1890; *Architecture, Commerce* (067)

**019 O** **Bristol Opera House;** 210 E Vistula St.; Italianate; 1897; *Architecture, Commerce, Performing Arts* (067)

**020 N** **The Red Bird;** 200 E Vistula St.; Italianate; c.1865; *Architecture, Commerce* (067)

**021 N** **House;** 110 Vistula St.; Greek Revival; 1836/1849; *Architecture* (067)

**022 C** **Hermance-Dussell Building;** 101 W Vistula St.; Two-part commercial block; c.1880; *Architecture, Commerce* (067)

**023 C** **House;** 110 W Vistula St.; Colonial Revival; c.1890; *Architecture* (067)

**024 C** **House;** 203 W Vistula St.; Center-gable I-house; c.1870; *Architecture* (067)

**025 C** **House;** 210 W Vistula St.; T-plan; c.1900; *Architecture* (067)

**026 O** **Washington Township School;** 304 W Vistula St.; Romanesque Revival; 1903/1923/1925 (George W. Selby, architect); *Architecture, Education* (067) **NR**

**027 C** **House;** 400 W Vistula St.; Colonial Revival; c.1935; *Architecture* (067)

**028 C** **House;** 402 W Vistula St.; English cottage; c.1925; *Architecture* (067)

06019 The Bristol Opera House is a rare example of a surviving framed commercial building. The Italianate building features clapboard siding on its main facade.

06020 The Red Bird is the name of the business housed in this Italianate commercial building that dates to c.1865.

**029 C** **House;** 406 W Vistula St.; Dutch Colonial Revival; c.1930; *Architecture* (067)

**030 N** **Yoder House;** 502 W Vistula St.; Greek Revival; c.1850; *Architecture* (067)

**031 C** **House;** 610 W Vistula St.; California bungalow; c.1925; *Architecture* (067)

**032 O** **Solomon Fowler Mansion and Cemetery;** 1105 W Vistula St.; Italianate; 1868; Cemetery: 1849; *Architecture* (067) **NR**

**033 C** **House;** 201 Elm St.; American foursquare; c.1925; *Architecture* (067)

**034 C** **House;** Elm St.; American foursquare; c.1925; *Architecture* (067)

**035 N** **House;** 205 Illinois St.; Midwest box; c.1925; *Architecture* (067)

**036 N** **House;** 117 Division St.; Queen Anne; c.1875; *Architecture* (067)

06026 The Washington Township School is a 1903 example of the Romanesque Revival style. Designed by George W. Selby, it is listed in the National Register of Historic Places.

06036 This Queen Anne house retains original clapboard siding and wood windows. Bay windows and the front porch further add character to the house.

**037 N** **Floyd Congdon House;** 112 Division St.; Gable-front; c.1870; *Architecture* (067)

**038 N** **House;** 108 Elkhart St.; Greek Revival; c.1870; *Architecture* (067)

**039 C** **House;** 110 Charles St.; Cape Cod; c.1945; *Architecture* (067)

**040 C** **House;** 207 Charles St.; Dormer-front bungalow; c.1920; *Architecture* (067)

**041 O** **Thomas Wheeler House;** 209 Charles St.; Greek Revival; c.1834; *Architecture* (067)

**042 C** **House;** 210 Charles St.; American foursquare; c.1915; *Architecture* (067)

**043 C** **House;** 409 Illinois St.; California bungalow; c.1925; *Architecture* (067)

06041 The Thomas Wheeler House dates to c.1834 and is said to have been moved to its current site in 1862 from a site along the St. Joseph River. The Greek Revival house exhibits a "Basilica" form.

# Osolo Township (10001-041)

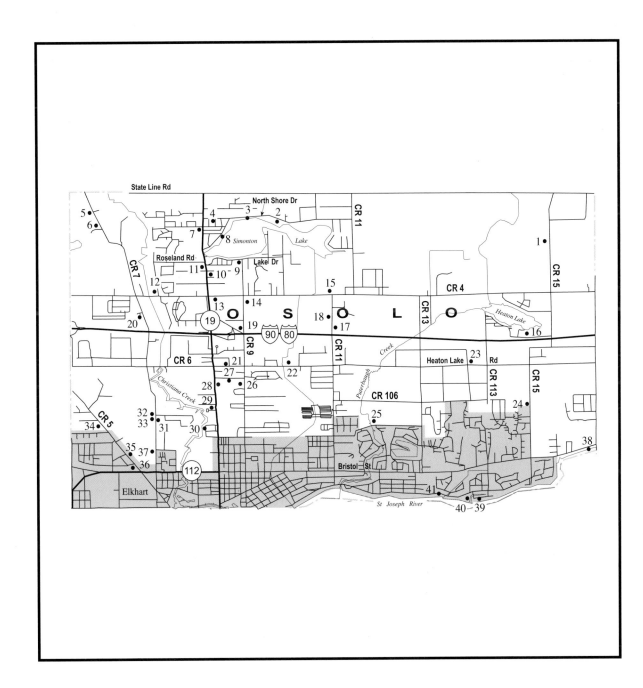

Osolo Township was established in 1838 when it was divided from Cleveland Township. The origin of the township's name is unknown. Early in its history, the township was nicknamed "The Barrens" because it was covered with a particularly thick growth of timber. The earliest reported resident in Osolo Township was Samuel Simonton, who settled there about 1834. Simonton Lake in the northern portion of the township was named after him.

Osolo Township is marshy and dotted with small lakes, especially in its northern half. After drainage, the marshy land was well suited for farming. Simonton and Heaton lakes are regional centers of recreation and residential development in the township.

No cities developed solely within the township, though a small portion of the city of Elkhart crosses into southern Osolo Township. Early in its history, the township briefly had its own post office in a cabin along Christiana Creek. The post office only operated for a couple years before closing as the city of Elkhart grew to be an important regional center. Corridors of commercial and industrial development grew in the township, linking Elkhart to Interstate 80/90. Interstate exits in the area provide easy access for people traveling to and from the township.

The township's first schoolhouse was built in 1838. Several one-room schoolhouses were used until consolidation in the 1920s. Banks School, located in the northeastern part of the township, is a fine example of those early schoolhouses (10001).

## OSOLO TOWNSHIP SCATTERED SITES (10001-041)

| No. | Rtg. | Description |
|---|---|---|

**001  N  Marsh School/Banks School/Osolo Township District No. 5 School;** 51201 CR 15; Gable-front; 1896; *Architecture, Education* (186)

**002  N  House;** 25656 North Shore Dr.; Contemporary shed-roof; c.1950 (Paul J. Grillo, architect); *Architecture* (186)

**003  C  House;** 26006 North Shore Dr.; Western bungalow; c.1920; *Architecture* (186)

**004  C  House;** 26292 Bell Ave.; Minimal traditional; c.1930; *Architecture* (186)

**005  N  Farm;** 50725 CR 7; Cape Cod; c.1940; Outbuilding: livestock barn; *Agriculture, Architecture* (186)

**006  C  Barn;** 50975 CR 7; Bank/basement barn; 1868; *Agriculture, Architecture* (186)

**007  C  House;** 50987 SR 19; Gable-front; c.1920; *Architecture* (186)

**008  C  House;** 51110 North Shore Dr.; Shotgun; c.1935; *Architecture* (186)

**009  C  House;** 26022 Lake Dr.; California bungalow; c.1920; *Architecture* (186)

**010  C  Simonton Lake Drive-In;** SR 19; House-with-canopy/Modern; c.1955; *Architecture, Commerce, Transportation* (186)

**10002  Notre Dame Professor of Architecture Paul J. Grillo designed his contemporary style home that features a shed roof. Interior ammenities include built-in seating and bookshelves, a hidden room, and convertible living spaces.**

**011  C  House;** 51579 SR 19; Western bungalow; c.1925; *Architecture* (186)

**012  O  House;** 51975 Winding Waters Ln.; Upright-and-wing/Greek Revival; 1854; *Architecture* (186)

**013  C  House;** 26260 CR 4; Minimal traditional; c.1940; *Architecture* (186)

**014  C  Farm;** 52084 CR 9; Gable-front; c.1900; Outbuilding: English barn; *Agriculture, Architecture* (186)

**015  NC  Houses;** 25051 CR 4; Geodesic domes; 1974; *Architecture* (186)

**016  C  Shady Nook Chapel;** 52256-7 Ideal Beach Rd.; 20th century rustic; c.1935; *Architecture* (186)

**017  C  House;** 52452 CR 11; Lazy-T; c.1885; *Architecture* (186)

**10025  The unfortunate victim of a fire, this c.1850 house was a stunning example of a double-pile Greek Revival.**

**018  C  House;** 52333 CR 11; English cottage; c.1925; *Architecture* (186)

**019  C  House;** 52399 CR 9; Ranch; c.1950; *Architecture* (186)

**020  C  House;** 52269 CR 7; California bungalow; c.1925; *Architecture* (186)

**021  C  House;** 2807 Cumberland Ave.; Colonial Revival; c.1935; *Architecture* (186)

**022  C  Osolo Township Cemetery;** CR 6; c.1838-present; *Religion* (186)

**023  C  Barn;** Marina Dr.; English barn; c.1930; *Agriculture, Architecture* (186)

**024  O  House;** 53585 CR 15; T-plan/Italianate; c.1880; Outbuilding: shed; *Architecture* (186)

**025  N  House;** 2620 Miller St.; Double-pile/Greek Revival; c.1850; *Architecture* (186) DESTROYED BY FIRE

**026  C  House;** 53217 CR 9; Minimal traditional; c.1940; *Architecture* (186)

**027  C  House;** 26152 Arlington Rd.; Minimal traditional; c.1940; *Architecture* (186)

**028  C  House;** 2624 SR 19; Ranch; c.1945; *Architecture* (186)

**029  C  House;** 415 North St.; Minimal traditional; c.935; *Architecture* (186)

**030  N  House;** 2031 Anna Dr.; Ranch/Prairie; c.1950; *Architecture* (186)

**10001 The 1896 Osolo Township District No. 5 School, also called the Marsh School and Banks School, retains its original slate roof. It remained a schoolhouse until consolidation in 1922; today it is a residence.**

**10024  This T-plan house features Italianate-style bay windows, decorative bargeboard in the gable ends, and round-arch windows.**

10030 This c.1950 ranch house is heavily influenced by the Prairie style and features a low-to-the-ground profile, wide, overhanging eaves, and ribbon windows.

10036 This c.1955 International-style house features smooth stucco walls, a flat roof with wide, overhanging eaves, and large, single-pane picture windows on each facade.

10038 This c.1880 upright-and-wing features a wide cornice and round-arched windows.

031  C  **Fair Acres Barn;** 53744 CR 7; English barn; c.1900; *Agriculture, Architecture* (186)

032  C  **House;** 55713 CR 7; California bungalow; c.1915; *Architecture* (186)

033  C  **House;** 53731 CR 7; Colonial Revival; c.1925; Outbuilding: garage; *Architecture* (186)

034  N  **House;** 53857 CR 5; Greek Revival; c.1860; *Architecture* (186)

035  C  **Double House;** 54268 CR 5; Minimal ranch; c.1950; *Architecture* (186)

036  N  **House;** 1541 CR 5; International; c.1955; *Architecture* (186)

037  C  **House;** 54257 CR 7; California bungalow; c.1920; *Architecture* (186)

038  N  **House;** 22150 CR 10; Upright-and-wing; c.1880; *Architecture* (186)

039  C  **House;** 23396 Shore Lane Dr.; Colonial Revival; c.1945; Outbuilding: garage; *Architecture* (186)

040  C  **House;** 23614 Greenleaf Blvd.; French Eclectic Revival; 1952; *Architecture* (186)

041  C  **House;** 23840 Greenleaf Blvd.; Ranch; c.1960; *Architecture* (186)

10034 This c.1860 Greek Revival house features a broad cornice with returns on the gable ends.

C.G. Conn's summer house, "Lawndale," date unknown. The house was located at the southeast corner of CR 6 and Osolo Road. *Photo from* Images of America, Elkhart, Indiana *by Amy (Lant) Wenger.*

# Cleveland Township (15001-075)

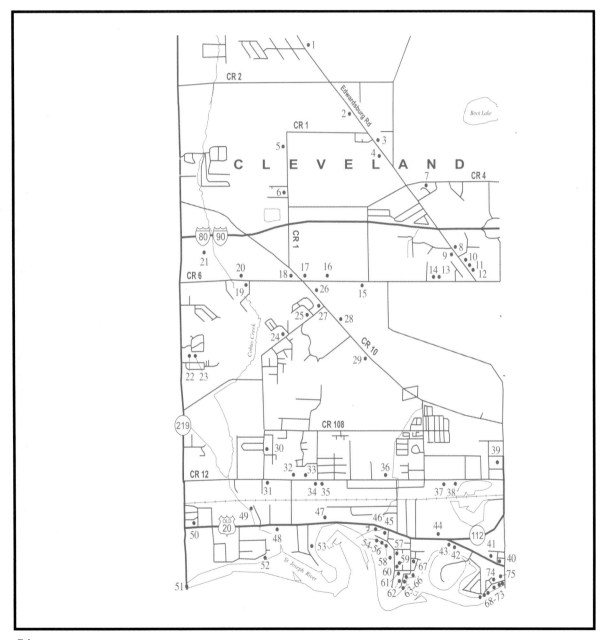

Cleveland Township was organized in January of 1835 and named after the Ohio city. Its original boundaries encompassed all the land currently in Cleveland and Osolo townships until 1837, when the two separated.

The first settler in the township is believed to have been Francis Rork, who settled along Cobus Creek in 1830. Five years later, residents organized the township's first school. Students attended classes held in a cabin owned by Rork and taught by fourteen-year-old Wealthy Evans. The first known commercial mill was built in 1856 along Cobus Creek, then known as Cobert's Creek.

Cleveland Township grew slowly because no cities developed within its boundaries. Although plans for a city called Bridgeport located at the confluence of Cobus Creek and the St. Joseph River were discussed, there is no evidence that anything ever materialized.

Census figures indicate that Cleveland Township's population decreased steadily between 1890 and 1920. However, after 1920 the township began to experience more rapid growth through the mid-20th century with the encroachment of the nearby city of Elkhart. Evidence of that growth is particularly apparent in the southern half of the township.

## CLEVELAND TOWNSHIP SCATTERED SITES (15001-075)

**No.  Rtg.  Description**

**001  C  House;** 50564 CR 5; Upright-and-wing; c.1865; Outbuilding: garage; *Architecture* (483)

**002  C  House;** 51365 CR 5; Double-entry Midwest box; c.1920; *Architecture* (483)

**003  N  Farm;** 51636 CR 5; Italianate; c.1890; Outbuilding: livestock barn; *Agriculture, Architecture* (483)

**004  N  Walter Ford House;** 51746 CR 5; Art Moderne; 1945 (Walter Ford, builder); Outbuilding: garage; *Architecture* (483)

**005  C  House;** CR 1; Double-entry, double-pile; c.1890; *Architecture* (483)

**006  N  House;** CR 1; Double-entry, double-pile; 1868; Outbuilding: fence posts; *Architecture* (483)

**007  C  Carleton Cemetery;** CR 4; c.1835-present; *Exploration/Settlement, Religion* (483)

**008  C  House;** 52684 CR 5; Ranch; c.1960; *Architecture* (483)

**009  C  Cleveland House;** 52725 CR 5; Upright-and-wing; c.1865; Outbuildings: garage, milk house; *Architecture* (483)

**010  C  House;** 52790 CR 5; Midwest box; 1920; *Architecture* (483)

15003 Elements of the Italianate style can be found on this brick house, most notably its tall, narrow windows with segmental-arched tops.

15006 This 1868 double-entry, double-pile house features cedar shake shingles and is well-preserved.

**011  C  House;** 52852 CR 5; Minimal traditional; c.1945; *Architecture* (483)

**012  C  House;** CR 5; California bungalow; c.1930; *Architecture* (483)

**013  C  House;** CR 6; English cottage; c.1937 (Architect's Small House Service Bureau); Outbuilding: garage; *Architecture* (483)

**014  C  House;** 28529 CR 6; Gable-front; c.1920; Outbuilding: garage; *Architecture* (483)

**015  C  Farm;** CR 6; Saltbox; c.1910; Outbuilding: transverse-frame barn; *Agriculture, Architecture* (483)

**016  C  House;** 29623 CR 6; Minimal traditional; c.1930; *Architecture* (483)

**017  C  House;** CR 6 & CR 10; Lazy-T; c.1880; *Architecture* (483)

**018  C  House;** CR 6 & CR 10; Ranch; c.1960; *Architecture* (483)

**019  N  Farm;** CR 6; Lazy-T/Italianate; c.1880; Outbuildings: bank/basement barn, garage, livestock barn, tool shed; *Agriculture, Architecture* (483)

**020  C  House;** 30371 CR 6; Shotgun; c.1920; *Architecture* (483)

**021  O  House;** 52740 Ash Rd.; Italianate cube; c.1840; *Architecture* (483)

**022  C  House;** 30904 Oakcrest Dr.; Ranch; c.1960; *Architecture* (483)

**023  C  House;** 30450 Oakcrest Dr.; Ranch; c.1960; *Architecture* (483)

**024  C  House;** CR 1; Dutch Colonial Revival/rustic; 1930; *Architecture* (483)

**025  C  House;** 53103 Tulain Rd.; Ranch; 1962; *Architecture* (483)

**026  C  Farm;** 29767 CR 10; Gable-front; c.1900; Outbuildings: English barn, transverse-frame barn; *Agriculture, Architecture* (483)

**027  N  House;** 29666 CR 10; Greek Revival; c.1855; Outbuilding: iron fence; *Architecture* (483)

15007 A Cleveland family monument in the Carleton Cemetery.

**15013** The Architects' Small House Service Bureau, Inc. called this house an "Economical Colonial Bungalow Designed For The Narrow Lot," and boasted that the location of rooms met modern needs.

**028  C  Farm;** CR 10; Dutch Colonial Revival; c.1920; Outbuilding: transverse-frame barn; *Agriculture, Architecture* (483)

**029  C  House;** 29160 CR 10; Upright-and-wing; c.1880; *Architecture* (483)

**030  C  House;** 54672 CR 1; Ranch; c.1955; *Architecture* (483)

**031  C  Commercial Building;** 30178 CR 12; Modern broadfront; c.1950; *Architecture, Commerce* (483)

**032  C  House;** CR 12; Ranch; c.1955; *Architecture* (483)

**033  N  Jensen's Orchard;** 29851 CR 12; Minimal traditional; c.1948 (Jensen, builder); *Architecture* (483)

**15019** This lazy-T house features Italianate-style windows and retains its original slate roof.

**15027** This c.1855 house retains many distinctive characteristics of the Greek Revival style, including a broad cornice with returns on the gable ends, and a door surround with transom and side lights.

**034  C  California Methodist Episcopal Church;** CR 12; Gable-front/Gothic Revival; 1878; *Architecture, Religion* (483)

**035  C  California Cemetery;** CR 12; c.1865-present; *Religion* (483)

**036  C  Farm;** 29099 CR 12; American foursquare; c.1900; Outbuilding: English barn; *Agriculture, Architecture* (483)

**037  C  House;** 2623 CR 12; Shed-roof/contemporary; 1956; *Architecture* (483)

**038  C  House;** 2531 CR 12; Gabled-ell; c.1900; *Architecture* (483)

**039  C  Riblet Manufacturing Factory;** 1125-1127 Nappanee St.; 20th century functional; c.1952; *Architecture, Industry* (483)

**15033** This minimal traditional house dates to c.1948 and includes features unusual to its time period, such as closets with door-activiated lights and retractable awnings controlled from the inside.

**15037** This 1956 Contemporary house has a shed-roof.

**040  C  House;** 2124 W Lexington Ave.; Western bungalow; c.1930; *Architecture* (483)

**041  C  House;** Lexington Ave.; American four-square; c.1910; *Architecture* (483)

**042  C  House;** 2597 Lexington Ave.; Double-entry minimal traditional; c.1945; *Architecture* (483)

**043  C  House;** 2599 Lexington Ave.; Double-entry minimal traditional; c.1945; *Architecture* (483)

**044  C  Commercial Building;** 2746 Old US 20; International; c.1950; *Architecture, Commercial* (483)

**045  N  Farm;** Old US 20; Upright-and-wing; c.1850/c.1890; Outbuildings: English barn, log house, spring house; *Agriculture, Architecture, Exploration/Settlement* (483)

**046  N  Bailey House;** Old US 20; Contemporary; 1962 (Albert Bailey, architect); *Architecture* (483)

**047  C  House;** 29713 Old US 20; Midwest box; c.1890; *Architecture* (483)

**048  C  House;** 30134 Old US 20; Western bungalow; c.1920; *Architecture* (483)

**15045** This log house is part of a farm that retains a number of representative outbuildings.

**15046** Albert Bailey designed and built this 1962 Contemporary-style home, which is owned by his son today. Bailey studied architecture in Chicago and was influenced by Frank Lloyd Wright.

**049** **C** **House;** Osborn Ave.; Ranch; c.1955; *Architecture* (483)

**050** **C** **Rib-a-Rama;** 30895 Old US 20; Contemporary; c.1955; *Architecture, Commerce* (483)

**051** **O** **County Line/Ash Road Bridge;** Ash Rd. over St. Joseph River; Concrete arch; 1929/1994; *Engineering, Transportation* (483) **HAER**

**052** **C** **House;** 30264 North Shore Dr.; Minimal traditional; c.1930; Outbuildings: log cabin, log crib barn; *Architecture* (483)

**053** **N** **Poorbaugh House;** 55632 Riverview Manor Dr.; Mediterranean Revival; c.1940; *Architecture* (483)

**054** **C** **House;** 29172 Frailey Dr.; Colonial Revival; c.1940; *Architecture* (483)

**055** **C** **House;** Frailey Dr.; Contemporary; c.1950; *Architecture* (483)

**056** **C** **House;** 55735 Riverdale Dr.; Ranch; c.1960; *Architecture* (483)

**057** **N** **House;** Riverdale Dr.; Contemporary; c.1950; *Architecture* (483)

**058** **C** **House;** 55877 Riverdale Dr.; Ranch; c.1955; *Architecture* (483)

**15050** The Rib-A-Rama building is a good example of 1950s roadside architecture.

**15051** This 1929 concrete arch bridge spans the St. Joseph River on Ash Road.

**059** **C** **House;** 55856 Kathryn Dr.; Ranch/split-level; c.1960; *Architecture* (483)

**060** **C** **House;** 28997 Oak Grove Dr.; Ranch; c.1955; *Architecture* (483)

**061** **C** **House;** 28790 Oak Grove Dr.; Ranch; c.1955; *Architecture* (483)

**062** **C** **House;** Rio Lindo Dr.; Colonial Revival; c.1950; *Architecture* (483)

**063** **C** **House;** Rio Lindo Dr.; Colonial Revival; c.1950; *Architecture* (483)

**064** **C** **House;** Rio Lindo Dr.; Colonial Revival; c.1935; *Architecture* (483)

**065** **C** **House;** 28916 Oak Manor Pl.; Gable-front/contemporary; c.1955; *Architecture* (483)

**066** **C** **House;** 28852 Oak Grove Dr.; Ranch; c.1955; *Architecture* (483)

**067** **C** **House;** Oak Manor Dr. & Oak Leaf Pl.; Ranch; c.1960; *Architecture* (483)

**068** **C** **House;** Rainbow Bend Blvd.; Ranch; 1959; *Architecture* (483)

**069** **C** **House;** 1945 Rainbow Bend Blvd.; Upright-and-wing/ranch; 1959; *Architecture* (483)

**15053** An unusual example of the Mediterranean Revival style is this c.1940 house that features brushed stucco walls.

**15055** This Contemporary house has a very low-pitch gabled roof.

**070** **C** **House;** 1939 Rainbow Bend Blvd.; Ranch; c.1955; *Architecture* (483)

**071** **C** **House;** 1909 Rainbow Bend Blvd.; Ranch; c.1955; *Architecture* (483)

**072** **C** **House;** Rainbow Bend Blvd.; Contemporary; c.1962 (John Lieberenz, architect); *Architecture* (483)

**073** **C** **House;** Rainbow Bend Blvd.; Ranch; c.1955; *Architecture* (483)

**074** **N** **House;** Aspin Dr. & Rainbow Bend Blvd.; Contemporary; c.1960 (John Lieberenz, architect); *Architecture* (483)

**075** **C** **House;** 1816 Rainbow Bend Blvd.; Ranch; c.1955; *Architecture* (483)

**15057** This c.1950 house is a notable example of the contemporary style. It features a low-pitched roof with broad overhangs, an integral carport, and a prominent chimney.

**15074** Local architect John Lieberenz designed this c.1960 ranch house that retains a high level of integrity.

# Baugo Township (20001-047)

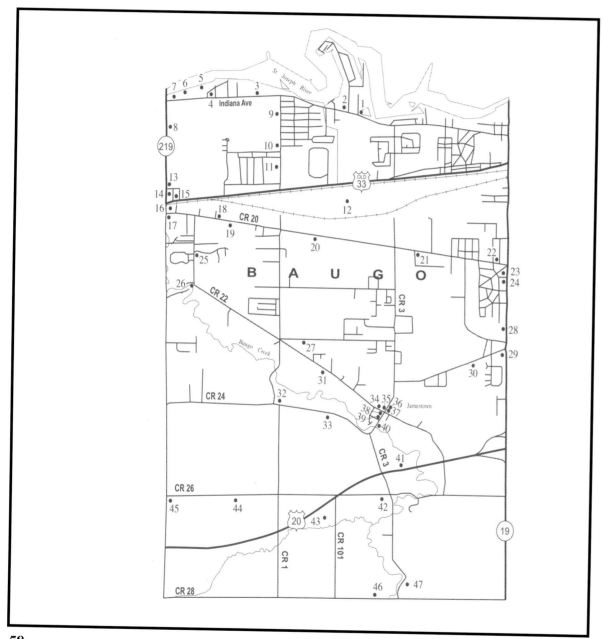

Baugo Township is located in west-central Elkhart County. Its land is mostly flat and contains some small creeks. It borders St. Joseph County to the west and the St. Joseph River creates its northern boundary.

Baugo Township was formed in 1836 and originally encompassed present-day Olive and Locke Townships until they were divided in 1839. The name of the township is a derivative of the Indian name given to a creek in the township. Indians called the creek *Baubaugo*, meaning "Devil River," due to its swift and sometimes dangerous current.

Little information about the township's earliest settlers is known. One source credits William Mote with being the first settler in 1830 and other families arrived in the following years.

In 1835, James Davis laid out the town of Jamestown on the banks of Baugo Creek, which came to be known as Jimtown. Jimtown had a saw mill, a few stores, and houses. Additionally, the township built the first schoolhouse in Jimtown. Unfortunately, Jimtown failed to develop as hoped and residents abandoned it for several years. However, in recent decades the area has reestablished itself as a bedroom community of Elkhart.

## BAUGO TOWNSHIP SCATTERED SITES (20001-047)

**No. Rtg. Description**

**001 N** **John Boss House & Brickyard;** 29291 CR 16; Lazy-T; c.1843; Outbuildings: privy, pumphouse; *Architecture, Industry* (483)

**002 C** **House;** 29463 CR 16; Italianate; c.1860; *Architecture* (483)

**003 C** **Barn;** CR 16; Basement barn; c.1880; Agriculture, Architecture (483)

**004 C** **House;** 30590 Edgewater Dr.; Ranch; c.1950; *Architecture* (483)

**005 C** **House;** 30665 CR 16; Colonial Revival; c.1920; *Architecture* (483)

**006 C** **House;** 30809 CR 16; Cape Cod; c.1950; *Architecture* (483)

**007 C** **House;** 30863 CR 16; I-house; c.1880; Outbuilding: pumphouse; *Architecture* (483)

**008 C** **House;** Ash Rd.; California bungalow; c.1925; *Architecture* (483)

**009 C** **Bethany Missionary Church;** 56295 CR 1; Contemporary; 1959; *Architecture, Religion* (483)

**010 C** **House;** CR 1; Dormer-front bungalow; c.1925; *Architecture* (483)

**011 C** **House;** 56767 CR 1; Dormer-front bungalow; c.1920; *Architecture* (483)

20001 The John Boss House is believed by its owner to date to 1843. It was originally twice its current size, but an east wing was demolished.

20020 The Henry Swartz House dates to c.1854.

**012 N** **Robert Young Memorial Yard;** US 33; Railroad yard; 1956; *Engineering, Industry, Transportation* (483)

**013 C** **House;** 30947 Carroll Ave.; Craftsman; c.1925; *Architecture* (483)

**014 C** **House;** 57092 Ash Rd.; Midwest box; c.1925; *Architecture* (483)

**015 C** **House;** 30895 Old US 33; Minimal traditional; c.1920; *Architecture* (483)

**016 C** **Osceola Cemetery;** Ash Rd. and CR 20; c.1831-present; *Exploration/Settlement, Religion* (483)

**017 C** **House;** 30880 CR 20; Minimal traditional; c.1950; *Architecture* (483)

**018 C** **House;** 30491 CR 20; Mission Revival; c.1930; *Architecture* (483)

**019 C** **Farm;** 30318 CR 20; Gabled-ell; c.1880; Outbuildings: English barn, privy, shed, transverse-frame barn; *Agriculture, Architecture* (483)

**020 N** **Henry Swartz House;** 29640 CR 20; I-house/Italianate; c.1854; *Architecture* (483)

**021 C** **Barn;** 28766 CR 20; Livestock barn; c.1930; *Agriculture, Architecture* (483)

**022 C** **House;** CR 20; Minimal traditional; c.1950; *Architecture* (483)

**023 C** **House;** SR 19; Massed ranch; c.1950; *Architecture* (483)

**024 C** **House;** 57867 SR 19; California bungalow; c.1925; *Architecture* (483)

Students and faculty pose in front of the original 1877 Jamestown School that was located at the northwest corner of CR 3 and CR 22 and closed in 1913. *Photo courtesy of the Elkhart County Historical Museum.*

**025 C** **House;** CR 100; Upright-and-wing; c.1900; *Architecture* (483)

**026 C** **House;** 57987 CR 100; Western bungalow; c.1920; *Architecture* (483)

**027 C** **House;** 29768 CR 118; Minimal traditional; c.1950; *Architecture* (483)

**028 C** **Farm;** SR 19; Double-pile; c.1860; Outbuildings: English barn, silo; *Agriculture, Architecture* (483)

**029 C** **Barn;** 28070 CR 24 W; Bank barn; 1916/1959; *Agriculture, Architecture* (483)

**030 C** **Farm;** 28336 CR 24; Upright-and-wing; c.1880; Outbuildings: English barn, silos, transverse-frame barn; *Agriculture, Architecture* (483)

**031 C** **House;** 29485 CR 22; Lazy-T; c.1890; *Architecture* (483)

20034 The 1929 Mission Revival Baugo Township High School.

**20040** This c.1935 English Cottage features an arched entryway and windows, historic double-hung sash windows, and a steeply-pitched roof.

**032 C Noffsinger Cemetery;** CR 24 & CR 1; c.1844-c.2001; *Exploration/Settlement, Religion* (483)

**033 C Farm;** CR 24; Upright-and-wing; c.1860/c.1880; Outbuildings: privy, Sweitzer barn, wood shed; *Agriculture, Architecture* (483)

**034 O Baugo Township High School;** CR 22; Mission Revival; 1929; *Architecture, Education* (483)

**035 C World War II Memorial;** CR 3; Memorial; 1945; *Social History* (483)

**036 C J.J. Frederick Building;** 59158 CR 3; Art Deco; 1947; *Architecture, Commerce* (483)

**037 C House;** 59188 CR 3; Western bungalow; c.1925; *Architecture* (483)

**038 C House;** 29088 CR 22; English cottage; c.1940; *Architecture* (483)

Two men and a young boy stand outside the Jamestown Store, c.1914. *Photo courtesy of the Elkhart County Historical Museum*

**20045** This house is a nice example of the popular American foursquare type. It features a pyramidal roof with hipped dormers and a full-width porch.

**039 C Cook House;** CR 3; Minimal traditional; c.1950; *Architecture* (483)

**040 N House;** 59320 CR 3; English cottage; c.1935; Outbuilding: garage; *Architecture* (483)

**041 C House;** 59710 CR 3; Free Classic; c.1890; *Architecture* (483)

**042 C House;** CR 3 & CR 26; New England 1 ½ cottage/Greek Revival; c.1850; *Architecture* (656)

**043 C Farm;** 60181 CR 101; Hall-and-parlor; c.1860; Outbuildings: bank/basement barn, pumphouse, shed, transverse-frame barn; *Agriculture, Architecture* (656)

**044 C Strubel Farm;** 30356 CR 26; Basement barn; c.1900; Outbuildings: drive-thru corn crib, transverse-frame barn; *Agriculture, Architecture* (656)

**045 N House;** 60020 County Line Rd.; American foursquare; c.1918; *Architecture* (656)

**046 C Barn;** CR 28; Bank barn; c.1930; *Agriculture, Architecture* (656)

**047 C Holdeman Farm;** 60848 CR 3; Gabled-ell; c.1893; Outbuildings: bank/basement barn, drive-thru corn crib, milk house, silo; *Agriculture, Architecture* (656)

Workers fire bricks at the Boss Brickyard, c.1900. The yard was located on CR 16 west of SR 19. *Photo courtesy of the Elkhart County Historical Museum.*

# Concord Township (25001-075)

Two prominent rivers cross Concord Township: the St. Joseph River flows west through the township's northern portion and the Elkhart River cuts diagonally through the township. The Elkhart River derives its name from an island located at the confluence of the Elkhart and St. Joseph Rivers, which is said to resemble the shape of an elk's heart.

The original 1830 boundaries of the township encompassed present-day Cleveland, Osolo, Washington, Baugo, Concord, and Jefferson townships. In 1834, Concord Township was greatly reduced in size as the lands of Washington and Jefferson townships became part of Middlebury Township. Less than a year later, Osolo and Cleveland Townships were divided to form Cleveland Township. In 1836 Concord Township's present boundaries were established when Baugo Township split off to become its own township.

The earliest settler in the township was Joseph Noffsinger, who arrived on the north side of the St. Joseph River near the mouth of Christiana Creek as early as 1821. A few years later more settlers arrived and formed the village of Pulaski. Pulaski consisted of a post office, gristmill, and several houses. In 1831, Dr. Havilah Beardsley purchased a tract of land just south of the St. Joseph River from the Indian Chief Pierre Moran. In 1832, Dr. Beardsley hired George Crawford to survey and plat the village of Elkhart and it began to grow steadily. In 1858, it was incorporated as a town and chartered as a city in 1875.

The rapid growth of Elkhart was largely due to its location along the rivers and the coming of the railroad. In the 1870s, the hydraulic works were developed, harnessing the power of the Elkhart River and allowing growth of industry in Elkhart. In 1870, the Lake Shore & Michigan Southern Railroad opened engine works and repair shops in Elkhart. The shops created many jobs and opportunities for the people of Elkhart. Between 1870 and 1900 the population of Elkhart grew almost five-fold. Following the period of rapid growth, the city continued to steadily grow.

Outside the city of Elkhart, the township's landscape combines industry and agriculture. The majority of agricultural activity is located in the southwestern corner of the township, while large industrial parks dominate the township's northeastern portion. A large commercial strip was developed along the Route 33 corridor linking Elkhart to the nearby city of Goshen.

On Palm Sunday of 1965, several tornadoes touched down in Elkhart County. The most heavily affected area was the community of Dunlap, located southeast of Elkhart. Two separate tornadoes were reported on the ground at the same time in the small community. The tornadoes destroyed or heavily damaged many homes in the area and, tragically, fifty-two people lost their lives in the storm.

## CONCORD TOWNSHIP SCATTERED SITES (25001-075)

**No. Rtg. Description**

**001 N Pine Creek Acres;** SR 120; Sweitzer barn; c.1900; Outbuilding: silo; *Agriculture, Architecture* (186)

**002 N John Garman House;** 22767 SR 120; Italianate cube; c.1870; *Architecture* (186)

**003 C Barn;** SR 120; English barn; c.1915; Outbuildings: sheds; *Agriculture, Architecture* (186)

**004 C House;** 4040 SR 120; Italianate cube; c.1870; *Architecture* (483)

**005 C Middleton Run Cemetery;** SR 120; 1852-2000; *Religion* (186)

**006 C House;** 300 Middleton Run Rd.; Dormer-front bungalow; c.1925; *Architecture* (186)

**007 C House;** 1529 Middlebury St.; Colonial Revival; c.1930; *Architecture* (186)

**25002 The Italianate cube John Garman House dates to c.1870 and features brick walls, decorative brackets along the cornice line, round-arched windows, and a full-width porch.**

**008 C Farm;** 2130 Middlebury St.; American foursquare; c.1915; Outbuilding: bank/basement barn; *Agriculture, Architecture* (186)

**009 C House;** 3203 Middlebury St.; Ranch; c.1945; *Architecture* (186)

**010 C Farm;** 56082 CR 15; California bungalow; c.1925; Outbuildings: chicken house, English barn, garage; *Agriculture, Architecture* (186)

**011 C Farm;** 21895 CR 14; T-plan; c.1915; Outbuildings: corn crib, English barn, hog house, machine shed, transverse-frame barn; *Agriculture, Architecture* (186)

**012 N Log House;** 22954 Old US 20; Double-pen saltbox; c.1840 (Ziba Winget, builder); *Architecture, Exploration/Settlement* (186)

**013 C Barn;** Old US 20; Sweitzer barn; c.1890; *Agriculture, Architecture* (186)

**014 C House;** 1927 Toledo Rd.; Gable-front; c.1958; *Architecture* (186)

**015 C House;** 1660 Toledo Rd.; Dutch Colonial Revival; c.1925; *Architecture* (186)

**016 C House;** 1650 Toledo Rd.; Gable-front; c.1915; *Architecture* (186)

**017 C House;** 1640 Toledo Rd.; Gable-front; c.1890; *Architecture* (186)

**018 C House;** 24136 CR 16; American foursquare; c.1930; *Architecture* (186)

**25007 This c.1930 Colonial Revival house exhibits cornice returns on the gable ends, double-hung sash windows, and a columned entry porch.**

**019 C Rowe Cemetery;** CR 16; c.1848-present; *Exploration/Settlement, Religion* (186)

**020 C House;** 57207 CR 17; Minimal traditional; c.1940; *Architecture* (186)

**021 C House;** US 20 & CR 18; Gabled-ell; c.1890; *Architecture* (186)

**022 C Barn;** 22956 CR 18; Sweitzer barn; c.1890; Outbuilding: silo; *Agriculture, Architecture* (186)

**023 C House;** 24560 Ne Ce Dah Ave.; English Cottage; c.1935; *Architecture* (186)

**024 C House;** 24664 Perkins Ave.; Minimal traditional; c.1955; *Architecture* (186)

**25008 This American foursquare has flared eaves and a columned full-width porch with stone walls.**

25010 This California bungalow boasts exposed rafter tails and original windows.

025   C   **House;** 57755 Newman St.; American four-square; c.1920; *Architecture* (186)

026   C   **House;** 1301 Hively Ave.; English cottage; c.1935; *Architecture* (186)

027   C   **House;** 903 Hively Ave.; American four-square; c.1910; *Architecture* (186)

028   C   **House;** 2715 Pleasant Plain Ave.; California bungalow; c.1920; *Architecture* (186)

029   C   **House;** 2901 Pleasant Plain Ave.; Side-gable bungalow/Craftsman; c.1925; *Architecture* (186)

030   C   **House;** 534 Hively Ave.; Gabled-ell; c.1900; *Architecture* (186)

031   N   **Markel House;** 2555 Oakland Ave.; Lazy-T; c.1847 (David Markel, builder); *Architecture* (186)

032   C   **House;** 2822 Oakland Ave.; California bungalow; c.1920; Outbuilding: garage; *Architecture* (186)

033   C   **House;** 27306 CR 20; Pyramidal-roof cottage; c.1940; Outbuilding: garage; *Architecture* (186)

034   C   **House;** 58005 CR 105; Dormer-front bungalow; c.1920; *Architecture* (186)

035   C   **House;** 1220 CR 20; Colonial Revival; c.1890; *Architecture* (186)

036   C   **Pleasant Plain/Oakland Avenue School;** 57968 CR 7; T-plan; 1893; *Architecture, Education* (186)

037   C   **Farm;** 58416 CR 7; Sweitzer barn; c.1875; Outbuildings: corn crib, silo, transverse-frame barn; *Agriculture, Architecture* (186)

038   C   **Barn;** 58555 CR 7; Livestock barn; c.1910; *Agriculture, Architecture* (186)

039   C   **Barn;** 58658 CR 9; English barn; c.1900; *Agriculture, Architecture* (186)

040   C   **House;** 58201 CR 9; California bungalow; c.1920; *Architecture* (186)

041   C   **Moore Farm;** 209 CR 20; English barn; c.1915; Outbuilding: spring house; *Agriculture, Architecture* (186)

042   C   **House;** 3401 Pleasant Plain Ave.; Gable-front cottage; c.1935; *Architecture* (186)

043   C   **House;** 3439 S Main St.; Art Moderne; c.1950; *Architecture* (186)

25023 This English cottage dates to c.1935 and features brick walls, a steeply-pitched roof, and original windows.

044   C   **Farm;** 22605 CR 118; Greek Revival; c.1870; Outbuildings: garage, transverse-frame barn; *Agriculture, Architecture* (186)

045   C   **Sugar Grove Cemetery;** 58500 CR 17; c.1858-present; *Exploration/Settlement, Religion* (186)

046   C   **Hearts Delight Farm;** CR 115; T-plan; c.1880; Outbuilding: bank/basement barn; *Agriculture, Architecture* (186)

047   C   **Farm;** 24994 CR 20; Cape Cod; c.1930; Outbuilding: English barn; *Agriculture, Architecture* (186)

048   C   **House;** 58855 CR 11; Gable-front; c.1930; *Architecture* (186)

049   O   **Joseph & Sarah Puterbaugh Farm;** 59123 CR 9; Italianate; 1850; Outbuilding: Sweitzer barn; *Agriculture, Architecture* (186) **NR**

050   C   **Farm;** 59701 CR 11; American foursquare; c.1925; Outbuilding: bank/basement barn; *Agriculture, Architecture* (186)

051   C   **Farm;** 59702 CR 11; Sweitzer barn; Outbuilding: transverse-frame barn; *Agriculture, Architecture* (186)

052   C   **Elkhart Valley Church of the Brethren;** 24955 CR 24; Gable-front; c.1866/1956; *Architecture, Religion* (186)

053   C   **Farm;** 24491 CR 24; Cross-plan/Gothic Revival; c.1873; Outbuilding: English barn; *Agriculture, Architecture* (186)

054   C   **House;** 59403 CR 13; Upright-and-wing; c.1910; Outbuildings: garage, shed; *Architecture* (186)

055   C   **Farm;** 59207 CR 17; T-plan; c.1880; Outbuildings: bank/basement barn, drive-thru corn crib; *Agriculture, Architecture* (186)

25013 Sweitzer barns are common throughout Elkhart County and northern Indiana. This good example dates to c.1890 and possesses board and batten siding.

25016 This gable-front house retains its original clapboard siding and wood windows with decorative moldings.

**056 C Farm;** 59263 CR 17; Sweitzer barn; Outbuilding: silo; *Agriculture, Architecture* (186)

**057 C House;** 59403 CR 17; Upright-and-wing; c.1900; *Architecture* (186)

**058 C Farm;** CR 45; American foursquare; c.1920; Outbuilding: English barn; *Agriculture, Architecture* (210)

**059 C Frame/Burkett Cemetery;** CR 113; c.1850-present; *Exploration/Settlement, Religion* (210)

**060 N Farm;** 60108 CR 13; Queen Anne; 1895; Outbuildings: drive-thru corn crib, English barn; *Agriculture, Architecture* (210)

**061 C House;** 60101 CR 13; Cross-gable; 1874; *Architecture* (210)

**062 C Farm;** 59851 CR 13; T-plan; c.1880; Outbuildings: bank/basement barn, chicken house, spring house; *Agriculture, Architecture* (210)

**063 C House;** CR 9; Double-pile/Greek Revival; c.1860; *Architecture* (210)

**064 C Barn;** CR 7; Bank barn; c.1890; *Agriculture, Architecture* (210)

**065 C Farm;** 60264 CR 9; Lazy-T; c.1875; Outbuildings: bank/basement barn, corn crib, hog house; *Agriculture, Architecture* (210)

**066 C House;** CR 7; Lazy-T; c.1900; *Architecture* (210)

**067 C House;** 60629 CR 7; Midwest box; c.1900; *Architecture* (210)

**068 C Bigler Farm;** 60578 CR 9; Central-passage; c.1865; Outbuildings: Sweitzer barn, silos, windmill; *Agriculture, Architecture* (210)

**069 C House;** 25270 CR 126; Gable-front/Greek Revival; c.1865; *Architecture* (210)

25029 This side-gable bungalow has many features of the Craftsman style, including battered porch columns and knee braces beneath overhanging eaves.

25031 The Markel House was home to former state senator, Orrin Markel.

**070 N Farm;** 80545 CR 11; I-house/Greek Revival; c.1850; Outbuilding: bank/basement barn; *Agriculture, Architecture* (210)

**071 C Farm;** 60692 CR 13; Lazy-T; c.1880; Outbuildings: bank/basement barn, drive-thru corn crib, sheds, silo, transverse-frame barn; *Agriculture, Architecture* (210)

**072 C Farm;** 60940 CR 13; American foursquare; c.1925; Outbuildings: bank/basement barn, silo, transverse-frame barn; *Agriculture, Architecture* (210)

**073 C House;** CR 17; T-plan; c.1900; *Architecture* (210)

**074 C House;** 2914 W Wilden Ave.; California bungalow/Craftsman; c.1920; Outbuilding: garage; *Architecture* (210)

**075 C House;** 3001 Marshwood Rd.; Italianate; c.1870; *Architecture* (243)

25049 The 1850 Joe & Sarah Puterbaugh House is an outstanding example of the Italianate style. Stylistic elements include a heavy cornice with paired decorative brackets, windows accentuated by flat stone sills and lintels, and an entry porch supported by classical columns.

25060 This 1895 Queen Anne house boasts an elaborate wrap-around porch with ten turned supports, decorative brackets, and gingerbread.

25036 Two classes of students and teachers pose in front of Pleasant Plain School. Above, c.1915; below, c.1922. *Photos courtesy of the Elkhart County Historical Museum.*

# Elkhart Downtown Commercial Historic District (039-186-26001-098)

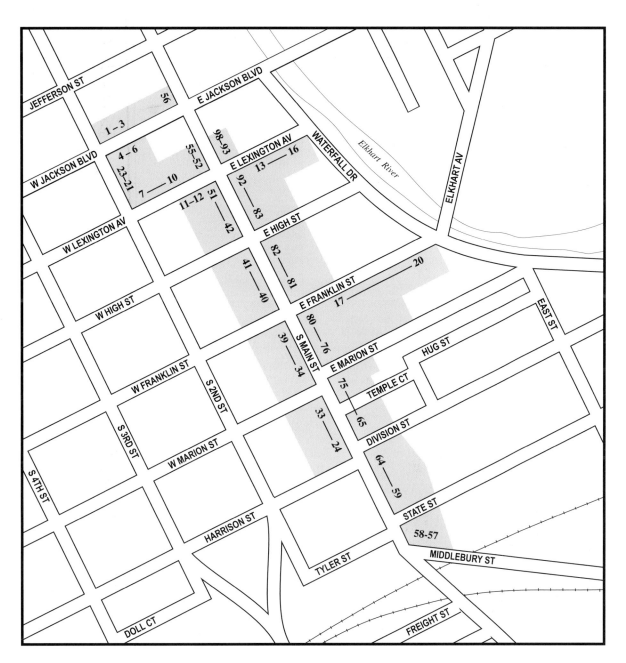

Nestled close to the railroad and the Elkhart and St. Joseph rivers lies the Elkhart Downtown Commercial Historic District. Its location along the railroad and rivers spurred its development and growth. The district includes approximately eight blocks of Main Street, a block of East Franklin Street, two blocks of Lexington Avenue, and a block of Second Street. The district's development began in 1870 and continued until 1930. Listed in the National Register of Historic Places, the district is mostly comprised of commercial buildings dominated by the Italianate, Queen Anne, and Neoclassical styles.

In the 1870s, railroad repair shops were built southwest of downtown and the hydraulic works were completed on the Elkhart River. Those two establishments were catalysts for increased industrial and commercial activity downtown.

Two noted local architects designed buildings in the district. Bristol's A. H. Ellwood designed the exuberant Green Block on East Lexington Street in 1895 (26013). Individually listed in the National Register of Historic Places, the Green Block is an excellent example of the Queen Anne style applied to a commercial building. The most prominent architect represented in the district is E. Hill Turnock. Turnock designed several Craftsman- and Prairie-influenced buildings downtown including the YWCA (26009) and the Elkhart Water Company (26093).

The railroad repair shops closed in 1930, marking the beginning of downtown Elkhart's decline. The Great Depression deepened the local economy's struggle. The Indiana Toll Road was built during the 1950s, passing north of downtown Elkhart and pulling business away from the historic commercial center. Several historic buildings were lost during the district's decline. Fortunately, a renewed interest in revitalization and a riverwalk project leads efforts to draw new businesses downtown.

# ELKHART DOWNTOWN COMMERCIAL HISTORIC DISTRICT (039-186-26001-098) NR

No.  Rtg.  Add.  Description

**WEST JACKSON BOULEVARD** *(north side)*

001 NC NA **Parking Lot**

002 NC 116 **Commercial Building;** Modern commercial; c.1970

003 C 112 **Commercial Building;** Italianate; 1868

**WEST JACKSON BOULEVARD** *(south side)*

004 NC NA **Vacant Lot**

005 C 117 **Commercial Building;** Italianate; c.1870

006 NC 115 **Commercial Building;** Italianate; c.1870

**WEST LEXINGTON AVENUE** *(north side)*

007 C 130 **Commercial Building;** Queen Anne; c.1910

008 N 124-28 **Menges Building;** Free Classic; 1908

26009  The Prairie style Lexington Building dates to c.1919. Designed by E.H. Turnock, it is listed in the National Register of Historic Places.

26010  This Queen Anne commercial building features a decorative cornice and patterned frieze, oriel windows, and a corner turret.

009 O 120 **Lexington Building/Young Women's Christian Association;** Prairie; 1919 (E. Hill Turnock, architect) **NR**

010 N 106-12 **Commercial Building;** Queen Anne; c.1895

**EAST LEXINGTON AVENUE** *(north side)*

**No Sites**

**WEST LEXINGTON AVENUE** *(south side)*

011 N 115-11 **Commercial Building;** Italianate; c.1880

012 N 109 **Commercial Building;** Italianate; c.1880

26013  The 1895 Green Block is another Queen Anne commercial building featuring oriel windows and corner turrets. It is listed in the National Register of Historic Places.

26030  This Italianate commercial building possesses a decorative cornice with central peak and a paneled frieze.

**EAST LEXINGTON AVENUE** *(south side)*

013 O 109-15 **Green Block;** Queen Anne; 1895 **NR**

014 NC NA **Parking Lot**

015 C 125 **Commercial Building;** Italianate; c.1880

016 NC NA **Vacant Lot**

**HIGH STREET** *(north side)*

**No sites**

**HIGH STREET** *(south side)*

**No Sites**

26034 The Neoclassical Midwest Museum of American Art dates to 1922 and exhibits stylistic details including a dentilated cornice and fluted classical columns.

**FRANKLIN STREET** *(north side)*

**No Sites**

**WEST FRANKLIN STREET** *(south side)*

**No Sites**

**EAST FRANKLIN STREET** *(south side)*

017  NC  109-15 **Commercial Building;** Modern commercial; c.1960

018  NC  NA  **Parking Lot**

019  NC  121  **Industrial Building;** Parapet-front; c.1920

020  N  131  **Commercial Building;** Romanesque Revival; 1895

26055 This Italianate commercial block dates to 1888 and features a bracketed cornice.

26056 This Neoclassical bank building features a dentilated cornice with a central pediment. The projecting entry is flanked by Ionic columns.

**MARION STREET**

**No Sites**

**DIVISION STREET**

**No Sites**

**HARRISON STREET**

**No Sites**

**STATE STREET**

**No Sites**

**SOUTH SECOND STREET** *(east side)*

021  NC  NA  **Parking Lot**

022  C  116  **Dreves Building;** Parapet-front; c.1910

023  O  112  **F.K.A. Masonic Temple;** Neoclassical; c.1910 (E. Hill Turnock, architect)

**SOUTH MAIN STREET** *(west side)*

024  NC  NA  **Vacant Lot**

025  C  523  **Commercial Building;** Neoclassical; c.1900

026  C  521  **Dill Building;** Four-part commercial block; 1911

027  C  519  **Commercial Building;** Beaux Arts; c.1920

028  C  511-15 **Commercial Building;** Two-part commercial block; c.1920

029  C  509  **Commercial Building;** One-part commercial block; c.1940

030  N  507  **Commercial Building;** Italianate; c.1880

031  C  505  **Commercial Building;** Three-part commercial block; c.1920

032  NC  503  **Commercial Building;** c.1970

033  NC  501  **Commercial Building;** c.1970

034  O  429  **Midwest Museum of American Art;** Neoclassical; 1922

035  NC  NA  **Sculpture;** Modern; 1994

036  NC  419  **Commercial Building;** c.1920

037  NC  NA  **Parking Lot**

038  C  409-11 **Commercial Building;** Romanesque Revival; c.1900

039  NC  401  **Commercial Building;** Modern; c.1965

040  NC  NA  **Parking Lot**

041  NC  301-19 **Commercial Building;** Contemporary; c.1970

26060 This Italianate commercial building features round-arched windows that are mimicked in the cornice line.

26061 This Italianate commercial building features a bracketed cornice and projecting oriel window.

042  NC  227  **Commercial Building;** c.1970

043  NC  223  **Commercial Building;** c.1970

044  NC  221  **Commercial Building;** c.1970

045  NC  219  **Commercial Building;** Parapet-front; c.1960

046  C  213-15 **Commercial Building;** Italianate; c.1880

047  C  211  **Commercial Building;** Italianate; c.1890

048  NC  209  **Commercial Building;** c.1890

049  NC  205-07 **Commercial Building;** c.1940

050  C  203  **Dalton Building;** Romanesque Revival; c.1880

051  N  201  **Commercial Building;** Italianate; c.1870

26071 This Queen Anne commercial building boldly features a highly-stylized projecting oriel window and heavy cornice.

052  C  131  **Commercial Building;** Three-part commercial block; c.1920

053  N  129  **Commercial Building;** Three-part commercial block; c.1900

054  C  127  **Commercial Building;** Three-part commercial block; c.1890

055  N  119-23 **Commercial Building;** Italianate; 1888

056  O  101  **Bank;** Neoclassical; 1905

## SOUTH MAIN STREET *(east side)*

057  C  706-08 **Commercial Building;** One-part commercial block; c.1920

26072 The Odd Fellows Building dates to 1899 and features round-arch windows on the upper stories and a rounded corner bay.

058  C  700-04 **Rowe Building;** Romanesque Revival; 1900 (A.H. Ellwood, architect)

059  C  618-22 **Weiler Block;** Italianate; 1904

060  N  614-16 **Commercial Building;** Italianate; c.1870

061  N  612  **Commercial Building;** Italianate; c.1880

062  C  610  **Commercial Building;** Queen Anne; c.1880

063  C  606  **Commercial Building;** Two-part commercial block; c.1910

064  C  600  **Commercial Building;** Italianate; 1888

065  C  534  **Commercial Building;** Two-part commercial block; c.1910

066  C  532  **Commercial Building;** Craftsman; c.1920

067  C  530  **Commercial Building;** Queen Anne; c.1880

26075 The 1923 Hotel Elkhart features limestone accents, including vertical bands that accent the corner bays.

068  C  528  **S.B. Shurt Building;** Queen Anne; c.1900

069  C  526  **Theater;** Art Deco; c.1920

070  NC  522-24 **Commercial Building;** Parapet-front; c.1965

071  N  520  **Commercial Building;** Queen Anne; c.1870

072  N  516  **Odd Fellows Building;** Romanesque Revival; 1899

073  C  514  **Commercial Building;** Parapet-front; c.1920

074  NC  512  **Commercial Building;** Two-part commercial block; c.1950

075  N  500  **Hotel Elkhart;** Italian Renaissance Revival; 1923

076  NC  NA  **Parking Lot**

077  C  418  **Commercial Building;** Neoclassical; c.1910

078  O  401  **Lerner/Elco Theatre;** Neoclassical; 1924 **NR**

079  NC  404  **Commercial Building;** Parapet-front; c.1965

26087 This 1892 commercial building is an example of the Romanesque Revival style.

080  NC  400  **Commercial Building;** Parapet-front; c.1965

081  NC  NA  **Fountain;** Modern; c.1990

082  NC  NA  **Clock Tower;** Modern; c.1990

083  C  230  **Borneman Building;** Craftsman; c.1910

084  C  224-26 **Commercial Building;** Art Deco; c.1920

085  NC  220  **Commercial Building;** c.1965

086  NC  NA  **Parking Lot**

087  O  214  **Commercial Building;** Romanesque Revival; 1892

088  NC  210  **Commercial Building;** c.1960

26093 Designed by E. Hill Turnock, the Water Company building is an exhuberant example of the Craftsman style.

089  C  208  **Commercial Building;** Two-part commercial block; c.1920

090  C  206  **Commercial Building;** Parapet-front; c.1920

091  C  202-04 **C.E. Frye Building;** Prairie; 1919

092  N  200  **Commercial Building;** Italianate; c.1880

093  O  130  **Water Company Building;** Craftsman; c.1910 (E. Hill Turnock, architect)

094  C  128  **Commercial Building;** Parapet-front; c.1920

095  C  124-26 **Commercial Building;** Parapet-front; c.1920

096  C  120  **Commercial Building;** Two-part commercial block; c.1920

097  C  118  **Commercial Building;** Italianate; c.1870

098  C  116  **Commercial Building;** Three-part commercial block; c.1920

# East Jackson/St. Joseph Manor Historic District  (039-186-27001-105)

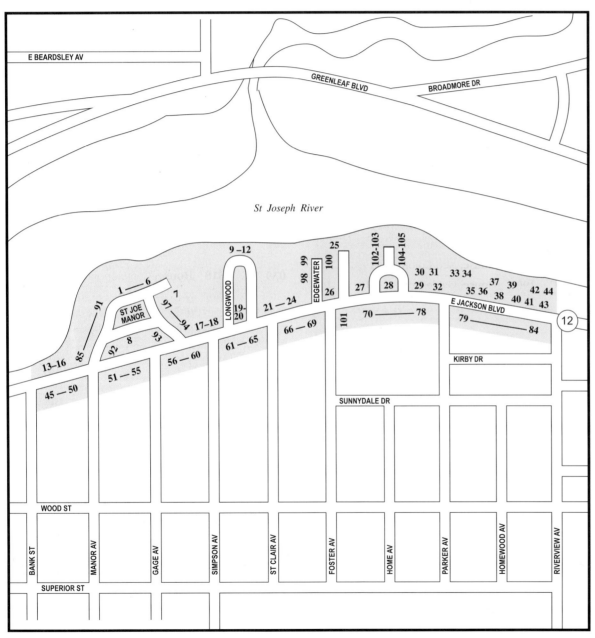

The East Jackson/St. Joseph Manor Historic District is located in the northern part of the city of Elkhart and lies along the southern bank of the St. Joseph River. The residential district includes a mixture of modest homes and luxury estates.

Due largely to its advantageous setting along the St. Joseph River, the area became a fashionable neighborhood, especially within St. Joseph Manor and along the northern side of East Jackson Boulevard. The families of Elkhart business and industry leaders settled along the river, while the area to the south became an attractive middle-class neighborhood.

Most homes in the district were built in the 1910s and 1920s in a variety of architectural styles. Several prominent homes are located in the district including the John Livers House (27010), designed by local architect E. Hill Turnock. The district has notable examples of Prairie (27021, 27087), Mediterranean Revival (27023, 27090), and Craftsman (27024, 27038) style houses.

Unfortunately, the district suffered a major loss when private owners demolished the Foster Mansion in 2002. The St. Joseph Manor mansion was deteriorated, but hope existed for its rehabilitation until its unexpected and sudden demolition. The mansion's vacant site represents a detracting gap in the otherwise cohesive district.

## EAST JACKSON/ST. JOSEPH MANOR HISTORIC DISTRICT (039-186-27001-105)

No. Rtg. Add.  Description

**NORTH ST. JOSEPH MANOR (north side)**

| 001 | NC | NA | Vacant Lot |
|---|---|---|---|
| 002 | NC | NA | Vacant Lot |
| 003 | N | 12 | House; Colonial Revival; c.1910 |
| 004 | NC | 13 | House; Colonial Revival; c.1930 |
| 005 | NC | 14 | House; Colonial Revival; c.1930 |
| 006 | C | 15 | House; Colonial Revival; c.1940 |

**NORTH ST. JOSEPH MANOR (south side)**

| 007 | C | 16 | House; Cape Cod; c.1940 |
|---|---|---|---|

**SOUTH ST. JOSEPH MANOR (south side)**

| 008 | C | 21 | House; Dutch Colonial Revival; c.1925 |
|---|---|---|---|

**LONGWOOD COURT (north side)**

| 009 | N | 6 | House; Classical Revival; c.1945 |
|---|---|---|---|
| 010 | N | 8 | House; Colonial Revival; c.1945 |
| 011 | NC | 10 | House; Ranch; c.1975 |
| 012 | NC | 12 | House; Ranch; c.1975 |

27021  This Prairie style house has a hipped clay tile roof, wide overhanging eaves, and ribbon windows.

**EAST JACKSON BOULEVARD (north side)**

| 013 | N | 1600 | House; Mediterranean Revival; c.1925 |
|---|---|---|---|
| 014 | N | 1604 | House; French Eclectic; c.1920 |
| 015 | C | 1608 | House; Colonial Revival; c.1920 |
| 016 | C | 1610 | House; Dormer-front bungalow; c.1930 |
| 017 | C | 1826 | House; Colonial Revival; c.1920 |
| 018 | C | 1828 | House; Colonial Revival; c.1920 |
| 019 | NC | 1900 | House; Neo-Colonial; c.1990 |
| 020 | C | 1902 | House; Gable-front; c.1910 |
| 021 | O | 1906 | House; Prairie; c.1920 |
| 022 | C | 1928 | House; Dormer-front bungalow; c.1920 |
| 023 | N | 2000 | House; Mediterranean Revival; c.1910 |
| 024 | O | 2002 | House; California bungalow/Craftsman; 1926 |

| 025 | O | 2020 | House; Prairie; c.1910 |
|---|---|---|---|
| 026 | C | 2022 | House; Ranch; c.1950 |
| 027 | C | 2100 | House; Ranch/Modern; c.1950 |
| 028 | C | 2114 | House; Colonial Revival; c.1920 |
| 029 | C | 2202 | House; California bungalow/Craftsman; c.1910 |
| 030 | O | 2206 | House; Tudor Revival; c.1910 |
| 031 | C | 2210 | House; Ranch/Contemporary; c.1960 |
| 032 | NC | 2218 | House; Colonial Revival; c.1940 |
| 033 | NC | 2220 | House; Split-level ranch; c.1970 |
| 034 | NC | 2224 | House; Ranch; c.1980 |
| 035 | C | 2226 | House; Side-gable bungalow; c.1910 |
| 036 | N | 2300 | House; American foursquare/Prairie; c.1910 |
| 037 | NC | 2310 | House; Ranch; c.1965 |
| 038 | N | 2312 | House; American foursquare/Craftsman; c.1900 |
| 039 | NC | 2318 | House; Contemporary; c.1980 |
| 040 | O | 2324 | House; Mediterranean Revival; c.1910 |
| 041 | N | 2402 | House; American foursquare/Craftsman; c.1920 |
| 042 | NC | 2414 | House; Contemporary; c.1980 |
| 043 | C | 2416 | House; Gable-front/Craftsman; c.1920 |
| 044 | C | 2422 | House; c.1920 |

27003  This St. Joseph Manor House is a good example of the Colonial Revival style and features a clay tile roof, cornice returns, and brick chimneys on each gable end.

27024  This California bungalow has many Craftsman-style elements, including paired knee braces, exposed rafter tails, and ribbon windows.

27025  Prairie-style influence is evident on this house in its low-pitched clay tile roof with wide, overhanging eaves.

27030  This Tudor Revival house features a slate roof, prominent chimney, and central tower-like entry.

### EAST JACKSON BOULEVARD (*south side*)

| 045 | N | 1601 | **House;** Colonial Revival; c.1910 |
|---|---|---|---|
| 046 | C | 1607 | **House;** Prairie; c.1910 |
| 047 | C | 1611 | **House;** Colonial Revival; c.1910 |
| 048 | C | 1621 | **House;** American foursquare; c.1910 |
| 049 | C | 1625 | **House;** Dormer-front bungalow; c.1920 |
| 050 | C | 1629 | **House;** Craftsman; c.1910 |
| 051 | NC | 1701 | **House;** Ranch; c.1965 |
| 052 | C | 1705 | **House;** Dormer-front bungalow; c.1920 |
| 053 | C | 1715 | **House;** Colonial Revival; c.1925 |
| 054 | C | 1719 | **House;** Colonial Revival; c.1930 |
| 055 | C | 1721 | **House;** Colonial Revival; c.1930 |
| 056 | N | 1801 | **House;** French Eclectic; c.1930 |
| 057 | C | 1807 | **House;** American foursquare; c.1920 |
| 058 | NC | 1813 | **House;** Ranch; c.1970 |
| 059 | C | 1823 | **House;** Craftsman; c.1925 |
| 060 | NC | 1825 | **House;** Pyramidal-roof cottage; c.1940 |
| 061 | N | 1901 | **House;** Prairie; c.1910 |
| 062 | C | 1907 | **House;** Craftsman; c.1910 |
| 063 | C | 1913 | **House;** Craftsman; c.1915 |

27061  Another Prairie-style influenced house is this bungalow that boasts a clay tile roof with jerkinheads, curved knee braces, and a tall chimney.

| 064 | C | 1919 | **House;** Dormer-front bungalow/ Craftsman; c.1920 |
|---|---|---|---|
| 065 | N | 1923 | **House;** Craftsman; c.1916 (Aladdin, builder) |
| 066 | C | 2001 | **House;** Dormer-front bungalow/ Craftsman; c.1920 |
| 067 | C | 2003 | **House;** Craftsman; c.1910 |
| 068 | C | 2005 | **House;** American foursquare; c.1915 |
| 069 | C | 2009 | **House;** American foursquare; c.1915 |
| 070 | C | 2107 | **House;** Tudor Revival; c.1910 |
| 071 | C | 2111 | **House;** English cottage; c.1930 |
| 072 | C | 2113 | **House;** Craftsman; c.1925 |
| 073 | NC | 2115 | **House;** American foursquare; c.1920 |

27065  This Craftsman-style house appears to be the "Shadow Lawn" model from the 1916 Aladdin catalog.

27076  This Mediterranean Revival house has a hipped clay tile roof, overhanging eaves supported by paired brackets, original windows, and a round-arch entryway.

| 074 | N | 2117 | **House;** Craftsman; c.1910 |
|---|---|---|---|
| 075 | C | 2207 | **House;** Dutch Colonial Revival; c.1920 |
| 076 | N | 2211 | **House;** Mediterranean Revival; c.1910 |
| 077 | C | 2217 | **House;** Craftsman; c.1910 |
| 078 | C | 2227 | **House;** Ranch; c.1960 |
| 079 | C | 2301 | **House;** Dutch Colonial Revival; c.1920 |
| 080 | NC | 2311 | **House;** Craftsman; c.1920 |
| 081 | NC | 2317 | **House;** Colonial Revival; c.1930 |
| 082 | NC | 2403 | **House;** Cape Cod; c.1940 |
| 083 | C | 2407 | **House;** English cottage; c.1930 |
| 084 | C | 2417 | **House;** California bungalow; c.1920 |

### WEST ST. JOSEPH MANOR (*west side*)

| 085 | NC | 1 | **House;** Midwest box; c.1925 |
|---|---|---|---|
| 086 | N | 2 | **House;** Prairie; c.1925 |
| 087 | O | 3 | **House;** Prairie; 1929 |
| 088 | C | 4 | **House;** Colonial Revival; c.1925 |
| 089 | O | 6 | **House;** Italian Renaissance Revival; c.1925 |
| 090 | O | 7 | **House;** Mediterranean Revival; c.1925 |

27087 This 1929 Prairie-style influenced house features a hipped clay tile roof with wide, overhanging eaves, leaded glass windows, and a grand porch.

| 091 | O | 8 | **John Livers House;** Italian Renaissance Revival; 1917 (E. Hill Turnock, architect) |

**WEST ST. JOSEPH MANOR** *(east side)*

| 092 | C | 5 | **House;** Ranch; 1950 |

**EAST ST. JOSEPH MANOR** *(west side)*

| 093 | NC | 22 | **House;** Ranch; c.1960 |

**EAST ST. JOSEPH MANOR** *(east side)*

| 094 | N | 20 | **House;** English cottage; c.1930 (Architects' Small House Service Bureau, design) |
| 095 | C | 19 | **House;** Dutch Colonial Revival; 1918 |

27089 This Italian Renaissance Revival house features a hipped clay tile roof, a symmetrical plan, and columned porch.

27090 This Mediterranean Revival house features a hipped clay tile roof, central tower with a round-arched entry, and second story balconies.

| 096 | C | 18 | **House;** Colonial Revival; c.1930 |
| 097 | N | 17 | **House;** Colonial Revival; c.1925 |

**EDGEWATER PLACE** *(west side)*

| 098 | N | 2 | **House;** Colonial Revival; c.1930 (Architects' Small House Service Bureau, design) |
| 099 | C | 3 | **House;** Mediterranean Revival; c.1925 |

**EDGEWATER PLACE** *(east side)*

| 100 | N | 4 | **House;** Mediterranean Revival; c.1925 |

27091 Local architect E. H. Turnock designed the John Livers House in 1917. The Italian Renaissance Revival house features wide overhanging eaves supported by oversized brackets and a grand corner tower.

27100 This Mediterranean Revival house features stuccoed walls, original casement windows, and a protruding entry bay.

**FOSTER AVENUE** *(east side)*

| 101 | C | 102 | **House;** Ranch; c.1960 |

**CLARENDON DRIVE** *(west side)*

| 102 | C | 3 | **House;** Cape Cod; c.1940 |
| 103 | NC | 5 | **House;** Ranch; c.1970 |

**CLARENDON DRIVE** *(east side)*

| 104 | NC | 8 | **House;** Ranch; c.1970 |
| 105 | C | 6 | **House;** French Eclectic; c.1935 |

This c.1955 aerial photo shows a winter scene in St. Joseph Manor. The now demolished Foster Mansion is prominently shown at the top of the photo. *Photo courtesy of the Elkhart County Historical Museum.*

73

# Beardsley Avenue Historic District (039-186-28001-054)

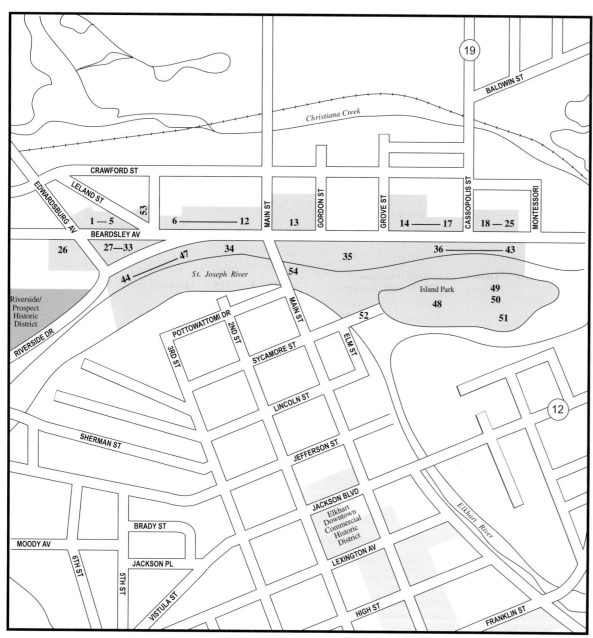

The Beardsley Avenue Historic District is located just north of downtown Elkhart, along the north side of the St. Joseph River in Osolo Township. The district is composed mostly of residential structures, but also contains a church, monument, bridge, and two parks. The majority of the buildings date to the turn of the century. Included in the district are two properties that are individually listed in the National Register of Historic Places (28012, 28014).

The land along the north side of the St. Joseph River originally belonged to the Beardsley family. Dr. Havilah Beardsley operated paper and flour mills; the race for these mills is still visible in the district. The oldest building in the district is the 1848 Havilah Beardsley House (28012).

By the turn of the century the Beardsley family began to subdivide their land. Because of its close proximity to downtown and the factories to the west along Beardsley Avenue, the neighborhood became popular with prominent local businessmen and industrialists. A streetcar line that ran on West Beardsley Avenue further contributed to the neighborhood's growth.

Located in the district are several large, impressive houses. Arguably the most impressive is Ruthmere (28014). Local architect Enoch Hill Turnock designed Ruthmere and at least two other houses in the district (28020, 28047). In addition to the houses, Turnock designed St. Paul's Methodist Episcopal Church (28026) and the Beardsley Memorial located at the intersection of Riverside and Beardsley.

# BEARDSLEY AVENUE HISTORIC DISTRICT (039-186-28001-054) NR

| No. | Rtg. | Add. | Description |
|-----|------|------|-------------|

## WEST BEARDSLEY AVENUE *(north side)*

| No. | Rtg. | Add. | Description |
|-----|------|------|-------------|
| 001 | O | 334 | **House;** Prairie; c.1915 |
| 002 | C | 326 | **House;** Gable-front; c.1900 |
| 003 | C | NA | **Mill Race Site** |
| 004 | C | 316 | **House;** Gable-front; 1903 |
| 005 | N | 306 | **House;** Prairie; c.1920 |
| 006 | C | 216 | **House;** Dutch Colonial Revival; c.1900 |
| 007 | C | 208 | **House;** Colonial Revival; c.1920 |
| 008 | N | 202 | **House;** Mediterranean Revival; c.1910 |
| 009 | C | 130 | **House;** American foursquare/ Colonial Revival; c.1920 |
| 010 | O | 120 | **House;** Colonial Revival; c.1910 |
| 011 | O | 114 | **Chamberlain-Bucklen House;** American foursquare/Colonial Revival; c.1906 |
| 012 | O | 102 | **Dr. Havilah Beardsley House;** Italianate; 1848/1875 **NR** |

## EAST BEARDSLEY AVENUE *(north side)*

| No. | Rtg. | Add. | Description |
|-----|------|------|-------------|
| 013 | O | 116 | **Floyd C. Best House;** French Eclectic; 1941 |
| 014 | O | 302 | **Ruthmere/Albert R. Beardsley House;** Beaux Arts; 1908-10 (E. Hill Turnock, architect) **NR** |

28001 This Prairie-style house boasts a hipped clay tile roof, oversized brackets supporting overhanging eaves, and a segmental-arch entryway surround.

28012 The Dr. Havilah Beardsley House is the oldest house in the district, dating to 1848. The Italianate house exhibits round-arched openings and a full-width porch. It is individually listed in the National Register of Historic Places.

| No. | Rtg. | Add. | Description |
|-----|------|------|-------------|
| 015 | C | 330 | **House;** Midwest box; c.1910 |
| 016 | C | 334 | **House;** Dutch Colonial Revival; c.1910 |
| 017 | C | 340 | **House;** Free Classic; c.1920 |
| 018 | N | 400 | **House;** Neoclassical; c.1910 |
| 019 | C | 414 | **House;** Dutch Colonial Revival; c.1910 |
| 020 | N | 418 | **House;** American foursquare/ Prairie; c.1920 (E. Hill Turnock, architect) |
| 021 | C | 422 | **Robert Schell House;** Dutch Colonial Revival; c.1920 |
| 022 | C | 426 | **House;** Midwest box; c.1920 |
| 023 | C | 430 | **House;** Dormer-front bungalow/ Craftsman; c.1910 |
| 024 | C | 434 | **House;** Colonial Revival; c.1910 |
| 025 | C | 438 | **Floyd C. Best House;** Dutch Colonial Revival; c.1920 |

28013 The 1941 Floyd C. Best House is an example of the French Eclectic style. The house features a slate roof, prominent chimney, and original windows.

28014 The 1908 Ruthmere Mansion is an example of the exuberant Beaux-Arts style. Individually listed in the National Register of Historic Places, Ruthmere features a flat roof with a dentilated cornice and round windows with decorative surrounds.

## WEST BEARDSLEY AVENUE *(south side)*

| No. | Rtg. | Add. | Description |
|-----|------|------|-------------|
| 026 | N | 403 | **St. Paul's M.E. Church;** Late-Gothic Revival; 1910 (E. Hill Turnock, architect) |
| 027 | C | 319 | **House;** American foursquare; c.1920 |
| 028 | C | 315 | **House;** Queen Anne; c.1890 |
| 029 | C | 311 | **House;** Gabled-ell/Free Classic; c.1890 |
| 030 | C | 307 | **House;** Dutch Colonial Revival; c.1920 |
| 031 | C | 303 | **House;** American foursquare; c.1890 |

28020 Designed by local architect E.H. Turnock, this American foursquare displays Prairie-style influences, including its shed-roof porch.

28026 E.H. Turnock designed the 1910 St. Paul's Methodist Episcopal Church in the late-Gothic Revival style.

032 NC 223 **House;** Gabled-ell; c.1900

033 C NA **Dr. Havilah Beardsley Memorial;** 1913 (E. Hill Turnock, designer)

034 N 125 **A.C. Collins House;** Mediterranean Revival/Neoclassical; 1910

### EAST BEARDSLEY AVENUE (south side)

035 C NA **Beardsley Park;** 1922

036 C 331 **House;** Upright-and-wing; c.1930

037 N 337 **House;** Prairie; c.1910

038 O 401 **Collins-Stanton House;** Stick; c.1895 (A.H. Ellwood, architect)

039 C 417 **House;** Prairie; c.1910

040 N 425 **Martin E. Crow House;** Prairie; c.1910

041 C 431 **House;** Colonial Revival; c.1915

28034 The A.C. Collins House has elements of both the Mediterranean Revival style and the Neoclassical style.

28038 The Collins/Stanton House is an example of the Stick style with its clapboard and wood-shingle walls.

042 C 437 **House;** Colonial Revival; c.1915

043 C 441 **House;** Dutch Colonial Revival; c.1900

### RIVERSIDE DRIVE (south side)

044 NC 736 **House;** Colonial Revival; c.1945

045 N 750 **House;** Prairie; c.1910

046 N 756 **House;** Colonial Revival; c.1915

047 N 760 **Dr. George Harter House;** Prairie; c.1910 (E. Hill Turnock, architect)

### ISLAND PARK

048 C NA **Park;** 1887

049 C NA **Water Fountain;** Rustic; c.1930 (WPA, builders)

28045 This Prairie-style house exhibits stylistic signatures such as a low-pitched roof and limestone accents that emphasize the horizontal.

050 C NA **Bandstand;** c.1905

051 N NA **Pavilion;** 1937 (WPA, builders)

### SYCAMORE STREET

052 NC NA **Bridge;** 2003

### CHRISTIANA STREET (west side)

053 C 801 **Percival M. Cochran House;** American foursquare/Prairie; c.1900

### MAIN STREET

054 N NA **Main Street Memorial Bridge;** Filled spandrel concrete arch/Art Moderne; 1918 (W.S. Moore, designer/Miller-Taylor Construction, builder)

28047 The Dr. George Harter House is another example of the Prairie style designed by E.H. Turnock. It features a low-pitched hipped roof with wide overhanging eaves. Horizontal bands above and below the leaded glass ribbon windows emphasize the horizontal.

# Riverside/Prospect Historic District (039-186-29001-036)

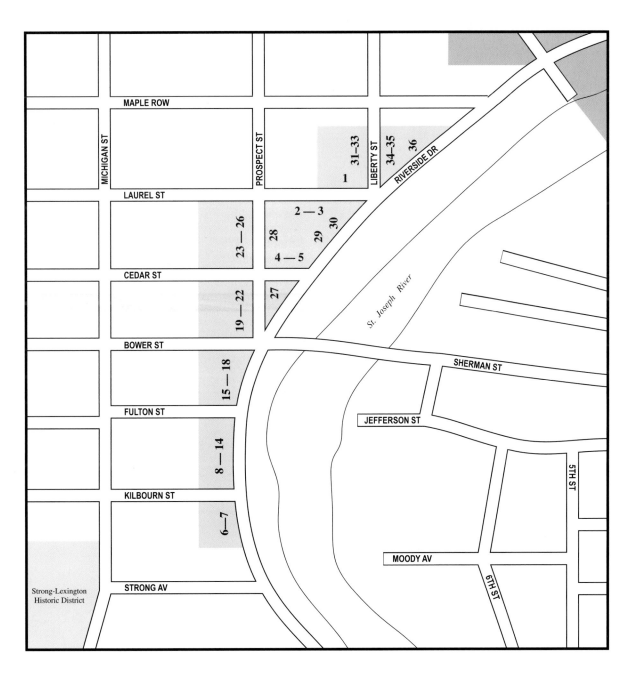

The Riverside/Prospect Historic District lies on the west side of the St. Joseph River in the northern portion of the city of Elkhart. It encompasses about four blocks of Riverside Drive and portions of Prospect and Liberty Streets. The district is residential in nature, having many well-situated homes with views of the river.

A portion of the district was platted as Johnson's Riverside Addition, named for R. M. Johnson, and what is today Riverside Drive was once known as Johnson Street. In 1895, lots in this area sold for $300 each. Advertisements proclaimed the benefits of the area as being free of diphtheria and other diseases that were common at the time. They also claimed that the area had good "magnetic water" that could serve as a cure for a variety of ailments. Developers hoped that a bridge would be built across the river at nearby Eighth Street to provide easy access to the railroad yards, but the bridge was never built. However, a bridge was built on Bower Street to provide the area with access to downtown Elkhart. As a result, the area became more popular with downtown merchants and laborers than railroad workers.

Most of the houses in the district were built in the late-19th through early-20th century. A variety of architectural styles are present including Second Empire (29021), Prairie (29031), and Craftsman (29014).

## RIVERSIDE-PROSPECT HISTORIC DISTRICT
## (039-186-29001-036)

| No. | Rtg. | Add. | Description |
|---|---|---|---|

**LAUREL STREET** *(north side)*

001 C 440 **House;** Queen Anne; c.1890

**LAUREL STREET** *(south side)*

002 N 523 **House;** Craftsman; c.1910

003 C 509 **House;** Colonial Revival; c.1910

**CEDAR STREET** *(north side)*

004 N 528 **House;** Italian Renaissance Revival; c.1920

005 C 520 **House;** Midwest box; c.1900

**NORTH RIVERSIDE DRIVE** *(west side)*

006 C 119 **House;** Tudor Revival; c.1920

007 O 125 **House;** Prairie; c.1920

008 C 201 **House;** Free Classic; c.1910

009 C 207 **House;** Craftsman; c.1920

010 C 209 **House;** Craftsman; c.1910

011 NC 213 **House;** Midwest box; c.1915

012 C 217 **House;** Midwest box; c.1910

**29022** This Craftsman-style house has wide overhanging eaves with exposed rafter tails, a wrap-around porch supported by columns, and half-timbering in the gable end.

**78**

**29031** This Prairie-style house features a hipped clay tile roof, original double-hung sash windows, and bracketed entry-stoop.

013 C 221 **House;** American foursquare; c.1920

014 N 227 **Charles Isbell House;** Craftsman; c.1900

015 C 301 **House;** Western bungalow; c.1910

016 C 305 **House;** American foursquare; c.1910

017 NC 309 **House;** American foursquare; c.1910

018 NC 313-15 **House;** Pyramidal-roof duplex; c.1910

**NORTH PROSPECT STREET** *(west side)*

019 C 403 **House;** Free Classic; c.1907

020 C 409 **House;** American foursquare; c.1900

021 O 417 **House;** Second Empire; c.1880

022 N 423 **House;** Craftsman; c.1900

023 C 501 **House;** Free Classic; c.1880

024 C 509 **House;** T-plan; c.1890

025 C 515 **House;** T-plan; c.1890

026 C 523 **House;** T-plan; c.1890

**NORTH PROSPECT STREET** *(east side)*

027 C NA **Park;** 1877

028 C 520 **House;** Gabled-ell; c.1880

**NORTH RIVERSIDE DRIVE** *(west side)*

029 N 515 **House;** Italian Renaissance Revival; c.1925

030 C 521 **House;** T-plan; c.1880

**LIBERTY STREET** *(west side)*

031 N 601 **House;** Prairie; c.1920

032 NC 615 **House;** Gable-front; c.1915

033 C 621 **House;** American foursquare; c.1920

**LIBERTY STREET** *(east side)*

034 N 616 **House;** Dormer-front bungalow; c.1915

035 NC 608 **House;** T-plan; c.1900

**RIVERSIDE DRIVE** *(west side)*

036 N 513 **House;** Prairie; c.1910

**29036** Another Prairie-style house is this c.1910 example that boasts a hipped clay tile roof, broad eaves, and original double-hung sash windows.

# Strong/Lexington Historic District (039-186-30001-060)

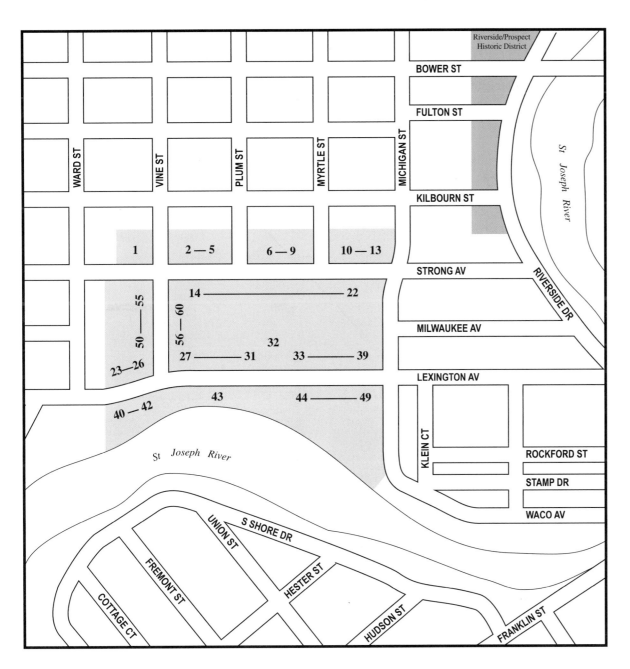

The Strong/Lexington Historic District is located along Strong and Lexington Avenues between Michigan and Ward Streets. It is on the north edge of the St. Joseph River, west of downtown Elkhart. Much of the area was originally platted as the Strong Addition.

The district is entirely residential in nature. The majority of the district's houses were built in the second half of the 19th century through the early-20th century as Elkhart grew west from downtown. The area had direct access to downtown via the Pigeon Street bridge. Pigeon Street was later renamed Lexington Avenue. The neighborhood's easy access encouraged the families of businessmen and laborers alike to settle west of the river.

Many of the houses along Lexington Avenue are fairly modest in terms of scale and architectural details, but more elaborate examples are found in the western end of the district. Strong Avenue is home to several notable houses, including the outstanding Conn Mansion (30020), which might be the most recognizable home in Elkhart. C. G. Conn was a prominent local businessman who founded the Conn band instrument factory. He was widely known as an innovator in the production of musical instruments. The mansion was originally built as an Italianate style home, but Conn drastically altered the house after purchasing it. The most notable addition is the colossal Neoclassical porch featuring massive fluted columns encircling the house.

## STRONG/LEXINGTON HISTORIC DISTRICT (039-186-30001-060)

| No. | Rtg. | Add. | Description |
|-----|------|------|-------------|

**WEST STRONG AVENUE** (*north side*)

| 001 | N | 1000 | **House;** Italianate; c.1875 |
| 002 | C | 920 | **House;** American foursquare; c.1910 |
| 003 | C | 914 | **House;** Queen Anne; c.1890 |
| 004 | C | 908 | **House;** Pyramidal-roof; c.1920 |
| 005 | C | 900 | **House;** Colonial Revival; c.1940 |
| 006 | N | 820 | **House;** Italian Renaissance Revival; c.1920 |
| 007 | C | 814 | **House;** American foursquare; c.1920 |
| 008 | C | 808 | **House;** T-plan/Queen Anne; c.1880 |
| 009 | N | 804 | **House;** Colonial Revival; c.1910 |
| 010 | C | 718 | **House;** Dormer-front bungalow; c.1920 |
| 011 | C | 714 | **House;** No style; c.1920 |
| 012 | C | 702 | **House;** Pyramidal-roof; c.1910 |
| 013 | C | 700 | **House;** American foursquare/ Prairie; c.1910 |

**WEST STRONG AVENUE** (*south side*)

| 014 | N | 921 | **House;** Colonial Revival; c.1910 |
| 015 | C | 915 | **House;** Midwest box/Craftsman; c.1940 |

**30001** This Italianate house dates to c.1875 and displays segmental arch windows with decorative hoods.

**30006** This Italian Renaissance Revival house boasts a hipped clay tile roof, broad eaves, and original double-hung sash windows.

| 016 | N | 905 | **House;** Prairie; c.1910 |
| 017 | O | 901 | **House;** Craftsman; c.1915 |
| 018 | C | 819 | **House;** Prairie; c.1915 |
| 019 | N | 811 | **House;** Colonial Revival; c.1925 |
| 020 | O | 723 | **Conn Mansion;** Italianate/Neoclassical; c.1870 |
| 021 | C | 709 | **House;** Cape Cod; c.1930 |
| 022 | C | 701 | **House;** American foursquare; c.1910 |

**WEST LEXINGTON AVENUE** (*north side*)

| 023 | N | 1024 | **House;** Colonial Revival; c.1920 |
| 024 | C | 1020 | **House;** T-plan; c.1880 |

**30009** This Colonial Revival house features a full-width stone porch with a columned balcony.

**30014** This Colonial Revival house exhibits a symmetrical plan, bay windows with copper roofs, and an ocular window above the entry.

| 025 | C | 1014 | **House;** Gable-front; c.1930 |
| 026 | NC | 1012 | **House;** Pyramidal-roof; c.1920 |
| 027 | N | 920 | **House;** Italianate; 1858 |
| 028 | N | 912 | **House;** Italianate; 1882 |
| 029 | NC | 904 | **House;** Colonial Revival; c.1920 |
| 030 | NC | 902 | **House;** T-plan; c.1910 |
| 031 | O | 900 | **House;** Craftsman; c.1910 |
| 032 | C | 804 | **House;** T-plan; c.1890 |
| 033 | C | 730 | **House;** Western bungalow; c.1920 |
| 034 | C | 726 | **House;** Free Classic; c.1920 |
| 035 | C | 722 | **House;** Western bungalow; c.1940 |

**30017** This Craftsman-style house has a clay tile roof with jerkinhead, broad eaves supported by large brackets, and diamond-paned windows.

30019 This Colonial Revival house exhibits a symmetrical plan, three dormer windows, and an entry flanked by sidelights and topped by a fanlight.

036 NC 718 **House;** T-plan; c.1900

037 C 714 **House;** Gable-front; 1908

038 C 710 **House;** Dormer-front bungalow; c.1920

039 C 706 **House;** Craftsman; c.1920

## WEST LEXINGTON AVENUE *(south side)*

040 C 1029 **House;** Gabled-ell; c.1910

041 N 1021 **House;** Italianate; 1880

042 N 1017 **House;** English cottage/Tudor Revival; c.1910

30020 The C.G. Conn Mansion was built in the Italianate style c.1870 and later updated to the Neoclassical style with its grand porch, complete with fluted Corinthian columns, dentilated cornice, and large, arched, leaded glass windows.

043 NC NA **Vacant Lot**

044 C 731 **House;** Dormer-front bungalow; c.1920

045 NC 725 **House;** T-plan; c.1900

046 C 717 **House;** Dormer-front bungalow; c.1920

047 NC 713 **House;** Lazy-T; c.1900

048 C 709 **House;** Pyramidal roof/bungalow; c.1910

049 C 705 **House;** American foursquare; c.1910

## SOUTH VINE STREET *(west side)*

050 C 141 **House;** Gable-front; c.1910

051 C 135 **House;** Colonial Revival; c.1910

052 C 131 **House;** Dutch Colonial Revival; c.1910

053 C 123 **House;** Bungalow; c.1920

054 NC 119 **House;** English cottage; c.1930

055 C 115-17 **Double House;** Bungalow; c.1910

30023 This Colonial Revival house features original windows and a rounded entry topped by an iron balustrade.

30028 This 1882 Italianate house has narrow segmental-arched window openings, a bracketed entry stoop, and original door.

## SOUTH VINE STREET *(east side)*

056 N 112 **House;** Cross-gabled square; c.1880

057 C 124 **House;** American foursquare; c.1910

058 NC 120 **House;** Gable-front; c.1920

059 NC 116 **House;** Gable-front; c.1920

060 C 112 **House;** Dormer-front bungalow; c.1910

30031 This Craftsman-style house is an outstanding example with its clay tile roof, large brackets beneath broad eaves, and multi-pane windows.

# State-Division Historic District (039-186-31001-133)

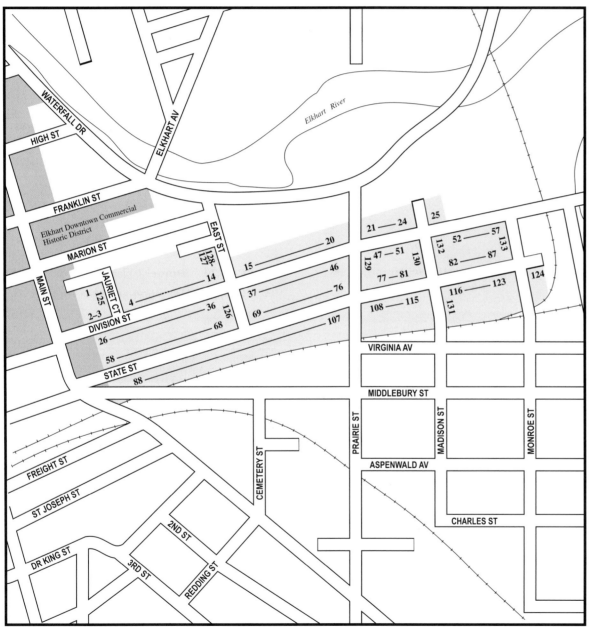

The State-Division Historic District borders downtown Elkhart and the former New York Central Railroad; additionally, the Elkhart River is easily accessible from the neighborhood. Due to its advantageous location, the area developed quickly as a working-class residential neighborhood. The district developed between 1870 and 1930, and it retains much of its integrity from that time period. It is a locally designated historic district and is also listed in the National Register of Historic Places.

The railroad and industries located along the river spurred the development of the district. In the 1870s, the Lake Shore & Michigan Southern Railroad constructed its repair shops southwest of downtown and the hydraulic works on the Elkhart River were completed. These establishments brought many jobs to the area and helped shape its working-class character. Although primarily a residential neighborhood, the district contains several commercial properties, including a former neighborhood grocery (31126) and a severely altered warehouse originally built for the Dr. Miles Medical Company (31091).

Homes in the district range from modest Italianate-influenced homes to Craftsman-influenced bungalows. The most outstanding house is the E. Hill Turnock-designed house (31031). It is a superb example of Craftsman-style architecture by Elkhart's premier architect. Also of note is one of the only Queen Anne houses in the district that retains the majority of its stylistic details (31002).

The neighborhood began to decline in 1930 with the onset of the Great Depression and the closing of the railroad repair shops. However, with its local and national designation as a historic district, a renewed interest in the area's rehabilitation has begun and the neighborhood's future is promising.

## STATE STREET/DIVISION STREET HISTORIC DISTRICT (039-186-31001-133) NR

**No. Rtg. Add.     Description**

### TEMPLE COURT *(south side)*

001  C   117-19 **Apartment Building;** Italianate; c.1890

### DIVISION STREET *(north side)*

002  N   112   **House;** Queen Anne; c.1870

003  N   116-18 **Apartment Building;** Neoclassical; c.1910

004  C   126   **House;** Italianate; c.1870

005  C   128   **House;** Queen Anne/Prairie; c.1890/c.1915

006  NC  NA    **Vacant Lot**

007  NC  138-40 **House;** T-plan; c.1890

008  C   144   **House;** Gable-front; c.1900

009  NC  150   **Apartment Building;** c.1965

010  C   156   **House;** Lazy-T; c.1890

011  C   160   **House;** Free Classic; c.1885

012  C   162   **House;** T-plan; c.1890

013  C   166   **House;** Gabled-ell; c.1890

**31002** This c.1870 house is the best example of the Queen Anne style remaining in the district. It features a wrap-around porch with turned posts and spindlework.

**31003** This apartment building boasts a Neoclassical two-story porch with Ionic columns.

014  C   172   **House;** Dutch Colonial Revival; c.1900

015  NC  NA    **Vacant Lot**

016  NC  214   **Norman Sage House;** Italianate; c.1870

017  NC  NA    **Parking Lot**

018  C   234-36 **Double House;** American four-square; c.1920

019  N   240   **House;** American foursquare/Prairie; c.1920

020  N   244   **House;** Italianate; c.1870

021  C   300   **House;** Gable-front; c.1880

022  NC  310   **Apartment Building;** c.1960

023  C   316   **Church;** Gable-front; 1939

024  C   320   **House;** T-plan; c.1880

025  NC  400   **House;** Double-pile

### DIVISION STREET (south side)

026  N   117-21 **Row House;** Italianate; c.1890

027  C   125   **House;** Gable-front; c.1900

028  C   129   **House;** T-plan; c.1890

029  NC  137   **Church;** Gothic Revival; 1893

030  N   147   **House;** Italianate/Craftsman; c.1890/c.1915

031  O   149   **House;** Craftsman; 1921 (E. Hill Turnock, architect)

**31016** A man stands on the porch of the Norman Sage House, date unknown. Today, the altered home houses the Stemm Funeral Home. *Photo courtesy of the Elkhart County Historical Museum*

032  C   155   **House;** Gable-front; c.1900

033  C   163   **House;** Italianate; c.1890

034  C   167   **House;** Lazy-T; c.1890

035  C   173   **House;** Italianate; c.1880

036  C   179   **House;** T-plan/Free Classic; c.1880

037  C   201-03 **Double House;** American four-square; c.1920

038  C   207   **House;** T-plan; c.1870

039  C   211   **House;** Upright-and-wing; c.1880

040  NC  217   **House;** Side-gable bungalow; c.1910

041  C   221-23 **House;** Gable-front/Free Classic; c.1915

**31019** This American foursquare has a hipped roof with broad eaves and hipped dormers.

31020 This Italianate house possesses tall, narrow windows with segmental-arched tops.

042 C 229 **Double House;** American four-square; c.1920

043 C 231 **House;** Gabled-ell/Free Classic; c.1910

044 C 237 **House;** T-plan; c.1890

045 C 241 **House;** Gabled-ell; c.1890

046 NC NA **Vacant Lot**

047 C 305 **House;** Gable-front; c.1900

048 C 309 **House;** California bungalow; c.1930

049 C 311 **House;** Colonial Revival; c.1910

050 C 315 **House;** Gable-front/Italianate; c.1880

051 C 321 **House;** Midwest box/Italianate; c.1880

052 C 401 **House;** Italianate; c.1870

31026 A rare example of row houses in Elkhart is this Italianate-style building.

053 C 409 **House;** Upright-and-wing; c.1880

054 NC 415 **House;** Modular; c.1970

055 C 419 **House;** California bungalow; c.1920

056 C 425 **House;** American foursquare; c.1920

057 C 429 **House;** Center-gable I-house; c.1910

**STATE STREET** (*north side*)

058 NC 116 **Commercial Building;** International; c.1965

059 NC NA **Parking Lot**

060 C 132 **House;** Queen Anne; c.1875/c.2000

061 NC NA **Parking Lot**

062 C 142 **House;** Gable-front; c.1880

063 C 146 **House;** Queen Anne; c.1870

064 C 148 **House;** Gable-front; c.1900

065 C 152 **House;** T-plan/Free Classic; c.1900

066 C 156 **House;** Gable-front; c.1890

067 C 160 **House;** Gable-front; c.1900

068 NC 174 **Office Building;** c.1970

069 C 200 **House;** Queen Anne; c.1880

070 N 208-10 **Double House;** Free Classic; c.1910

31030 This house was initially built in the Italianate style with later Craftsman-era updates. It features a slate roof, brick walls with half-timbering in the gable end, and ribbon windows.

31031 Designed by local architect E.H. Turnock, this 1921 house is an excellent example of the Craftsman style with a clay tile roof, oversized brackets, and arched openings.

071 NC 214 **House;** Manufactured; c.1970

072 C 216 **House;** Gable-front/Italianate; c.1880

073 C 222 **House;** Gabled-ell; c.1910

074 C 226 **House;** Gabled-ell; c.1920

075 C 232 **House;** Gabled-ell; 1895

076 N 236 **House;** T-plan/Italianate; c.1870

077 C 300 **House;** Saltbox; c.1890

078 C 308 **House;** T-plan; c.1880

079 C 316 **House;** Upright-and-wing; c.1900

080 C 320-22 **Double House;** Midwest box; c.1920

081 C 324-26 **House;** Lazy-T; c.1910

082 C 400 **House;** California bungalow; c.1920

083 C 405 **House;** Gable-front; c.1910

084 C 408 **House;** Gable-front; c.1910

085 C 416 **House;** Gable-front; c.1890

086 NC 422 **Apartment Building;** c.1965

087 C 428 **House;** American foursquare; c.1920

**STATE STREET** (*south side*)

088 C 113-15 **Commercial Building;** Two-part commercial block; c.1905

089 NC NA **Parking Lot**

090 C 125 **Commercial Building;** One-part commercial block; c.1920

31070 This double house is an example of the Free Classic style and has a two-story porch with balcony supported by Doric columns.

091 NC 133 **Warehouse;** 20th century functional; 1906

092 NC 147 **Commercial Building;** c.1950

093 NC NA **Vacant Lot**

094 NC 169 **Apartment Building;** c.1965

095 C 173 **House;** T-plan; c.1890

096 C 175-77 **Double House;** American foursquare/Craftsman; c.1910

097 C 181 **House;** Free Classic; c.1900

098 NC NA **Vacant Lot**

099 C 201-03 **Double House;** Midwest box; c.1910

100 C 205 **House;** California bungalow/Craftsman; c.1920

101 C 209 **House;** Gable-front; c.1890

102 C 211 **House;** Lazy-T; c.1910

103 C 215 **House;** Gable-front; c.1890

104 C 217 **House;** Lazy-T; c.1900

105 C 223 **House;** Gable-front; c.1880

106 C 229 **House;** Lazy-T; c.1900

107 NC NA **Vacant Lot**

108 C 301 **House**; American foursquare; c.1920

109 NC NA **Vacant Lot**

110 C 309-11 **Double House;** Prairie; c.1890

111 N 315 **House;** T-plan/Italianate; c.1880

112 C 319 **House;** Lazy-T; c.1940

113 C 323 **House;** Gable-front; c.1920

114 C 325 **House;** Free Classic; c.1890

115 C 329 **House;** Gable-front; c.1890

116 C 401-03 **House;** Italianate; c.1880

117 NC 411 **House;** Modular; c.1965

118 C 413 **House;** T-plan; c.1880

119 C 417 **House;** Lazy-T; c.1900

120 C 419 **House;** Gable-front; c.1900

121 C 423 **House;** T-plan; c.1890

122 C 425 **House;** California bungalow; c.1920

123 C 429 **House;** T-plan; c.1910

124 C 501 **House;** Gable-front; c.1920

**JAURIET COURT** *(west side)*

125 C 517 **House;** T-plan; c.1880

**EAST STREET** *(west side)*

126 C 615 **Commercial Building;** Two-part commercial block; c.1910

127 C 527 **House;** Gable-front; c.1920

31076 This T-plan house has Italianate-style segmental-arched windows that are tall and narrow.

31111 Another T-plan house, this example also has tall, narrow windows with segmental-arch tops, as well as a corniced bay window.

128 C 515 **Commercial Building;** 20th century functional; c.1900

**PRAIRIE STREET** *(east side)*

129 NC 600 **House;** Modular; c.1965

**MADISON STREET** *(west side)*

130 C 617 **House;** Free Classic; c.1910

**MADISON STREET** *(east side)*

131 C 710 **House;** Center-gable I-house; c.1910

132 C 608 **House;** Upright-and-wing; c.1900

**MONROE STREET** *(west side)*

133 C 611 **House;** Colonial Revival; c.1920

# Morehouse Historic District (039-186-32001-099)

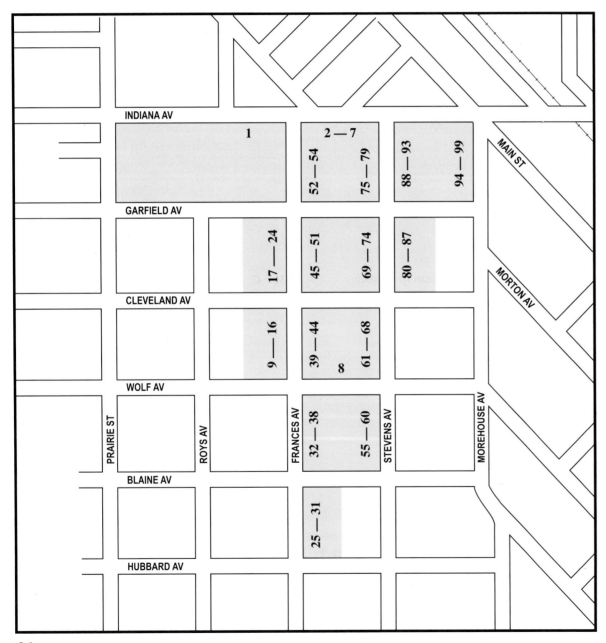

The Morehouse Historic District encompasses a collection of modest houses in the southern portion of the city of Elkhart. The district is a portion of approximately eighty acres once owned by Philo Morehouse. His holdings stretched from Indiana Avenue in the north to Lusher Avenue on the south, and Prairie Street on the west to Morehouse Avenue on the east. A 1915 plat map calls this area the Morehouse Addition and several of the streets in the district were named for members of the Morehouse family. For example, Frances Avenue was named for Frances Morehouse and Roys Avenue was named for Cyrus Roys, the husband of Katherine Morehouse.

The district appears to have been largely developed in the late 1910s and early 1920s. Modest bungalows and Craftsman-style houses dominate the area. Despite alterations to many of the homes, the neighborhood still retains much of its historic character.

The Morehouse Historic District contains one school and one church. The Late-Gothic Revival church, built in 1913, is located in the northeast corner of the district and has had several later additions (32099). Roosevelt School, on the northern end of the district, was built in 1921 and has been renovated six times (32001). The school is an outstanding example of early 1920s architecture and greatly adds to the character of the neighborhood. Plans are set to close Roosevelt School and the structure's future is unclear. Unfortunately, unless a plan for an alternative use for the building can be found, it will be demolished and the land will become a park.

## MOREHOUSE HISTORIC DISTRICT (039-186-32001-099)

| No. | Rtg. | Add. | Description |
|---|---|---|---|

### EAST INDIANA AVENUE (south side)

| | | | |
|---|---|---|---|
| 001 | O | 215 | **Roosevelt Elementary School;** Arts & Crafts; 1921 |
| 002 | NC | 301 | **House;** American foursquare; c.1920 |
| 003 | C | 305 | **House;** Prairie; c.1920 |
| 004 | C | 309 | **House;** American foursquare; c.1920 |
| 005 | NC | 315 | **House;** Craftsman; c.1920 |
| 006 | C | 319 | **House;** Western bungalow; c.1920 |
| 007 | C | 321 | **House;** American foursquare; c.1920 |

### EAST WOLF AVENUE

| | | | |
|---|---|---|---|
| 008 | NC | 304 | **House;** Modular; c.1990 |

### SOUTH FRANCES AVENUE (west side)

| | | | |
|---|---|---|---|
| 009 | C | 1729 | **House;** Side-gable bungalow; c.1915 |
| 010 | C | 1723 | **House;** American foursquare; c.1920 |
| 011 | NC | 1721 | **House;** Gable-front; c.1920 |

32001  The 1921 Roosevelt School is an outstanding example of the Arts & Crafts style. It boasts crenelated parapet walls and an arched entryway with keystones.

32044  This dormer-front bungalow displays board and batten siding on the the gable ends, clapboard siding on the first floor, and original windows.

| | | | |
|---|---|---|---|
| 012 | C | 1719 | **House;** Dormer-front bungalow; c.1920 |
| 013 | N | 1711 | **House;** California bungalow; c.1920 |
| 014 | C | 1709 | **House;** American foursquare; c.1920 |
| 015 | NC | 1705 | **House;** American foursquare; c.1920 |
| 016 | C | 1701 | **House;** Dormer-front bungalow; c.1915 |
| 017 | NC | 1629 | **House;** Dormer-front bungalow; c.1920 |
| 018 | C | 1627 | **House;** Gable-front bungalow; c.1920 |
| 019 | NC | 1625 | **House;** American foursquare; c.1920 |
| 020 | NC | 1621 | **House;** Dormer-front bungalow; c.1920 |
| 021 | C | 1615 | **House;** Side-gable bungalow; c.1920 |
| 022 | NC | 1611 | **House;** Dormer-front bungalow; c.1920 |
| 023 | C | 1605 | **House;** Dutch Colonial Revival; c.1920 |
| 024 | C | 1601 | **House;** American foursquare; c.1920 |

### SOUTH FRANCES AVENUE (east side)

| | | | |
|---|---|---|---|
| 025 | NC | 1926 | **House;** California bungalow; c.1920 |
| 026 | C | 1922 | **House;** California bungalow; c.1920 |
| 027 | C | 1918 | **House;** Dormer-front bungalow; c.1920 |
| 028 | C | 1912 | **House;** Dutch Colonial Revival; c.1920 |
| 029 | NC | 1908 | **House;** Midwest box; c.1920 |
| 030 | C | 1904 | **House;** Dutch Colonial Revival; c.1920 |
| 031 | NC | 1900 | **House;** Dutch Colonial Revival; c.1920 |
| 032 | C | 1828 | **House;** American foursquare; c.1920 |
| 033 | NC | 1826 | **House;** Dormer-front bungalow; c.1920 |
| 034 | C | 1816 | **House;** Side-gable bungalow; c.1920 |
| 035 | NC | 1814 | **House;** Side-gable bungalow; c.1920 |
| 036 | C | 1812 | **House;** California bungalow; c.1920 |
| 037 | C | 1806 | **House;** Craftsman; c.1920 |
| 038 | C | 1800 | **House;** American foursquare; c.1910 |
| 039 | C | 1726 | **House;** California bungalow; c.1920 |
| 040 | NC | 1722 | **House;** California bungalow; c.1920 |
| 041 | NC | 1720 | **House;** American foursquare; c.1920 |
| 042 | C | 1716 | **House;** Dormer-front bungalow; c.1920 |

32068  This dormer-front bungalow features exposed rafter tails and a partially-enclosed gabled porch.

32086 This bungalow retains original clapboard siding and windows, exposed rafter tails, and an integral porch with tapered wood supports.

043  C   1710  **House;** Dutch Colonial Revival; c.1920

044  N   1702  **House;** Dormer-front bungalow; c.1920

045  C   1630  **House;** Dormer-front bungalow; c.1920

046  NC  1622  **House;** Ranch; c.1960

047  C   1610  **House;** Dormer-front bungalow; c.1920

048  C   1608  **House;** American foursquare; c.1910

049  NC  1606  **House;** American foursquare; c.1920

050  C   1604  **House;** American foursquare; c.1920

051  C   1600  **House;** English cottage; c.1930

052  NC  1528  **House;** California bungalow; c.1940

053  NC  1524  **House;** Modular; c.1980

054  NC  1520  **House;** California bungalow; c.1920

## SOUTH STEVENS AVENUE *(west side)*

055  C   1829  **House;** English cottage; c.1935 (Sears & Roebuck)

056  C   1827  **House;** Midwest box; c.1920

057  NC  1817  **House;** English cottage; c.1930

058  NC  1815  **House;** Western bungalow; c.1920

059  NC  1809  **House;** American foursquare; c.1920

060  NC  1801  **House;** Ranch; c.1960

061  C   1731  **House;** California bungalow; c.1920

062  C   1725  **House;** California bungalow; c.1920

063  C   1717  **House;** California bungalow; c.1920

064  NC  1715  **House;** American foursquare; c.1920

065  C   1713  **House;** Dormer-front bungalow; c.1920

066  C   1711  **House;** Western bungalow; c.1920

067  C   1709  **House;** California bungalow; c.1920

068  N   1701  **House;** Dormer-front bungalow; c.1920

069  C   1627  **House;** American foursquare; c.1920

070  NC  1625  **House;** Gable-front; c.1920

071  NC  1623  **House;** Split-level; c.1960

072  C   1621  **House;** American foursquare; c.1920

073  NC  1609  **House;** American foursquare; c.1920

074  NC  1605  **House;** American foursquare; c.1920

075  C   1531  **House;** Western bungalow; c.1920

076  NC  1525  **House;** American foursquare; c.1920

077  NC  1519  **House;** American foursquare; c.1920

078  C   1517  **House;** American foursquare; c.1920

079  NC  1515  **House;** American foursquare; c.1920

## SOUTH STEVENS AVENUE *(east side)*

080  C   1628  **House;** California bungalow; c.1920

081  C   1626  **House;** Dormer-front bungalow; c.1920

082  C   1624  **House;** Dormer-front bungalow; c.1920

083  NC  1616  **House;** California bungalow; c.1920

32099 This 1913 church is an excellent example of the Romanesque Revival style with its corner bell tower and round-arched openings.

084  C   1610  **House;** American foursquare; c.1920

085  C   1606  **House;** Side-gabled bungalow; c.1920

086  N   1604  **House;** Bungalow; c.1920

087  N   1602  **House;** Dormer-front bungalow; c.1920

088  C   1530  **House;** Midwest box; c.1920

089  NC  1522  **House;** Pyramidal-roof; c.1930

090  NC  1518  **House;** California bungalow; c.1940

091  C   1516  **House;** American foursquare; c.1920

092  C   1514  **House;** American foursquare; c.1920

093  NC  NA    **Parking Lot**

## SOUTH MOREHOUSE *(west side)*

094  NC  1531  **House;** Midwest box; c.1920

095  C   1527  **House;** Western bungalow; c.1920

096  C   1523  **House;** Side-gable bungalow; c.1920

097  C   1517  **House;** Side-gable bungalow; c.1920

098  C   1515  **House;** American foursquare; c.1920

099  N   1501  **Church;** Romanesque Revival; 1913

# Elkhart Scattered Sites Key Map

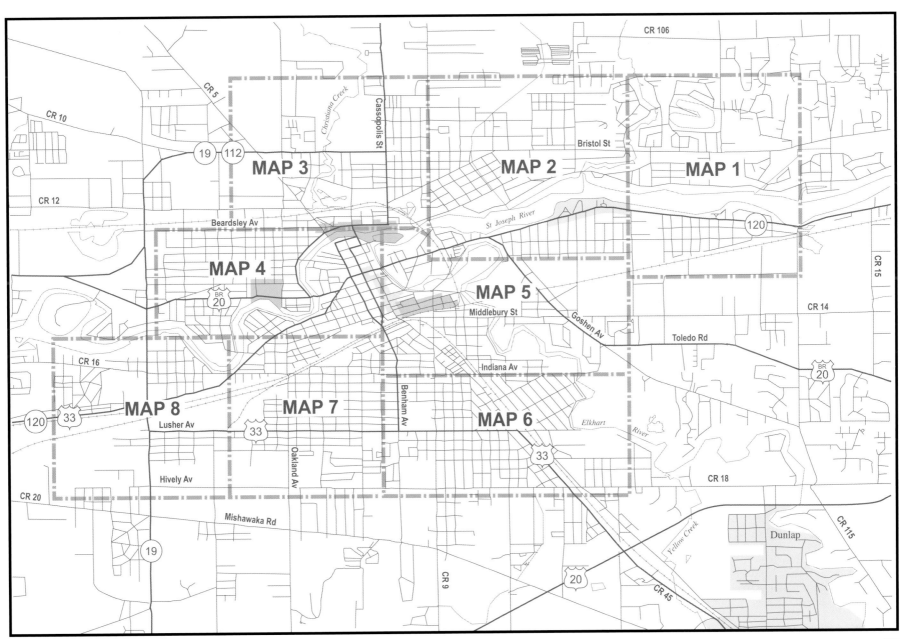

Settlement began in the Elkhart area as early as 1821 when Joseph Noffsinger settled on the north side of the St. Joseph River. Other settlers quickly followed and developed a small community known as Pulaski. Situated on the north side of the river, it consisted of a post office, grist mill, and several houses. In 1830, Dr. Havilah Beardsley came to the area and recognized its potential as the site for a new city. In 1831, he purchased a large tract of land south of the river from the Indian Chief Pierre Moran for $1,500. The following year, Dr. Beardsley hired George Crawford to survey and plat the original section of the city of Elkhart. The construction of various mills along the St. Joseph River immediately attracted people to Elkhart. However, in 1835 Richard Godfroy slowed Elkhart's early progress when he claimed that he was the rightful owner of the land on which Elkhart was being built. The case was disputed in the courts for several years until a compromise was reached giving Godfroy some land east of the Elkhart River.

Much of Elkhart's early development focused on harnessing the power of the St. Joseph and Elkhart Rivers and Christiana Creek. By the end of the 1840s, corn, saw, paper, grist, and flour mills were located in Elkhart. In 1844, the first steamboat arrived in Elkhart on the St. Joseph River, but its influence was short-lived as the railroad soon arrived. The first train came to Elkhart in 1851 and the railroad became instrumental in the city's growth. Railroad traffic grew steadily through the years; at its peak it was estimated that 124 trains passed over the Main Street crossing each day. Additionally, all trains stopped in Elkhart because it was a railroad division point, meaning that train crews switched at Elkhart.

By 1858, Elkhart had grown to the point that it officially incorporated as a town. In 1875, another vote incorporated Elkhart as a city. At the time, Elkhart was experiencing a dramatic population boom. Between 1860 and 1880, Elkhart's population more than quadrupled to nearly 7,000. The city's growth was spurred by the increase of industry in the area. The hydraulic works opened in 1870, allowing for greater industrial use of the

Elkhart River. Additionally, the Lake Shore and Michigan Southern Railroad (later known as the New York Central) built its first repair shops in 1867, with the rest completed by 1871. As the importance of the railroad increased, it became Elkhart's leading employer. By 1890, Elkhart's population reached 11,360.

Other prominent industries in Elkhart included the Conn Band Instrument Company, which started making instruments in 1875. Among the company's achievements was producing the first cornet and saxophone in America and the first sousaphone in the world. Elkhart became known as the "Band Instrument Capital of the World."

Another prominent Elkhart company was Miles Laboratories. Dr. Franklin Miles was a local physician specializing in eye and ear problems. In 1885, he formed a business to produce and distribute medicines. Miles Laboratories' most famous product was Alka-Seltzer. Introduced in 1931, Alka-Seltzer was an immediate success with sales reaching $2 million by 1934.

Despite the decline of the railroad and band instrument industries, the economy of Elkhart remains viable. Today, the largest industry in Elkhart is the manufacturing of mobile homes and recreational vehicles. Production of trailers in Elkhart began in 1935 with the Schult Company. By 1969, there were approximately 80 mobile home companies in the Elkhart area. As a result, Elkhart is today known as the "Mobile Home and Recreational Vehicle Capital of the World."

**An automobile passes in front of 801 Christiana Street (28053) in the Beardsley Avenue Historic District, c.1905.** *Photo courtesy of the Elkhart County Historical Museum*

# Elkhart Scattered Sites Map 1 (33001-017)

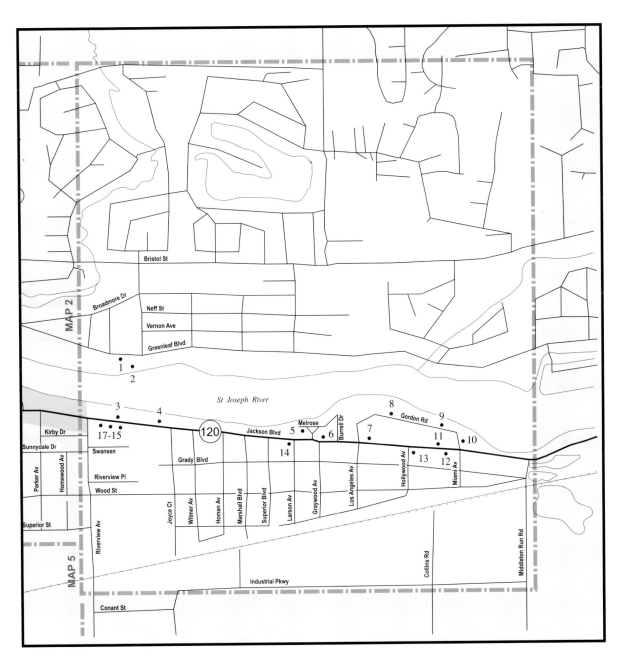

**No. Rtg. Description**

**001 O** **William and Helen Koerting House;** 2625 Greenleaf Blvd.; Prairie; 1936 (Alden Dow, architect); *Architecture* (186)

**002 N** **House;** 2629 Greenleaf Blvd.; Neoclassical; c.1920; *Architecture* (186)

**003 N** **House;** 2624 E Jackson Blvd.; French Eclectic; c.1935; *Architecture* (186)

**004 C** **House;** 2726 E Jackson Blvd.; Side-gable bungalow/Craftsman; c.1920; *Architecture* (186)

**005 N** **House;** 9 Melrose Manor; French Eclectic; c.1940; *Architecture* (186)

**006 C** **House;** 3404 E Jackson Blvd.; Cape Cod; c.1945; *Architecture* (186)

**007 O** **Gordon House;** 3520 E Jackson Blvd.; Italianate cube; 1855-1860; *Architecture* (186)

**008 N** **House;** 3556 Gordon Rd.; International; 1958; *Architecture* (186)

**009 N** **House;** 3630 Gordon Rd.; Colonial Revival; 1949; *Architecture* (186)

**010 C** **House;** 3668 Gordon Rd.; Tudor Revival; c.1940; *Architecture* (186)

**33001 Alden Dow designed the 1936 William and Helen Koerting House, which is an outstanding example of the Prairie style.**

33002 This Neoclassical house features a pedimented front gable with a fanlight above a Doric-columned integral porch.

33005 This French Eclectic house boasts a crenellated entry tower and stuccoed walls.

33009 This 1949 Colonial Revival house displays a hipped slate roof, symmetrical plan, and segmental-arched openings.

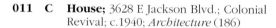

011  C  **House;** 3628 E Jackson Blvd.; Colonial Revival; c.1940; *Architecture* (186)

012  C  **House;** 2639 E Jackson Blvd.; Dormer-front bungalow/Dutch Colonial Revival; c.1920; *Architecture* (186)

013  N  **House;** 3603 E Jackson Blvd.; Chicago bungalow; c.1920; *Architecture* (186)

014  C  **House;** 3221 E Jackson Blvd.; American foursquare/Prairie; c.1920; *Architecture* (186)

015  C  **House;** 2623 E Jackson Blvd.; French Eclectic; c.1930; *Architecture* (186)

016  C  **House;** 2617 E Jackson Blvd.; Gabled-ell/Mediterranean Revival; c.1930; *Architecture* (186)

017  C  **House;** 2609 E Jackson Blvd.; English cottage; 1930; *Architecture* (186)

33013 This Chicago bungalow has a hipped roof, brick walls, and original double-hung sash windows.

33003 This French Eclectic house has a wood shake shingle roof, round tower with arched entryway, and diamond pane leaded glass windows.

33007 The Gordon House is an outstanding example of an Italianate cube. It features a reconstructed cupola, painted brick walls, and a paneled frieze with paired decorative brackets.

33015 This French Eclectic house dates to c.1930 and exhibits a steeply-pitched roof with several hipped dormer windows.

# Elkhart Scattered Sites Map 2 (33018-068)

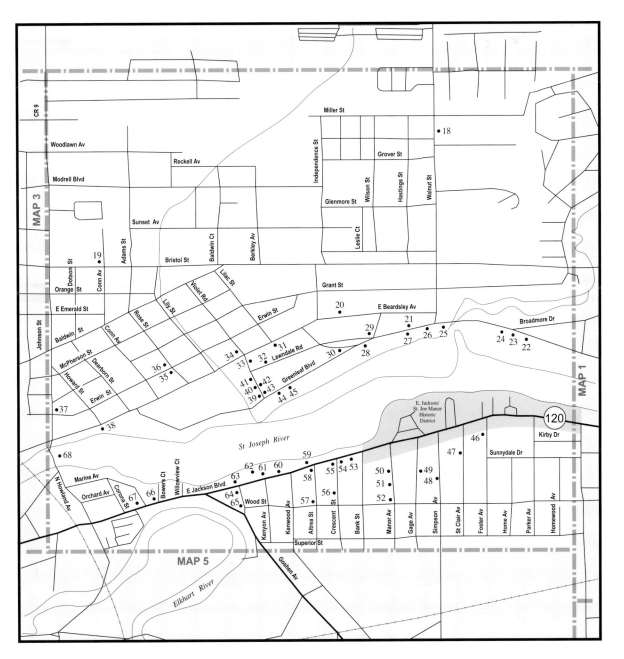

**33024** This house is an outstanding example of the Neoclassical style. It boasts a dentilated cornice and full length two-story porch with fluted Ionic columns.

035   C   **House;** 1139 Erwin St.; Gable-front bungalow; c.1930; *Architecture* (186)

036   C   **House;** 1126 Erwin St.; California bungalow; c.1925; *Architecture* (186)

037   N   **House;** 825 Grant St.; California bungalow/Craftsman; c.1920; Outbuilding: garage; *Architecture* (186)

038   O   **Mark L. and Harriett E. Monteith House;** 871 E Beardsley Ave.; Tudor Revival; 1910; Outbuildings: boathouse, studio; *Architecture* (186) **NR**

039   C   **House;** 1312 Greenleaf Blvd.; Prairie; c.1920; *Architecture* (186)

040   C   **House;** 721 Violet Rd.; Western bungalow; c.1920; *Architecture* (186)

041   C   **House;** 725 Violet Rd.; Western bungalow; c.1920; *Architecture* (186)

042   C   **House;** 716 Violet Rd.; Midwest box; c.1915; *Architecture* (186)

**33025** This Tudor Revival house exhibits stuccoed walls with half-timbering on the second floor, a clay tile roof, and original double-hung sash windows.

**33026** This Colonial Revival house retains a slate roof, three gabled dormer windows, and a dentilated cornice.

043   N   **Conrad Ziesel House;** 1418 Greenleaf Blvd.; Colonial Revival; 1919 (A.H. Ellwood, architect); *Architecture* (186)

044   O   **Greenleaf House;** 1449 Greenleaf Blvd.; French Eclectic; c.1935; Outbuilding: garage; *Architecture* (186)

045   N   **House;** 1501 Greenleaf Blvd.; Tudor Revival; c.1920; *Architecture* (186)

046   C   **House;** 119 Foster Ave.; Minimal traditional; c.1940; *Architecture* (186)

047   C   **House;** 141 St. Claire Ave.; Western bungalow; c.1920; *Architecture* (186)

048   C   **House;** 169 Simpson Ave.; California bungalow; c.1920; *Architecture* (186)

049   C   **House;** 138 Gage Rd.; Dormer-front bungalow/Craftsman; c.1920; *Architecture* (186)

**33028** This house is an outstanding example of the Tudor Revival style. It features brick walls with half-timbering beneath the gable, a prominent chimney, and original casement windows.

**33030** This English cottage displays a steeply-pitched gable roof with flared eaves, brick walls, and wood shake-sided dormer windows.

050   N   **House;** 153 Manor Ave.; French Eclectic; c.1940; *Architecture* (186)

051   N   **House;** 179 Manor Ave.; English Cottage; 1937; *Architecture* (186)

052   C   **House;** 199 Manor Ave.; English cottage; c.1910; *Architecture* (186)

053   N   **House;** 1513 E Jackson Blvd.; Colonial Revival; c.1930; *Architecture* (186)

054   O   **House;** 1501 E Jackson Blvd.; Mediterranean Revival; c.1910; *Architecture* (186)

055   C   **House;** 1425 E Jackson Blvd.; Gable-front/Free Classic; c.1910; *Architecture* (186)

**33038** The Monteith House is an outstanding example of the Tudor Revival style. It has brick walls with stucco and half-timbering on the second story and original diamond-paned leaded glass windows.

33044 The Greenleaf House is an outstanding example of the French Eclectic style. It boasts a round tower, a number of dormer windows, and original leaded glass windows.

33050 This French Eclectic house has a round tower with conical roof, flared walls, and original casement windows.

33062 The prominent arched entryway gives this Mediterranean Revival house a striking appearance. The house is believed to have been designed by local architect E. Hill Turnock.

**056  C  House;** 139 Crescent St.; California bungalow/Craftsman; c.1920; *Architecture* (186)

**057  C  House;** 1321 Wood St.; English cottage; c.1940 (ASHSB, builders); *Architecture* (186)

**058  C  House;** 1321 E Jackson Blvd.; American foursquare/Prairie; c.1920; *Architecture* (186)

**059  C  Wood Haven;** 1312 E Jackson Blvd.; Double-entry, dormer-front bungalow/Craftsman; c.1920; *Architecture* (186)

**060  N  House;** 1214 E Jackson Blvd.; Tudor Revival; c.1915; *Architecture* (186)

**061  N  House;** 1126 E Jackson Blvd.; American foursquare/Arts & Crafts; c.1910; *Architecture* (186)

**062  O  House;** 1118 E Jackson Blvd.; Mediterranean Revival; 1920 (E. Hill Turnock); *Architecture* (186)

**063  N  House;** 1034 E Jackson Blvd.; Colonial Revival; c.1935; *Architecture* (186)

**064  N  House;** 1035 E Jackson Blvd.; Prairie; c.1920; *Architecture* (186)

**065  C  House;** 144 Goshen Ave.; California bungalow/Craftsman; c.1920; *Architecture* (186)

**066  C  House;** 104-06 Marine Ave.; Colonial Revival; c.1915; *Architecture* (186)

**067  C  House;** 822 E Jackson Blvd.; Side-gable bungalow/Craftsman; c.1920; *Architecture* (186)

**068  O  St. Joseph River Dam;** 20th century functional; 1912; *Engineering, Industry* (186)

33045 This Tudor Revival house displays brick walls with half-timbering beneath the front-facing gable. Rusticated surrounds adorn window and door openings.

33054 This Mediterranean Revival house retains many key decorative elements, including exposed rafter ends and arched window openings, original clay tile roof, brick and stucco walls and wood windows.

33068 The St. Joseph Dam was constructed in 1912 along the St. Joseph River. The hydroelectric plant has brick walls and original multi-pane windows.

# Elkhart Scattered Sites Map 3 (33069-102)

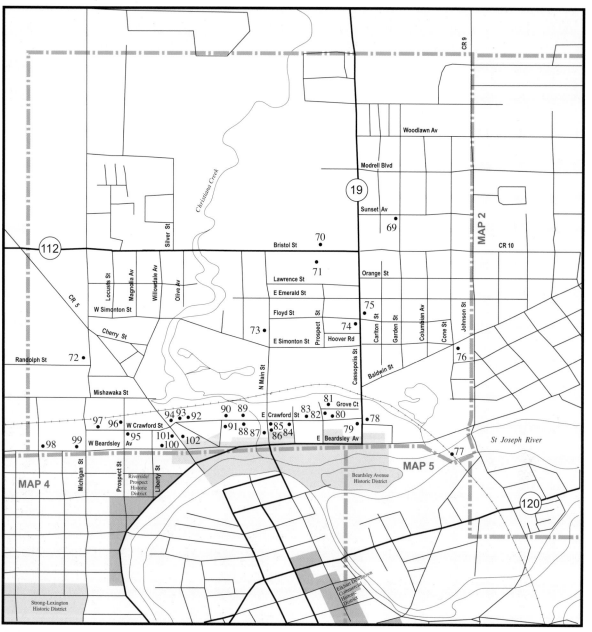

## ELKHART SCATTERED SITES (33069-102)

| No. | Rtg. | Description |
|---|---|---|
| 069 | N | **House;** 513 Sunset Ave.; Art Moderne; c.1935; *Architecture* (186) |
| 070 | C | **House;** 220 E Bristol St.; Side-gable bunga-low; c.1925; *Architecture* (186) |
| 071 | N | **North Side Gymnasium;** 300 Lawrence St.; Modern; 1953; *Architecture, Entertainment/Recreation* (186) |
| 072 | N | **House;** 1101 N Michigan St.; Side-gable bungalow/Craftsman; c.1920; *Architecture* (186) |
| 073 | C | **House;** 1247 N Main St.; T-plan; c.1910; *Architecture* (186) |
| 074 | N | **Simonton House;** 1241 Cassopolis St.; Italianate; 1890 (Lawrence Simonton, builder); *Architecture* (186) |
| 075 | C | **House;** 1242 Cassopolis St.; Gable-front; c.1910; *Architecture* (186) |
| 076 | O | **Albright United Brethren Church;** 1114 Cone St.; Mission Revival; 1915; *Architecture, Religion* (186) |
| 077 | C | **Railroad Bridge;** over St. Joseph River; c.1910; *Engineering, Transportation* (186) |
| 078 | C | **House;** 900 N Cassopolis St.; California bungalow; c.1920; *Architecture* (186) |
| 079 | N | **Beardsley House;** 323 E Crawford St.; Gable-front/Craftsman; 1917; *Architecture* (186) |
| 080 | C | **House;** 912 Grove St.; Western bungalow; c.1920; *Architecture* (186) |
| 081 | C | **House;** 920 Grove St.; Colonial Revival; c.1915; *Architecture* (186) |
| 082 | C | **House;** 912 Grove St.; California bungalow; c.1920; *Architecture* (186) |
| 083 | C | **House;** 220 E Crawford St.; Side-gable bungalow/Craftsman; c.1920; *Architecture* |

33072 This side-gabled bungalow retains wood shake siding, knee braces beneath overhanging eaves, and original double-hung sash windows with decorative moldings.

**084  N  House;** 831 Gordon St.; Mediterranean Revival; c.1915; *Architecture* (186)

**085  C  House;** 826-28 N Main St.; Colonial Revival; c.1930; *Architecture* (186)

**086  C  House;** 818 N Main St.; English cottage; c.1930; Outbuilding: garage; *Architecture* (186)

**087  C  House;** 819 N Main St.; Cross-gable square/English cottage; c.1920; *Architecture* (186)

33074 The 1890 Simonton House is a notable example of the Italianate style. It features tall, narrow window openings with segmental-arch tops and has only had three owners in its long history.

33076 The Albright United Brethren Church was built in 1915 in the Mission Revival style. It is an unusual style for a Protestant church.

**088  N  House;** 131 W Crawford St.; American foursquare/Free Classic; c.1910; *Architecture* (186)

**089  C  House;** 202 W Crawford St.; Free Classic; c.1910; *Architecture* (186)

**090  C  Double House;** 212 W Crawford St.; American foursquare; c.1920; *Architecture* (186)

**091  C  House;** 217 W Crawford St.; Free Classic; c.1900; *Architecture* (186)

**092  C  House;** 334 W Crawford St.; Free Classic; c.1910; *Architecture* (186)

**093  C  House;** 340 W Crawford St.; Side-gable bungalow; c.1920; *Architecture* (186)

**094  C  House;** 352 W Crawford St.; Lazy-T; c.1910; Outbuilding: garage; *Architecture* (186)

**095  C  House;** 822 Prospect St.; T-plan; c.1900; *Architecture* (186)

**096  C  Factory Fabrics & Linen Center;** 600 W Crawford St.; Parapet-front; c.1900; *Architecture, Industry* (186)

**097  C  House;** 626 W Crawford St.; Lazy-T/Italianate; c.1885; *Architecture* (186)

**098  N  Firehouse No. 4;** 822 W Beardsley Ave.; American foursquare/20th century functional; 1904; *Architecture, Public Safety* (186)

33088 This American foursquare house displays elements of the Free Classic style including wide columns supporting the full-width porch.

**099  N  Pratt-Elkhart Factory;** 700 W Beardsley Ave.; 19th century functional; c.1880; *Architecture, Commerce, Industry, Transportation* (186)

**100  N  House;** 422 W Beardsley Ave.; Queen Anne; c.1890; *Architecture* (186)

**101  C  House;** 827 Edwardsburg Rd.; Mediterranean Revival; c.1920; Outbuilding: garage; *Architecture* (186)

**102  N  House;** 816 Edwardsburg Rd.; Mediterranean Revival; c.1910; *Architecture* (186)

33102 This Mediterranean Revival house features a clay tile roof, brick walls, and original double-hung sash windows. The recessed entry has pilasters, a dentilated cornice, and leaded-glass sidelights.

# Elkhart Scattered Sites Map 4 (33103-260)

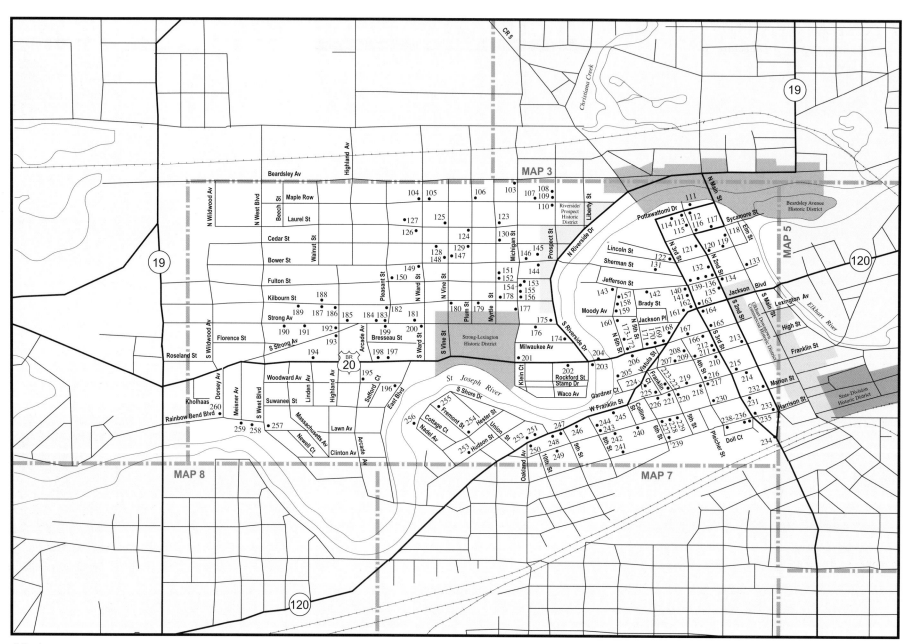

**No. Rtg. Description**

**103 C Commercial Building;** 729 N Michigan St.; Italianate; c.1900; *Architecture, Commerce* (186)

**104 C House;** 1100 Maple Row; California bungalow; c.1920; *Architecture* (186)

**105 C House;** 1014 Maple Row; Side-gable bungalow; c.1920; *Architecture* (186)

**106 C House;** 705 Plum St.; Italianate; c.1900; *Architecture* (186)

**107 C Double House;** 616-18 Maple Row; Double-entry California bungalow/Craftsman; c.1920; *Architecture* (186)

**108 C Double House;** 707-09 Prospect St.; Craftsman; c.1920; *Architecture* (186)

**109 C House;** 600 Maple Row; Italianate; c.1883; *Architecture* (186)

**110 N House;** 631 Prospect St.; Western bungalow; c.1925; *Architecture* (186)

**111 C House;** 126 Pottawattomi Dr.; Dormer-front bungalow; c.1920; *Architecture* (186)

**112 C Temple Israel;** 430 N Second St.; Contemporary; 1948; *Architecture, Religion* (186)

**113 C House;** 427 N Second St.; Gable-front; 1884; *Architecture* (186)

**33123 Riverside Christian Church displays a cross plan with side bell tower, pointed-arch openings, and original stained glass windows.**

**33136 This 1887 Queen Anne house features clapboard siding with a decorative sunburst pattern beneath the front gable. Fishscale shingles adorn the side gable.**

**114 C House;** 213 Pottawattomi Dr.; Gable-front; c.1910; Outbuilding: garage; *Architecture* (186)

**115 C House;** 423 N Second St.; Shingle Style; c.1910; *Architecture* (186)

**116 C House;** 404 N Second St.; Gabled-ell; c.1880; *Architecture* (186)

**117 C House;** 114 Sycamore St.; Gable-front; c.1895/c.1970; *Architecture* (186)

**118 C House;** 321 N Main St.; Italianate; 1877; *Architecture* (186)

**119 C House;** 114 Washington St.; American foursquare; c.1920; *Architecture* (186)

**120 C House;** 302 N Second St.; Shingle Style; c.1890; *Architecture* (186)

**121 C House;** 317 N Second St.; Free Classic; c.1910; *Architecture* (186)

**122 C House;** 324 Washington St.; American foursquare/Free Classic; c.1920; *Architecture* (186)

**123 N Riverside Christian Church;** 600 Myrtle St.; Gothic Revival; c.1885; *Architecture, Religion* (186)

**124 C House;** 521 Plum St.; T-plan; c.1905; *Architecture* (186)

**125 C House;** 521 N Vine St.; Dormer-front bungalow; c.1920; *Architecture* (186)

**33139 Compton House is an unusual example of the Shingle style, which is reminiscent of east coast examples.**

**126 C House;** 1111 Laurel St.; American foursquare; c.1922; *Architecture* (186)

**127 C House;** 1118 Laurel St.; Dormer-front bungalow; c.1925; *Architecture* (186)

**128 C House;** 1015 Cedar St.; Dormer-front bungalow; c.1920; *Architecture* (186)

**129 C House;** 903 Cedar St.; T-plan; c.1910; *Architecture* (186)

**130 N House;** 423 Myrtle St.; Lazy-T; c.1890; *Architecture* (186)

**131 C House;** 412-14 Sherman St.; Double-entry, double-pile; c.1880; *Architecture* (186)

**132 C Cook House;** 209 N Second St.; I-house/Greek Revival; 1862; *Architecture* (186)

**33152 The 1930 Hagerty House was designed by its original owner and is a nice example of an English Cottage.**

**133 N Armory Building;** 200 N Main St.; Craftsman; 1911 (E. Hill Turnock); *Architecture, Military* (186)

**134 C Apartment Building;** 130 N Second St.; Romanesque Revival; c.1910; *Architecture* (186)

**135 C James Cornish House;** 129 N Second St.; Italianate; 1871; *Architecture* (186)

**136 N House;** 201 N Second St.; Queen Anne; 1887; *Architecture* (186)

**137 C House;** 212 W Jefferson St.; Gabled-ell; c.1870; *Architecture* (186)

**138 C House;** 216 Jefferson St.; T-plan; c.1890; *Architecture* (186)

**139 N Compton House;** 220-222 Jefferson St.; Shingle Style; 1904 (E. Hill Turnock, architect); *Architecture* (186)

**140 C House;** 129 N Third St.; T-plan; c.1900; *Architecture* (186)

**141 C House;** 125 N Third St.; American foursquare; c.1920; *Architecture* (186)

**142 C House;** 405 Jefferson St.; Free Classic; c.1910; *Architecture* (186)

**143 C House;** 601 Jefferson St.; T-plan; c.1890; Outbuilding: garage; *Architecture* (186)

**144 C House;** 619 Bower St.; T-plan; c.1900; *Architecture* (186)

**33161** This house is an outstanding example of a gable-front house with Greek Revival details. It features a dentilated cornice with returns, clearstory windows, and an elaborate entry surround.

**33163** This apartment building displays a crenellated parapet wall that alludes to the Craftsman style.

**145 O Emmanuel C. Bickel House;** 614 Bower St.; Gabled-ell/Italianate; c.1870; *Architecture* (186)

**146 C House;** 626 Bower St.; Gabled-ell; c.1890; *Architecture* (186)

**147 C House;** 412 N Vine St.; Dutch Colonial Revival; c.1920; *Architecture* (186)

**148 C House;** 409 N Vine St.; Dormer-front bungalow/Craftsman; c.1925; *Architecture* (186)

**149 N House;** 1101 Bower St.; Bungalow/Craftsman; c.1920; *Architecture* (186)

**150 C House;** 1136 Fulton St.; Bungalow; c.1920; *Architecture* (186)

**151 N House;** 310 N Myrtle St.; Colonial Revival; c.1920; *Architecture* (186)

**152 O Hagerty House;** 300 Myrtle St.; English cottage; 1930 (H. Hagerty, designer); Outbuilding: garage; *Architecture* (186)

**153 C House;** 669 Fulton St.; Gabled-ell; 1891; *Architecture* (186)

**154 C House;** 222 N Michigan St.; Free Classic; 1900; Outbuilding: garage; *Architecture* (186)

**155 C House;** 214 N Michigan St.; Queen Anne; c.1900; *Architecture* (186)

**156 C House;** 210 N Michigan St.; Dormer-front bungalow/Craftsman; c.1925; *Architecture* (186)

**33166** This house exhibits Craftsman-style details, such as the knee braces beneath overhanging eaves, a front gable with a jerkinhead, and original double-hung sash and casement windows.

**157 C House;** 176 N Sixth St.; Gable-front; c.1900; *Architecture* (186)

**158 C House;** 174 N Sixth St.; Gable-front; c.1900; *Architecture* (186)

**159 C House;** 164 N Sixth St.; T-plan; c.1900; *Architecture* (186)

**160 C House;** 156 N Sixth St.; Gable-front; c.1910; *Architecture* (186)

**161 O House;** 320 W Jackson Blvd.; Gable-front/Greek Revival; c.1870; *Architecture* (186)

**162 N House;** 302 W Jackson Blvd.; Craftsman; c.1920; *Architecture* (186)

**163 N Apartment Building;** 230 W Jackson Blvd.; Craftsman; c.1910; *Architecture* (186)

**33168** Local architect E. Hill Turnock designed the 1917 Fred Gampher House in the Prairie style. It boasts a clay tile roof, decorative brackets beneath broad eaves, and original windows.

**33179** This dormer-front bungalow has wood shake siding, large knee braces beneath overhanging eaves, and original windows topped with decorative molding.

**164 N Apartment Building;** 229 W Jackson Blvd.; Classical Revival; c.1915 (E. Hill Turnock, architect); *Architecture* (186)

**165 O St. John's Episcopal Church;** 226 W Lexington Ave.; Gothic Revival; 1896 (A.H. Ellwood, architect); *Architecture, Religion* (186)

**166 N House;** 315 W Lexington Ave.; Craftsman; c.1920; *Architecture* (186)

**167 N Elkhart High School/Samuel Strong School;** 330 W Lexington Ave.; Romanesque Revival; 1892; *Architecture, Education* (186)

**168 O Fred Gampher House;** 414 Vistula St.; Prairie; 1917 (E. Hill Turnock, architect); *Architecture* (186)

**33186** This Prairie style house possesses a hipped roof, original windows, and a protruding entry bay with flared walls.

**169 N House;** 432 W Lexington Ave.; Free Classic; c.1890; *Architecture* (186)

**170 N Apartment Building;** 424-428 W Lexington Ave.; Free Classic; c.1900; *Architecture* (186)

**171 C House;** 436 W Lexington St.; Craftsman; c.1920; *Architecture* (186)

**172 C House;** 518 W Lexington St.; Gabled-ell; c.1900; *Architecture* (186)

**173 C House;** 122 N Sixth St.; American four-square; c.1910; *Architecture* (186)

**174 N House;** 117 S Riverside Dr.; T-plan; c.1890; *Architecture* (186)

**175 C House;** 660 Strong Ave.; Dutch Colonial Revival; c.1910; *Architecture* (186)

**176 C House;** 671 Strong Ave.; Gable-front; c.1890; *Architecture* (186)

**177 C House;** 117 N Michigan St.; Gabled-ell; c.1890; *Architecture* (186)

**178 C House;** 714 Kilbourn St.; American four-square; c.1920; *Architecture* (186)

**179 N House;** 815 Kilbourn St.; Dormer-front bungalow/Craftsman; c.1920; *Architecture* (186)

**33191** This English cottage retains stuccoed walls with half-timbering in the dormer windws and wood shake shingles beneath the gables.

**33198** This Queen Anne cottage features original clapboard siding with corner boards, a porch with turned posts, and historic double-hung sash windows.

**180 C House;** 915 Kilbourn St.; American four-square; c.1910; *Architecture* (186)

**181 N House;** 1110 Strong Ave.; Dormer-front bungalow/Craftsman; c.1920; *Architecture* (186)

**182 C House;** 1203 Kilbourn St.; American four-square; c.1920; *Architecture* (186)

**183 C House;** 1146 Strong Ave.; American four-square; c.1920; *Architecture* (186)

**184 N House;** 1150 Strong Ave.; American four-square; c.1920; *Architecture* (186)

**185 C House;** 1210 Strong Ave.; Bungalow; c.1920; *Architecture* (186)

**186 N House;** 1401 Kilbourn St.; American four-square/Prairie; c.1915; *Architecture* (186)

**187 C House;** 1421 Kilbourn St.; Bungalow; c.1920; *Architecture* (186)

**188 C House;** 1422 Kilbourn St.; English cottage; c.1930; *Architecture* (186)

**189 C House;** 1439 Kilbourn St.; Eclectic Revival; c.1930; *Architecture* (186)

**190 C House;** 1505 Strong Ave.; Eclectic Revival; c.1930; *Architecture* (186)

**191 N House;** 1433 Strong Ave.; English cottage; c.1930; *Architecture* (186)

**192 C House;** 1407 Strong Ave.; English cottage; c.1920; Outbuilding: garage; *Architecture* (186)

33203 The Dr. Stamp House is an outstanding example of a variation on the American foursquare type. Dr. Stamp was a local dentist. The house has had only two owners since its 1923 construction.

33215 The Neoclassical Elkhart High School displays a dentilated cornice and protruding entry bay with a segmental-arched window flanked by classical columns.

193   C   **House;** 101 S Highland Ave.; Spanish Colonial Revival; c.1930; Outbuilding: garage; *Architecture* (186)

194   C   **House;** 1322 W Lexington Ave.; Tudor Revival; c.1930; *Architecture* (186)

195   C   **House;** 1146 Woodward Ave.; English cottage; c.1925; *Architecture* (186)

196   C   **House;** 301 East Blvd.; American foursquare; c.1925; *Architecture* (186)

197   C   **House;** 1148 W Lexington Ave.; Bungalow; c.1925; *Architecture* (186)

198   N   **House;** 1154 W Lexington Ave.; Queen Anne cottage; c.1890; *Architecture* (186)

199   N   **House;** 1151 Strong Ave.; English cottage; 1932; *Architecture* (186)

200   N   **Curtis House;** 1103 Strong Ave.; Tudor Revival; c.1925 (P. Lindhout, architect); *Architecture* (186)

201   C   **House;** 690 W Lexington Ave.; American foursquare; c.1920; *Architecture* (186)

202   C   **House;** 637 W Lexington Ave.; Dormer-front bungalow; c.1920; *Architecture* (186)

203   O   **Dr. Stamp House;** 619 W Lexington Ave.; American foursquare; 1923; *Architecture* (186)

204   N   **Bridge;** W Lexington Ave. over St. Joseph River; Filled spandrel arch; 1926; *Engineering, Transportation* (186)

205   C   **House;** 616 W High St.; Free Classic; c.1910; *Architecture* (186)

206   O   **Phelps House/Knickerbocker Weddings;** 525 W Lexington Ave.; Gothic Revival; c.1875; *Architecture* (186) **IRHSS**

207   C   **House;** 414 W High St.; American foursquare/Craftsman; c.1920; *Architecture* (186)

208   C   **House;** 219 Fourth St.; California bungalow/Craftsman; c.1910; *Architecture* (186)

209   N   **Charles B. Broderick House;** 328 W High St.; Italianate; c.1870; *Architecture* (186)

210   C   **Four Arts Club;** 311 W High St.; Italianate; c.1872 (Albert R. Beardsley, builder); *Architecture* (186)

211   N   **House;** 300 W High St.; Queen Anne; c.1890; *Architecture* (186)

212   C   **House;** 221 S Third St.; Colonial Revival; c.1925; *Architecture* (186)

213   O   **Municipal Building;** 229 S Second St.; Classical Revival; 1915 (E. Hill Turnock, architect); *Architecture* (186)

214   C   **Commercial Building;** 215 W Franklin St.; Italianate; c.1880; *Architecture* (186)

215   N   **Elkhart High School;** 216 W Franklin St.; Neoclassical; c.1910 (E. Hill Turnock, architect); *Architecture* (186)

216   N   **House;** 328 W Franklin St.; Shingle Style; c.1900; *Architecture* (186)

217   C   **House;** 329 W Franklin St.; Colonial Revival; c.1890; *Architecture* (186)

218   C   **Franklin Miles House;** 403 W Franklin St.; Italianate; c.1885; *Architecture* (186)

219   N   **Central Christian Church;** 418 W Franklin St.; Late Gothic Revival; 1925/1952; *Architecture, Religion* (186)

220   N   **House;** 429 W Franklin St.; American foursquare; c.1910; *Architecture* (186)

221   C   **House;** 515 W Franklin St.; T-plan/Italianate; c.1870; *Architecture* (186)

222   C   **House;** 502 W Franklin St.; Italianate; c.1875; *Architecture* (186)

223   C   **House;** 323 S Fifth St.; Italianate; c.1880; *Architecture* (186)

33213 E. Hill Turnock designed the 1915 Elkhart Municipal Building. The Classical Revival style structure features a dentilated cornice, segmental-arched and flat openings, and limestone accents.

33225 The Bierce House was owned by the parents of the nationally-prominent journalist and author Ambrose G. Bierce who lived and worked in Elkhart in 1860-1861.

**224  C  House;** 320 S Sixth St.; T-plan/Free Classic; c.1890; *Architecture* (186)

**225  N  Bierce House & Historical Marker;** 518 W Franklin St.; Free Classic; c.1880; *Architecture* (186)

**226  C  House;** 519 W Franklin St.; Italianate; c.1870; *Architecture* (186)

**227  N  House;** 529 W Marion St.; Queen Anne; c.1890; *Architecture* (186)

**228  C  House;** 517 W Marion St.; T-plan; c.1880; *Architecture* (186)

**229  N  Apartment Building;** 501 W Marion St.; Italianate; c.1870; *Architecture* (186)

**230  C  Colonial Apartments;** 330-328 W Marion St.; 20th century functional; c.1910; *Architecture* (186)

**231  N  F.O.E. No. 395;** 225 W Marion St.; Neoclassical Revival; c.1903; *Architecture* (186)

**232  N  Elkhart Truth Building;** 421-417 S Second St.; Italianate/Classical Revival; c.1910; *Architecture* (186)

**233  O  Winchester-Knickerbocker Mansion;** 529 S Second St.; Italian Renaissance Revival; 1905 (E. Hill Turnock, architect); *Architecture* (186)

**234  C  Railroad Bridge;** Over Benham Ave.; 1955; *Engineering, Transportation* (186)

33229 These Italianate apartments have painted brick walls with a highly ornamental cornice line that features scroll decorations, brackets, and corner cupolas.

33233 The Winchester-Knickerbocker Mansion was built in 1905 for Charles H. Winchester, who was president of First National Bank from 1887 to 1917. Designed by E. Hill Turnock, Winchester's daughter and son-in-law, Nellie and William H. Knickerbocker, also lived in the house.

**235  C  Memorial;** Third St. & Harrison St.; *Social History* (186)

**236  N  House;** 601 S Third St.; Queen Anne; c.1880; *Architecture* (186)

**237  N  House;** 311 Harrison St.; Second Empire; c.1870; *Architecture* (186)

**238  C  House/Apartment Building;** 325-327 Harrison St.; Greek Revival; c.1870; *Architecture* (186)

**239  C  Commercial Building;** 528 Harrison St.; Italianate; c.1880; *Architecture, Commerce* (186)

**240  C  House;** 615 W Marion St.; T-plan; c.1890; *Architecture* (186)

**241  C  House;** 714 Harrison St.; Lazy-T/Italianate; c.1880; *Architecture* (186)

**242  C  House;** 717 W Marion St.; T-plan/Italianate; c.1880; *Architecture* (186)

**243  C  Apartment Building;** 724-730 W Marion St.; Italianate; c.1890; *Architecture* (186)

**244  C  Double-House;** 410-412 Eighth St.; Double-entry I-house; c.1890; *Architecture* (186)

**245  N  House;** 629 W Franklin St.; American four-square; c.1920; *Architecture* (186)

**246  C  House;** 819 Franklin St.; T-plan/Italianate; c.1880; *Architecture* (186)

**247  C  House;** 903 Franklin St.; Gable-front; c.1900; *Architecture* (186)

**248  C  House;** 917 Franklin St.; T-plan/Italianate; c.1880; *Architecture* (186)

**249  C  House;** 913 Marion St.; Queen Anne; c.1890; *Architecture* (186)

**250  C  House;** 931 Franklin St.; Dormer-front bungalow; c.1910; *Architecture* (186)

**251  C  House;** 928 Franklin St.; Gable-front/Craftsman; c.1920; *Architecture* (186)

**252  C  House;** 930 Franklin St.; Gable-front/Craftsman; c.1920; *Architecture* (186)

**253  C  House;** 1300 Hudson St.; Gabled-ell/Italianate; c.1890; *Architecture* (186)

**254  C  House;** 1218 Hester St.; Western bungalow; c.1920; *Architecture* (186)

**255  C  House;** 116 Fremont St.; California bungalow; c.1920; *Architecture* (186)

**256  C  House;** 102 Nadel Ave.; American four-square; c.1920; *Architecture* (186)

**257  N  Evangelical Lutheran Dreieinigkeits Kirche;** 400 S West Blvd.; Tudor Revival/Late Gothic Revival; c.1925; *Architecture, Ethnic Heritage, Religion* (186)

**258  C  House;** 1617 Rainbow Bend Blvd.; Italian Renaissance Revival; c.1925; *Architecture* (186)

**259  C  House;** 1623 Rainbow Bend Blvd.; Tudor Revival; 1935; *Architecture* (186)

**260  N  House;** 1700 Rainbow Bend Blvd.; French Eclectic Revival; c.1930; *Architecture* (186)

33257 The Evangelical Lutheran Dreieinigkeits Kirche has elements of both the Tudor Revival and late-Gothic Revival styles.

# Elkhart Scattered Sites Map 5 (33261-320)

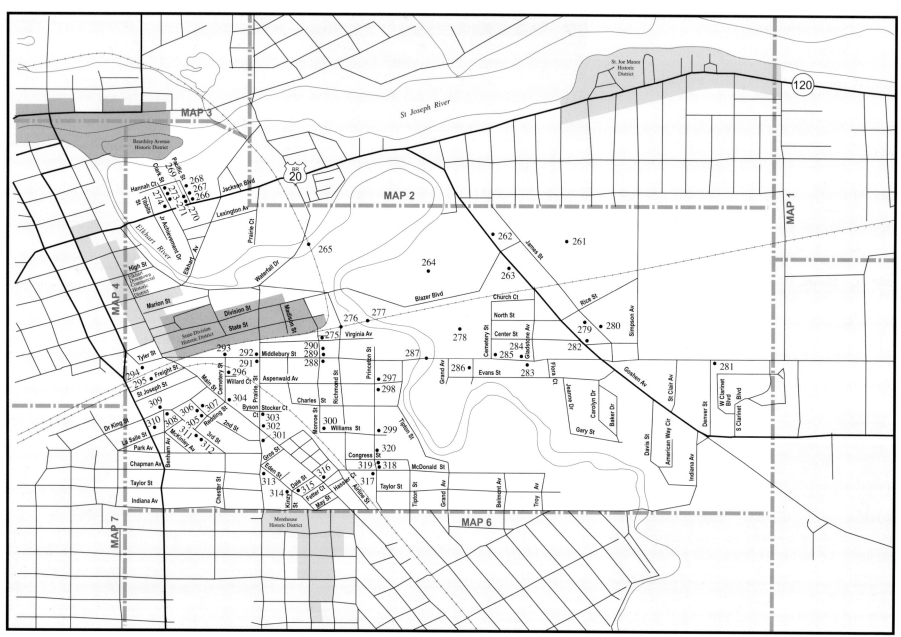

## ELKHART SCATTERED SITES (33261-320)

**No. Rtg. Description**

**261 N** **Rice Cemetery;** 400 James St.; 1913-present; Outbuildings: Neoclassical Revival Office Building (E. Hill Turnock, architect); *Architecture, Landscape Architecture, Social History* (186)

**262 N** **House;** 360 Goshen Ave.; Tudor Revival; c.1935; *Architecture* (186)

**263 O** **Rice School;** 425 Goshen Ave.; Collegiate Gothic; c.1915 (E. Hill Turnock, architect); Outbuilding: smokestack; *Architecture, Education* (186)

**264 N** **Rice Field;** 1 Blazer Blvd.; Prairie; 1939; Outbuildings: administration building, concession stand; *Architecture, Entertainment/Recreation* (186)

**265 C** **Railroad Bridge;** Over Elkhart River; Plate-girder; c.1910; *Engineering, Transportation* (186)

**266 C** **House;** 124 Pacific St.; English cottage; c.1940; *Architecture* (186)

**267 C** **House;** 130 Pacific St.; Gabled-ell; c.1915; *Architecture* (186)

**268 C** **House;** 132 Pacific St.; T-plan; c.1915; *Architecture* (186)

**269 C** **House;** 121 Pacific St.; Gable-front; c.1915; *Architecture* (186)

**270 C** **House;** 117 Pacific St.; Gable-front; c.1915; *Architecture* (186)

**271 N** **Hospital;** 126 Clark St.; Italianate; c.1860; *Architecture, Health/Medicine* (186)

**33261** Rice Cemetery and its office building pictured here were designed by local architect E. Hill Turnock.

**33262** This Tudor Revival house has varied wall surfaces, including brick, stucco, and shingle siding.

**272 C** **House;** 136 N Clark St.; Queen Anne; c.1890; *Architecture* (186)

**273 C** **House;** 150 N Clark St.; California bungalow; c.1935; *Architecture* (186)

**274 C** **House;** 119 N Clark St.; T-plan; c.1880; *Architecture* (186)

**275 C** **House;** 500 Virginia Ave.; T-plan; c.1890; *Architecture* (186)

**276 C** **Bridge;** Over Richmond St.; Plate-girder; c.1900; *Engineering, Transportation* (186)

**277 C** **Railroad Bridge;** Over Elkhart River; c.1910; *Engineering, Transportation* (186)

**278 C** **Grace Lawn Cemetery;** Middlebury St.; c.1864-present; *Religion, Social History* (186)

**279 C** **House;** 619 James St.; California bungalow; c.1920; *Architecture* (186)

**280 C** **House;** 636 James St.; Lazy-T; c.1900; *Architecture* (186)

**281 C** **House;** 1501 Middlebury St.; Dormer-front bungalow; c.1920; *Architecture* (186)

**282 N** **Seventh-Day Adventist Church;** 638 Goshen Ave.; Gable-front/Colonial Revival; 1947; *Architecture, Religion* (186)

**283 C** **House;** 1025 Middlebury St.; 1 ½ I-house; c.1910; *Architecture* (186)

**284 C** **House;** 1022 Middlebury St.; Upright-and-wing/Italianate; c.1885; *Architecture* (186)

**285 C** **House;** 1002 Middlebury St.; Pyramidal-roof cottage; c.1920; *Architecture* (186)

**33263** Rice School is an example of the Collegiate Gothic style, which was popular on college and high school campuses.

**286 C** **House;** 817 Grace Ave.; California bungalow; c.1920; *Architecture* (186)

**287 N** **Middlebury Street Bridge;** Middlebury St. over Elkhart River; Concrete arch; 1931; *Engineering, Transportation* (186)

**288 C** **Castle United Brethren Church;** 501 Middlebury St.; Neoclassical; 1910/1950; *Architecture, Religion* (186)

**289 N** **House;** 500 Middlebury St.; Queen Anne; 1896; *Architecture* (186)

**290 C** **House;** 748 Monroe St.; Center-gable cottage; c.1900; *Architecture* (186)

**291 C** **House;** 235 Middlebury St.; T-plan/Italianate; c.1880; *Architecture* (186)

**292 O** **School;** 222 Middlebury St.; Neoclassical; c.1915; *Architecture, Education* (186)

**293 C** **House;** 154 Middlebury St.; T-plan/Italianate; c.1880; *Architecture* (186)

**294 O** **LS & MS Passenger Depot;** 131 Tyler St.; Romanesque Revival; 1900; *Architecture, Transportation* (186)

**33264** Rice Field features this Prairie-style administration building.

**33292** This Neoclassical school exhibits a symmetrical facade and prominent arched entryway.

**295 N** **LS & MS Freight Depot;** 721 S Main St.; 19th century functional; 1885/1906/c.1920; *Architecture, Commerce, Industry, Transportation* (186)

**296 C** **House;** 826 Willard Ct.; Lazy-T; c.1880; *Architecture* (186)

**297 C** **House;** 830 Princeton St.; Midwest box; c.1920; *Architecture* (186)

**298 C** **House;** 912 Princeton St.; Side-gable bungalow; c.1920; *Architecture* (186)

**299 C** **House;** 1030 Princeton St.; California bungalow; c.1930; *Architecture* (186)

**300 C** **House;** Monroe St.; T-plan; c.1900; *Architecture* (186)

**301 O** **House;** 11055 S Main St.; I-house/Italianate; c.1860; Outbuilding: garage; *Architecture* (186)

**302 O** **St. Vincent DePaul Catholic Church and School;** 1108 S Main St.; Gothic Revival; 1868: school/1886: church/1996; Outbuildings: houses, monument 1948, school 1868/1909; *Architecture, Religion* (186)

**303 C** **House;** 1000 Prairie St.; American foursquare; c.1915; *Architecture* (186)

**304 N** **House;** 920 S Main St.; Queen Anne; 1890; *Architecture* (186)

**305 C** **House;** 931 S Second St.; T-plan; c.1890; *Architecture* (186)

**306 C** **House;** 927 S Second St.; T-plan; c.1890; *Architecture* (186)

**307 C** **House;** 912 S Second St.; Gabled-ell; c.1890; *Architecture* (186)

**308 C** **House;** 227 Dr. Martin Luther King Jr. Dr.; T-plan/Italianate; c.1880; *Architecture* (186)

**309 C** **House;** 236 Dr. Martin Luther King Jr. Dr.; Gabled-ell/Italianate; c.1880; *Architecture* (186)

**310 C** **Water Tower;** Benham Ave.; c.1940; *Engineering* (186)

**311 N** **House;** 1005 S Third St.; American foursquare; c.1915; *Architecture* (186)

**312 C** **House;** 1017 S Third St.; T-plan; c.1890; *Architecture* (186)

**313 C** **House;** 1230 Eden St.; American foursquare; c.1920; *Architecture* (186)

**314 C** **House;** 1301 Kinzy St.; Upright-and-wing; c.1900; *Architecture* (186)

**33316** This Craftsman style house features a hipped roof, ribbon windows on the second story, and an integral, full-width front porch.

**315 C** **House;** 315 Dale St.; American foursquare; c.1915; *Architecture* (186)

**316 N** **House;** 1304 S Main St.; Craftsman; c.1925; *Architecture* (186)

**317 N** **Jones-Murray House;** 629 McDonald St.; Italianate; 1873; *Architecture* (186)

**318 N** **House;** 1220 Princeton St.; American foursquare; c.1920; *Architecture* (186)

**319 C** **House;** 1216 Princeton St.; Side-gable bungalow; c.1920; *Architecture* (186)

**320 C** **House;** 1118 Princeton St.; Side-gable bungalow; c.1930; *Architecture* (186)

**33301** This Italianate house features a bracketed cornice line, round-arched window and door openings, and a porch supported by thin, classical columns.

**33311** This American foursquare has a clay tile roof, enclosed front porch, and some original windows.

**33318** This American foursquare exhibits brick and wood shingle sided walls, decorative brackets beneath overhanging eaves, and original double-hung sash windows.

# Elkhart Scattered Sites Map 6 (33321-380)

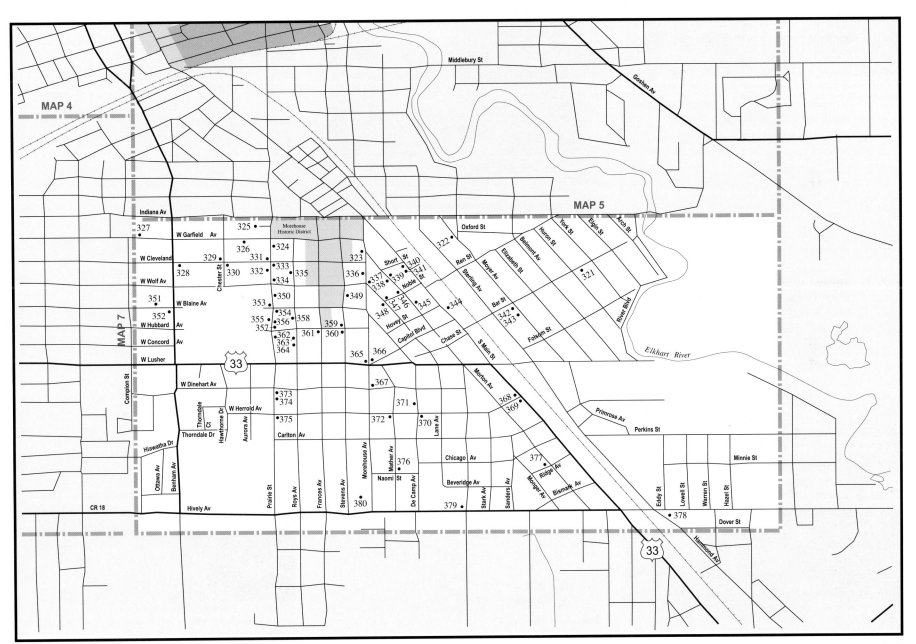

# ELKHART SCATTERED SITES (33321-380)

| No. | Rtg. | Description |
|-----|------|-------------|

**321 N McQuiston School/Concord Township District No. 15;** 1800 Huron St.; Pyramidal-roof; c.1890; *Architecture, Education* (186)

**322 C House;** 1525 Moyer Ave.; Midwest box; c.1920; *Architecture* (186)

**323 N House;** 1611 Morehouse Ave.; Dormer-front bungalow; c.1910; *Architecture* (186)

**324 C House;** 1614 Prairie St.; Dormer-front bungalow; c.1920; *Architecture* (186)

**325 N Abraham F. Wolf House;** 121 Lambert Ct.; Italianate; c.1850; *Architecture* (186)

**326 C House;** 141 W Garfield Ave.; Gable-front; c.1910; *Architecture* (186)

**327 C House;** 348 W Garfield Ave.; American foursquare; c.1920; *Architecture* (186)

**328 C House;** 235 W Cleveland Ave.; Western bungalow/Craftsman; c.1920; *Architecture* (186)

**329 C House;** 202 W Cleveland Ave.; Side-gable bungalow; c.1920; Outbuilding: garage; *Architecture* (186)

**330 N House;** 155 W Cleveland Ave.; English cottage; c.1930; *Architecture* (186)

**331 C House;** 1629 Prairie St.; T-plan; c.1910;

33323 This dormer-front bungalow retains original clapboard siding with fishscale siding beneath the dormer's gable, original windows with decorative moldings, and a full-width front porch.

108

33330 This English cottage has brick walls with half-timbering and clapboard siding beneath gable ends. It retains original casement windows.

**332 C House;** 1711 Prairie St.; American foursquare; 1915 (Bechtel, architect); *Architecture* (186)

**333 N House;** 1700-1702 Prairie St.; American foursquare/Craftsman; c.1920; *Architecture* (186)

**334 N House;** 1720 Prairie St.; English cottage; c.1930; *Architecture* (186)

**335 C House;** 1717 Roys Ave.; California bungalow/Craftsman; c.1920; *Architecture* (186)

**336 C House;** 1717 Morehouse Ave.; Bungalow; c.1920; *Architecture* (186)

**337 C House;** 1732 Morehouse Ave.; Bungalow/Craftsman; c.1920; *Architecture* (186)

**338 C House;** 1617 Morton Ave.; California bungalow/Craftsman; c.1920; *Architecture* (186)

**339 C House;** 1608 Morton Ave.; American foursquare; c.1915; *Architecture* (186)

**340 C House;** 1605 S Main St.; Dormer-front bungalow; c.1920; *Architecture* (186)

**341 C House;** 1611 S Main St.; Dormer-front bungalow; c.1920; *Architecture* (186)

**342 C House;** 1905 Moyer Ave.; American foursquare; c.1915; *Architecture* (186)

**343 C House;** 1909 Moyer Ave.; American foursquare; c.1915; *Architecture* (186)

**344 N Schult Warehouse;** 1800 S Main St.; 19th century functional; 1897; *Architecture, Industry* (186)

**345 C House;** 1712 Morton Ave.; American foursquare; c.1920; *Architecture* (186)

**346 C House;** 1635 Morton Ave.; T-plan; c.1900; *Architecture* (186)

**347 C House;** 1626 Lane Ave.; T-plan; c.1880; *Architecture* (186)

**348 N House;** 1629 Lane Ave.; Prairie; c.1915; *Architecture* (186)

**349 C House;** 1816 Stevens Ave.; Dormer-front bungalow; c.1920; Outbuilding: garage; *Architecture* (186)

**350 C House;** 1812 Prairie St.; Dutch Colonial Revival; c.1930; *Architecture* (186)

**351 C House;** 333 W Blaine Ave.; Midwest box; c.1920; *Architecture* (186)

**352 N House;** 1901 Benham Ave.; California bungalow; c.1930; *Architecture* (186)

**353 C House;** 1821 Prairie St.; American foursquare; c.1920; *Architecture* (186)

**354 N House;** 1900 Prairie St.; English cottage; c.1920; *Architecture* (186)

**355 C House;** 1907 Prairie St.; California bungalow/Craftsman; c.1920; *Architecture* (186)

33334 This English cottage has brick walls, a paritally covered porch with brick piers, and original double-hung sash windows.

33344 The Schult Warehouse, 1948. Schult Trailers, Inc. began as the Sportsman Trailer Company in 1934 as a trailer manufacturer. The 1897 building was once home to the Noyes Carriage Company. *Photo courtesy of Schult Warehouse, Inc.*

356  N  **House;** 1908 Prairie St.; Side-gable bungalow/Craftsman; c.1920; *Architecture* (186)

357  C  **House;** 1912 Prairie St.; Colonial Revival; c.1920; *Architecture* (186)

358  C  **House;** 1913 Roys Ave.; Dormer-front bungalow/Craftsman; c.1920; *Architecture* (186)

359  C  **House;** 1927 Stevens Ave.; American four-square; c.1910; *Architecture* (186)

360  N  **House;** 2001 Stevens Ave.; Prairie; c.1910; *Architecture* (186)

33348 Characteristics of the Prairie style found on this house include its broad overhanging eaves, while its windows are Craftsman in style.

33352 This California bungalow has brick walls, original windows, and a small gabled front porch.

361  C  **House;** 2001 Frances Ave.; Side-gable bungalow; c.1930; *Architecture* (186)

362  N  **House;** 2010 Prairie St.; English cottage; c.1920; *Architecture* (186)

363  C  **House;** 2015 Roys Ave.; American four-square; c.1920; *Architecture* (186)

364  C  **House;** 2019 Roys Ave.; Colonial Revival; c.1920; *Architecture* (186)

365  C  **Relay Station;** Morehouse Ave.; Parapet-front; c.1920; *Architecture, Industry* (186)

366  C  **House;** 506 Capitol Blvd.; California bungalow/Craftsman; c.1920; *Architecture* (186)

367  C  **House;** 2120 Morehouse Ave.; California bungalow; c.1920; Outbuilding: garage; *Architecture* (186)

368  C  **House;** 2229 S Main St.; American four-square; c.1920; *Architecture* (186)

369  N  **House;** 2323 S Main St.; Mission Revival; c.1930; *Architecture* (186)

370  C  **House;** 2308 DeCamp Ave.; Minimal traditional; c.1920; *Architecture* (186)

371  C  **House;** DeCamp Ave.; California bungalow/Craftsman; c.1920; *Architecture* (186)

372  C  **House;** 2301 Mather Ave.; Dormer-front bungalow; c.1920; *Architecture* (186)

373  N  **Leonard Dinehart House;** 2200 Prairie St.; Italianate; c.1860 (Leonard Dinehart, builder); *Architecture* (186)

374  C  **House;** 2206 Prairie St.; Side-gable bungalow; c.1920; *Architecture* (186)

375  C  **House;** 2300 Prairie St.; Western bungalow; c.1920; *Architecture* (186)

33354 This English cottage features a prominent chimney and limestone accents surrounding the entryway.

376  C  **House;** 2215 W Indiana Ave.; T-plan; c.1900; *Architecture* (186)

377  C  **House;** 2525 Morton Ave.; California bungalow; c.1920; *Architecture* (186)

378  C  **Concord Township District No. 10 School ;** 2700 Hammond Ave.; Romanesque Revival; c.1890 (A.H. Ellwood, architect); *Architecture, Education* (186)

379  C  **House;** 2625 Pleasant Plain Ave.; Colonial Revival; c.1930; *Architecture* (186)

380  C  **Prairie Street Cemetery;** 401 E Hively Ave.; c.1898-present; *Religion, Social History* (186)

33362 This English cottage displays a steeply-pitched roof and exposed rafter tails.

# Elkhart Scattered Sites Map 7 (33381-417)

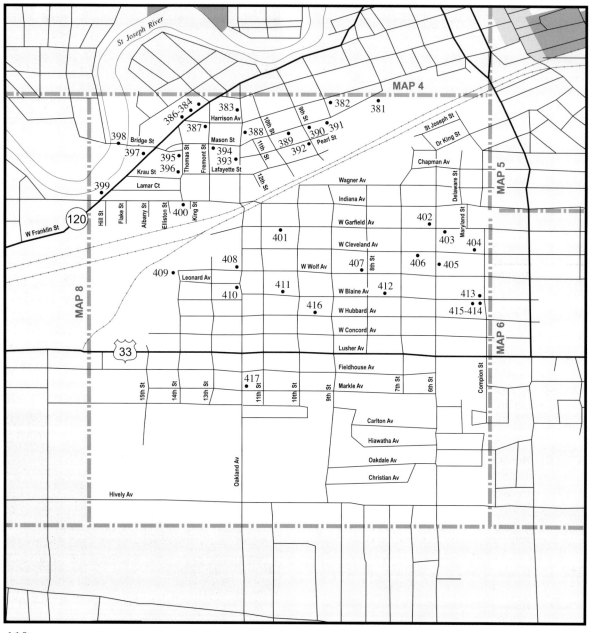

## ELKHART SCATTERED SITES (33381-417)

| No. | Rtg. | Description |
|---|---|---|
| 381 | N | **Railroad Repair Shops;** 605 Mason St.; Greek Revival; c.1850; *Architecture, Commerce, Industry, Transportation* (186) |
| 382 | C | **House;** 731 Harrison St.; T-plan/Italianate; c.1880; *Architecture* (186) |
| 383 | C | **House;** 521 Oakland Ave.; Lazy-T; c.1910; *Architecture* (186) |
| 384 | N | **House;** 1304 W Franklin St.; Lazy-T/Italianate; c.1870; *Architecture* (186) |
| 385 | C | **House;** 1334 W Franklin St.; Gable-front Italianate; c.1875; *Architecture* (186) |
| 386 | C | **House;** 1342-1344 W Franklin St.; T-plan; c.1900; *Architecture* (186) |
| 387 | C | **House;** 1301 Harrison St.; T-plan; c.1900; *Architecture* (186) |
| 388 | N | **Lincoln School;** 608 Oakland Ave.; Collegiate Gothic; c.1920; *Architecture, Education* (186) |
| 389 | C | **House;** 921 Mason St.; T-plan/Italianate; 1880; *Architecture* (186) |
| 390 | C | **House;** 831 Mason St.; T-plan/Italianate; c.1870; *Architecture* (186) |
| 391 | C | **House;** 809 Mason St.; T-plan/Italianate; c.1870; *Architecture* (186) |
| 392 | C | **House;** 901 Pearl St.; Free Classic; c.1890; *Architecture* (186) |
| 393 | C | **House;** 717 Oakland Ave.; Western bungalow; c.1920; *Architecture* (186) |
| 394 | C | **House;** 718 Fremont St.; Side-gable bungalow/Craftsman; c.1920; *Architecture* (186) |
| 395 | C | **House;** 803 Thomas St.; Gabled-ell/Italianate; c.1880; *Architecture* (186) |
| 396 | C | **House;** 821 Thomas St.; T-plan/Italianate; c.1880; *Architecture* (186) |

33384 This lazy-T house has Italianate details, including a highly decorative cornice and tall, round-arched windows with drip moldings.

**397 C House;** 1518 W Franklin St.; T-plan; c.1880; *Architecture* (186)

**398 N Bridge Street Bridge;** Over St. Joseph River; 1939 (William S. Moore/PWA); *Engineering, Transportation* (186)

**399 C House;** 1588 W Franklin St.; American foursquare; c.1925; Outbuilding: garage; *Architecture* (186)

**400 N Fire Station;** 1409 W Indiana Ave.; Colonial Revival; 1926 (Russell M. Kistner, contractor/A.H. Ellwood & Son, architect); *Architecture* (186)

**401 C House;** 1015 W Garfield Ave.; California bungalow; c.1920; *Architecture* (186)

**402 C House;** 600 W Garfield Ave.; Gable-front; c.1900; *Architecture* (186)

33388 Lincoln School has brick walls with engaged buttresses. Brick pilasters with limestone accents emphasize the vertical.

33398 The Bridge Street Bridge dates to 1939 and is an example of a concrete arch bridge with continuous framed box beams. Its construction was a project of the Federal Works Agency, Public Works Administration.

**403 C House;** 513 W Garfield Ave.; American foursquare; c.1920; *Architecture* (186)

**404 C House;** 412 W Cleveland Ave.; Side-gable bungalow; c.1920; *Architecture* (186)

**405 C House;** 1714 Sixth St.; California bungalow/Craftsman; c.1920; *Architecture* (186)

**406 C House;** 621 W Cleveland Ave.; Gable-front; c.1910; *Architecture* (186)

**407 C House;** 800 W Wolf Ave.; Side-gable bungalow/Craftsman; c.1920; *Architecture* (186)

**408 C House;** 1723 Oakland Ave.; Lazy-T; c.1890; *Architecture* (186)

**409 C Warehouse;** 1400 Wolf Ave.; Neoclassical; c.1900; *Architecture, Industry* (186)

**410 N Oakland Avenue Evangelical Church;** 1829 Oakland Ave.; Neoclassical; 1921; *Architecture, Religion* (186)

33400 This 1926 fire station has elements of the Colonial Revival style, such as its heavy cornice with exaggerated returns.

33410 The Oakland Avenue Evangelical Church is a notable example of the Neoclassical style dating to 1921. It features a pedimented portico supported by paired classical columns.

**411 C House;** 1016 W Blaine Ave.; Western bungalow; c.1920; *Architecture* (186)

**412 C House;** 716 W Blaine Ave.; T-plan/Italianate; c.1880; *Architecture* (186)

**413 C House;** 400 W Blaine Ave.; Midwest box; c.1920; *Architecture* (186)

**414 C House;** 401 W Blaine Ave.; American foursquare; c.1920; *Architecture* (186)

**415 C House;** 411 W Blaine Ave.; California bungalow; c.1920; *Architecture* (186)

**416 C House;** 908 Hubbard Ave.; Gabled-ell; c.1900; *Architecture* (186)

**417 N House;** 2220 Oakland Ave.; Double-entry, double-pile; c.1846-1850; *Architecture* (186)

33417 This double-entry, double-pile house dates to c.1846 and features clerestory windows.

# Elkhart Scattered Sites Map 8  (33418-423)

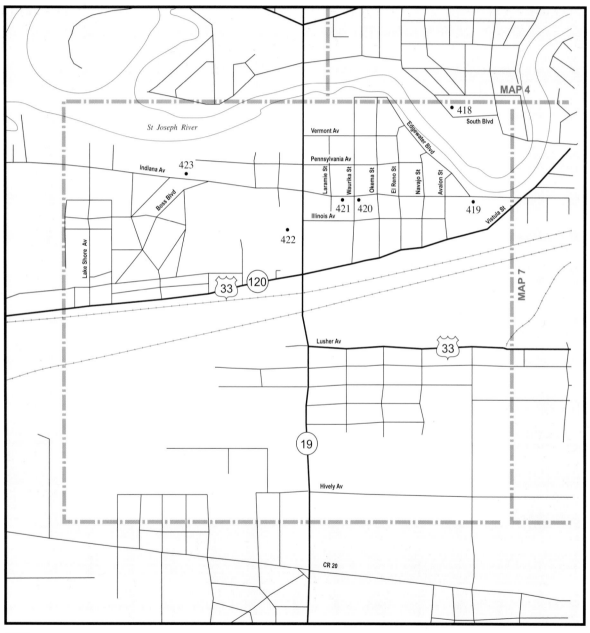

## ELKHART SCATTERED SITES (33418-423)

**No. Rtg. Description**

**418** N **House;** 608 West Blvd. S; Dormer-front bungalow/Craftsman; c.1920; *Architecture* (186)

**419** C **House;** 1657 W Indiana Ave.; T-plan/ Italianate; c.1870; *Architecture* (186)

**420** C **House;** W Indiana Ave.; Gabled-ell; c.1890; *Architecture* (186)

**421** C **House;** 2508 Mather Ave.; English cottage; c.1920; *Architecture* (186)

**422** C **St. Vincent DePaul Cemetery;** Nappannee Rd; 1881-present; *Religion* (483)

**423** O **Jacob Boss House;** 28273 CR 16; Queen Anne.; 1897; Outbuilding: carriage house; *Architecture* (186)

**33423** The Jacob Boss House is an exuberant example of the Queen Anne style and features a slate roof with decorative cresting. Boss was the owner of Boss Brickyard and the walls of the house measure between ten and fourteen inches thick.

# Dunlap Scattered Sites (34001-015)

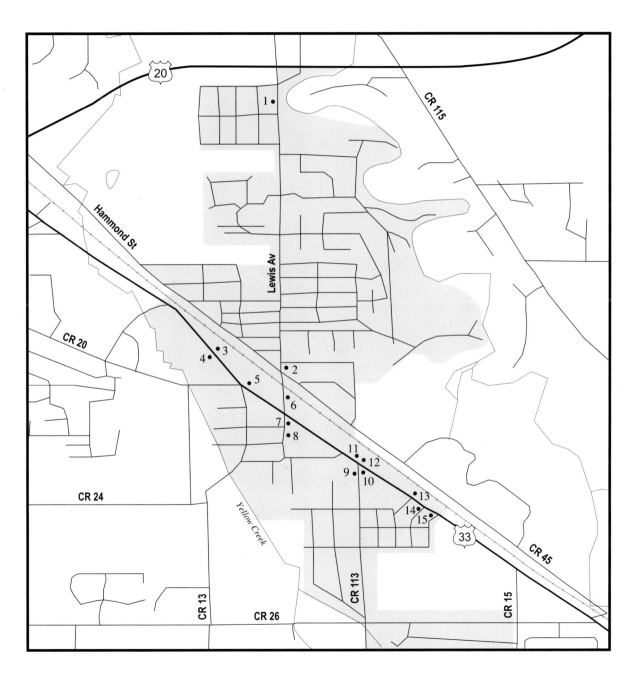

Located in Concord Township, Dunlap is bordered on the east by the winding Elkhart River, while the New York Central Railroad cuts through town from the northwest to the southeast.

When Elkhart County organized in 1830, a plat of land in Concord Township near what became the town of Dunlap briefly served as the first Elkhart County seat. However, as more western townships became part of neighboring St. Joseph County, residents wanted to relocate the seat to a more central location. As a result, Goshen became the new county seat in 1831.

The town's name has changed many times over the years. First named Cat Town, then Middleport, the town eventually became known as Dunlaps or Dunlaps Station. The town was renamed after the New York Central Railroad built a station there, in honor of an official of the Lake Shore Railroad. Today it is simply called Dunlap.

Dunlap was the site of the county's first infirmary and asylum, the Elkhart County Home. Built from 1886-87 on an existing farmstead of 123 acres, the County Home boasted state-of-the-art conveniences for its patients in a modern setting. The home took in the indigent and elderly who had previously been left to eke out their own existence from charitable individuals in the community. Its farm was used for the asylum's sustenance and for profit. The home continued operation until its demolition in 1982. Today Oxbow Park is located where the county home once stood.

## DUNLAP SCATTERED SITES (34001-015)

| No. | Rtg. | Description |
|-----|------|-------------|
| 001 | C | **House;** 57839 CR 13; Minimal traditional; c.1950; *Architecture* (186) |
| 002 | C | **House;** 58938 CR 13; California bungalow; c.1925; *Architecture* (186) |
| 003 | C | **House;** 23903 US 33 E; Bungalow/Colonial Revival; c.1930; Outbuilding: garage; *Architecture* (186) |
| 004 | C | **House;** 23811 US 33; Dutch Colonial Revival; c.1925; *Architecture* (186) |
| 005 | C | **House;** 23775 US 33; Dormer-front bungalow; c.1920; *Architecture* (186) |
| 006 | N | **House;** 59048 CR 13; Western bungalow; c.1920; *Architecture* (186) |
| 007 | N | **Dunlap United Methodist Church;** 23674 US 33; Tudor Revival; 1927/1956; *Architecture, Religion* (186) |
| 008 | C | **House;** 59178 CR 13; Gable-front; c.1915; *Architecture* (186) |
| 009 | C | **House;** 59379 CR 113; California bungalow; c.1925; *Architecture* (186) |
| 010 | C | **House;** 23452 US 33; Dormer-front bungalow; c.1925; *Architecture* (186) |
| 011 | C | **House;** 23455 US 33; Dormer-front bungalow; c.1920; *Architecture* (186) |
| 012 | C | **House;** 23451 US 33; California bungalow; c.1925; *Architecture* (186) |

**34005** This dormer-front bungalow retains original clapboard siding and board-and-batten siding on the dormer and gable ends. Knee braces support overhanging eaves and original double-hung sash windows are retained.

**34006** This western bungalow possesses original clapboard siding and windows. Knee braces support overhanging eaves and rafter tails are exposed.

| 013 | N | **House;** 23325 US 33; Italianate; c.1870; *Architecture* (186) DEMOLISHED |
|-----|---|---------------------------------------------------------------------------|
| 014 | C | **House;** 23290 US 33; Dormer-front bungalow; c.1925; *Architecture* (186) |
| 015 | C | **House;** 59543 Glenmore St.; English cottage; c.1930; *Architecture* (186) |

**34007** The Dunlap United Methodist Church's congregation dates to 1856, while the building dates to 1927 with 1956 updates.

**34009** This California bungalow retains its original clapboard siding and double-hung sash windows.

**34013** This Italianate house featured ornate curved brackets along the cornice and segmental-arched window openings. Unfortunately, it was demolished in 2004.

**34014** This dormer-front bungalow has a shed dormer with ribbon windows, and an integral front porch.

An aerial photo shows the Elkhart County Home, c.1955. The County Home was demolished in 1982. *Photo courtesy of the Elkhart County Historical Museum.*

# Jefferson Township (35001-045)

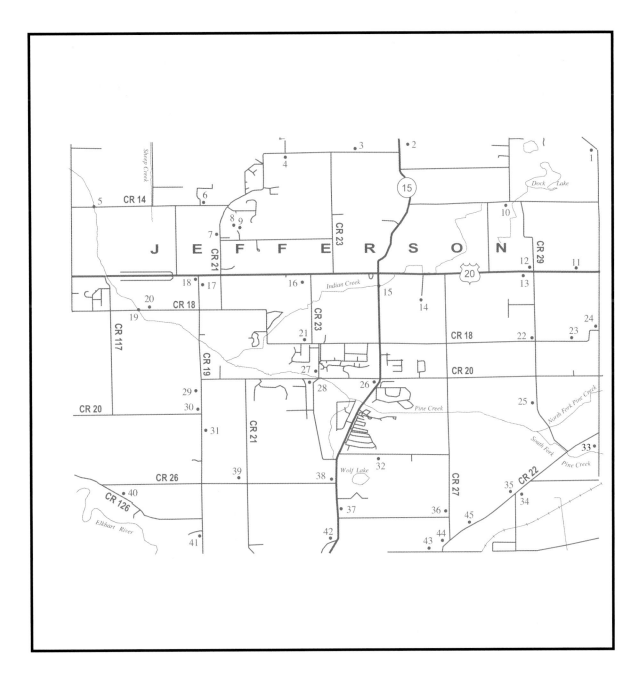

Jefferson Township is located in the north-central part of Elkhart County. Goose Pond and Dock Lake are located in the northeastern part of the township and Wolf Lake is located in the southern part. Pine Creek flows in a northwesterly direction through the township. The abandoned right-of-way of the Goshen and Michigan Branch of the Lake Shore and Michigan Southern Railroad (later the Pennsylvania Railroad) bisects the southeastern part of the township. The former rail bed is being made into a linear park stretching from Goshen to Shipshewana in LaGrange County.

The first settlers in the area were Thomas Carick, a trapper, his father, and Daniel Stutsman who arrived in about 1830. The township was officially formed in 1836 from part of Washington Township. Other early settlers who became prominent in the township include Benjamin Cornell, who came in 1831 and is buried in the Cornell Cemetery (35033); and Richard C. Lake, a farmer and carpenter who came in 1836 and is buried in the Pine Creek Cemetery (35017). The Goshen and Bristol Road, now State Road 15, was laid out in 1846.

Fruit, including plums, strawberries and grapes, was once a prominent crop in the hilly northeastern portion of the township. Colonel Henry G. Davis and his son, Charles A. Davis, operated a saw mill and furniture factory on Pine Creek, and Henry Bemenderfer operated a brickyard near his house (35037). No towns developed in the township, most likely due to its central location between Bristol, Middlebury, Goshen, and Elkhart, but also because there were no direct railroad crossings. In 1929, upon the completion of the consolidated Jefferson School, the township's one-room schools closed. This included the Bemenderfer School (35038), built with bricks from Bemenderfer's brickyard, the Frog Pond School (35022), the Pine Creek School (35018), and the White Brick School (35004).

**115**

## JEFFERSON TOWNSHIP SCATTERED SITES (35001-045)

**No. Rtg. Description**

**001 N** **Farm;** 55119 CR 31; L-plan; c.1890; Outbuildings: bank/basement barn, garages, pumphouse; *Agriculture, Architecture* (067)

**002 C** **House;** 55114 SR 15; English cottage; c.1940; Outbuilding: garage; *Architecture* (067)

**003 C** **Bishop House;** 18705 CR 14; Gable-front/Upright-and-wing; c.1860/c.1910; *Architecture* (067)

**004 N** **White Brick School;** 19500 CR 14; Gable-front; c.1889; *Architecture, Education* (067)

**005 C** **County Bridge No. 166;** Concrete; 1963 (C.W. Nicholson, engineer); *Engineering, Transportation* (186)

**006 C** **House;** 20429 CR 14; American foursquare; c.1892; Outbuildings: hog house, house; *Architecture* (067)

35009 The James Mills House was originally built near New Paris in Jackson Township and was moved to its current location in 1970.

35016 C.A. Barthel built his stone house c.1875. Barthel came to Elkhart County from Germany in 1849 and was a farmer and a mason.

**007 N** **Farm;** 56389 CR 21; L-plan; c.1872; Outbuildings: bank/basement barn, drive-thru corn crib, well; *Agriculture, Architecture* (067)

**008 C** **Daniel Lower Log House;** 20033 CR 16; Stack house; c.1834 (Daniel Lower, builder); *Architecture, Exploration/Settlement* (067)

**009 N** **James Mills Log House;** 20033 CR 16; Stack house; c.1834 (James Mills, builder); *Architecture, Exploration/Settlement* (067)

**010 C** **Farm;** 17064 CR 14; Hall-and-parlor; c.1850; Outbuildings: bank/basement barn, sheds; *Agriculture, Architecture* (067)

**011 C** **House;** 16329 US 20; American foursquare; c.1920; *Architecture* (067)

**012 C** **Farm;** 56961 CR 29; T-plan; c.1890; Outbuildings: bank/basement barn, granary; *Agriculture, Architecture* (067)

**013 C** **House;** 16868 US 20; Dutch Colonial Revival; c.1920; Outbuilding: garage; *Architecture* (067)

**014 C** **Farm;** 18012 US 20; Double-pile; c.1860; Outbuildings: chicken house, English barns, silo; *Agriculture, Architecture* (067)

**015 C** **Bridge;** SR 15 over Indian Creek; Reinforced concrete; c.1948; *Engineering, Transportation* (067)

35032 The stone Benjamin Zigler House has Greek Revival details including a wide cornice. Zigler moved to Elkhart County from Pennsylvania, settling in Jefferson Township in 1853.

**016 O** **C.A. Barthel House;** 57105 CR 23; Double-pile; c.1875 (C.A. Barthel, builder); *Architecture* (067)

**017 C** **Pine Creek Church and Cemetery;** CR 19; Steeple-front; 1959; Outbuilding: chapel; Cemetery: 1841-2002; *Architecture, Religion* (067)

**018 N** **Pine Creek School/Seminary;** 20528 US 20; Side-gable; c.1888; *Architecture, Education* (067)

35037 The Italianate Henry Bemenderfer House features a bracketed cornice, original windows, and decorative entry porch. Bemenderfer was a carpenter, contractor, farmer, and brick manufacturer who came to Elkhart County in 1865 from Virginia.

019  C  **County Bridge No. 167;** CR 18 over Pine Creek; Concrete girder; 1961; *Engineering, Transportation* (067)

020  C  **Mast Cemetery;** CR 18; 1849-1854; *Exploration/Settlement, Religion* (067)

021  C  **Farm;** 19381 CR 18; L-plan; c.1900; Outbuildings: dairy barn, drive-thru corn crib, pumphouse; *Agriculture, Architecture* (067)

022  N  **Frog Pond School;** 16767 CR 18; Italianate; 1899; *Architecture, Education* (067)

023  C  **Farm;** 16329 CR 18; American foursquare; c.1920; Outbuildings: English barn, milk house; *Agriculture, Architecture* (067)

024  C  **Neff-Adams Cemetery;** CR 31; c.1842-c.1912; *Exploration/Settlement, Religion* (067)

025  C  **Farm;** 58871 CR 29; Gable-front; c.1880; Outbuildings: bank/basement barn, granary, grain bin, livestock barn, machine shed, milk house, silo, smokehouse; *Agriculture, Architecture* (067)

026  C  **Jefferson Township School Monument;** SR 15 & CR 20; 1998; *Education* (067)

027  C  **House;** 58399 CR 23; T-plan; c.1860; Outbuilding: garage; *Architecture* (067)

028  C  **Pleasant View Cemetery;** CR 20; 1838-present; *Exploration/Settlement, Religion* (067)

029  N  **Farm;** 58617 CR 19; Midwest box; c.1920; Outbuildings: chicken house, Sweitzer barn; *Agriculture, Architecture* (067)

35038  The 1886 Bemenderfer School was made with bricks produced at Henry Bemenderfer's nearby brick factory. The school closed in 1929 and was later converted into a residence.

35039  This double-entry, double pile house is a well preserved example of the Italianate style. It features paired brackets on a wide cornice and an original bracketed porch.

030  N  **Farm;** 58913 CR 19; Center-gable cottage; c.1880; Outbuildings: transverse-frame barn, garage, shed; *Agriculture, Architecture* (067)

031  C  **Farm;** 59276 CR 19; Double-pile; c.1870; Outbuildings: bank/basement barn, chicken house, drive-thru corn crib, English barn, windmill, workshop; *Agriculture, Architecture* (067)

032  O  **Benjamin Ziglar Farm;** 18596 CR 24; Upright-and-wing/Greek Revival; c.1853; Outbuildings: drive-thru corn crib, livestock barn, silos; *Agriculture, Architecture* (067)

033  C  **Cornell Cemetery;** CR 31; 1834-present; *Exploration/Settlement, Religion* (067)

034  C  **Farm;** 16958 CR 22; Midwest box; c.1910; Outbuildings: bank/basement barn, garage, granary, summer kitchen; *Agriculture, Architecture* (243)

035  C  **Farm;** 16993 CR 22; Hall-and-parlor; c.1870; Outbuildings: chicken house, corn crib, stable; *Agriculture, Architecture* (243)

036  N  **Smith Chamberlain Farm;** 60417 CR 27; T-plan; c.1856 (Smith Chamberlain, builder); Outbuildings: cold cellar, dairy barn, ; *Agriculture, Architecture* (243)

037  O  **Henry Bemenderfer House;** 60390 SR 15; Italianate; c.1865 (Henry Bemenderfer, builder); Outbuildings: garage; *Architecture* (243)

038  N  **Bemenderfer School;** 60031 SR 15; Italianate; 1886 (E.J. Lower, builder); *Architecture, Education* (243)

039  O  **Farm;** 20093 CR 26; Double-entry, double-pile/Italianate; c.1860; Outbuildings: milk house, silo; *Agriculture, Architecture* (243)

040  C  **John W. Simmons House;** 21301 CR 126; L-plan; c.1870 (John W. Simmons, builder); Outbuildings: chicken house, machine shed, smokehouse; *Architecture* (210)

041  N  **George P. Rowell, Sr. Farm;** 60749 CR 19; L-plan; c.1875; Outbuildings: bank/basement barn, windmill; *Agriculture, Architecture* (243)

042  N  **House;** 60850 Old SR 15; Free Classic; c.1900; Outbuilding: shed; *Architecture* (243)

043  C  **Morris Cemetery;** CR 28; 1865-1867; *Exploration/Settlement, Religion* (243)

044  C  **House;** 17739 CR 22; American foursquare; c.1920; *Architecture* (243)

045  C  **House;** 17477 CR 22; Dormer-front bungalow/Craftsman; c.1920; *Architecture* (243)

35041  The George P. Rowell, Sr. House is an example of an L-plan constructed using glacial stone.

# Middlebury Township (40001-047)

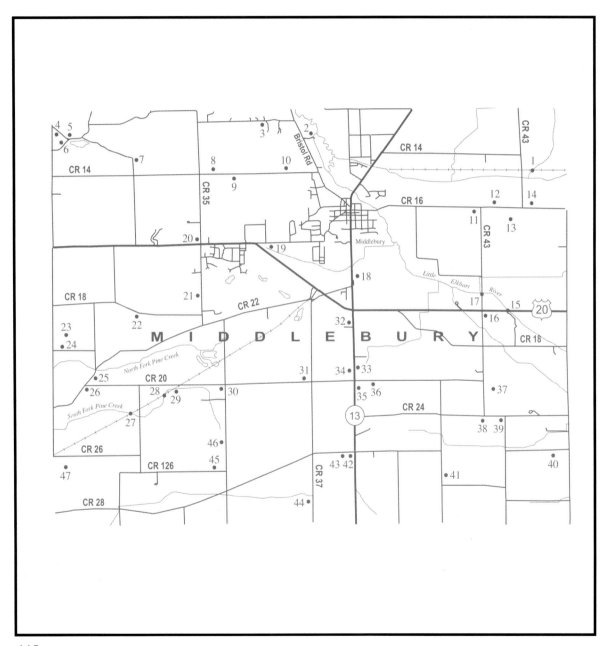

Middlebury Township is located in the east-central part of Elkhart County and is bordered to the east by LaGrange County. Lake Grange is located in the northwestern part of the township and the Little Elkhart River flows to the northwest through the township. The abandoned right-of-way of the Goshen and Michigan Branch of the Lake Shore and Michigan Southern Railroad (later the Pennsylvania Railroad) cuts diagonally through the township from the southwest to northeast. The former rail bed is being made into a linear park stretching from Goshen to Shipshewana in LaGrange County. The town of Middlebury is located in the north central part of the township.

The township was heavily forested prior to its settlement. A Potawatomi Indian village once existed about two miles southeast of Middlebury. The county organized Middlebury Township in 1834 from part of Elkhart Township. The original Middlebury Township also encompassed what became York, Jefferson, and Washington Townships. In 1835, Washington Township was divided out (and from that, Jefferson Township), followed by York Township in 1837. Original settler Enoch Woodbridge and his family came from Vermont and named Middlebury Township after the town near their home. Settler Squier Lee came in 1830 and was a carpenter who assisted in the construction of many early buildings. Other prominent settlers included Solomon Landis Hixon, who came in 1834, and David B. Mather, who came in 1837 and whose farm still stands (40010). Mather was a descendant of the Reverends Increase and Cotton Mather, who gained notoriety during the Salem witchcraft trials. Many of the township's early settlers were Mennonite and Old Order Amish.

Forest Grove, also known as Sugar Grove, was settled in 1830 and a log school was built there in 1836. Located in the southeastern part of the township, the community did not develop, having a post office only between 1880 and 1887. The Forest Grove Cemetery is an extant reminder of the settlement (40038).

The firm of Winslow, Warren and Brown of Niles, Michigan laid out the town of Middlebury in 1835; it would grow to be the township's largest community. A post office was established there in 1836 and Middlebury incorporated in 1868. The coming of the Canada and St. Louis Railway in 1888 ensured Middlebury's economic viability.

## MIDDLEBURY TOWNSHIP SCATTERED SITES (40001-047)

No. Rtg. Description

**001 C** **Lake Shore and Michigan Southern Railroad Bridge;** Over East Lake Ditch; c.1900; *Engineering, Transportation* (408)

**002 O** **Myers Mill;** CR 8; 19th century functional; c.1892; Outbuildings: hog house, milk house, windmill; *Architecture, Commerce* (408)

**003 C** **House;** 13528 CR 12; Lazy-T; c.1870; Outbuilding: pumphouse; *Architecture* (408)

**004 C** **Farm;** 15850 CR 129; Single-pen; c.1850; Outbuildings: chicken house, English barn, garage, privy; *Agriculture, Architecture* (067)

**005 N** **Lake Grange Hall;** 15723 CR 129; Gable-front; 1922; Outbuilding: privy; *Architecture, Social History* (067)

**006 C** **Farm;** 55683 CR 131; Dormer-front bungalow/Craftsman; c.1920; Outbuilding: Sweitzer barn; *Agriculture, Architecture* (067)

**007 C** **House;** 55826 CR 33; Gabled-ell; c.1870; Outbuilding: privy; *Architecture* (067)

**008 C** **Farm;** 14129 CR 14; Lazy-T; c.1880; Outbuildings: chicken house, garage, milk house, privy, Sweitzer barn, silos; *Agriculture, Architecture* (408)

**009 C** **Farm;** 13828 CR 14; Lazy-T; c.1880; Outbuildings: drive-thru corn crib, English barn, granary, hog house, house; *Agriculture, Architecture* (408)

40002 Myers Mill was rebuilt in 1892 after the original 1864 structure burned down. Over the years it has been used as a cider, grist, and feed mill.

**010 N** **David B. Mather Farm;** 13229 CR 14; Lazy-T/Greek Revival; c.1845; Outbuildings: bank/basement barn, privy, stable; *Agriculture, Architecture, Exploration/Settlement* (408)

**011 C** **House;** 11092 CR 16; American foursquare; c.1910; Outbuilding: chicken house; *Architecture* (408)

**012 C** **Farm;** 10785 CR 16; Lazy-T; c.1880; Outbuildings: chicken houses, corn cribs, English barn, privy, summer kitchen, transverse-frame barn; *Agriculture, Architecture* (408)

**013 C** **Mast Cemetery;** CR 16; c.1890-c.1998; *Religion* (408)

**014 N** **Farm;** 10405 CR 16; Side-gable; c.1880; Outbuildings: bank/basement barn, buggy shed, chicken houses, corn crib, drive-thru corn crib, hog house, pumphouse, summer kitchen, wood shed, workshops; *Agriculture, Architecture* (408)

**015 C** **Bridge;** US 20 over Little Elkhart River; Reinforced concrete girder; 1952; *Engineering, Transportation* (408)

40005 Lake Grange Hall was built in 1922 on the site of the former Lake School.

**016 C** **House;** 58072 CR 43; L-plan; c.1900; *Architecture* (408)

**017 C** **Elkhart County Bridge No. 183;** CR 43 over Little Elkhart River; Reinforced concrete bridge; 1960; *Engineering, Transportation* (408)

**018 O** **Farm;** 57500 SR 13; L-plan; c.1860; Outbuildings: bank/basement barn, milk house, silo, smokehouse, stable; *Agriculture, Architecture* (408)

**019 C** **Log House and School;** 240 US 20; Log house: hall-and-parlor; 1835; School: single-pen; 1857; *Architecture, Education, Exploration/Settlement* (408)

**020 N** **Jug Hardle School/District No. 9 School;** US 20; Gable-front; 1892; *Architecture, Education* (408)

**021 C** **House;** 57761 CR 35; Hall-and-parlor; c.1850; Outbuilding: chicken house; *Architecture* (408)

**022 C** **Geisinger Cemetery;** CR 18; c.1850-c.1910; *Exploration/Settlement, Religion* (067)

**023 C** **Log House;** 15901 CR 20; Single-pen; c.1840; *Architecture, Exploration/Settlement* (067)

**024 O** **Farm;** 15903 CR 20; L-plan; c.1870; Outbuilding: English barn; *Agriculture, Architecture* (067)

40024 This L-plan house has brick walls, segmental-arched window openings, and a porch supported by square columns.

40036 This decorative fretwork is found on the porch of a lazy-T/Italianate house.

40039 A Queen Anne porch was added onto this cross plan house.

40047 This Upright and Wing house is a noteworthy example of glacial stone construction.

025 C **Pleasant Ridge Methodist Church;** 15510 CR 22; Gothic Revival; 1900; *Architecture, Religion* (067)

026 C **Farm;** 15629 CR 20; 1 ½ hall-and-parlor; c.1890; Outbuilding: corn crib; *Agriculture, Architecture* (067)

027 C **Lake Shore and Michigan Southern Railroad Bridge;** Over South Fork Pine Creek; c.1900; *Engineering, Transportation* (067)

028 C **Lake Shore and Michigan Southern Railroad Bridge;** Over South Fork Pine Creek; c.1900; *Engineering, Transportation* (408)

029 N **Farm;** 14414 CR 20; T-plan; c.1870; Outbuildings: corn crib, English barn, summer kitchen; *Agriculture, Architecture* (408)

030 C **Farm;** 59029 CR 20; Dormer-front bungalow/Craftsman; c.1920; Outbuildings: chicken house, stable, well; *Agriculture, Architecture* (408)

031 C **Farm;** 13099 CR 20; Second Empire; c.1870; Outbuildings: barn, machine shed; *Agriculture, Architecture* (408)

032 C **Simon Griner House;** 911 S Main St.; L-plan; 1880 (Simon Griner, builder); *Architecture* (408)

033 C **Farm;** 58782 SR 13; Greek Revival; c.1850; Outbuildings: drive-thru corn crib, English barn, garage, milk house, pumphouse, summer kitchen; *Agriculture, Architecture* (408)

034 C **Farm;** 58873 SR 13; Side-gable; 1892; Outbuildings: privy, stable; *Agriculture, Architecture* (408)

035 C **Griner Cemetery;** SR 13 & CR 20; 1999-2001; *Religion* (408)

036 N **Farm;** 12186 CR 20; Lazy-T/Italianate; c.1875; Outbuildings: English barn, house, privy, silo, smokehouse; *Agriculture, Architecture* (408)

037 C **Hostetler Cemetery;** CR 43; 1856; *Exploration/Settlement, Religion* (408)

038 C **Forest Grove Cemetery;** CR 24; c.1835-present; *Exploration/Settlement, Religion* (408)

039 N **J. O. Shoup Farm;** 10742 CR 24; Cross-plan/Queen Anne; c.1860; Outbuildings: privy, Sweitzer barn; *Agriculture, Architecture* (408)

040 C **Eldridge Cemetery;** CR 26; 1838-1984; *Exploration/Settlement, Religion* (412)

041 C **Farm;** 60340 CR 41; Side-gable; c.1880; Outbuildings: English barn, shed, silo, summer kitchen; *Agriculture, Architecture* (412)

042 C **House;** 12502 CR 26; Side-gable; c.1900; Outbuilding: garage; *Architecture* (412)

043 C **AT&T Telephone Repeater Station;** CR 26; Pyramidal-roof; c.1935; *Architecture, Communications* (412)

044 N **Kauffman Farm;** 60425 CR 37; American foursquare; 1906; Outbuildings: bank/basement barn, butcher house, grain bins, hog house, oven shed, smokehouse, shed, water tank; *Agriculture, Architecture* (412)

045 C **Miller Cemetery;** CR 126; 1855-present; *Ethnic Heritage, Religion* (412)

046 N **Farm;** 59841 CR 35; Cross-plan; c.1870; Outbuildings: bank/basement barn, garage, milk house, silo; *Agriculture, Architecture* (408)

047 O **Farm;** 15784 CR 26; Upright-and-wing/Greek Revival; c.1850; Outbuildings: hog house/corn crib, machine shed, silo; *Agriculture, Architecture* (243)

Leona Blakemore poses with her bicycle in front of the Putt House at 113 North Brown Street in Middlebury, c.1890. *Photo courtesy of the Elkhart County Historical Museum*

# Middlebury Scattered Sites (41001-078)

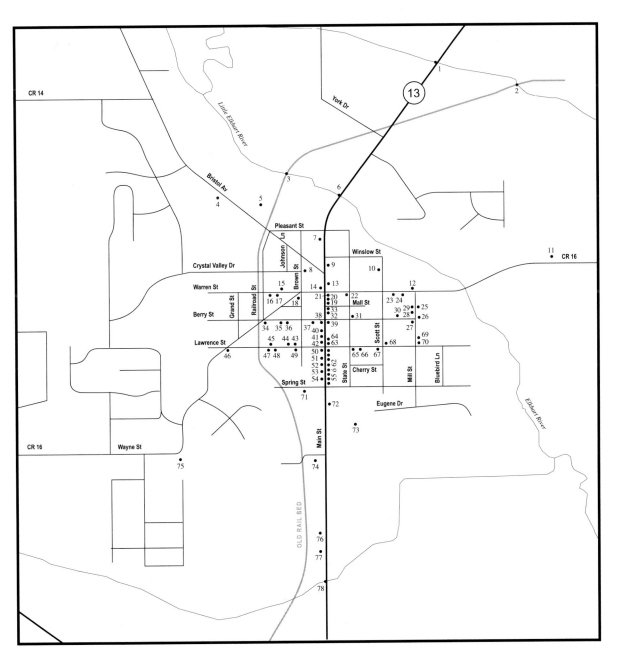

The first settlers of what became the town of Middlebury were the Enoch Woodbridge family, John C. Holmes, George A. Buffam, and Jonathan Pratt, who arrived in 1832 from near Middlebury, Vermont. Grace Lawn Cemetery (41011) is the burial place of many Middlebury Township settlers, including Squier Lee, Solomon Landis Hixon, and David B. Mather. Several mills were located on the Little Elkhart River in Middlebury and Enoch Woodbridge, Jr. built a saw mill that was instrumental in the construction of many of the town's early buildings.

The real estate speculation firm of Winslow, Warren, and Brown of Niles, Michigan laid out Middlebury in 1835. A public square was centered on the Logansport and White Pigeon Road (now North Main Street). Bristol and Wayne Avenues radiated out diagonally from the north- and southwestern corners of the square. A continuation of Wayne Avenue that was to radiate out from the southeastern corner of the square was not realized. By 1868, the town was large enough to incorporate. Bristol Avenue was eventually extended into the square to meet North Main Street. Initially green space, the square was built upon over the years, most notably with the Middlebury Town Hall in 1912 (41013). The square's remaining open areas divided by North Main Street are now Memorial and East Parks. Warren and South Main Streets became the primary commercial district.

A post office was established in 1836 and was housed in several locations before the completion of its present building in 1937 (41039). Also in 1836, Middlebury's first school was built. It was replaced in 1857 with a school on West Berry Street. The consolidated Middlebury Township School (41073), built in 1939 at a new location, replaced a 1907 school.

Until 1888, the closest railroad connection was York Township's Middlebury Station (Vistula). The completion of the Canada and St. Louis Railway through Middlebury, spurred development, ensuring the town's economic viability. A depot stood on the east side of the tracks between West Berry and West Warren Streets. After the turn of the 20th century, Interurban service came to Middlebury when the St. Joseph Valley Railway built a depot on the north side of town (41007).

## MIDDLEBURY SCATTERED SITES (41001-078)

**No. Rtg. Description**

**001  C  Bridge;** N Main St. over Mather Ditch; Concrete girder; c.1958; *Engineering, Transportation* (408)

**002  C  Lake Shore and Michigan Southern Railroad Bridge;** Over Mather Ditch; c.1900; *Engineering, Transportation* (408)

**003  N  Lake Shore and Michigan Southern Railroad Bridge;** Over Little Elkhart River; c.1900; *Engineering, Transportation* (408)

**004  O  House;** 313 Bristol Ave.; Second Empire/Italianate; c.1880; Outbuildings: garage, summer kitchen; *Architecture* (408)

**005  O  Krider Nurseries World's Fair Garden;** Bristol Ave.; 1933/1935/1995; Outbuildings: concrete mushrooms, gazebos, historical marker, miniature mill; *Horticulture, Landscape Architecture* (408)

**006  C  Bridge;** N Main St. over Little Elkhart River; 1953; *Engineering, Transportation* (408)

**007  C  St. Joseph Valley Traction Company Middlebury Depot;** 209 N Main St.; Craftsman; 1913; *Architecture, Commerce, Transportation* (408)

**008  O  St. Paul's Evangelical Lutheran Church;** 110 N Brown St.; Late Gothic Revival; 1910; *Architecture, Religion* (408)

**009  C  Boy Scout Cabin;** N Main St.; Minimal traditional/parks rustic; 1938; *Architecture, Recreation* (408)

**010  C  House;** 111 N Scott St.; Hall-and-parlor; c.1890; Outbuilding: garage; *Architecture* (408)

41008 St. Paul's Evangelical Lutheran Church was dedicated in 1910 and is a good example of the late-Gothic Revival style.

**011  C  Grace Lawn Cemetery;** E Warren St.; 1815-present; *Military, Religion* (408)

**012  C  House;** 308 W Warren St.; I-house; c.1880; Outbuilding: garage; *Architecture, Exploration/Settlement* (408)

**013  N  Middlebury Town Hall;** 104 N Main St.; Spanish Revival/Arts & Crafts; 1912 (J.C. Hershberger, builder); *Architecture, Politics* (408)

**014  C  Commercial Building;** 101 W Warren St.; Italianate; c.1890; *Architecture, Commerce* (408)

**015  C  House;** 204 W Warren St.; English cottage; c.1930; *Architecture* (408)

**016  N  Dr. B.F. Teters House;** 207 W Warren St.; Free Classic; c.1896; Outbuilding: carriage house; *Architecture* (408)

**017  O  Dr. B.F. Teters Office;** 203 W Warren St.; Eastlake; c.1890; Outbuilding: garage; *Architecture, Health/Medicine* (408)

**018  N  Middlebury Gymnasium;** 101 Wayne St.; Art Deco; 1923 (Freed Hershberger, builder); *Architecture, Education* (408)

**019  N  Dr. Myers Office;** 106 S Main St.; Gable-front; 1887; *Architecture, Health/Medicine* (408)

**020  C  Commercial Building;** 104 S Main St.; Italianate; 1881; *Architecture, Commerce* (408)

**021  O  Varns & Wise Hardware Store;** 102 S Main St.; Italianate; c.1886; *Architecture, Commerce* (408)

**022  N  Commercial Building;** 113 W Warren St.; One-part commercial block; c.1890; *Architecture, Commerce* (408)

**023  C  House;** 305 E Warren St.; Western bungalow; c.1910; Outbuilding: garage; *Architecture* (408)

**024  C  House;** 307 E Warren St.; Dormer-front bungalow; c.1910; *Architecture* (408)

**025  C  House;** 106 Mill St.; Hall-and-parlor; c.1860; *Architecture* (408)

**026  C  Henry Karch House;** 110 Mill St.; California bungalow; 1926; Outbuilding: garage; *Architecture* (408)

**027  C  House;** 311 E Berry St.; T-plan; c.1890; Outbuilding: garage; *Architecture* (408)

**028  C  House;** 107 Mill St.; Cape Cod; c.1930; *Architecture* (408)

**029  C  House;** 105 Mill St.; Dormer-front bungalow; c.1910; *Architecture* (408)

**030  C  House;** 308 E Berry St.; Stack house; c.1850; *Architecture, Exploration/Settlement* (408)

**031  C  House;** 200 E Berry St.; Dutch Colonial Revival; c.1900; *Architecture* (408)

**032  N  House;** 114 S Main St.; Dormer-front bungalow/Craftsman; c.1910; *Architecture* (408)

**033  N  House;** 112 S Main St.; American foursquare; c.1900; *Architecture* (408)

41013 J.C. Hershberger built the 1912 Middlebury Town Hall, which served as the town hall and fire station until 1970.

**41017** The Dr. B. F. Teters Office housed the doctor's office between 1890 and 1927, and his son's office until 1972. The Eastlake style house has a very unusual porch construction.

**034 C** **House;** 209 W Berry St.; Gable-front; c.1900; Outbuilding: garage; *Architecture* (408)

**035 C** **House;** 205 W Berry St.; T-plan; 1900; *Architecture* (408)

**036 C** **House;** 203 W Berry St.; T-plan; 1900; Outbuilding: garage; *Architecture* (408)

**037 O** **House;** 105 W Berry St.; Gable-front/Greek Revival; 1846; Outbuilding: garage; *Architecture, Exploration/Settlement* (408)

**038 C** **Alvin Farrar House/Mott Funeral Home;** 201 S Main St.; Colonial Revival; c.1930/c.1946; *Architecture, Commerce* (408)

**039 O** **Middlebury Post Office;** 200 S Main St.; Depression Modern; 1937 (Louis A. Simon, architect); *Architecture, Art* (408)

**040 C** **House;** 203 S Main St.; Dormer-front bungalow/Craftsman; c.1910; Outbuilding: garage; *Architecture* (408)

**041 N** **Ellsworth Varns House;** 205 S Main St.; Free Classic; 1898; *Architecture* (408)

**042 N** **House;** 207 S Main St.; Gable-front bungalow/Craftsman; 1918; *Architecture* (408)

**043 C** **House;** 200 W Lawrence St.; Upright-and-wing; c.1900; Outbuilding: garage; *Architecture* (408)

**044 C** **House;** 202 W Lawrence St.; Side-gable bungalow/Craftsman; c.1910; Outbuilding: garage; *Architecture* (408)

**045 C** **House;** 208 W Lawrence St.; Italianate; c.1880; Outbuilding: chicken house; *Architecture* (408)

**046 N** **Karch Lumber Company;** 304 W Lawrence St.; 19th century functional; c.1895; Outbuilding: office; *Architecture, Commerce* (408)

**047 C** **House;** 209 W Lawrence St.; Gable-front; c.1880; Outbuilding: garage; *Architecture* (408)

**048 C** **House;** 207 W Lawrence St.; Dormer-front bungalow/Craftsman; c.1920; *Architecture* (408)

**049 N** **House;** 201 W Lawrence St.; Queen Anne; c.1890; Outbuilding: garage; *Architecture* (408)

**050 N** **First United Methodist Church of Middlebury;** 301 S Main St.; Side-steeple/Greek Revival; 1890/1913; *Architecture, Religion* (408)

**051 N** **David F. Blough House;** 307 S Main St.; Second Empire; 1883; *Architecture* (408)

**052 C** **House;** 311 S Main St.; Western bungalow; c.1910; Outbuilding: garage; *Architecture* (408)

**41019** The 1887 Dr. Myers Office is an example of a simple gable-front commercial building.

**053 N** **House;** 313 S Main St.; L-plan/Italianate; c.1845; *Architecture, Exploration/Settlement* (408)

**054 C** **House;** 317 S Main St.; T-plan; c.1890; *Architecture* (408)

**055 C** **House;** 320 S Main St.; American foursquare; 1907; Outbuilding: stable; *Architecture* (408)

**056 C** **House;** 316 S Main St.; American foursquare; 1912; Outbuildings: chicken house, garage; *Architecture* (408)

**057 N** **House;** 312 S Main St.; Dormer-front bungalow/Craftsman; 1927; Outbuilding: shed; *Architecture* (408)

**058 N** **House;** 310 S Main St.; Upright-and-wing; c.1870; *Architecture* (408)

**41021** The Varns & Wise Hardware Store was established in this building in 1886. The Italianate building features a cast iron storefront and original round-arch windows.

123

41039 The Middlebury Post Office dates to 1937 and is a good example of a depression-era post office. Both the interior murals by artist Raymond Redell and the building itself by supervising architect Louis A. Simon are significant WPA projects.

**059 C House;** 308 S Main St.; Dormer-front bungalow; c.1910; *Architecture* (408)

**060 C House;** 306 S Main St.; Italianate; c.1875; *Architecture* (408)

**061 C House;** 304 S Main St.; American foursquare; c.1910; Outbuilding: garage; *Architecture* (408)

**062 N House;** 302 S Main St.; Italianate cube; c.1870; Outbuilding: garage; *Architecture* (408)

**063 C Truman Blough House/First United Methodist Church Parsonage;** 210 S Main St.; American foursquare; c.1910 (Truman Blough, builder); *Architecture, Religion* (408)

41046 Adam Griner established a lumber company here in the early 1890s that was known for most of its early years as the Karch Lumber Company.

**064 C House;** 208 S Main St.; L-plan/Greek Revival; c.1850; *Architecture, Exploration/Settlement* (408)

**065 N House;** 201 E Lawrence St.; Free Classic; c.1900; *Architecture* (408)

**066 C First Mennonite Church of Middlebury;** 203 E Lawrence St.; Late Gothic Revival; 1911/1951/1969; *Architecture, Religion* (408)

**067 C House;** 209 E Lawrence St.; Cross-gable square/Craftsman; c.1910; *Architecture* (408)

**068 C House;** 300 E Lawrence St.; Gable-front; c.1870; *Architecture* (408)

**069 C Middlebury Church of the Brethren;** 206 Mill St.; T-plan; 1911; *Architecture, Religion* (408)

**070 C House;** 210 Mill St.; Hall-and-parlor/English cottage; c.1850/c.1920; *Architecture* (408)

**071 C House;** 201 W Spring St.; T-plan; c.1880; *Architecture* (408)

**072 C House;** 412 S Main St.; Italianate; c.1870; Outbuilding: garage; *Architecture* (408)

**073 N Middlebury Township School;** 432 S Main St.; Art Deco; 1939 (Henkel & Hanson, architects/C.R. Acherman, engineer/Peter Schumacher & Sons, builders); Outbuilding: Industrial Arts Annex; *Architecture, Education* (408)

**074 O J.F. Nusbaum House;** 455 S Main St.; Free Classic; 1894; Outbuilding: garage; *Architecture* (408)

**075 C Cecil Eby House;** 525 Wayne Ave.; Cape Cod; c.1935; Outbuilding: shed; *Architecture* (408)

**076 C Dr. C. Russell Carson House and Veterinary Clinic;** 517 S Main St.; Prairie; 1938/1955; Outbuilding: stable; *Architecture, Health/Medicine* (408)

**077 N House;** 523 S Main St.; Gable-front/French Eclectic; c.1920; *Architecture* (408)

**078 C Bridge;** S Main St. over creek; Concrete girder; c.1958; *Engineering, Transportation* (408)

41041 The 1898 Ellsworth Varns House was home to the hardware merchant who established Varns and Wise Hardware. The Free Classic house features original clapboard siding and wood shingles.

41051 The 1883 David F. Blough House is a good example of a late Second Empire house with a transitional Queen Anne porch.

41062 This Italianate cube house retains original clapboard siding and windows.

# Clinton Township (45001-050)

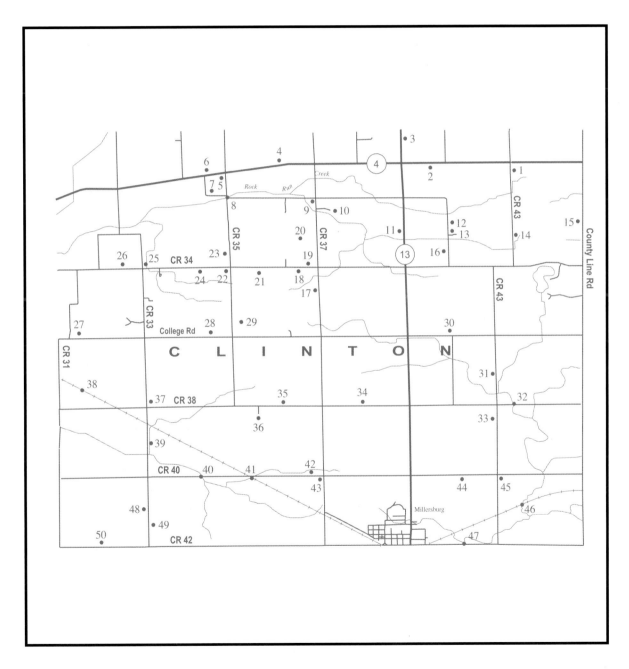

Clinton Township is located in east-central Elkhart County and bordered to the east by LaGrange County. Fish Lake is located in the northeastern part of the moderately flat township, which was originally heavily forested. The Lake Shore and Michigan Southern Railroad bisected the southwestern part of the township and the abandoned right-of-way of the Wabash Railroad cuts through the southeastern part of the township, meeting south of Millersburg, the township's only town.

Clinton Township was formed out of Elkhart Township in 1836 and named after the son of William Denney, an early settler. Settler Michael C. Cook arrived in 1840 and became prominent in the township. Many of the settlers were Mennonite, Old Order Amish, and German Baptist (also known as Dunkards or Church of the Brethren). The Rock Run Church of the Brethren was established in 1850 to serve members in the eastern part of Elkhart County (45037).

Several one-room schools in the southern part of Clinton Township closed upon completion of the consolidated Millersburg School in 1914. These included Cooper (45045) and Pleasant Hill (45043) schools. Likewise, when the Clinton Community School opened in 1924 (45019), one-room schools in the northern part of the township closed, including the Schrock School (45006).

Captain Solomon T. Miller settled Millersburg in 1842 on land he had purchased in 1834. He platted the town in 1855 after becoming aware of the Michigan Southern and Northern Indiana Railroad's plan to build through the area. The railroad called Millersburg "Cook's Station" after a prominent local farmer, but its original name was used when Millersburg incorporated as a town in 1866. In 1892, the Wabash Railroad completed its line across the county and through Millersburg. The town did not develop as quickly as some other nearby towns, partially due to its location away from a water source that could provide power for industries. However, its status as a railroad shipping point ensured its survival.

## CLINTON TOWNSHIP SCATTERED SITES (45001-050)

**No. Rtg. Description**

**001  C  Farm;** 61554 CR 43; American foursquare; c.1900; Outbuildings: bank/basement barn, drive-thru corn crib, garage, machine shed; *Agriculture, Architecture* (412)

**002  C  Samuel F. Ulery Farm;** 11616 CR 32; L-plan; 1889; Outbuilding: bank/basement barn; *Agriculture, Architecture* (412)

**003  C  House;** 619162 SR 13; L-plan; c.1860; Outbuildings: pumphouse, smokehouse, windmill; *Architecture* (412)

**004  C  Thomas Cemetery;** SR 4; 1867-present; *Religion* (412)

**005  C  House;** 61613 CR 35; T-plan; c.1870; Outbuildings: garage, shed; *Architecture* (412)

**006  N  Schrock School;** SR 4; Gable-front; c.1880; *Architecture, Education* (412)

**007  C  Farm;** 14169 CR 30; American foursquare; c.1900; Outbuildings: chicken houses, English barn, house, milk house, privy; *Agriculture, Architecture* (412)

**008  C  County Bridge No. 201;** CR 35 over Rock Run Creek; 1961; *Engineering, Transportation* (412)

**009  C  Farm;** 61935 CR 37; I-house; c.1860; Outbuildings: chicken house, English barn; *Agriculture, Architecture* (412)

**010  C  Peter Phillips Farm;** 62148 CR 37; Italianate; 1881 (Peter Phillips, builder); Outbuildings: machine shed, privy, Sweitzer barn, smokehouse; *Agriculture, Architecture* (412)

**011  C  Clinton Brick Mennonite Church and Cemetery;** 62499 SR 13; Gable-front;1946; Cemetery: 1849-present; *Architecture, Exploration/Settlement, Religion* (412)

**45006 The Schrock School replaced an earlier frame school and closed its doors to students in 1924.**

**012  N  Farm;** 62376 CR 41; L-plan; c.1870; Outbuildings: dairy barn, privy, silo, smokehouse; *Agriculture, Architecture* (412)

**013  N  Noah Miller Farm;** 62520 CR 41; American foursquare; 1942 (Noah Miller, builder); Outbuildings: chicken house, hog house, house (Dutch Colonial Revival, 1948), milk house, privy, Sweitzer barn, shed, silo, wood shed, workshop; *Agriculture, Architecture* (412)

**014  N  Farm;** 62598 CR 43; T-plan; c.1880; Outbuilding: bank/basement barn; *Agriculture, Architecture* (412)

**015  O  St. John's Evangelical Lutheran Church;** 62437 E County Line Rd.; Gable-front/Gothic Revival; 1878; *Architecture, Religion* (412)

**016  C  Woodlawn Amish Mennonite Cemetery;** CR 41; 1979-present; *Religion* (412)

**017  C  Millersburg Wabash Railroad Depot;** 63275 CR 37; Stick; 1892; *Architecture, Transportation* (412)

**018  N  Farm;** 13234 CR 34; Upright-and-wing; c.1880; Outbuildings: bank/basement barn, garage, granary, milk house, privy; *Agriculture, Architecture* (412)

**019  C  Clinton Community School;** 13151 CR 34; Neoclassical Revival; 1924 (Griffith & Goodrich, architects/Freed Hershberger & George P. Weaver, builders); *Architecture, Education* (412)

**020  C  Jacob Hay House;** 62745 CR 37; Single-pen/log construction; c.1850; *Architecture, Exploration/Settlement* (412)

**021  C  AT & T Microwave Tower;** CR 34; c.1955; *Communications* (412)

**022  C  House;** 14028 CR 34; Hall-and-parlor; c.1860; Outbuildings: chicken house, garage; *Architecture* (412)

**023  C  Nisley Cemetery;** CR 35; 1862-2002; *Religion* (412)

**024  N  Farm;** 14448 CR 34; Double-pile; c.1860/1951; Outbuildings: bank/basement barn, brooder houses, chicken house, corn crib, hog house, machine shed, privies, shed, windmill, wood shed, workshop; *Agriculture, Architecture* (412)

**025  C  Silver Street School;** 14955 CR 34; Side-gable; c.1892; *Architecture, Education* (243)

**026  C  Weaver Farm;** 15229 CR 34; T-plan; c.1870; bank/basement barn, chicken house, garage, pumphouse, shed, silos; *Agriculture, Architecture* (243)

**027  C  Farm;** 15555 CR 36; L-plan; 1898; Outbuilding: drive-thru corn crib; *Agriculture, Architecture* (243)

**028  C  Clinton Union Cemetery;** CR 36; 1840-present; *Exploration/Settlement, Religion* (243)

**45012 This L-plan house has brick walls and segmental-arched windows.**

45013 Noah Miller built this house in 1942 on the foundation of a brick house that burned down. A 1948 Dutch Colonial Revival house is also on the farm.

029  C  **Clinton Frame Mennonite Cemetery;** 63846 CR 35; 2002-2003; *Religion* (412)

030  N  **Farm;** 11642 CR 36; Pennsylvania farmhouse; c.1870; Outbuilding: English barn; *Agriculture, Architecture* (412)

031  C  **South East Clinton Cemetery;** CR 43; 1994-2002; Religion (412)

032  C  **County Bridge No. 190;** CR 38 over McAllister Ditch; 1960; *Engineering, Transportation* (412)

033  C  **Jacob Groff House;** 65147 CR 43; Italianate; 1872; Outbuildings: workshop; *Architecture* (412)

034  C  **House;** 12615 CR 38; I-house; c.1860; *Architecture* (034)

035  C  **Pleasant Grove Conservative Mennonite Church;** 13465 CR 35; Gable-front; 1948; *Architecture, Religion* (412)

036  C  **Farm;** 13744 CR 38; I-house; c.1860; Outbuildings: bank/basement barn, milk house; *Agriculture, Architecture* (412)

037  C  **Rock Run Church of the Brethren and Rock Run Cemetery;** 64985 CR 33; 1928; Cemetery: 1873-present; *Architecture, Religion* (412)

038  C  **Lake Shore and Michigan Southern Railroad Bridge;** Over Lateral K Lohri-Cripe Ditch; Plate girder; c.1900; *Engineering, Transportation* (243)

039  C  **House;** 65546 CR 33; Central-passage; c.1860; Outbuildings: machine shed, smokehouse; *Architecture* (243)

040  C  **Bridge;** CR 40 over Horn Ditch; concrete girder; c.1948; *Engineering, Transportation* (412)

041  N  **Lake Shore and Michigan Southern Railroad Bridge;** Over CR 40; Plate girder; c.1900; *Engineering, Transportation* (412)

042  C  **Farm;** 13141 CR 40; Gable-front; c.1870; Outbuildings: bank/basement barn, chicken house; *Agriculture, Architecture* (412)

043  N  **Clinton Township District No. 5/Pleasant Hill School;** CR 40; T-plan; 1888; *Architecture, Education* (412)

044  C  **Farm;** 11446 CR 40; Double-pile; c.1860; Outbuildings: English barn, milk house; *Agriculture, Architecture* (412)

45043 This oval tablet beneath the Pleasant Hill School's front gable identifies it as the Clinton Township District No. 5 school, built in 1888.

045  C  **Cooper School/Clinton Township District No. 9;** CR 40; Gable-front; 1883; Outbuilding: house; *Architecture, Education* (412)

046  C  **Wabash Railroad Stony Creek Bridge;** Over Stony Creek; wood girder; 1892; *Engineering, Transportation* (412)

047  C  **County Bridge No. 194;** CR 42 over Stony Creek; concrete girder; 1957 (G.W. Nicholson, engineer); *Engineering, Transportation* (412)

048  N  **Farm;** 66495 CR 33; American foursquare; c.1910; Outbuildings: English barn, garage; *Agriculture, Architecture* (243)

049  C  **House;** 66732 CR 33; Side-gable bungalow; c.1920; Outbuildings: carriage house, privy, shed; *Architecture* (243)

050  C  **Farm;** 15507 CR 42; T-plan; c.1870; Outbuildings: bank/basement barn, garage, milk house; *Agriculture, Architecture* (243)

45024 This double pile retains original clapboard siding and six-over-six windows dating to the house's 1951 remodeling.

45030 This Pennsylvania farmhouse features original clapboard siding with corner pilasters, a wood frieze board, and original windows.

45048 This American foursquare is a classic example of the type with its hipped roof, front dormer window, and full-width porch.

# Millersburg Scattered Sites (46001-022)

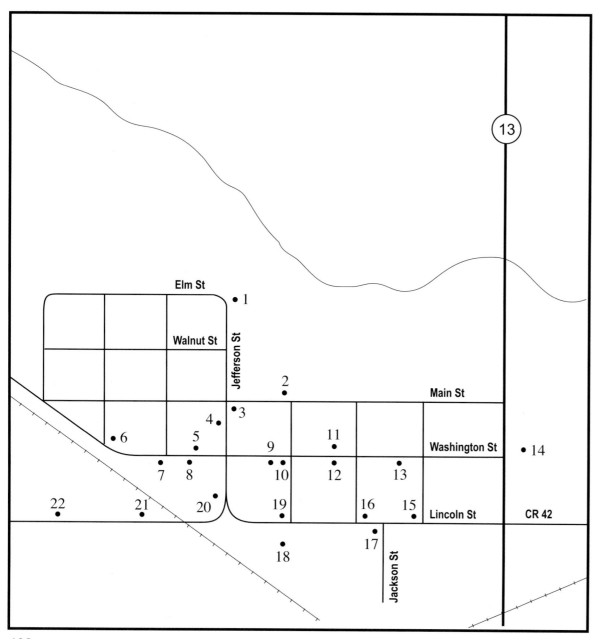

Captain Solomon T. Miller bought the land that became Millersburg in 1834, but did not settle on it until 1842. In 1855, he became aware of the Michigan Southern and Northern Indiana Railroad's plans to build through the area, so he platted the town of Millersburg. His son, James C. Miller, built the first house in the new town and David Eldridge established a dry goods and grocery store. An addition to the north side of town was made in 1860, followed by several additions to the east side of town and south of Lincoln Street. Millersburg incorporated in 1866.

The Michigan Southern and Northern Indiana Railroad (later called the Lake Shore and Michigan Southern Railroad) completed its line across the county in 1856. They built a depot the following year and replaced it in 1878. The railroad referred to Millersburg as "Cook's Station," named after prominent farmer Michael C. Cook, whose farm adjoined the west side of town. J. L. Davis became postmaster in 1861 and successfully insisted that the town's original name be used. In 1892, the Wabash Railroad completed a line across the county and through Millersburg, crossing the Lake Shore and Michigan Southern Railroad just south of town in Benton Township.

Shortly after the town's establishment, it built its first school, which was replaced with a new building in 1866. In 1914, the town built a large consolidated school that replaced an 1878 building and resulted in the closing of several one-room school houses in Clinton Township. The St. Peter's Evangelical Lutheran Church completed their present building in 1922 (46002), replacing its 1867 structure. In 1868, the Zion Reformed Church (now Zion Community Church), was built (46015).

Millersburg did not develop as quickly as some other nearby towns, partially due to its location away from water that could supply power for industries. For many years, it served primarily as a railroad shipping point for agricultural products from nearby farms. Fires in Millersburg's commercial district occurred in 1898 and 1909, destroying a number of frame structures. The Knights of Pythias, established in Millersburg in 1892, built their building in 1910 after the second fire (46008). In 1901, concrete sidewalks replaced 1877 boardwalks and beginning in 1914, Hawks Electric Light Company provided electricity to the town. The Millersburg Water Company (46007) began supplying water to the town in 1924.

Today Millersburg still reflects its rural heritage. Agricultural icons like the Lyon and Greenleaf Grain Elevator (46018) built in 1920 continues to service area farmers. Additionally, other buildings that housed agriculture-related services still stand in Millersburg. These are Wilson's Feed Mill (46006), built c.1855, and the blacksmith shop (46004) located on North Jefferson St., both of which are vacant.

Millersburg's historical domestic architecture predominantly dates from the late 1800s to the early 1900s, and is mostly simple and vernacular in nature. One of the earliest examples is an Italianate house located on E. Washington St. (46010) that features decorative lintels and paired cornice brackets, resting on a stone foundation. A common style is the bungalow with Craftsman influences. An outstanding example of this is the Clark A. Rink House (46009), built around 1916, that has a full front porch, gabled dormer, knee braces, and original windows. Similar houses include the Mikel B. Rink House (46013), the house at 315 W. Lincoln Street (46022), and 215 E. Washington St. (46011). Other common styles found in Millersburg from this period are American foursquares (46003) and Colonial Revivals (46001).

**MILLERSBURG SCATTERED SITES (46001-022)**

**No.  Rtg.  Description**

**001  C  Roy E. Rogers House;** 324 N Jefferson St.; Colonial Revival; 1939; Outbuilding: garage; *Architecture* (412)

**002  N  St. Peter's Evangelical Lutheran Church;** 125 E Main St.; Late Gothic Revival; 1922; *Architecture, Religion* (412)

**003  C  House;** 126 N Jefferson St.; American foursquare; c.1920; Outbuilding: garage; *Architecture* (412)

**004  C  Blacksmith Shop;** 115 N Jefferson St.; Parapet-front; c.1900; Outbuilding: house; *Architecture, Commerce* (412)

**005  C  Commercial Building;** 105 W Washington St.; Parapet-front; c.1874; *Architecture, Commerce* (412)

**006  N  Opera House/Wilson's Feed Mill;** Railroad St.; Greek Revival; c.1855; *Agriculture, Architecture, Commerce* (412)

**007  N  Millersburg Water Company;** 200 W Washington St.; Pyramidal-roof; 1924; *Architecture* (412)

**008  N  Knights of Pythias Millersburg Lodge 328;** 114-116 W Washington St.; Two-part commercial block; 1910; *Architecture, Social History* (412)

**009  O  Clark A. Rink House;** 118 E Washington St.; Dormer-front bungalow/Craftsman; c.1916; Outbuilding: garage; *Architecture* (412)

**010  N  Hotel;** 124 E Washington St.; Italianate; c.1860; *Architecture* (412)

**011  C  House;** 215 E Washington St.; Western bungalow; c.1910; Outbuilding: garage; *Architecture* (412)

**46002** St. Peter's Evangelical Lutheran Church was built in the late-Gothic Revival style in 1922. It features a corner tower with battlements.

**46022** This dormer-front bungalow has a shed-roof dormer, original clapboard siding, and an integral full-width porch with tapered piers.

**012  C  House;** 216 E Washington St.; American foursquare; c.1920; Outbuilding: garage; *Architecture* (412)

**013  N  Mikel B. Rink House;** 316 E Washington St.; Dormer-front bungalow; 1918; Outbuilding: garage; *Architecture* (412)

**014  C  House;** 513 E Washington St.; Double-pile; c.1890; *Architecture* (412)

**015  C  Zion Reformed Church;** 143 E Lincoln St.; Gothic Revival; 1868 (John Gehring & F. Moseman, builders); *Architecture, Religion* (412)

**016  C  House/Clinton Township Farmers Telephone Exchange Office;** 301 E Lincoln St.; Gable-front; c.1880; *Architecture, Communications* (412)

**017  C  House;** 310 E Lincoln St.; L-plan; c.1870; *Architecture* (412)

**018  C  Lyon & Greenleaf Grain Elevator;** 130 E Lincoln St.; 1920; Outbuildings: grain bin, shed, silos; *Agriculture, Architecture, Commerce* (412)

**019  C  House;** 127 Sherman St.; Gable-front; c.1900; *Architecture* (412)

**020  C  Potter Dry Goods Store;** 317 S Jefferson St; Octagon House; c.1860; *Architecture, Commerce* (412)

**021  C  House;** 211 W Lincoln St.; Side-gable; c.1890; Outbuilding: shed; *Architecture* (412)

**022  N  House;** 315 W Lincoln St.; Dormer-front bungalow/Craftsman; c.1920; Outbuilding: carriage house; *Architecture* (412)

# Elkhart Township (50001-050)

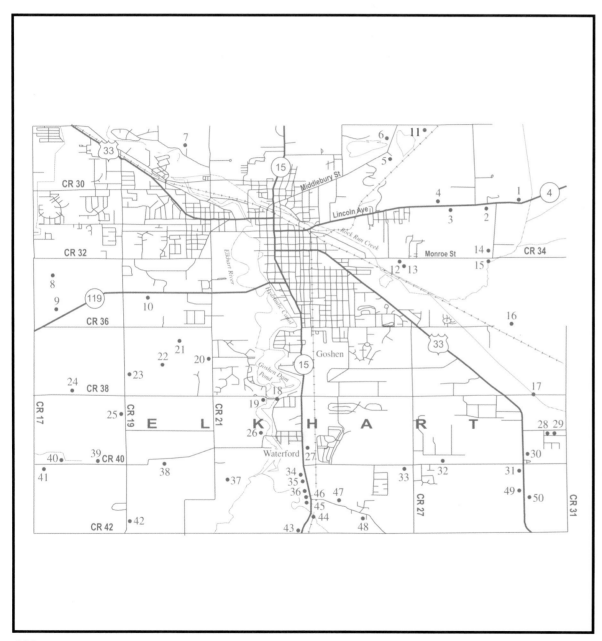

Elkhart Township is located in central Elkhart County and is home to the county seat, Goshen. Norton and Butts Lakes are situated in the hilly northern part of the township and the Elkhart River flows in a northwestwardly direction through the township. Turkey and Rock Run Creeks flow into the Elkhart River. The hydraulic canal flows to the north from the Goshen Dam Pond and also empties into the Elkhart River. The former Lake Shore and Michigan Southern Railroad tracks bisect the northern part of the township and the abandoned right-of-way of its Goshen and Michigan Branch begins in Goshen, heading northeast. The Cincinnati, Wabash, and Michigan Railroad runs north through the township, meeting the Lake Shore and Michigan Southern Railroad in Goshen; its abandoned right-of-way continues northwest.

The first settlers in the area were Elias Riggs and William Simpson in 1828. Many other settlers came the following year, including Balser Hess, a Baptist minister buried in the Hess Cemetery (50020). The house of his son Israel still stands (50031). Major John W. Violett came from Ohio, settled just north of Waterford, and became the first county recorder, while James Frier became the first county assessor. Azel Sparklin, a Methodist minister, settled south Waterford and is buried in the Sparklin Cemetery (50035).

Elkhart Township is one of two original townships established when Elkhart County was formed in 1830. Several townships were subsequently formed from Elkhart Township, including York, Middlebury, Olive, Harrison, Clinton, Locke, Union, Jackson, and Benton. Elkhart Township acquired its present boundaries in 1837, when it was still heavily forested.

Two towns, Goshen and Waterford, developed in the township. Goshen, which became the Elkhart

County seat in 1831, occupies much of the north-central part of the township. Daniel Cripe was a German Baptist (also called Dunkards or Church of the Brethren) minister who came from Ohio and settled in what would become Goshen. The house of Cripe's son Daniel still stands (50008). In about 1830, John Carpenter built a grist mill on Rock Run Creek in what would become Goshen. Goshen developed at the crossing of the Fort Wayne Road and the Logansport and White Pigeon Road (today's Lincoln Avenue and Main Street), and this area became the center of Goshen's commercial activity. Goshen incorporated as a village in 1854 and as a city in 1868, the same year the construction of the hydraulic canal and its dam on the Elkhart River was completed. The power harnessed from the canal was essential to the industrial development of Goshen and the canal also provided the town's first water system in 1875.

Goshen became a hub of much railroad activity in the latter half of the 20th century. The Northern Indiana Railroad completed a branch line from Elkhart to Goshen in 1852. Six years later, that line became the through line of the merged Michigan Southern and Northern Indiana Railroad (later called the Lake Shore and Michigan Southern Railroad). Streetcar service came to Goshen in 1896, eventually connecting the town to Elkhart and points south.

The small community of Waterford developed to Goshen's south in 1833, when William Layton Baker built a grist mill on the eastern side of the Elkhart River. In 1835, Cephas Hawks, who had come with his family from Michigan, purchased the grist mill. Hawks, his son, and David Ballentine laid out the town in 1838 between the Elkhart River and the Logansport and White Pigeon Road (State Road 15). By the 1840s, Waterford was a thriving community having several mills and businesses. Between 1854 and 1904, the town had a post office and was known as Waterford Mills. After the completion of the hydraulic canal in Goshen in 1868, Waterford's gristmill and other businesses moved to Goshen. In 1870, the Warsaw, Goshen, and White Pigeon Railroad built a depot on the

eastern side of Waterford. The Winona Interurban Railway later built a waiting station in Waterford; however, with no industry to serve, Waterford remained a small hamlet.

## ELKHART TOWNSHIP SCATTERED SITES (50001-050)

**No. Rtg. Description**

**001** N **McCullough Farm;** 16523 SR 4; Lazy-T; c.1870; Outbuildings: bank/basement barn, garage; *Agriculture, Architecture* (243)

**002** C **House;** 16902 SR 4; American foursquare; c.1910; Outbuildings: garage, machine shed; *Architecture* (243)

**003** C **Farm;** 17346 SR 4; Ranch; c.1952; Outbuildings: chicken house, dairy barn, garage; *Agriculture, Architecture* (243)

**004** C **House;** 17477 SR 4; Cape Cod; c.1930; Outbuildings: chicken house, garage; *Architecture* (243)

**005** N **Ebenezer Brown Farm;** 18078 CR 22; Greek Revival; c.1834; Outbuildings: bank/basement barn, pumphouse; *Agriculture, Architecture, Exploration/Settlement* (243)

**006** C **Farm;** 17947 CR 22; Cape Cod; c.1930; Outbuildings: chicken houses, garage; *Agriculture, Architecture* (243)

50001 The McCullough House is a notable example of a Lazy-T house, in part because it retains its original front porch, a rare feat.

**50005 Despite its replacement siding, this c.1834 house is a good early example of the Greek Revival style. It retains original windows and features a wide cornice with returns.**

**007** N **House;** 20269 CR 19; Gable-front/Gothic Revival; c.1870; Outbuildings: cold cellar, garage; *Architecture* (243)

**008** C **Daniel Cripe House;** 21752 CR 32; Cross-plan; 1862; *Architecture* (210)

**009** C **Gorsuch Farm;** 21703 SR 119; L-plan; c.1870; Outbuildings: iron fence, milk house, summer kitchen, Sweitzer barn; *Agriculture, Architecture* (210)

**010** O **Eli Cripe Farm;** 20522 SR 119; Double-pile; c.1870 (Eli Cripe, builder); Outbuildings: chicken house, garage, granary, smokehouse, summer kitchen; *Agriculture, Architecture* (243)

**011** C **Fuller Farm;** 17466 CR 28; Lazy-T; c.1870; Outbuildings: bank/basement barn, chicken house, garage, machine shed, shed, smokehouse; *Agriculture, Architecture* (243)

**012** C **Barn;** 17746 CR 34; Bank barn; 1890; Outbuildings: blacksmith shop, milk house, privy, wagon shed, wood shop; *Agriculture, Architecture* (243)

**013** C **Goshen National Guard Armory;** 17746 CR 34; 20th century functional; 1950 (Everett Brown, architect/Curry Construction Company, builders); *Architecture, Military* (243)

**014 C Cripe Cemetery;** CR 29; 1834-1893; *Exploration/Settlement, Religion* (243)

**015 C Farm;** 16784 CR 34; Double-pile; c.1850; Outbuildings: dairy barn, milk house, workshop; *Agriculture, Architecture* (243)

**016 C Kaufmann Farm;** 16629 CR 36; American foursquare; c.1900; Outbuildings: chicken house, corn crib, drive-thru corn crib, garage, grain bin, milk house, silo, stable; *Agriculture, Architecture* (243)

**017 C County Bridge No. 213;** CR 38 over Horn Ditch; Concrete girder; 1959; *Engineering, Transportation* (243)

**018 C County Bridge No. 409;** CR 38 over Elkhart River; Concrete girder; 1962; *Engineering, Transportation* (243)

**019 N Violett House/Tall Pines;** 19478 CR 38; Gable-front; c.1855 (Kaylor, builder); Outbuildings: garage, pumphouse; *Architecture* (243)

**020 C Hess Cemetery;** CR 21; 1856-present; *Religion* (243)

**021 N Hoke Farm;** 20382 CR 36; L-plan/Italianate; c.1865; Outbuildings: garage, Sweitzer barn; *Agriculture, Architecture* (243)

**022 C Farm;** 20419 CR 38; American foursquare; c.1910; Outbuildings: bank/basement barn, garage; *Agriculture, Architecture* (243)

50010 The Eli Cripe Farm features this double-pile house, as well as a number of outbuildings, including a chicken house, granary, smokehouse, and summer kitchen.

50019 The Violett House, also known as Tall Pines, is a brick gable-front house with segmental-arched openings.

**023 C Inbody Farm;** 64624 CR 19; T-plan; c.1870; Outbuildings: garage, machine shed, Sweitzer barn, shed; *Agriculture, Architecture* (243)

**024 C William Miltenberger Farm;** 21523 CR 38; T-plan; c.1870; Outbuildings: chicken house, drive-thru corn crib, English barn, privy, shed, smokehouse, summer kitchen; *Agriculture, Architecture* (210)

**025 C House;** 65261 CR 19; American foursquare; c.1910; Outbuilding: windmill; *Architecture* (243)

**026 C Farm;** 19467 CR 40; American foursquare; c.1910; Outbuildings: drive-thru corn crib, shed; *Agriculture, Architecture* (243)

**027 N Rarich House;** 65736 SR 15; Italianate; 1865; *Architecture* (243)

**028 N Yoder House;** 16234 CR 138; Double-pile; c.1855; Outbuilding: house; *Architecture* (243)

**029 C House;** 16170 CR 138; American foursquare/Prairie; c.1922; *Architecture* (243)

50021 This Italianate house features a wide cornice and segmental-arched window openings.

**030 C House;** 65940 US 33; American foursquare; c.1920; *Architecture* (243)

**031 N Israel Hess House;** 66063 US 33; Cross-plan; 1863 (Israel Hess, builder); Outbuilding: smokehouse; *Architecture* (243)

**032 C Yoder House;** 17393 CR 40; Lazy-T; c.1870; Outbuilding: chicken house; *Architecture* (243)

**033 N Clark Farm;** 17848 CR 40; T-plan; c.1870; Outbuilding: English barn; *Agriculture, Architecture* (243)

50027 The 1865 Rarich House is a fine example of the Italianate style with its central tower, overhanging eaves supported by paired brackets, and segmental-arched openings.

50033 The Clark House is a T-plan that features clapboard siding with fishscale shingles in the gable end, a slate roof, and original windows.

034 C **Sparklin House;** 66149 SR 15; Italianate; c.1895; *Architecture* (243)

035 C **Sparklin Cemetery;** SR 15; 1829-1968; *Exploration/Settlement, Religion* (243)

036 C **House;** 66325 SR 15; English cottage; c.1930; *Architecture* (243)

037 C **Echleberger Farm;** 66154 CR 21; T-plan; c.1870; Outbuildings: bank/basement barn, milk house; *Agriculture, Architecture* (243)

038 N **Lower Farm;** 20480 CR 40; Cross-plan; c.1870; Outbuildings: bank/basement barn, windmill; *Agriculture, Architecture* (243)

50038 The Lower House is a cross plan that has original wood siding and fishscale shingles in the gable ends, original windows, and a wrap-around porch.

50042 The Miller House is a well-preserved example of a T-plan; it retains original clapboard siding, most original windows, and a wrap-around porch with turned posts.

039 C **Farm;** 21305 CR 40; American foursquare; c.1910; Outbuildings: bank/basement barn, machine shed; *Agriculture, Architecture* (243)

040 C **House;** 21683 CR 40; American foursquare; c.1910; *Architecture* (210)

041 N **House;** 21874 CR 40; I-house/Federal; c.1835; *Architecture, Exploration/Settlement* (210)

042 N **Miller Farm;** 66816 CR 19; T-plan; c.1900; Outbuildings: English barn, granary, summer kitchen, windmill, workshop; *Agriculture, Architecture* (243)

043 C **Samuel Rodibaugh House;** 19047 CR 121; Double-pile/Greek Revival; 1851; Outbuilding: shed; *Architecture* (243)

50047 The J. Abraham Neff House is a c.1912 American foursquare.

50050 This 1929 Colonial Revival house is a refined and large-scale example of the "Neo-Federal" style. Its estate-like grounds add to the property's significance.

044 C **Cincinnati, Wabash, and Michigan Railroad Bridge;** Over Elkhart River; Plate girder; c.1900; *Engineering, Transportation* (243)

045 C **House;** 66491 SR 15; American foursquare; c.1910; Outbuildings: chicken house, garage; *Architecture* (243)

046 C **House;** 66467 SR 15; American foursquare; c.1910; Outbuilding: garage; *Architecture* (243)

047 N **J. Abraham Neff Farm;** 18725 CR 42; American foursquare; c.1912 (J. Abraham Neff, builder); Outbuildings: English barn, grain bins, maple syrup shed, stable, workshop; *Agriculture, Architecture* (243)

048 C **Clark Farm;** 18440 CR 42; Center-gable I-house; c.1865; Outbuildings: bank/basement barn, milk house; *Agriculture, Architecture* (243)

049 C **Morehouse Farm;** 66278 US 33; Lazy-T; c.1880; Outbuildings: chicken house, English barn, garage, pumphouse; *Agriculture, Architecture* (243)

050 O **House;** 66398 US 33; Colonial Revival; 1929; Outbuilding: stable; *Architecture* (243)

# Goshen Historic District (039-243-51001-858)

The Goshen Historic District is situated in the heart of Goshen, Indiana and many of its buildings have served as the city's commercial center for over a century. The district is roughly bounded to the north by Pike Street, to the east by Cottage Avenue, to the south by Plymouth, Main, and Purl Streets, and to the west by the Hydraulic Canal and Second Street. The district was listed in the National Register of Historic Places in 1981. The heart of the district is the courthouse square, which is surrounded by commercial buildings. Outside the commercial area are residential and religious structures. The once-booming industrial area along the Hydraulic Canal has declined in recent years; however, many of its structures and buildings remain intact (51124, 51144).

Goshen was platted in 1831 and it is believed that the city was chosen as the county seat due to its central location. The original courthouse was built in 1833 on a block of land reserved for public use. In 1871, a second courthouse to replace the original structure was completed, designed by the Chicago architectural firm of Barrows and Garnsey. Patton and Miller, also of Chicago, remodeled the building in 1905 by adding wings and a new tower. The Elkhart County Courthouse was individually listed in the National Register of Historic Places in 1980.

Many of Goshen's prominent residential structures were built in the mid-1800s, while its most remarkable commercial structures were built between the late 1800s and early 1900s. The 1847 Rowell/Champion House was built by George P. Rowell and is Goshen's oldest brick home (51304). The Italianate Wickam House was built in 1857 for Dr. William Wickam, a Goshen physician (51515).

Between 1898 and 1919, steel magnate Andrew Carnegie funded libraries in 1,406 communities throughout the nation. Goshen was the first Indiana community to take advantage of his generosity to build its 1901 public library (51554), also designed by Patton and Miller. Listed in the National Register of Historic Places in 1983, it has housed Goshen's City Hall since 2002. The Spohn Building was built in 1909 and originally housed a veterinary supply manufacturer owned by Samuel F. Spohn, who also served as Goshen's mayor for one term (51469). The building has had few alterations made to its exterior.

Small portions of the Goshen Historic District were demolished and replaced with modern infill. Main street was expanded to accommodate four lanes of traffic and old businesses have made way for new ones, but the heart of the district is still intact. An era of preservation and restoration is dawning in Goshen. The movement is spearheaded by several local property and business owners who are looking to invigorate Goshen with ideas such as angled parking along Main Street and second-story apartments that will bring greater pedestrian traffic.

## GOSHEN HISTORIC DISTRICT (039-243-51001-858) NR

| No. | Rtg. | Add. | Description |
|---|---|---|---|

**WEST PIKE STREET** *(south side)*

| No. | Rtg. | Add. | Description |
|---|---|---|---|
| 001 | NC | NA | Parking Lot |
| 002 | NC | 214 | Commercial Building; c.1985 |
| 003 | NC | NA | House; American foursquare; c.1915 |
| 004 | NC | NA | Parking Lot |
| 005 | NC | NA | Commercial Building; c.1980 |
| 006 | NC | NA | Gas Station; c.1995 |
| 007 | NC | NA | Parking Lot |

**EAST PIKE STREET** *(south side)*

| No. | Rtg. | Add. | Description |
|---|---|---|---|
| 008 | NC | NA | Gas Station; c.1985 |
| 009 | NC | NA | Parking Lot |
| 010 | NC | NA | Parking Lot |
| 011 | NC | 114-16 | House; I-house; c.1890 |

51024 Chicago architects J.H. Barrows & George O. Garnsey designed the 1870 Elkhart County Courthouse shortly after the end of the Civil War. Between 1904 and 1906 it underwent an extensive renovation that added the central domed tower and north and south extensions.

**WEST CLINTON STREET** *(north side)*

| No. | Rtg. | Add. | Description |
|---|---|---|---|
| 012 | C | NA | First Brethren Church; Colonial Revival; 1927 |
| 013 | C | 213 | House; Colonial Revival; c.1925 |
| 014 | NC | NA | Parking Lot |
| 015 | NC | 119 | Commercial Building; c.1975 |
| 016 | NC | 117 | Commercial Building; c.1990 |
| 017 | NC | NA | Parking Lot |

**EAST CLINTON STREET** *(north side)*

| No. | Rtg. | Add. | Description |
|---|---|---|---|
| 018 | C | 201 | Commercial Building; International; 1958 |
| 019 | NC | NA | Parking Lot |
| 020 | C | NA | House; Free Classic; c.1900 |
| 021 | NC | NA | Vacant Lot |

**WEST CLINTON STREET** *(south side)*

| No. | Rtg. | Add. | Description |
|---|---|---|---|
| 022 | NC | NA | Parking Lot |
| 023 | C | 204-06 | Carriage House/Commercial Building; Cross-gable; c.1930 |

**COURTHOUSE SQUARE**

| No. | Rtg. | Add. | Description |
|---|---|---|---|
| 024 | O | NA | Elkhart County Courthouse; Neoclassical; 1870/1906 (J.H. Barrows & George O. Garnsey/Patton and Miller, architects) NR |
| 025 | C | NA | Veteran Memorial; c.1945 |
| 026 | C | NA | Fountain; 1912 |
| 027 | C | NA | Historical Marker |
| 028 | C | NA | Goshen Police Booth; 1939 |

**EAST CLINTON STREET** *(south side)*

| No. | Rtg. | Add. | Description |
|---|---|---|---|
| 029 | NC | NA | Commercial Building; Post Modern; c.2000 |
| 030 | C | 114 | Commercial Building; One-part commercial block; c.1950 |
| 031 | C | 116 | House; T-plan/Queen Anne; c.1890 |
| 032 | NC | 118 | Commercial Building; c.1970 |

51044 The Bank Building dates to 1875 and features a dentilated cornice with decorative brackets, round-arched windows in a Palladian arrangement, and cast iron storefront members.

135

**51054** Goshen's United States Post Office dates to 1912 and is an example of the Italian Renaissance Revival style.

033 NC 122 **Commercial Building;** c.1990

034 C NA **House;** Gable-front; c.1900

035 NC NA **House;** Lazy-T; c.1900

036 NC 212 **House;** Shotgun; c.1900

037 C 214 **House;** California bungalow; c.1920

038 C NA **House;** Gable-front; c.1900

039 C 308 **House;** Double-entry I-house; c.1900

## WEST LINCOLN AVENUE *(north side)*

040 NC NA **Parking Lot**

041 NC 215 **Commercial Building;** c.1980

042 NC 211 **Commercial Building;** c.1980

043 C 209 **Commercial Building;** One-part commercial block; c.1930

## EAST LINCOLN AVENUE *(north side)*

044 O 109-11 **Bank Building;** Italian Renaissance Revival; 1875

045 C 113-15 **A.J. & H.D. Irwin Building;** Parapet-front; 1917

046 N 119 **Commercial Building;** Italianate; c.1890

047 C 123 **Crary Building;** Italianate; 1890

048 N 125 **Commercial Building;** Queen Anne; c.1890

049 C NA **Commercial Building;** Queen Anne; c.1890

050 C 129 **Commercial Building;** Italianate; c.1890

051 NC 203 **Commercial Building;** Two-part commercial block; c.1940

052 C NA **Commercial Building;** Two-part commercial block; c.1900

053 N 215 **First Presbyterian Church;** Side-steeple/Romanesque Revival; c.1910

054 N NA **United States Post Office;** Italian Renaissance Revival; 1912 (James Knox Taylor, architect)

055 NC NA **Parking Lot**

056 N 313 **John Lesh House;** Italianate; 1879 (Cass Chapman, architect)

057 N NA **House;** Queen Anne; c.1880

058 C NA **House;** T-plan; c.1890

059 C 403 **House;** T-plan; c.1890

060 C 409 **House;** Gabled-ell; c.1890

## WEST LINCOLN AVENUE *(south side)*

061 NC 212 **Commercial Building;** c.1985

062 C 208-10 **Hamilton Iron Works;** 20th century functional; c.1920

**51057** This Queen Anne house features a decorative slate roof with pointed towers and a wrap-around porch with a central pediment

**51101** The Hydraulic Canal's Central Generating Station, which was the main power source for Goshen, Middlebury, Millersburg, Benton, New Paris, Wakarusa, Bremen, Syracuse, and Milford until the 1920s.

063 NC 200 **Commercial Building;** Two-part commercial block; c.1910

064 NC NA **Parking Lot**

065 NC NA **Commercial Building;** Contemporary; c.1980

066 NC 102 **Commercial Building;** Contemporary; c.1970

## EAST LINCOLN AVENUE *(south side)*

067 C 100-08 **Commercial Building;** Italianate; 1876

068 C 110 **Commercial Building;** Italianate; c.1875

069 C NA **Shoots Building;** Italian Renaissance Revival; c.1880

070 NC NA **Parking Lot**

071 C 206-08 **Benham Block;** Queen Anne; 1893

072 N 210 **Hotel;** Italianate; c.1890

073 NC NA **Parking Lot**

074 C 302 **House;** Free Classic; c.1900

075 C 304 **Commercial Building;** Italianate/Neoclassical; c.1880/c.1910

076 C 306 **House;** Gabled-ell; c.1900

077 N 308 **House;** Queen Anne; c.1900

078 NC NA **House;** c.1900

51124 The Old Stone Bridge crosses the Hydraulic Canal and was built by the Hawks Furniture Company to carry goods between its two buildings on each side of the canal.

079 C 314 **House;** Lazy-T; c.1900

080 C 316 **House;** Midwest box/Craftsman; c.1900

081 NC NA **Commercial Building;** c.1975

082 NC 408 **House;** Free Classic; c.1910

### WEST WASHINGTON STREET (north side)

083 NC NA **Parking Lot**

084 NC NA **House;** Free Classic; c.1900

085 C 207 **House;** Gable-front; c.1900

086 C 121 **Gas Station;** 20th century functional; c.1940

087 C NA **Commercial Building;** One-part commercial block; c.1940

088 C 117 **Commercial Building;** Two-part commercial block; c.1940

089 C 113 **Dembufsky Building;** Parapet-front; 1926

090 C 111 **Commercial Building;** Parapet-front; c.1900

### EAST WASHINGTON STREET (north side)

091 C NA **Commercial Building;** Italianate; c.1885

092 C 115 **Commercial Building;** Two-part commercial block; c.1890

093 C NA **Parking Lot**

094 C NA **Memorial**

095 NC NA **Parking Lot**

096 C 307 **House;** T-plan; c.1890

097 N 309 **House;** T-plan/Craftsman; c.1910

098 C 311 **House;** L-plan; c.1890

099 C 313 **House;** T-plan; c.1900

100 NC NA **Parking Garage**

### WEST WASHINGTON STREET (south side)

101 O NA **Hydraulic Canal Central Generating Station;** 1898

102 N NA **Tailgates Building;** 19th century functional; 1898

103 NC NA **Shed;** 20th century functional; c.1990

104 NC NA **Commercial Building;** c.1990

105 NC 212 **Commercial Building;** c.1980

106 C 210 **House;** Gabled-ell; c.1890

107 C 208 **House;** Gabled-ell; c.1890

108 NC NA **Parking Lot**

109 NC 111 **Commercial building;** One-part commercial block; c.1965 DEMOLISHED

110 NC NA **Commercial Building;** Colonial Revival; c.1950

51289 This Italianate cube house features a wide cornice with paired brackets supporting overhanging eaves and a later wrap-around porch.

51304 The c.1847 Rowell/Champion House is an outstanding example of the Greek Revival style and is believed by many to be the oldest home in Goshen. The house appears in Wilbur Peat's influential 1962 book *Indiana Houses of the Nineteenth Century.*

111 C 116 **Commercial Building;** Italianate; c.1880/c.1980

### EAST WASHINGTON STREET (south side)

112 C NA **Central Block;** Italianate; 1882

113 C 108 **Commercial Building;** Italianate; c.1885

114 C 112 **Commercial Building;** Two-part commercial block; c.1920

115 C 118 **Commercial Building/Garage;** Italianate/20th century functional; c.1890/c.1950

116 NC 124 **Commercial Building;** c.1970

117 NC NA **Parking Lot**

118 NC 212-14 **Double House;** c.1900

119 C 310 **House;** Minimal traditional; c.1945

120 C 312 **House;** Center-gable I-house; c.1890

121 N 314 **House;** Prairie; c.1910

122 C 316 **House;** Gable-front; c.1900

123 C 410 **House;** Gabled-ell; c.1915

## WEST JEFFERSON STREET *(north side)*

124 N NA **Old Stone Bridge;** Stone; c.1880

125 NC NA **Parking Lot**

126 N 209 **House;** Free Classic; c.1890

127 NC NA **Commercial Building;** c.1980

128 C NA **Commercial Building;** 20th century functional; c.1960

129 NC NA **Commercial Building;** Contemporary; c.1960

130 NC NA **Parking Lot**

## EAST JEFFERSON STREET *(north side)*

131 NC NA **Parking Lot**

132 NC NA **Marker;** 1978

133 NC NA **Marker**

134 NC 111 **Government Building;** c.1990

135 NC NA **Monument;** 1998

136 C 209 **House;** Free Classic; c.1900

137 C 211 **House;** Lazy-T; c.1890

138 C 309 **House;** Queen Anne; c.1880

139 C 311 **House;** Gable-front; c.1880

140 NC 313 **House;** Free Classic; c.1900

141 C 401-03 **House;** Queen Anne; c.1890/c.1960

51336 This Queen Anne house features sawtooth and scalloped decorative shingles in its gable peaks, original clapboard siding, and wood double-hung windows.

51350 The Queen Anne Mayfield block dates to 1901 and boasts a corner entry and turret with pressed-tin detailing.

142 C 405 **House;** Gable-front/Craftsman; c.1910

143 C 409 **House;** Queen Anne cottage; c.1885

## WEST JEFFERSON STREET *(south side)*

144 C 214 **Industrial Building;** 19th century functional; c.1880

145 C 210 **House;** Gabled-ell; c 1890

146 NC 120 **Commercial Building;** Colonial Revival; c.1925

147 C 116 **House;** American foursquare; c.1930

148 NC 114 **Commercial Building;** c.1965

149 C 112 **Garage;** Parapet-front; c.1915

150 NC NA **Parking Lot**

## EAST JEFFERSON STREET *(south side)*

151 NC 106 **Gas Station;** House-with-canopy; c.1970

152 NC NA **Parking Lot**

153 C 212 **House;** T-plan/English cottage; c.1920

154 NC 312 **House;** Gabled-ell; c.1890

155 C 314 **House;** Lazy-T; c.1900

156 C 406 **House;** Dutch Colonial Revival; c.1915

157 N 410 **House;** American foursquare; c.1920

## WEST MADISON STREET *(north side)*

158 NC NA **Bridge**

159 C NA **Industrial Factory;** 20th century functional; c.1930

160 NC NA **Vacant Lot**

161 NC NA **Vacant Lot**

162 NC NA **Parking Lot**

## EAST MADISON STREET *(north side)*

163 NC NA **Parking Lot**

51449 This building dates to 1880 and its current storefront was completed c.1938.

164   C   109   **House;** T-plan; c.1890

165   N   113   **House;** Tudor Revival; c.1920

166   NC   NA   **Parking Lot**

167   NC   211   **Dentist Office;** Contemporary; c.1970

168   C   309   **House;** Craftsman; c.1915

169   C   311   **House;** Colonial Revival; c.1920

170   NC   NA   **Parking Lot**

171   NC   333   **House;** Gable-front; c.1910

172   NC   NA   **Parking Lot**

173   NC   401   **Commercial Building;** Contemporary; c.1966

174   C   409   **House;** Colonial Revival; c.1915

## WEST MADISON STREET (*south side*)

175   C   NA   **Carriage House;** Craftsman; c.1915

51460 This commercial building features a metal cornice decorated with an egg & dart motif and acanthus leaves.

176   C   212   **House;** Craftsman; c.1915

177   C   204   **House;** Cross-gable square; c.1880

178   NC   NA   **Vacant Lot**

179   NC   NA   **Parking Lot**

## EAST MADISON STREET (*south side*)

180   NC   NA   **Commercial Building;** c.2000

181   NC   112   **House;** Gable-front; c.1950

182   NC   NA   **Parking Lot**

183   C   306   **House;** Dutch Colonial Revival; c.1920

184   NC   308   **House;** Central-passage; c.1930

185   C   310   **House;** T-plan/Queen Anne; c.1880

186   C   NA   **Garage;** Craftsman; c.1915

187   C   320   **House;** Gabled-ell; c.1890

188   C   406   **House;** T-plan

189   C   408   **House;** California bungalow; c.1920

190   NC   410   **House;** Free Classic; c.1910

## WEST MONROE STREET (*north side*)

191   NC   NA   **Garage;** c.1965

192   NC   209   **House;** Upright-and-wing; c.1900

193   NC   117   **Office Building;** c.2000

## EAST MONROE STREET (*north side*)

194   C   109   **House;** T-plan; c.1900

195   C   NA   **Garage;** Pyramidal-roof; c.1950

196   NC   209   **House;** English cottage; c.1925

197   C   211   **House;** American foursquare; c.1915

198   C   NA   **Carport;** International; c.1955

199   C   301   **House;** Cape Cod; c.1940

200   C   307   **House;** Craftsman; c.1910

201   C   309   **House;** American foursquare; c.1920

202   C   311   **House;** Colonial Revival; c.1930

51484 This Free Classic house has a cross-gabled roof, decorative shingles in the gable peak and a full-width porch supported by wood columns on stone piers.

203   C   NA   **Garage;** Craftsman

204   NC   NA   **Garage**

## WEST MONROE STREET (*south side*)

205   NC   NA   **Parking Lot**

206   NC   208   **House;** Gable-front; c.1900

207   C   NA   **Park**

208   C   114   **Rectory;** Colonial Revival; c.1940

209   C   110   **House;** Gable-front; c.1900

## EAST MONROE STREET (*south side*)

210   NC   108   **House;** Gable-front; c.1900

211   C   110   **House;** Gabled-ell; c.1900

212   C   112   **House;** Upright-and-wing; c.1900

213   NC   NA   **Parking Lot**

214   C   210   **House;** Free Classic; c.1900

215   C   212   **House;** Dutch Colonial Revival; c.1900

216   C   NA   **House;** Tudor Revival; c.1915

217   N   310   **House;** American foursquare; c.1910

218   C   312   **House;** Craftsman; c.1915

51486 **This Free Classic house boasts a clay tile roof, prominent chimney and porte-cochere.**

219 NC NA **Vacant Lot**

220 N 316 **House;** Dutch Colonial Revival; c.1930

221 O 318 **House;** Craftsman; 1910

222 C 412 **House;** Upright-and-wing; c.1900

## WEST PURL STREET *(north side)*

223 NC NA **Barn;** Transverse-frame barn

224 C 205 **House;** Gable-front; c.1910

225 C NA **Garage;** Pyramidal-roof

226 C 113 **House;** Midwest box; c.1900

227 C 111 **House;** Dormer-front bungalow/ Craftsman; c.1920

228 C 109 **House;** Dormer-front bungalow; c.1920

229 C 107 **House;** English cottage; c.1925

230 NC NA **Vacant Lot**

231 C 103 **House;** Dormer-front bungalow/ Craftsman; c.1920

## EAST PURL STREET *(north side)*

232 NC NA **Parking Lot**

233 C 207 **House;** Midwest box, c.1915

234 NC 209 **House;** Upright-and-wing

235 C 211 **House;** Gable-front; c.1900

236 C 307 **Commercial Building;** Two-part commercial block; c.1930

237 NC 313 **House;** T-plan

238 NC 409 **House;** Gable-front; c.1910

## WEST PURL STREET *(south side)*

**No Sites**

## EAST PURL STREET *(south side)*

239 C 210 **House;** Ranch; c.1950

240 C 212 **House;** Minimal traditional; c.1935

241 N 310 **House;** Queen Anne cottage; c.1900

242 C 314 **House;** Gabled-ell; c.1910

243 C 410 **House;** Gable-front/Free Classic; c.1890

## EAST DOUGLAS STREET *(north side)*

244 NC 209 **House;** Free Classic; c.1900

245 C 211 **House;** American foursquare; 1901

246 C 215 **House;** Minimal ranch; c.1950

247 C 309 **House;** Minimal ranch; c.1950

248 NC 311 **House;** Gable-front; c.1900

## EAST DOUGLAS STREET *(south side)*

249 C NA **Garage;** Pyramidal-roof

250 C 210 **House;** Gable-front; c.1890

251 C 212 **House;** Gabled-ell; c.1900

252 NC 214 **House;** Free Classic; c.1900

253 C 310 **House;** Minimal ranch; c.1930

254 NC NA **Parking Lot**

255 C 406 **House;** Dormer-front bungalow; c.1915

256 C 410 **House;** American foursquare; c.1915

## GARFIELD AVENUE *(south side)*

**No Sites**

## PLYMOUTH AVENUE *(north side)*

**No Sites**

## HYDRAULIC CANAL *(east side)*

257 C **Industrial Building;** c.1940

258 NC **Garage;** c.1950

## SOUTH 2ND STREET *(east side)*

259 NC 120 **Commercial Building;** Contemporary; c.1999

260 NC NA **Commercial Building;** c.2000

## NORTH 2ND STREET *(east side)*

261 NC NA **Parking Lot**

262 NC NA **Parking Lot**

## SOUTH 3RD STREET *(west side)*

263 C 535 **House;** I-house; c.1890/c.1920

264 N 531 **House;** T-plan; c.1890

265 C 529 **House;** Gable-front; c.1910

266 C 527 **House;** Center-gable I-house; c.1880

267 C 525 **House;** Mediterranean Revival; c.1925

51487 **The Simmons House is an outstanding example of the Queen Anne style. It features decorative spindle work in the peaks, a Palladian style window, and wrap-around porch with a dentilated cornice.**

268 C 523 **House;** Gable-front; c.1890

269 C 521 **House;** T-plan; c.1890

270 C 519 **House;** Gable-front; c.1890

271 NC 517 **House;** Lazy-T; c.1890

272 N 513 **House;** Free Classic; c.1900

273 NC 511 **House;** Colonial Revival; c.1945

274 C NA **House;** Gable-front; c.1890

275 NC NA **Vacant Lot**

276 C 505 **House;** Free Classic; c.1890

277 N 503 **House;** T-plan; c.1890

278 NC 501 **House;** Gabled-ell; c.1920

279 NC 419 **House;** Gabled-ell; c.1920

280 C 413 **House;** Gabled-ell; c.1920

281 C 415 **House;** Lazy-T; c.1920

282 C 413 **House;** Dutch Colonial Revival; c.1920

283 NC 411 **Commercial Building;** c.1970

284 C NA **House;** Gable-front; c.1890

285 C 405 **House;** Lazy-T; c.1900

286 C 401 **House;** Gable-front/Italianate; c.1880

287 NC NA **Commercial Building;** Classical Revival; c.2000

288 NC NA **Parking Lot**

51492 **The 1875 John H. Baker House features a wide, bracketed cornice, tall, narrow windows with arched openings, and an assymetrical plan, typical of the Italianate style.**

289 N NA **House;** Italianate cube; c.1880

290 NC 307 **House;** Lazy-T; c.1880

291 C 305 **House;** Gable-front; c.1890

292 C 303 **House;** L-plan; c.1890

293 C 301 **House;** Gable-front; c.1900

294 C 223 **House;** T-plan/Queen Anne; c.1890

295 C 219 **House;** Lazy-T; c.1900

296 NC 213 **House;** American foursquare; c.1910

297 C NA **House;** Italianate; c.1880

298 NC NA **Vacant Lot**

299 C 123 **House;** American foursquare; c.1900

300 NC NA **Parking Lot**

301 NC NA **Parking Lot**

302 C 109 **Commercial Building;** Contemporary; c.1960

303 C 105 **House;** Colonial Revival; c.1917

**NORTH 3ᴿᴰ STREET** (*west side*)

304 O 101 **Rowell/Champion House;** Greek Revival; c.1847 (George P. Rowell, builder)

305 NC 111 **Sheriff Department & Detention Center;** Brutalist; c.1985

306 NC 119 **House;** Minimal ranch; c.1950

307 N 121 **House;** Italianate; c.1885/c.1910

308 C NA **House;** Colonial Revival; c.1925

309 NC NA **Central Fire Station;** 20th century functional; c.1970

310 NC NA **Parking Lot**

311 C 213 **House;** Free Classic; c.1890

312 NC NA **Vacant Lot**

313 C 217 **House;** American foursquare; c.1910

314 NC 219 **House;** American foursquare; c.1910

51493 **This outstanding Greek Revival house possesses a two-story porch with a dentilated pediment and cornice supported by paired Ionic columns.**

**SOUTH 3ᴿᴰ STREET** (*east side*)

315 N 528 **House;** American foursquare; c.1920

316 C 526 **House;** Gable-front; c.1920

317 NC 524 **House;** Gable-front; c.1900

318 NC 522 **House;** Gabled-ell; c.1890

319 C 520 **Baptist Church;** Gable-front; 1859

320 C 516 **House;** Gable-front; c.1910

321 NC 512 **House;** Gable-front; c.1910

322 C 510 **House;** Cross-gable; c.1920

323 C 508 **House;** Cape Cod; c.1930

324 NC NA **Playground/Parking Lot**

325 NC NA **Vacant Lot**

326 C 316 **House;** Free Classic; c.1900

327 C 312 **House;** American foursquare; c.1910 DEMOLISHED

328 NC NA **Commercial Building;** One-part commercial block; c.1950

329 C 306 **House;** Mediterranean Revival; c.1920

330 NC NA **Parking Lot**

331 NC 116 **Celebration Center;** Contemporary; c.2000

332 NC NA **Parking Lot**

333 NC NA **Parking Lot**

51495 This elaborate take on an American foursquare exhibits stuccoed walls, diamond pane windows, and a partially covered front porch.

**NORTH 3RD STREET** (*east side*)

| 334 | NC | NA | **Parking Lot** |
| 335 | NC | NA | **Parking Lot/Garage;** c.1980 |
| 336 | O | 214 | **House;** Queen Anne; c.1885 |
| 337 | NC | NA | **Parking Lot** |

**SOUTH MAIN STREET** (*west side*)

| 338 | NC | NA | **Vacant Lot** |
| 339 | C | 809 | **House;** Gabled-ell; c.1900 |
| 340 | C | 805 | **House;** Gabled-ell; c.1900 |
| 341 | C | 801 | **House;** Gable-front; c.1900 |
| 342 | NC | 723 | **House;** Gabled-ell; c.1890 |
| 343 | NC | NA | **Vacant Lot** |
| 344 | NC | 719 | **House;** Gabled-ell; c.1890 |
| 345 | C | 715 | **House;** Gable-front; c.1900 |
| 346 | C | 713 | **House;** Gabled-ell; c.1890 |
| 347 | C | 711 | **House;** American foursquare; c.1910 |
| 348 | C | 707 | **House;** Gabled-ell; c.1890 |
| 349 | C | 705 | **House;** Lazy-T; c.1890 |
| 350 | N | 701 | **Mayfield Block;** Queen Anne; 1901 |
| 351 | NC | NA | **House;** Gabled-ell; c.1900 |
| 352 | NC | NA | **Parking Lot** |
| 353 | NC | 623 | **House;** T-plan; c.1890 |
| 354 | C | 621 | **House;** English cottage; c.1930 |

| 355 | NC | 619 | **House;** Gable-front; c.1920 |
| 356 | C | 617 | **House;** Gable-front; c.1900 |
| 357 | NC | 615 | **House;** Lazy-T; c.1900 |
| 358 | C | 611 | **House;** Gable-front; c.1890 |
| 359 | C | 609 | **House;** T-plan; c.1890 |
| 360 | C | 605 | **House;** T-plan; c.1890 |
| 361 | C | 601 | **House;** Cross-gable square; c.1900 |
| 362 | NC | 527 | **House;** Minimal traditional; c.1930 |
| 363 | C | 523 | **House;** Dormer-front bungalow/ Craftsman; c.1920 |
| 364 | N | 521 | **House;** Second Empire; c.1870 |
| 365 | C | 517 | **House;** American foursquare; c.1910 |
| 366 | NC | 513-15 | **House;** Gabled-ell; c.1920 |
| 367 | N | 509 | **House;** Dormer-front bungalow; c.1910 |
| 368 | C | 505 | **House;** Italianate; c.1900 |
| 369 | C | 503 | **House;** Free Classic; c.1910 |
| 370 | NC | 501 | **House;** c.1900 |
| 371 | NC | NA | **St. John's Catholic Church;** Neo-classical; 1970 |
| 372 | NC | NA | **Parking Lot** |
| 373 | C | NA | **Bank;** Contemporary; c.1960 |
| 374 | NC | NA | **Parking Lot** |
| 375 | C | 311 | **C.W. Kerstetter House;** Second Empire; 1868 |
| 376 | NC | NA | **Parking Lot** |

51497 The Masonic Temple has a copper cornice, brick pilasters, and limestone accents.

51515 The Wickam House is an 1857 example of an Italianate cube. It features a very heavy cornice line with paired brackets, a cupola, and an elaborate door surround.

| 377 | NC | 301 | **Commercial Building;** c.1970 |
| 378 | NC | 233 | **Commercial Building/Garage;** 20th century functional; c.1980 |
| 379 | NC | 229 | **Commercial Building;** One-part commercial block; c.1970 |
| 380 | C | 225-27 | **Commercial Building;** Queen Anne; c.1890 |
| 381 | C | 223 | **Ednie Block;** Italianate; 1890 |
| 382 | C | 219-21 | **Platter Building;** Parapet-front; 1912 |
| 383 | C | 215 | **Commercial Building;** Parapet-front; 1884 |
| 384 | N | 211-13 | **Commercial Building;** Romanesque Revival; c.1880 |
| 385 | C | 209 | **Commercial Building;** Two-part commercial block; c.1880 |
| 386 | NC | 207 | **Commercial Building;** Italianate; c.1880 |
| 387 | C | 201 | **Kindy Block;** Italianate; c.1880 |
| 388 | C | NA | **Commercial Building;** Italianate; c.1880 |
| 389 | C | NA | **Commercial Building;** Italianate; c.1880 |
| 390 | C | NA | **Commercial Building;** Italianate; c.1880 |
| 391 | C | 129 | **Commercial Building;** Italianate; c.1880 |
| 392 | C | 129 | **Commercial Building;** Italianate; c.1880 |

51516 This Craftsman-style exhibits a front-facing gable with wide, overhanging eaves supported by knee braces, stucco walls with half-timbering, and original doors and windows.

| 393 | C | 127 | Commercial Building; Italianate; c.1880 |
| 394 | C | 125 | Commercial Building; Italianate; 1878 |
| 395 | C | 123 | Commercial Building; Art Deco; c.1930 |
| 396 | C | 119 | German Block; Italianate; c.1890 |
| 397 | NC | 117 | Commercial Building; Parapet-front; c.1910 |
| 398 | C | 115 | Commercial Building; One-part commercial block; c.1920 |
| 399 | NC | 113 | Commercial Building; c.1960 |
| 400 | C | 111-07 | Commercial Building; Two-part commercial block; c.1920 |

**NORTH MAIN STREET** *(west side)*

| 401 | NC | 201 | Bank; Post Modern; c.1985 |

**SOUTH MAIN STREET** *(east side)*

| 402 | C | 812 | House; Gabled-ell; c.1900 |
| 403 | C | NA | Garage; c.1940 |
| 404 | C | 806 | House; Free Classic; c.1910 |
| 405 | C | 804 | House; Dormer-front bungalow; c.1910 |
| 406 | C | 802 | House; Gabled-ell; c.1890 |

| 407 | C | 724 | Commercial Building; Italianate; c.1890 |
| 408 | NC | 722 | House; Gable-front; c.1910 |
| 409 | NC | 720 | House; T-plan; c.1890 |
| 410 | C | 718 | House; Craftsman; c.1920 |
| 411 | NC | 716 | House; Gable-front; c.1910 |
| 412 | C | 714 | House; Free Classic; c.1910 |
| 413 | C | 708 | House; Cross-gable; c.1890 |
| 414 | C | 706 | House; T-plan; c.1890 |
| 415 | NC | 704 | House; Gabled-ell; c.1900 |
| 416 | C | 702 | House; Free Classic; c.1890 |
| 417 | C | NA | Park |
| 418 | NC | NA | Vacant Lot |
| 419 | C | 510 | House; California bungalow; c.1910 |
| 420 | C | 508 | House; Gable-front; c.1890 |
| 421 | NC | NA | House; Gable-front; c.1890 |
| 422 | C | 502 | House; Free Classic; c.1900 |
| 423 | C | NA | House; American foursquare; c.1910 |
| 424 | C | NA | House; American foursquare; c.1920 |
| 425 | C | 320 | House; T-plan; c.1910 |
| 426 | C | 318 | House; Gable-front; c.1900 |
| 427 | NC | 316 | Market; Box; c.1970 |
| 428 | NC | NA | Parking Lot |

51539 This Free Classic house retains original wood siding and fish-scale shingles in the gable peaks.

51540 A fine example of the Prairie style, this house has wide overhanging eaves that, combined with decorative banding, create an emphasis on the horizontal.

| 429 | NC | 312 | House; Free Classic; c.1900 |
| 430 | NC | 310 | House; Free Classic; c.1900 |
| 431 | NC | 308 | House; T-plan; c.1900 |
| 432 | NC | NA | Commercial Building; House-with-canopy |
| 433 | NC | 232-34 | Visitor Center; c.1960 |
| 434 | C | 230 | Commercial Building; Two-part commercial block; c.1890 |
| 435 | C | 228 | Commercial Building; Italianate; 1882 |
| 436 | C | 224-26 | Garage; Parapet-front/Art Nouveau; 1917 |
| 437 | C | NA | Commercial Building; Classical Revival; c.1900 |
| 438 | C | 210-16 | Jefferson Theater; Romanesque Revival; c.1907 (Colonel J.M. Woods, Architect) |
| 439 | C | 208 | Commercial Building; Italianate; c.1880 |
| 440 | C | 206 | Commercial Building; Italianate; c.1880 |
| 441 | C | 204 | Commercial Building; Italianate; 1882 |
| 442 | C | NA | Commercial Building; Italianate; 1882 |
| 443 | C | NA | Commercial Building; Italianate; 1885 |
| 444 | C | 132 | Commercial Building; Italianate; c.1885 |

445 C 130 **Cunningham Building;** Italianate; 1885

446 C NA **Commercial Building;** Colonial Revival; c.1890

447 N 124 **Harper Block;** Italianate Renaissance Revival; 1888

448 C 122 **Commercial Building;** Two-part commercial block; c.1960

449 O 120 **Commercial Building;** Italian Renaissance Revival; 1880/1938

450 C 118 **Commercial Building;** Art Deco; c.1940

451 NC NA **The Goshen News;** c.1965

452 C 110 **Law Office;** Italianate; c.1880

453 C NA **Commercial Building;** Italianate; c.1880

454 C NA **Commercial Building;** Italianate; c.1880

455 C NA **Commercial Building;** Italianate; 1876

## NORTH MAIN STREET (east side)

456 C NA **Bank;** Neoclassical; c.1900

457 C 106 **Commercial Building;** Romanesque Revival; c.1890

458 N 108 **Noble Building;** Italianate; c.1890

459 C 110 **Commercial Building;** Italianate; c.1890

51541 This Free Classic house features a mansard-type roof, rounded tower with conical roof, and a large wrap-around porch supported by square columns.

51542 This 1876 Gothic Revival church has a corner tower and steeple, brick corbeling in a rounded pattern, and pointed-arch openings, including stained glass windows.

460 N 112 **Commercial Building;** Italianate; c.1890

461 C 114 **Commercial Building;** Italianate; c.1890

462 C 116 **State Bank;** Neoclassical; c.1891

463 C 118 **Law Office;** Two-part commercial block; c.1940

464 NC NA **Commercial Building;** No style; c.1965

465 NC 130 **Commercial Building;** c.1970

466 NC NA **Commercial Building;** Parapet-front; c.1960

467 NC NA **Commercial Building;** Two-part commercial block; c.1900/c.1945

468 N 136 **Commercial Building;** Two-part commercial block; c.1890

469 N 202-04 **Spohn Building;** Italian Renaissance Revival; 1909

470 C NA **Democrat Building;** Two-part commercial block; 1907

471 NC NA **Parking Lot**

472 C 212 **Commercial Building;** Italianate; c.1900

473 NC 214 **Commercial Building;** Italianate; c.1910

474 C 216 **Commercial Building;** Two-part commercial block; c.1930

475 C 218 **Commercial Building;** Two-part commercial block; c.1930

476 NC 220 **Commercial Building;** One-part commercial block; c.1954

477 NC 222 **House/Commercial Building;** Gable-front; c.1900/1972

## SOUTH 5TH STREET (west side)

478 NC 601 **Goshen Public Library;** c.1990

479 C 517 **House;** American foursquare; c.1910

480 O 515 **House;** Gable-front; c.1890

481 C 513 **House;** Gable-front; c.1890

482 C 511 **House;** American foursquare; c.1920

483 C 507 **House;** Free Classic; c.1900

51544 This outstanding Italianate house displays a dentilated cornice with decorative brackets, tall, narrow windows with flat limestone sills and lentils, and a full-width porch supported by paired fluted columns.

484  N  505  **House;** Cross-gable/Free Classic; c.1900

485  N  501  **House;** Free Classic; c.1900

486  N  423  **House;** Free Classic; c.1910

487  O  419  **Simmons House;** Queen Anne; c.1890

488  N  413  **House;** Craftsman; 1920

489  N  411  **House;** Queen Anne; c.1890

490  C  407  **House;** Gable-front; c.1920

491  NC  405  **House;** Gabled-ell; c.1890

492  O  401  **John H. Baker House;** Italianate; 1875

493  O  317  **House;** Greek Revival; c.1875

494  NC  313  **House;** Italianate; c.1910

495  N  NA  **House;** American foursquare; c.1920

496  N  307  **House;** Mission Revival; c.1920

497  O  301  **Masonic Temple;** Neoclassical; c.1915

498  C  NA  **Historical Marker;** 1998

499  NC  NA  **Parking Lot**

500  C  NA  **Commercial Building;** Art Moderne; c.1950

501  NC  NA  **Parking Lot**

502  C  123  **American Legion;** Italianate; c.1900

503  NC  NA  **Parking Lot**

51545  This outstanding Free Classic house features scalloped shingles beneath the gable peak and a full-width porch supported by thin columns on stone piers.

51548  Architects Patton & Miller designed the 1903 Goshen High School.

504  NC  109  **Commercial Building;** c.1980

### NORTH 5TH STREET *(west side)*

505  NC  NA  **Parking Lot**

506  NC  105  **Commercial Building;** c.1980

507  C  111  **Church;** Steeple-front; c.1900

508  NC  NA  **Parking Lot**

509  C  203  **Goshen City Church of the Brethren;** One-part commercial block; 1950

510  NC  NA  **Parking Lot**

511  C  219  **House;** Midwest box; c.1910

512  NC  223  **House;** Gable-front; c.1900

513  NC  229  **House;** Hall-and-parlor; c.1890

### SOUTH 5TH STREET *(east side)*

514  C  634  **House;** English cottage; c.1920

515  O  628  **Wickam House;** Italianate cube; 1857

516  O  624  **House;** Craftsman; c.1915

517  C  622  **House;** Dormer-front bungalow; c.1920

518  N  618  **House;** T-plan; c.1890

519  C  616  **House;** Center-gable cottage; c.1900

520  NC  612  **House;** Upright-and-wing; c.1900

521  NC  610  **House;** L-plan; c.1900

522  C  608  **House;** Cross-plan; c.1900

523  N  604  **House;** Free Classic; c.1900

524  C  602  **House;** Free Classic; c.1900

525  C  524  **House;** Midwest box; c.1920

526  N  522  **House;** Midwest box; c.1920

527  C  520  **House;** American foursquare; c.1920

528  NC  518  **House;** Midwest box; c.1910/c.1960

529  NC  514  **House;** American foursquare; c.1910

530  C  512  **House;** Gabled-ell; c.1900

531  C  510  **House;** American foursquare; c.1890

51549  The 1874 First Methodist Episcopal Church (now the First United Methodist Church) is a grand example of the Gothic Revival style. It exhibits a side steeple, pointed-arch openings, stained glass windows, and stone accents.

**51550** This Tudor Revival building is part of the First United Methodist Church. The c.1900 building features paired casement windows with leaded glass and stone surrounds.

**532** NC NA **Vacant Lot**

**533** NC NA **Funeral Home;** American four-square; c.1910

**534** C NA **House;** American foursquare; c.1900

**535** C 502 **House;** American foursquare; c.1900

**536** C 424 **House;** American foursquare; c.1900

**537** NC 422 **House;** T-plan; c.1900

**538** N 420 **House;** Lazy-T/Queen Anne; c.1900

**539** N 418 **House;** Free Classic; c.1900

**540** N 414 **House;** Prairie; c.1920

**541** N 412 **House;** Free Classic; c.1900

**542** O NA **Church;** Gothic Revival; 1876

**543** O 324 **J.A.S. Mitchell House;** Eastlake; 1870 (Cass Chapman, architect)

**544** O 320 **House;** Italianate; c.1887

**545** O 316 **House;** Free Classic; c.1900

**546** NC 314 **House;** Free Classic; c.1900

**547** N 312 **House;** American foursquare/ Colonial Revival; c.1900

**548** O NA **Goshen High School;** Italian Renaissance Revival; 1903 Patton & Miller, architects)

**549** O 215 **First Methodist Episcopal Church;** Gothic Revival; 1874

**550** O NA **First United Methodist Church;** Tudor Revival; c.1900

**551** NC NA **Church Nursery School;** c.1990

**552** NC NA **Parking Lot**

**553** C NA **Historical Marker**

**554** O 202 **Goshen Carnegie Public Library/ City Hall;** Beaux-Arts; 1901 (Patton & Miller, architects) **NR**

**555** C 124 **House;** Italianate; c.1900

**556** C 118 **House;** American foursquare; c.1900

**557** O 114 **Dale-Zook House;** Queen Anne; 1890

**558** C 112 **House;** Greek Revival; c.1870

**559** N 110 **Church;** Parapet-front; 1893

## NORTH 5TH STREET *(east side)*

**560** C 108 **Commercial Building;** One-part commercial block

**561** NC NA **Parking Lot**

**562** C 120 **House;** American foursquare; c.1920

**563** C 124 **House;** Gable-front; c.1900

**564** C 206 **House;** Free Classic; c.1890

**565** NC 208 **House;** T-plan; c.1900

**51554** Goshen's Carnegie Library was constructed between 1901-02 and today houses City Hall.

**51584** This Free Classic house features pointed-arch insets beneath the gable peaks surrounded by wood shingles and a full-width porch supported by short, fluted columns atop a stone wall.

**566** NC 212-10 **House;** Gable-front; c.1900

**567** NC NA **Parking Lot**

**568** N 214 **House;** T-plan/Italianate; c.1880

**569** NC 218 **Commercial Building;** c.1950

**570** NC NA **Commercial Building;** c.1990

## SOUTH 6TH STREET *(west side)*

**571** C 815 **House;** Gabled-ell; c.1890

**572** C 813 **House;** Dutch Colonial Revival; c.1920

**573** C 811 **House;** Cross-gable square; c.1920

**574** C 809 **House;** Western bungalow; c.1910

**575** C 805 **House;** American foursquare; c.1900

**576** C 803 **House;** American foursquare; c.1900

**577** C 801 **House;** American foursquare; c.1900

**578** C 721 **House;** American foursquare; c.1900

**579** C 719 **House;** Free Classic; c.1900

**580** C 717 **House;** Dormer-front bungalow; c.1920

**581** C 715 **House;** American foursquare; c.1890

**51599** This 1904 late-Gothic Revival church has a crenellated side tower, pointed-arch openings, and a cut stone foundation.

**582** C 713 **House;** Cross-gable/Dutch Colonial Revival; c.1900

**583** C 711 **House;** American foursquare; c.1900

**584** O 705 **House;** Free Classic; c.1910

**585** NC 703 **House;** American foursquare; c.1910

**586** C 701 **House;** Dormer-front bungalow; c.1920

**587** NC 635 **House;** T-plan; c.1900

**588** NC 631 **House;** Gabled-ell; c.1900

**589** N 629 **House;** American foursquare; c.1910

**590** NC 627 **House;** I-house; c.1900

**591** C 623 **House;** Lazy-T; c.1900

**592** NC NA **Vacant Lot**

**593** NC 617 **House;** Gable-front; c.1900

**594** NC NA **Vacant Lot**

**595** C 611 **House;** Gable-front; c.1890

**596** C 609 **House;** Gable-front; c.1900

**597** C 605 **House;** Upright-and-wing; c.1900

**598** N 601 **House;** Queen Anne; c.1900

**599** N NA **Church;** Late Gothic Revival; 1904

**600** C 519 **House;** Lazy-T; c.1910/c.1950

**601** C 517 **House;** Lazy-T; c.1890

**602** C 513 **House;** Dormer-front bungalow; c.1930

**603** C 511 **House;** T-plan; c.1890

**604** NC 509 **House;** Cross-plan; c.1920

**605** NC 507 **House;** Gabled-ell; c.1900

**606** C 505 **House;** T-plan; c.1910

**607** C 423 **House;** American foursquare; c.1910

**608** C 421 **House;** Gable-front; c.1900

**609** C 419 **House;** Gable-front; c.1890

**610** NC 417 **House;** Gable-front; c.1900

**611** NC 413 **House;** American foursquare; c.1910

**612** C 411 **House;** Queen Anne; c.1890

**613** C 405 **House;** Cross-plan; c.1890

**614** N 323 **House;** Italianate; c.1880

**615** C 319 **House;** Lazy-T; c.1890

**616** C 317 **House;** T-plan/Greek Revival; c.1890

**617** O 313 **House;** Queen Anne; c.1890

**618** C 311 **House;** Free Classic; c.1890

**619** C 309 **House;** California bungalow; c.1920

**620** N 305 **House;** T-plan; c.1900

**621** C 301 **House;** Free Classic; c.1900

**622** N 223 **House;** Shingle style; c.1900

**51617** This Queen Anne house boasts a circular tower with a conical roof topped by a finial, original siding and windows, and a wrap-around front porch.

**51624** John Lesh built this Queen Anne house that features a circular tower with slate roof, some diamond-pane and double-hung windows, and a wrap-around porch with paired columns.

**623** N 217 **House;** Midwest box/Colonial Revival; c.1900

**624** O 213 **John Lesh House;** Queen Anne; c.1897 (John Lesh, builder)

**625** C 211 **House;** Free Classic; c.1900

**626** N 209 **House;** Free Classic; c.1900

**627** NC NA **Parking Lot**

**628** N 203 **Elias Gortner House;** Italianate; 1862

**629** N NA **First Baptist Church;** Gothic Revival; 1876

**630** C 117 **House;** Lazy-T; c.1900

**631** C 113 **House;** Midwest box; c.1900

**632** NC 111 **House;** Gable-front; c.1900

**633** NC 109 **House;** Midwest box; c.1900

**634** C 105 **St. James Episcopal Church;** Late Gothic Revival; 1959

**NORTH 6TH STREET** (*west side*)

**635** NC NA **Parking Lot**

**636** C 113 **House;** American foursquare; c.1910

**637** C 115 **House;** Midwest box; c.1910

**638** N 117 **House;** American foursquare; 1908

**639** C NA **House;** Double-entry I-house; c.1890

## SOUTH 6TH STREET (east side)

**640** C 816 **House;** American foursquare; c.1900

**641** C 814 **House;** Dutch Colonial Revival; c.1930

**642** NC 806 **House;** American foursquare; c.1910

**643** NC 804 **House;** T-plan; c.1900

**644** C 802 **House;** American foursquare; c.1910

**645** C 718 **House;** T-plan; c.1900

**646** N 716 **House;** Craftsman; c.1920

**647** C 714 **House;** Free Classic; c.1900

**648** NC 712 **House;** Free Classic; c.1900

**649** N 710 **House;** Free Classic; c.1900

**650** N 708 **House;** American foursquare; c.1900

**651** NC 706 **House;** American foursquare; c.1900

**652** NC 704 **House;** T-plan; c.1890

**653** C 702 **House;** American foursquare; c.1910

**654** C 636 **House;** T-plan; c.1890

**655** C 632 **House;** Free Classic; c.1890

**656** N 630 **House;** Free Classic; c.1900

**657** C 628 **House;** Dormer-front bungalow/ Craftsman; c.1920

**51646** This Craftsman house has stucco on the second level and wide clapboard siding on the first, ribbon windows, and a gabled front porch.

**51656** This Free Classic house features a diamond pane window surrounded by wood shingles beneath the gable peak, a swag motif on the cornice, flared corners, and a pedimented front porch.

**658** C 626 **House;** California bungalow; c.1920

**659** C 620 **House;** Lazy-T; c.1900

**660** C 618 **House;** American foursquare; c.1910

**661** C 616 **House;** American foursquare; c.1910

**662** C 614 **House;** T-plan; c.1890

**663** C 612 **House;** Gable-front; c.1890

**664** N 610 **House;** Gable-front; c.1890

**665** N 608 **House;** Gabled-ell; c.1890

**666** NC 606 **House;** Gable-front; c.1890

**667** NC 602 **House;** T-plan; c.1900

**668** C 524 **House;** Gable-front; c.1900

**669** C 522 **House;** Gabled-ell; c.1900

**670** NC 520 **House;** Bungalow; c.1920

**671** C 518 **House;** Gable-front; c.1890

**672** C 516 **House;** Gable-front; c.1890

**673** C 514 **House;** Gable-front/Greek Revival; c.1880

**674** C 512 **House;** T-plan; c.1890

**675** NC 508 **House;** Gable-front; c.1900

**676** NC 506 **House;** T-plan; c.1890

**677** C 504 **House;** American foursquare; c.1900

**678** C 502 **House;** Gable-front; c.1890

**679** C 420 **House;** Cape Cod; c.1940

**680** C 418 **House;** Gable-front; c.1890

**681** O 414 **House;** Queen Anne; c.1890

**682** C 412 **House;** Gabled-ell; c.1920

**683** C 410 **House;** Gabled-ell; c.1900

**684** C 406 **House;** Gabled-ell; c.1900

**685** C 402 **House;** Gable-front; c.1920

**686** NC 324 **House;** Gabled-ell; c.1890

**687** N 320 **House;** T-plan/bungalow; c.1920

**688** C 314 **House;** Dutch Colonial Revival; c.1910

**689** C 312 **House;** Free Classic; c.1915

**690** C 310 **House;** American foursquare; c.1910

**691** NC 304 **House;** Gable-front; c.1970

**692** N 302 **House;** American foursquare; c.1910

**693** N 224 **House;** Italianate; c.1900

**51681** This Queen Anne house retains a round turret with conical roof, fish scale and clapboard siding, original windows, and a curved front porch supported by turned posts.

694 C 222 **House;** Gable-front; c.1900

695 N 218 **House;** Shingle style; c.1910

696 N 214 **House;** Queen Anne; c.1910

697 O 212 **John Gortner House;** Italianate; 1861

698 NC NA **Vacant Lot**

699 O 204 **House;** Free Classic; c.1894

700 O 202 **Charles B. Harris House;** Free Classic; c.1894

701 N 124 **House;** American foursquare; c.1900

702 C 118-20 **House;** Gable-front; c.1900

703 C 114 **House;** American foursquare; c.1920

704 C 112 **House;** Midwest box; c.1900

705 O 108 **House;** Italianate; c.1890

706 C NA **House;** Second Empire; c.1900

### NORTH 6TH STREET (east side)

707 C 410 **House;** Midwest box; c.1910

708 C 112 **House;** Midwest box; c.1890

709 NA 114 **House;** Lazy-T; c.1910

710 C 116 **House;** Gabled-ell; c.1890

711 C 120 **House;** Gable-front; c.1900

712 NC NA **House;** Gable-front; c.1910

51697 The John Gartner House dates to 1861 and is a fine example of the Italianate style. It has a wide cornice with paired brackets, tall narrow windows, and a dentilated full-width porch supported by paired fluted columns.

51699 This Free Classic house features a slate roof, wood clapboard and shingle siding, original windows including some diamond-pane casements, and a full-width porch supported by narrow columns on brick piers.

### SOUTH 7TH STREET (west side)

713 C NA **House;** Colonial Revival; c.1920

714 C 819 **House;** Dormer-front bungalow; c.1920

715 C 817 **House;** Free Classic; c.1910

716 NC 815 **House;** American foursquare; c.1920

717 C 813 **House;** Dutch Colonial Revival; 1925

718 O 811 **House;** Tudor Revival; 1925

719 C 805 **House;** Midwest box; c.1920

720 C 803 **House;** Dormer-front bungalow; c.1920

721 C 801 **House;** California bungalow/Craftsman; c.1910

722 C 707 **House;** American foursquare; c.1910

723 NC 705 **House;** Dormer-front bungalow; c.1920

724 C 703 **House;** English cottage; c.1915

725 C 701 **House;** Side-gable bungalow/Craftsman; c.1920

726 C 631 **House;** T-plan; c.1910

727 C 629 **House;** T-plan; c.1900

728 NC 627 **House;** Gable-front; c.1900

729 C 625 **House;** T-plan/Queen Anne; c.1890

730 C 621-23 **House;** Free Classic; c.1900

731 C 619 **House;** Asymmetrical gable-front; c.1900

732 NC 615 **House;** T-plan; c.1890

733 NC 613 **House;** Dormer-front bungalow; c.1910

734 C 611 **House;** Gabled-ell; c.1900

735 C 605 **House;** Gabled-ell; c.1900

736 C 601 **House;** Free Classic; c.1900

737 C 523 **House;** Queen Anne; c.1900

738 C 517 **House;** Free Classic; c.1900

739 C 513 **House;** Gabled-ell; c.1900

740 C 511 **House;** Gabled-ell; c.1890

741 NC 509 **House;** Gabled-ell; c.1900

742 N 507 **House;** Gable-front/Craftsman; c.1910

743 C NA **House;** Queen Anne; c.1910

744 C 421 **House;** Gable-front; 1904

745 C 419 **House;** T-plan; c.1890

746 C NA **House;** Colonial Revival; c.1920

747 C 411 **House;** American foursquare; c.1910

748 NC 407 **House;** California bungalow; c.1910

749 C 405 **House;** Queen Anne; c.1900

51700 The Charles B. Harris House dates to c.1894. The Free Classic house received the 2001 Old Town Neighborhood Association Preservation Award.

51705 This Italianate house features overhanging eaves supported by paired scroll brackets, segmental-arch openings, and an original full-width porch.

750  C   321   **House;** Gable-front; c.1890

751  C   319   **House;** Queen Anne; c.1890

752  C   315   **House;** Lazy-T; c.1890

753  C   313   **House;** L-plan; c.1920

754  C   311   **House;** Gable-front; c.1910

755  C   307   **House;** Free Classic; c.1900

756  C   305   **House;** Gable-front; c.1890

757  C   223   **House;** Queen Anne; c.1900

758  C   219   **House;** Center-gable cottage; c.1900

759  N   215   **House;** Free Classic; c.1900

760  O   213   **House;** Second Empire; c.1880

761  C   211   **House;** American foursquare; c.1910

762  NC  209   **House;** Free Classic; c.1890

763  NC  207   **House;** Gable-front; c.1900

764  NC  NA    **House;** Ranch; c.1965

765  C   121-23 **Double House;** Gothic Revival; c.1875

766  C   117   **House;** Center-gable cottage; c.1900

767  O   NA    **House;** American foursquare; c.1900

768  N   111   **House;** Free Classic; c.1890

769  NC  109   **House;** Lazy-T; c.1900

770  C   107   **House;** Gable-front; c.1890

771  C   105   **House;** Center-gable cottage; c.1890

**NORTH 7TH STREET (west side)**

772  C   109   **House;** Free Classic; c.1900

773  NC  NA    **Vacant Lot**

774  NC  113   **House;** Center-gable cottage; c.1890

775  C   117   **House;** I-house; c.1890

**SOUTH 7TH STREET (east side)**

776  N   822   **House;** Tudor Revival; c.1900

777  C   820   **House;** Dutch Colonial Revival; c.1900

778  N   818   **House;** English cottage; c.1920

779  C   816   **House;** American foursquare; c.1920

780  C   814   **House;** Free Classic; c.1890

781  N   812   **House;** California bungalow/Craftsman; c.1920

782  C   810   **House;** Craftsman; c.1920

783  C   808   **House;** Free Classic; c.1910

784  C   806   **House;** American foursquare; c.1920

785  C   804   **House;** American foursquare; 1903

786  O   640   **House;** Colonial Revival; c.1900

787  C   634   **House;** Free Classic; c.1920

788  C   632   **House;** Dormer-front bungalow; c.1920

789  C   630   **House;** T-plan; c.1910

790  C   628   **House;** T-plan; c.1910

51718 This 1925 Tudor Revival house retains a slate roof, stuccoed walls with half-timbering, and a combination of casement and double-hung windows.

51742 This Craftsman house displays wide overhanging eaves supported by knee braces, wide clapboard siding on the second floor and stucco on the first, and original casement windows.

791  C   626   **House;** Gabled-ell; c.1900

792  NC  622   **House;** Gable-front; c.1910

793  C   620   **House;** American foursquare; c.1910

794  C   NA    **House;** T-plan; c.1910

795  C   614   **House;** Lazy-T; c.1900

796  C   612   **House;** Gable-front; c.1910

797  C   610   **House;** Gable-front; c.1900

798  C   608   **House;** Gable-front; c.1920

799  C   606   **House;** Minimal traditional; c.1935

800  C   602   **House;** Gabled-ell; c.1900

801  C   524   **House;** T-plan/Craftsman; c.1900

802  C   518   **House;** T-plan; c.1890

803  C   516   **House;** T-plan; c.1890

804  NC  514   **House;** Gable-front; c.1900

805  C   512   **House;** Colonial Revival; c.1920

806  C   510   **House;** Gable-front; c.1900

807  C   508   **House;** Free Classic; c.1900

808  C   506   **House;** American foursquare; c.1910

809  C   504   **House;** Side-gable bungalow/ Craftsman; c.1920

810  C   502   **House;** Pyramidal-roof/Queen Anne cottage; c.1910

**51760** This Second Empire house exhibits a mansard roof with dormers, a dentilated cornice with paired brackets, and windows with flat stone sills and lintels.

811  C  424  **House;** Gable-front/Craftsman; c.1920

812  C  418  **House;** Gabled-ell; c.1900

813  C  414  **House;** Gabled-ell; c.1900

814  NC  412  **Apartment Building;** Colonial Revival; c.1930

815  C  406  **House;** Gabled-ell; c.1890

816  NC  402  **House;** Dormer-front bungalow; c.1915

817  NC  NA  **House;** Gable-front; c.1900

818  NC  312  **House;** Gable-front; c.1900

819  NC  310  **House;** Gable-front; c.1900

820  C  308  **House;** T-plan/Queen Anne; c.1900

821  C  306  **House;** Gable-front; c.1900

822  C  NA  **House;** Free Classic; c.1900

823  C  222  **House;** Gable-front; c.1890/1900

824  C  220  **House;** Gabled-ell; c.1900

825  C  218  **House;** Gabled-ell; c.1900

826  C  216  **House;** Gable-front; c.1920

827  C  214  **House;** Free Classic; c.1890

828  C  212  **House;** Shotgun; c.1920

829  C  210  **House;** Gabled-ell; c.1890

830  C  206  **House;** Upright-and-wing; c.1920

831  C  202  **House;** Queen Anne; c.1900

832  NC  124  **House;** Ranch; c.1965

833  C  118  **House;** Gable-front; c.1890

834  C  NA  **House;** Free Classic; c.1900

835  C  110-12 **House;** Second Empire; c.1910

836  C  106-08 **Apartment Building;** Italianate; c.1880

## NORTH 7TH STREET *(east side)*

837  C  NA  **House;** Dutch Colonial Revival; c.1900

838  C  110  **House;** Hall-and-parlor; c.1900

839  C  112  **House;** T-plan; c.1890

840  C  114  **House;** Gable-front; c.1900

841  C  116  **House;** California bungalow; c.1920

## SOUTH COTTAGE AVENUE *(west side)*

842  C  513  **House;** Gabled-ell; c.1900

843  C  507  **House;** Gable-front; c.1900

844  NC  505  **House;** California bungalow; c.1920

845  NC  419  **House;** Colonial Revival; c.1930

846  C  317  **House;** Dutch Colonial Revival; c.1900

847  C  315  **House;** Gable-front; c.1910

**51767** This elaborate example of an American foursquare features a green barrel tile roof, full width porch with second story balcony, and original windows.

**51786** This Colonial Revival boasts a slate roof with three gabled dormers, side chimneys, and an elaborate entry with fan and sidelights.

848  C  305  **House;** Gable-front; c.1900

849  C  217  **House;** Gable-front; c.1920

850  C  215  **House;** California bungalow; c.1920

851  C  213  **House;** Airplane bungalow; c.1920

852  C  211  **House;** California bungalow; c.1910

853  C  209  **House;** Dormer-front bungalow; c.1920

854  NC  NA  **Vacant Lot**

855  C  111  **House;** Colonial Revival; c.1900

856  NC  NA  **House;** Midwest box; c.1900

## NORTH COTTAGE AVENUE *(west side)*

857  C  NA  **Barn;** English barn; c.1900

858  NC  NA  **Parking Lot**

# Goshen College Scattered Sites (52001-013)

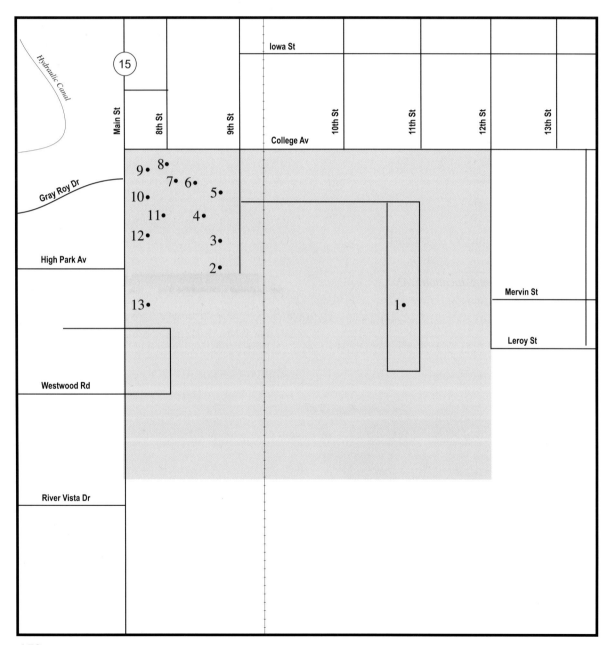

Goshen College began as The Elkhart Institute of Science, Industry and the Arts, and was located on Prairie Street in Elkhart. A Mennonite physician named H.A. Mumaw founded the Institute in 1894. In 1895, control of the institute was turned over to a Mennonite board of directors. Enrollment in the school increased steadily and it soon outgrew its original location. Several sites in Elkhart and Goshen were considered for relocation and a site in Elkhart was favored, but negotiations failed. Eventually, a field at the southern end of Eighth Street in Goshen was selected and the school moved to its current location in the summer of 1903. As part of the negotiations, the school changed its name to Goshen College.

The first buildings erected on the campus were East Hall (destroyed by fire) and the Administration Building (52011). Classrooms in the Administration Building were not finished before the start of the fall semester in 1903 and professors held classes in East Hall's empty dorm rooms. Shortly after its move to Goshen, the leadership of the school changed hands and the Mennonite Board of Education took control in 1904.

The school's growth was slowed by the Mennonite community's belief that the school was too liberal in its methods and theology. Those concerns, coupled with financial problems, caused the school to close its doors in 1923. When it reopened a year later, the college weathered its financial problems and strengthened relations with church leadership.

The college grew and the need for accreditation soon became apparent. The school received official accreditation in March of 1941. Rapid growth followed in the 1950s and 60s. Between 1954 and 1970, annual enrollment grew from 815 to over 1200. During that period, several new buildings were constructed, including the 1951 Westlawn Residence Hall (52009), the 1957 Wyse Building (52003), and the 1962 Yoder Hall (52001).

Goshen College continues to grow and hold a prominent place in the community. In 1981, it was estimated that the college contributed $35 million to the local economy in jobs, goods, and services.

## GOSHEN COLLEGE SCATTERED SITES (52001-013)

**No. Rtg. Description**

**001  C  Yoder Hall;** Contemporary; 1962; *Architecture, Education* (243)

**002  C  Heating Plant;** 20th century functional; 1945; *Architecture* (243)

**003  C  Wyse Building;** Modern; 1957; *Architecture, Education* (243)

**004  N  Science Hall;** Collegiate Gothic; 1915; *Architecture, Education* (243)

**005  N  John S. Coffman Residence Hall;** Depression Modern; 1929; *Architecture, Education* (243)

**006  C  Bench;** 1916; *Art, Education* (243)

**007  C  Adelphian Fountain;** 1904; *Art, Education* (243)

**008  C  Goshen College Gateway;** College Ave.; Stone wall; c.1904; *Education* (243)

**009  C  Westlawn Residence Hall;** Main St.; Modern; 1951-53; *Architecture, Education* (243)

**010  N  Kulp Hall;** Colonial Revival; 1906; *Architecture, Education* (243)

**011  N  Administration Building;** Colonial Revival; 1903; *Architecture, Education* (243)

**012  N  Memorial Library;** Neoclassical; 1940; *Architecture, Education* (243)

**013  C  Union Building;** Main St.; Modern; 1947-50; *Architecture, Education* (243)

**52005  The John S. Coffman Residence Hall was built in 1929. Its simple, blocky style can be classified as Depression Modern. The hall underwent renovations in 1960 and 1989.**

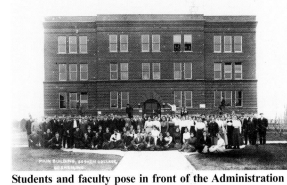

**52011  The Administration Building is one of the original buildings built for the school's new Goshen campus in 1903. The Colonial Revival building was renovated in 1907, 1972, and 1989.**

**Students and faculty pose in front of the Administration Building, c.1915.** *Photo courtesy of the Elkhart County Historical Museum*

**52004  Science Hall was built in the Collegiate Gothic style in 1915. It underwent renovations in 1953, 1980, and 1992. The Schrock Annex was added to its east side in 1992.**

**52010  Kulp Hall was the first permanent residence hall to serve students. It was built in 1906, three years after the school relocated to Goshen. Its basement housed the campus dining hall until 1950. The Colonial Revival building was renovated in 1953, 1980, 1989, and 1992.**

**52012  Memorial Library was built in the Neoclassical style in 1920. It features brick walls, a limestone belt course, and original multi-pane double- and triple-hung sash windows, as well as some casement windows.**

# Goshen Scattered Sites (53001-244)

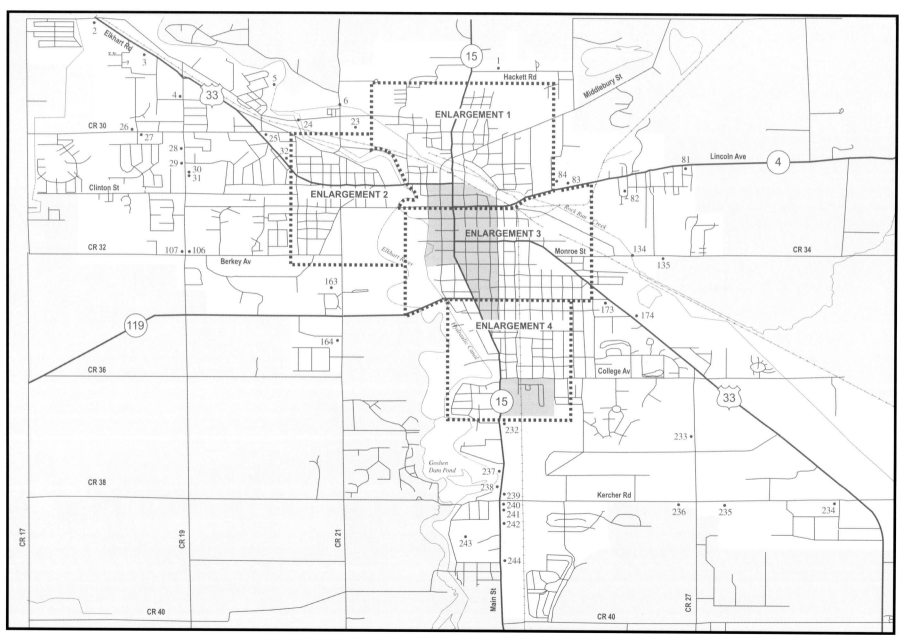

154

# Goshen Scattered Sites Enlargement 1 (53001-244)

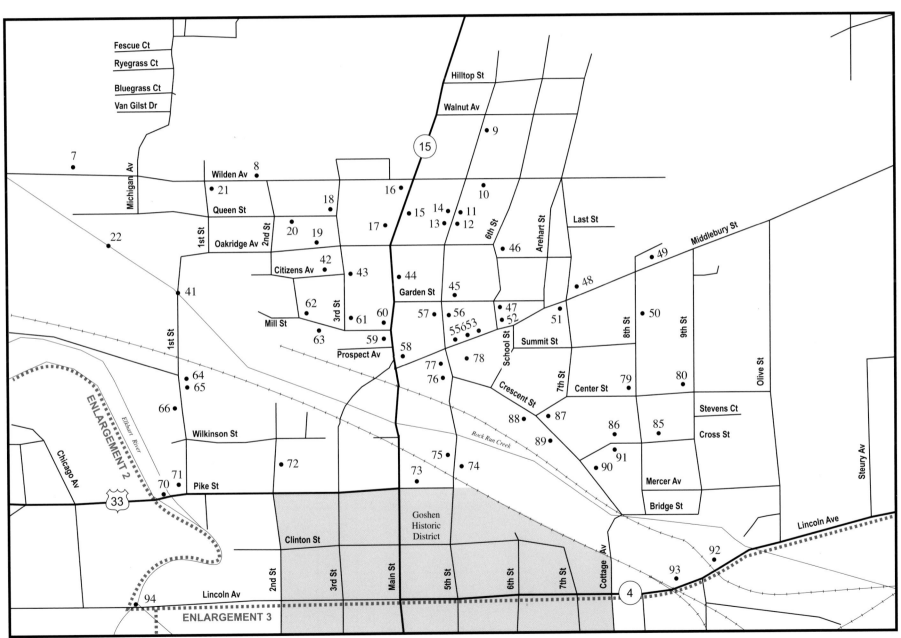

# Goshen Scattered Sites Enlargement 2 (53001-244)

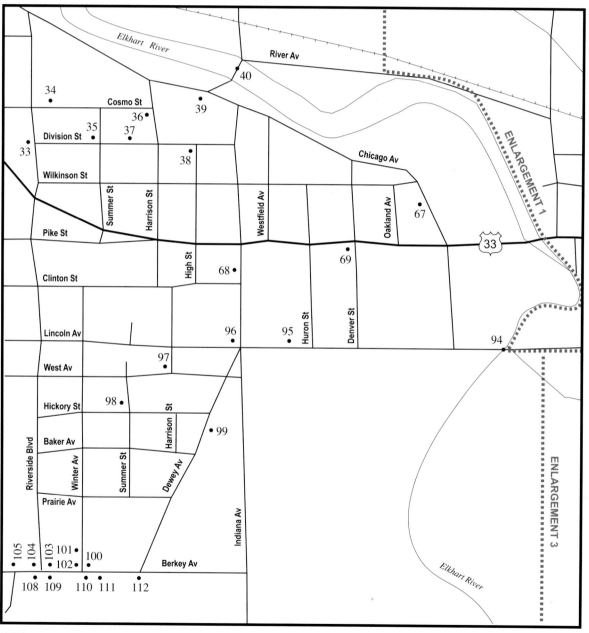

In 1831, Goshen became the new Elkhart County seat. That year, George Crawford platted the town, while Oliver Crane sold the first lots. Goshen was named after Goshen, New York, the hometown of Crane. William Bissell built the first house and store in the new town, and became its first postmaster in 1832. In 1833, Joseph Studebaker designed the first Elkhart County courthouse, modeling it after a courthouse in Dayton, Ohio. Studebaker is buried in the West Goshen Cemetery (53163). The original courthouse was replaced in 1870 with the present building (51024).

Goshen developed at the crossing of the Fort Wayne Road and the Logansport and White Pigeon Road (Lincoln Avenue and Main Street), which became Goshen's primary commercial district. Major John W. Violett, an early Elkhart Township settler, built the 1854 Violett House at the northwestern corner of North Main and West Clinton Streets, which later became the Hotel Hascall (53241). Major Violett is buried in the Violett Cemetery (53243). Goshen was incorporated as a village in 1854 and incorporated as a city in 1868.

The Northern Indiana Railroad completed a branch line from Elkhart to Goshen in 1852; Goshen citizens had built a roundhouse as an incentive for the line. Six years later, the line became the through line of the merged Michigan Southern and Northern Indiana Railroad (later called the Lake Shore and Michigan Southern Railroad).

Construction on the hydraulic canal and its dam on the Elkhart River began in 1866 and was completed two years later. Cephas Hawks, buried in the Oakridge Cemetery (53023), formed a company with several other businessmen to build the canal that was vital to the town's industrial and economic health. Hawks moved his grist mill from

*Continued on page 158*

# Goshen Scattered Sites Enlargement 3 (53001-244)

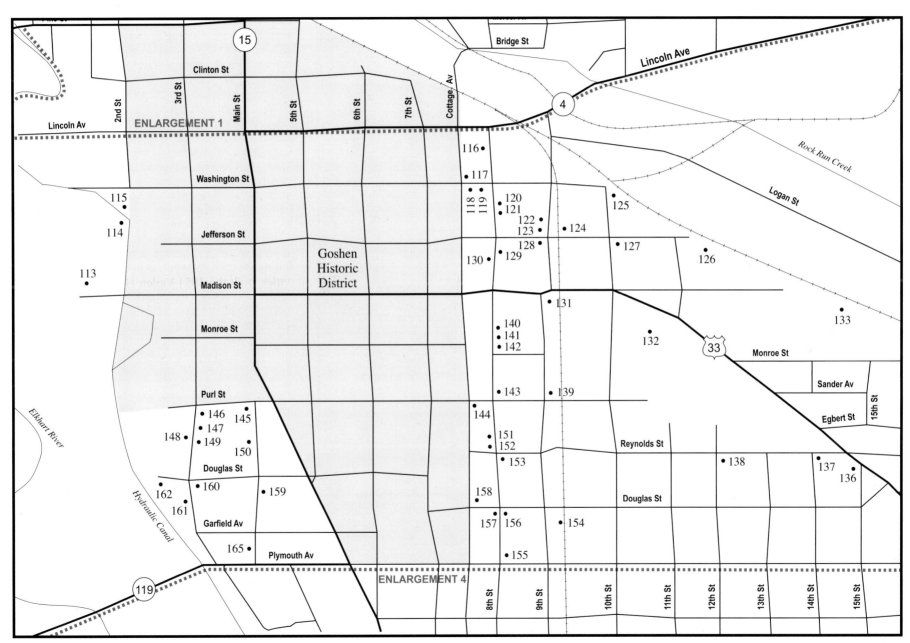

# Goshen Scattered Sites Enlargement 4 (53001-244)

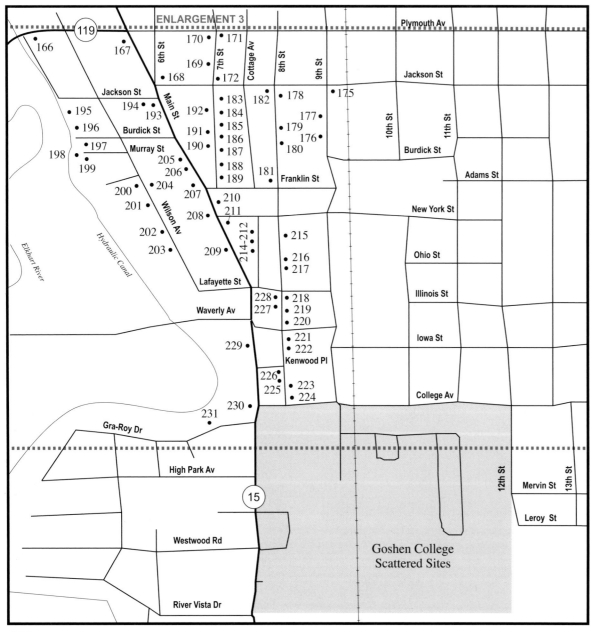

*Continued from page 156*

Waterford to the eastern side of the canal and it became the Goshen Milling Company. Hawks formed other industries along the canal to harness its power, including the Hawks Furniture and Electric Light Companies (51114-115). The Hawks Electric Light Company provided electricity generated from water and steam for Goshen, Middlebury, Millersburg, Benton, Wakarusa, and Bremen in Marshall County. In the 1890s, a stem from the Lake Shore and Michigan Southern Railroad was built to serve businesses along both sides of the canal.

The hydraulic canal provided the town's first water system in 1875. A pumping station was built along the canal with wooden water mains. In 1881, the Goshen Water Works moved to its present site (53074). The city replaced the original building with the present building, which also produced electricity for a time. The metal standpipe was built in 1896.

Early Goshen industries include the Goshen Sash and Door Company (53139). Established on the hydraulic canal in 1869, it moved to its Purl Street site in 1893. E.W. Walker and Company (53093) manufactured wood pumps and wheelbarrows, the Nash, Knox, and Hubbell Company (53063) manufactured tables, the Goshen Churn and Ladder Company (53092) manufactured lawn swings and stepladders, and the Thomas-Albright Company (53126) manufactured hydraulic presses.

Oil lamps originally lit the streets of Goshen. They were replaced by gas produced at the Goshen Gas Light and Fuel Company in 1874. In 1887, the city contracted with the Goshen Electric Light and Power Company to provide electric lighting for city streets and the city bought the system two years later.

Streetcar service came to Goshen in 1896. J. J. Burns was the promoter and principal stockholder of the Indiana Electric Railway. Burns designed and operated the Cosmo Buttermilk Soap Company, built the same year (53039). The Indiana Electric Railway ran from Burns' factory south to Fleetwood Park, which was renamed Burns Park. The steam boilers at the Cosmo Buttermilk Soap Company, later the headquarters of the Chase Bag Company, provided the electricity for the streetcars. Service between Goshen and Elkhart began in 1898 after Burns purchased the Citizens' Street Railway of Elkhart. The Winona Interurban Railway provided service from Goshen to towns south beginning in 1906.

Early Goshen churches include St. James Episcopal Church, built in 1861, and the First Presbyterian Church, built two years later. Both congregations now occupy newer buildings. Architect Cass Chapman of Chicago designed the First Methodist Episcopal Church (51549), as well as the John Lesh House (51056) and the J. A. S. Mitchell House (51543). Also of Chicago, the architectural firm of Patton and Miller designed the Goshen Public Library (51554), the state's first Carnegie library. Patton and Miller were also responsible for the Goshen High School (51548), the David W. Neidig House, and the courthouse's wings and tower (51024).

## GOSHEN SCATTERED SITES (53001-244)

**No. Rtg. Description**

**001 C House;** 309 Hackett Rd.; American foursquare; c.1915; *Architecture* (243)

**002 C Kunderd Gladiolus Memorial Marker;** US 33; *Horticulture* (243)

**003 C House;** US 33; English cottage; c.1940; *Architecture* (243)

**004 C House;** 1003 Greene Rd.; Cape Cod; c.1945; *Architecture* (243)

**005 C Studebaker Cemetery;** 1108 Jed Ln.; Unknown date; Religion (243)

**006 C County Bridge No. 402;** Indiana Ave. over Rock Run Creek; 1961; *Engineering, Transportation* (243)

53017 Walnut Hill was the name given to this property in the mid-1800s. The current 1903 house is an eclectic mix of Romanesque Revival, Neoclassical, and Prairie influences. Today it houses the Fourth Freedom Forum.

**007 C House;** 615 W Wilden Ave.; Gable-front; c.1945; *Architecture* (243)

**008 C House;** 301 W Wilden Ave.; T-plan; c.1870; *Architecture* (243)

**009 C House;** 416 N 5th St.; c.1930; Outbuilding: garage; *Architecture* (243)

**010 C House;** 206 W Wilden Ave.; Gable-front; c.1900; *Architecture* (243)

**011 C House;** 716 N 5th St.; Gable-front; c.1900; Outbuilding: garage; *Architecture* (243)

**012 C House;** 712 N 5th St.; Gable-front; c.1900; Outbuilding: shed; *Architecture* (243)

**013 C House;** 709 N 5th St.; Gable-front; c.1900; *Architecture* (243)

**014 C House;** 713 N 5th St.; Gable-front; c.1900; *Architecture* (243)

**015 C House;** 708 N Main St.; Gable-front; c.1900; *Architecture* (243)

**016 C House;** 811 Main St.; Cross-gable; c.1920; *Architecture* (243)

**017 O Walnut Hill/Judkins-Abshire House;** 803 N Main St.; Romanesque Revival; 1903 (E. Hill Turnock, architect); Outbuildings: carriage house, stable; *Architecture* (243)

**018 C House;** 803 Queen St.; T-plan; c.1890; Outbuilding: shed; *Architecture* (243)

**019 C House;** 207 Oakridge Ave.; T-plan; c.1900; Outbuilding: garage; *Architecture* (243)

**020 C House;** 218 Queen St.; Gable-front; c.1900; *Architecture* (243)

**021 C House;** 316 Wilden Ave.; T-plan; c.1880; *Architecture* (243)

**022 C Old County Bridge No. 401;** Over Rock Run Creek; Warren pony truss; c.1890; *Engineering, Transportation* (243)

**023 C Oakridge Cemetery;** Wilden Ave. & Indiana Ave.; c.1831-present; *Religion* (243)

**024 C Railroad Bridge;** Over Elkhart River; Plate girder; *Engineering, Exploration/Settlement, Transportation* (243)

**025 C Office Building;** 1715 Elkhart Rd.; Classical Revival; c.1950; *Architecture, Commerce* (243)

**026 C Farm;** 2303 Bashon Rd.; Colonial Revival; c.1880; Outbuildings: chicken house, dairy barn; *Agriculture, Architecture* (243)

**027 C House;** 2208 Bashon Rd.; Minimal traditional; c.1950; *Architecture* (243)

**028 C House;** 605 N Greene Rd.; Lazy-T; c.1880; *Architecture* (243)

**029 O House;** 409 N Greene Rd.; Italianate; c.1870; *Architecture* (243)

**030 C House;** 306 N Greene Rd.; Craftsman; c.1920; *Architecture* (243)

**031 C Dunkard Brethren Church;** Greene Rd.; Gable-front; c.1928; *Architecture, Ethnic Heritage, Religion* (243)

53029 This outstanding Italianate house features overhanging eaves supported by paired brackets, paired segmental-arch window openings and a front porch supported by fluted Ionic columns.

**53039** The Cosmo Buttermilk Soap Company/Chase Bag Company is a significant early industrial resource in Goshen.

**032 C Commercial Building;** 1501 Elkhart Rd.; Art Moderne; c.1950; *Architecture, Commerce* (243)

**033 C House;** 503 Riverside Blvd.; Lazy-T; c.1890; *Architecture* (243)

**034 C House;** 1311 Cosmo St.; Craftsman; c.1920; *Architecture* (243)

**035 C House;** 1307 Division St.; Gable-front; c.1890; *Architecture* (243)

**036 C House;** 1202 Cosmo St.; California bungalow; c.1920; *Architecture* (243)

**037 C House;** 1207 Division St.; Ranch; c.1940; *Architecture* (243)

**038 C House;** 1102 Division St.; Western bungalow; c.1915; *Architecture* (243)

**039 O Cosmo Buttermilk Soap Company/ Chase Bag Company;** Chicago Ave.; Italianate; 1896; Outbuildings: blacksmith shop, log cabin, smokestack, studio; *Architecture, Industry* (243)

**040 O Bridge;** Indiana Ave. over Elkhart River; Iron truss; 1898; *Engineering, Transportation* (243)

**041 C County Bridge No. 405;** N 1st St. over Rock Run Creek; 1963; *Engineering, Transportation* (243)

**042 C House;** 219 Citizens Ave.; California bungalow; c.1935; Outbuilding: garage; *Architecture* (243)

**043 C House;** 620 N 3rd St.; T-plan; c.1900; *Architecture* (243)

**044 C House;** 622 Main St.; American foursquare; c.1920; *Architecture* (243)

**045 C House;** 602 N 5th St.; Gable-front; c.1880; *Architecture* (243)

**046 C House;** 309 Oakridge Ave.; Cape Cod; c.1945; *Architecture* (243)

**047 C House;** 526 N 6th St.; American foursquare; c.1920; Outbuilding: chicken house; *Architecture* (243)

**048 C House;** 401 Middlebury St.; Gable-front; c.1900; *Architecture* (243)

**049 C House;** 507 Middlebury St.; American foursquare; c.1900; *Architecture* (243)

**050 C House;** 514 N 8th St.; Minimal traditional; c.1940; Outbuilding: garage; *Architecture* (243)

**051 C House;** 518 Middlebury St.; Gabled-ell; c.1890; *Architecture* (243)

**052 C House;** 301 Middlebury St.; English cottage; c.1920; *Architecture* (243)

**053 C North Side Fire Station;** Middlebury St.; Art Deco; 1949; *Architecture* (243)

**054 C House;** 205 Middlebury St.; Lazy-T; c.1880; *Architecture* (243)

**055 C House;** 203 Middlebury St.; Dutch Colonial Revival; c.1915; *Architecture* (243)

**056 C House;** 516 N 5th St.; Gable-front; c.1890; Outbuilding: shed; *Architecture* (243)

**057 C House;** 513 N 5th St.; Gable-front; c.1890; Outbuilding: shed; *Architecture* (243)

**058 C St. Mark's Methodist Episcopal Church;** 502 N Main St.; Tudor Revival/Arts & Crafts; 1927/1969/1994; *Architecture, Religion* (243)

**059 C House;** 513 Main St.; Dormer-front bungalow; c.1920; Outbuilding: garage; *Architecture* (243)

**53078** Chamberlain Elementry School features a symmetrical plan and a gabled central entry with Palladian windows.

**53119** This Queen Anne house retains original clapboard and wood shake siding, original double-hung sash windows and a decorative multi-pane window, and a porch supported by turned posts.

**060 C House;** 601 Main St.; Gable-front; c.1890; *Architecture* (243)

**061 C House;** 606 N 3rd St.; Gable-front; c.1890; *Architecture* (243)

**062 C House;** 211 Mill St.; California bungalow; c.1920; *Architecture* (243)

**063 C Nash, Knox, and Hubbell Company;** Mill St.; 19th century functional; c.1875; *Architecture, Industry* (243)

**064 C House;** 430 N 1st St.; Lazy-T; c.1870; *Architecture* (243)

**065 C House;** 424 N 1st St.; Gable-front; c.1915; *Architecture* (243)

**066 C House;** 415 N 1st St.; Italianate cube; c.1880; *Architecture* (243)

**067 C House;** N Chicago Ave.; Lazy-T; c.1880; *Architecture* (243)

**068 C House;** 207 N Indiana Ave.; American foursquare; c.1920; *Architecture* (243)

**069 C Commercial Building;** Pike St. and Denver St.; Parapet-front; c.1930; *Architecture* (243)

**070 N Pike Street Bridge;** Pike Street over Elkhart River; Concrete arch; 1926 (William S. Moore, designer/H.H. Stoddard, builder); *Engineering, Transportation* (243)

**071  C  House;** 301 N 1st St.; Craftsman; c.1920; *Architecture* (243)

**072  C  House;** 316 N 2nd St.; Gable-front; c.1890; *Architecture* (243)

**073  C  House;** 109 E Pike St.; T-plan; c.1880; *Architecture* (243)

**074  N  Goshen Water Works;** 308 N 5th St.; Art Deco; 1930/1949; Outbuildings: pump-houses, sheds, standpipe; *Architecture, Engineering* (243)

**075  C  House;** 319 N 5th St.; T-plan; c.1915; *Architecture* (243)

**076  C  House;** 423 N 5th St.; Gable-front; c.1900; Outbuilding: garage; *Architecture* (243)

**077  C  House;** 425 N 5th St.; Hall-and-parlor; c.1900; *Architecture* (243)

**078  N  Chamberlain Elementary School;** 5th St. & Middlebury St.; Classical Revival; c.1915; *Architecture, Education* (243)

**079  C  House;** 411 Center St.; Gabled-ell; c.1890; *Architecture* (243)

**080  C  House;** 515 Center St.; Hall-and-parlor; c.1890; *Architecture* (243)

**081  C  House;** 2206 E Lincoln Ave.; Craftsman; c.1920; *Architecture* (243)

**082  C  House;** 209 S 22nd St.; T-plan; c.1890; *Architecture* (243)

**53172  This American foursquare features original clapboard siding and wood windows, a full width porch with tapered posts on brick piers, and flared eaves.**

**53173  This dormer-front bungalow retains original clapboard siding and double-hung sash windows, knee braces beneath overhanging eaves, and an integral porch supported by wood piers on brick bases.**

**083  C  House;** 927 E Lincoln Ave.; Central-passage/Greek Revival; c.1850; *Architecture* (243)

**084  C  Commercial Building;** 921 Steury Ave.; Parapet-front; c.1940 (Cecil West, builder); *Architecture, Commerce* (243)

**085  C  House;** 505 Cross St.; Gabled-ell; c.1880; *Architecture* (243)

**086  C  House;** 413 Cross St.; T-plan; c.1870; *Architecture* (243)

**087  C  House;** 214 Crescent St.; T-plan; c.1880; *Architecture* (243)

**088  C  House;** 301 Crescent St.; Upright-and-wing/ Italianate; c.1880; *Architecture* (243)

**089  C  House;** 209-11 Crescent St.; Gothic Revival; c.1870; *Architecture* (243)

**090  C  Farm;** 122 Crescent St.; Gabled-ell; c.1850; Outbuilding: English barn; *Agriculture, Architecture* (243)

**091  C  House;** 406 Cross St.; Gable-front; c.1890; *Architecture* (243)

**092  C  Goshen Churn and Ladder Company;** E Lincoln Ave.; 19th century functional; c.1890; *Architecture, Industry* (243)

**093  N  E.W. Walker and Company;** 521 E Lincoln Ave.; 19th century functional; c.1860; *Architecture, Industry* (243)

**094  N  Lincoln Avenue Bridge;** W Lincoln Ave. over Elkhart River; Concrete arch; 1927 (William Moore, designer/Rieth-Riley, builder); *Engineering, Transportation* (243)

**095  C  House;** 903 W Lincoln Ave.; Lazy-T; c.1890; *Architecture* (243)

**096  C  House;** 1011 W Lincoln Ave.; American foursquare; c.1920; Outbuilding: garage; *Architecture* (243)

**097  C  House;** 1101 West Ave.; Dormer-front bungalow; c.1920; *Architecture* (243)

**098  C  House;** 1201 Hickory St.; American foursquare; c.1915; *Architecture* (243)

**099  C  Farm;** 328 Dewey Ave.; Gable-front; c.1910; Outbuildings: English barn, garage; *Agriculture, Architecture* (243)

**100  C  House;** 1211 Berkey Ave.; Western bungalow; c.1925; *Architecture* (243)

**101  C  House;** 517 Winter Ave.; Western bungalow; c.1925; *Architecture* (243)

**102  C  House;** 1301 Berkey Ave.; c.1880; *Architecture* (243)

**103  C  House;** 1307 Berkey Ave.; Upright-and-wing; c.1880; *Architecture* (243)

**104  C  House;** 1401 Berkey Ave.; California bungalow; c.1920; *Architecture* (243)

**105  C  House;** 1405 Berkey Ave.; English cottage; c.1940; *Architecture* (243)

**106  C  School;** 211 Berkey Ave.; Neoclassical; c.1910; *Architecture, Education* (243)

**107  C  Barn;** Greene Rd. & Berkey Ave.; English barn; c.1930; *Agriculture, Architecture* (243)

**108  C  House;** 1402 Berkey Ave.; 1 ½ I-house; c.1870; *Architecture* (243)

**109  C  House;** 1310 Berkey Ave.; T-plan; c.1880; *Architecture* (243)

**110  C  House;** 1214 Berkey Ave.; Dutch Colonial Revival; c.1915; *Architecture* (243)

**53177  This worker housing complex is a collection of eleven single-room boarding houses adjacent to the historically industrial area of Goshen.**

**53180** This bungalow has elements of the Craftsman style including knee braces beneath overhanging eaves, double-hung sash windows, and a gabled front porch.

**111**  **C**  **House;** 1210 Berkey Ave.; T-plan; c.1885; *Architecture* (243)

**112**  **C**  **West Goshen Church of the Brethren;** 1200 Berkey Ave.; Gothic Revival; 1886/ 1924/1955/1999; *Architecture, Religion* (243)

**113**  **C**  **Rieth-Riley Construction Company;** 311 W Madison St.; Parapet-front; c.1930; *Architecture, Commerce* (243)

**114**  **C**  **Hawks Electric Company Power Plant;** Hydraulic Canal; Gable-front; c.1910; *Architecture, Industry* (243)

**115**  **C**  **Hawks Electric Company Power Plant;** 315 W Washington St.; 20th century functional; c.1917; *Architecture, Industry* (243)

**116**  **C**  **House;** 111 S 8th St.; Upright-and-wing; c.1870; *Architecture* (243)

**117**  **C**  **House;** 411 E Washington St.; Gabled-ell; c.1870; *Architecture* (243)

**118**  **C**  **House;** 412 E Washington St.; Bungalow; c.1925; *Architecture* (243)

**119**  **N**  **House;** 416 E Washington St.; Queen Anne; c.1880; *Architecture* (243)

**120**  **C**  **House;** 212 S 8th St.; T-plan; c.1880; *Architecture* (243)

**121**  **C**  **House;** 218 S 8th St.; Craftsman; c.1910; *Architecture* (243)

**122**  **C**  **House;** 213 S 9th St.; Gable-front; c.1870; *Architecture* (243)

**123**  **N**  **House;** 217 S 9th St.; Double-pile; c.1870; *Architecture* (243)

**124**  **C**  **House;** 224 S 9th St.; Upright-and-wing; c.1900; *Architecture* (243)

**125**  **C**  **House;** 206 S 10th St.; Gable-front; c.1870; *Architecture* (243)

**126**  **N**  **Thomas-Albright Company;** 814 E Jefferson St.; Parapet-front; c.1911; *Architecture, Industry* (243)

**127**  **C**  **House;** 306 S 10th St.; Upright-and-wing; c.1880; *Architecture* (243)

**128**  **C**  **House;** 516 E Jefferson St.; Upright-and-wing; c.1900; *Architecture* (243)

**129**  **C**  **House;** 306 S 8th St.; California bungalow; c.1930; *Architecture* (243)

**130**  **C**  **House;** 311 S 8th St.; Dormer-front bungalow; c.1920; *Architecture* (243)

**131**  **C**  **General Crafts Corporation;** US 33; Gable-front; c.1890; *Architecture, Industry* (243)

**132**  **C**  **Goshen High School;** US 33; Collegiate Gothic; c.1920/1954; *Architecture, Education* (243)

**133**  **C**  **Hettrich Manufacturing Company;** 402 E Madison St.; 20th century functional; c.1937; *Architecture, Industry* (243)

**134**  **C**  **County Bridge No. 400;** E Monroe St. over Rock Run Creek; 1960; *Engineering, Transportation* (243)

**135**  **N**  **House;** 1809 E Monroe St.; Queen Anne; c.1880; *Architecture* (243)

**53185** This house is an unusual example of Craftsman detailing. It features wood shingle siding, knee braces beneath overhanging eaves, and a shed dormer with ribbon windows.

**53186** This Tudor Revival house features brick walls with clapboard siding on the gable ends and half-timbering on the cross gable.

**136**  **C**  **Fort Beane Historical Marker;** US 33; 1932; *Exploration/Settlement, Social History* (243)

**137**  **C**  **House;** 1102 Reynolds St.; California bungalow; c.1925; *Architecture* (243)

**138**  **C**  **House;** Reynolds St.; Colonial Revival; c.1930; *Architecture* (243)

**139**  **O**  **Goshen Sash & Door Company;** Purl St. & S 9th St.; 19th century industrial; 1893; *Architecture, Industry* (243)

**140**  **C**  **House;** 418 S 8th St.; English cottage; c.1940; *Architecture* (243)

**141**  **C**  **House;** 420 S 8th St.; Colonial Revival; c.1890; *Architecture* (243)

**142**  **C**  **House;** 418 S 8th St.; Dutch Colonial Revival; c.1890; *Architecture* (243)

**143**  **C**  **House;** 514 S 8th St.; Dutch Colonial Revival; c.1900; *Architecture* (243)

**144**  **C**  **House;** E Purl St.; Craftsman; c.1920; *Architecture* (243)

**145**  **C**  **House;** 601 Emerson St.; T-plan; c.1880; *Architecture* (243)

**146**  **C**  **House;** 606 S 3rd St.; Dormer-front bungalow; c.1915; *Architecture* (243)

**147**  **C**  **House;** 610 S 3rd St.; Bungalow; c.1925; Outbuilding: garage; *Architecture* (243)

**53192** This dormer-front bungalow has Craftsman styling apparent in its overhanging eaves, exposed rafter tails, and tapered wood piers on brick bases supporting the integral porch.

**148** **C** **House;** 615 S 3rd St.; American foursquare; c.1915; *Architecture* (243)

**149** **C** **House;** 616 S 3rd St.; American foursquare; c.1915; *Architecture* (243)

**150** **C** **House;** 609 Emerson St.; T-plan; c.1870; *Architecture* (243)

**151** **C** **House;** 613 S 8th St.; T-plan; c.1880; *Architecture* (243)

**152** **C** **House;** 623 S 8th St.; Lazy-T; c.1890; *Architecture* (243)

**153** **C** **House;** 708 S 8th St.; Craftsman; c.1910; *Architecture* (243)

**154** **C** **Western Rubber Company/Ariel Cycles;** Douglas St. & S 9th St.; 19th century industrial; c.1890/c.1930/1967; *Architecture, Industry* (243)

**155** **C** **House;** 818 S 8th St.; California bungalow; c.1920; *Architecture* (243)

**156** **C** **House;** 806 S 8th St.; Gable-front; c.1890; *Architecture* (243)

**157** **C** **House;** 807 S 8th St.; Gable-front; c.1870; *Architecture* (243)

**158** **C** **House;** 415 E Douglas St.; Colonial Revival; c.1910; Outbuilding: garage; *Architecture* (243)

**159** **C** **House;** 708 Emerson St.; Craftsman; c.1920; *Architecture* (243)

**160** **C** **House;** 702 S 3rd St.; Upright-and-wing; c.1870; *Architecture* (243)

**161** **C** **House;** 711 S 3rd St.; Gable-front; c.1880; *Architecture* (243)

**162** **C** **House;** 312 W Douglas St.; Gable-front; c.1880; *Architecture* (243)

**163** **C** **West Goshen Cemetery;** Berkey Ave.; c.1842-present; *Exploration/Settlement, Religion* (243)

**164** **C** **Farm;** 1215 Indiana Ave.; Lazy-T; c.1870; Outbuildings: shed, transverse-frame barn; *Agriculture, Architecture* (243)

**165** **C** **House;** 805 Emerson St.; T-plan; c.1890; *Architecture* (243)

**166** **C** **House;** 210 W Plymouth Ave.; T-plan; c.1880; *Architecture* (243)

**167** **C** **House;** 901 S Main St.; Gable-front; c.1890; *Architecture* (243)

**168** **C** **House;** 918 S Main St.; Lazy-T; c.1890; *Architecture* (243)

**169** **C** **House;** 915 S 7th St.; American foursquare; c.1920; *Architecture* (243)

**170** **C** **House;** 901 S 7th St.; Colonial Revival; c.1910; *Architecture* (243)

**171** **C** **House;** S 7th St.; Colonial Revival; c.1915; *Architecture* (243)

**172** **N** **House;** 924 S 7th St.; American foursquare; c.1915; *Architecture* (243)

**173** **N** **House;** 921 Lincoln Way East; Dormer-front bungalow/Craftsman; c.1920; *Architecture* (243)

**174** **C** **House;** Lincoln Way East; Gable-front; c.1880; *Architecture* (243)

**53197** This California bungalow has Craftsman detailing, including knee braces beneath overhanging eaves, a partially integral porch, and original windows.

**53201** This Colonial Revival house is a well detailed example of the style, displaying a slate roof with three gabled dormers, a central entry with elaborate surround, and broad cornice.

**175** **C** **Industrial Building;** E Jackson St.; 20th century functional; c.1930; *Architecture, Industry* (243)

**176** **C** **House;** 1021 S 9th St.; Dutch Colonial Revival; c.1930; *Architecture* (243)

**177** **N** **Worker Housing Complex;** 1013 S 9th St.; Single pen; 1946; *Architecture* (243)

**178** **C** **House;** 1004 S 8th St.; Midwest box/Colonial Revival; c.1930; *Architecture* (243)

**179** **C** **House;** 1104 S 8th St.; Dormer-front bungalow; c.1925; *Architecture* (243)

**180** **N** **House;** 1106 S 8th St.; Bungalow/Craftsman; c.1925; *Architecture* (243)

**181** **N** **House;** 1119 S 8th St.; Free Classic; c.1885; *Architecture* (243)

**182** **C** **House;** 1005 S 8th St.; Dormer-front bungalow/Craftsman; c.1925; *Architecture* (243)

**183** **C** **House;** 1014 S 7th St.; American foursquare; c.1915; *Architecture* (243)

**184** **C** **House;** 1018 S 7th St.; California bungalow/Craftsman; c.1915; *Architecture* (243)

**53210** Parkside Elementry School features brick walls, two-pane windows with limestone sills and lintels, and arched entry openings with an elaborate carved decoration above the main entry.

53219 This Free Classic house retains original clapboard siding and wood windows, cornice returns, and a full-width porch supported by battered piers on brick bases.

185 N **House;** S 7th St.; Craftsman; c.1925; *Architecture* (243)

186 N **House;** 1104 S 7th St.; Tudor Revival; c.1925; Outbuilding: garage; *Architecture* (243)

187 N **House;** 1112 S 7th St.; English cottage; c.1925; *Architecture* (243)

188 C **House;** 1116 S 7th St.; Dormer-front bungalow/Craftsman; c.1920; *Architecture* (243)

189 C **House;** 1120 S 7th St.; English cottage; c.1920; *Architecture* (243)

53227 This Free Classic house features clapboard and wood shingle siding, historic windows, and a porch with square posts.

190 C **House;** 1021 S 7th St.; California bungalow; c.1925; Outbuilding: garage; *Architecture* (243)

191 C **House;** 1019 S 7th St.; American four-square; c.1920; *Architecture* (243)

192 N **House;** 1015 S 7th St.; Dormer-front bungalow; c.1925; Outbuilding: garage; *Architecture* (243)

193 C **House;** 106 W Jackson St.; Gable-front/ Free Classic; c.1890; *Architecture* (243)

194 C **House;** 112 W Jackson St.; California bungalow; c.1920; *Architecture* (243)

195 C **House;** Hydraulic Canal; Mission Revival; c.1930; *Architecture* (243)

196 C **House;** Burdick St.; Mission Revival; c.1930; Outbuilding: garage; *Architecture* (243)

197 N **House;** Murray St.; California bungalow/ Craftsman; c.1915; *Architecture* (243)

198 N **Murray Street Bridge;** Murray St. over Hydraulic Canal; Pratt pony truss; 1909; *Engineering, Transportation* (243)

199 C **House;** 212 Murray St.; Free Classic; c.1890; *Architecture* (243)

200 C **House;** 1211 Wilson Ave.; Western bungalow/Craftsman; c.1920; *Architecture* (243)

53233 The 1854 Dierdorf House exhibits clapboard siding with decorative fishscale shingles in the gable ends, a slate roof, and historic windows.

53234 The Smoker Farm is home to this c.1870 Italianate house. John Smoker, who lived in the house as a child, started Smoker Craft Inc. in New Paris. The house is now home to the Brick House Restaurant.

201 N **House;** 1245 Wilson Ave.; Colonial Revival; c.1940; *Architecture* (243)

202 C **House;** 1307 Wilson Ave.; Dormer-front bungalow; c.1920; *Architecture* (243)

203 C **House;** 1309 Wilson Ave.; California bungalow; c.1930; *Architecture* (243)

204 N **House;** 1216 Wilson Ave.; English cottage; c.1930; *Architecture* (243)

205 N **House;** 1115 S Main St.; Lazy-T; c.1870; *Architecture* (243)

206 C **House;** S Main St.; Dormer-front bungalow/Craftsman; c.1920; *Architecture* (243)

207 C **House;** 1121 S Main St.; Bungalow/Craftsman; c.1920; *Architecture* (243)

208 C **House;** 1301 S Main St.; Gabled-ell; c.1880; *Architecture* (243)

209 N **House;** S Main St.; Craftsman; c.1920; *Architecture* (243)

210 N **Parkside Elementary School;** S Main St.; Collegiate Gothic; c.1930; *Architecture, Education* (243)

211 C **House;** 1306 S Main St.; Bungalow; c.1915; *Architecture* (243)

212 C **House;** 1323 S 8th St.; Italianate; c.1880; *Architecture* (243)

213 C **House;** 1325 8th St.; Italianate cube; c.1880; *Architecture* (243)

214 C **House;** 1407 S 8th St.; Free Classic; c.1890; *Architecture* (243)

**215  C  House;** 1320 S 8th St.; Dutch Colonial Revival; 1925/1947; *Architecture* (243)

**216  N  House;** S 8th St.; Colonial Revival; c.1915; *Architecture* (243)

**217  N  House;** 1406 S 8th St.; Colonial Revival; c.1930; *Architecture* (243)

**218  C  House;** 1502 S 8th St.; California bungalow; c.1925; *Architecture* (243)

**219  N  House;** 1504 S 8th St.; Free Classic; c.1915; *Architecture* (243)

**220  C  House;** 1508 S 8th St.; American foursquare; c.1915; *Architecture* (243)

**221  N  House;** 1602 S 8th St.; Craftsman; c.1925; Outbuilding: garage; *Architecture* (243)

**222  C  House;** 1610 S 8th St.; American foursquare; c.1925; *Architecture* (243)

**223  C  House;** 1626 S 8th St.; American foursquare/Free Classic; c.1915; Outbuilding: garage; *Architecture* (243)

**224  C  House;** 1628 S 8th St.; Gable-front/Free Classic; c.1890; *Architecture* (243)

**225  C  House;** 1615 S 8th St.; English cottage; c.1925; *Architecture* (243)

**226  C  Kenwood House;** 1613 S 8th St.; Queen Anne; c.1880; Outbuilding: garage; *Architecture* (243)

**227  N  House;** 1505 S 8th St.; Free Classic; c.1915; *Architecture* (243)

53237  The striking groin-vaulted roof of this Italianate Cube makes it one of the most distinctive buildings in the county.

53238  This Free Classic house features original clapboard siding, historic windows including a Palladian window in the gable end, and a full width porch with stone walls and thin columns.

**228  N  House;** 100 E Lafayette St.; Colonial Revival; c.1935; *Architecture* (243)

**229  C  House;** 1613 S Main St.; Gable-front/Free Classic; c.1915; *Architecture* (243)

**230  C  House;** 1637 S Main St.; California bungalow/Craftsman; c.1925; *Architecture* (243)

**231  N  House;** Gra-Roy Dr.; English cottage; c.1935; *Architecture* (243)

**232  C  Dierdorf Cemetery;** S Main St.; 1838-1893; *Exploration/Settlement, Religion* (243)

**233  O  Dierdorf Farm;** 64439 Dierdorf Rd.; Crossplan; 1854; Outbuildings: English barn, shed, windmill; *Agriculture, Architecture* (243)

**234  N  Smoker Farm;** 16820 CR 38; Italianate; c.1870; Outbuildings: Sweitzer barn, silo; *Agriculture, Architecture* (243)

**235  C  Farm;** 17510 CR 38; Italianate; c.1870; Outbuildings: dairy barn, silos; *Agriculture, Architecture* (243)

**236  C  Elkhart Prairie Cemetery;** CR 38; c.1855-present; *Exploration/Settlement, Religion* (243)

**237  O  House;** 2309 S Main St.; Italianate; c.1860; Outbuilding: fence; *Architecture* (243)

**238  N  House;** 2401 S Main St.; Free Classic; c.1890; *Architecture* (243)

53241  The Major John W. Violett House is significant not only for its Italianate architecture, but also for landscape features including a fountain, grotto, and arbor.

**239  N  House;** 2510 S Main St.; English cottage; c.1935; *Architecture* (243)

**240  N  House;** S Main St.; Colonial Revival; c.1900; *Architecture* (243)

**241  O  Major John W. Violett House;** 2612 S Main St.; Italianate; c.1850; Outbuilding: garage; *Architecture, Landscape Architecture* (243)

**242  C  House;** 2706 S Main St.; English cottage; c.1945; Outbuilding: garage; *Architecture* (243)

**243  C  Violett Cemetery;** 2818 Violett Rd.; c.1839-present; *Exploration/Settlement, Religion* (243)

**244  O  William N. Violett House;** 3004 S Main St.; Italianate; c.1854; Outbuilding: garage, shed; *Architecture* (243) **NR**

53244  The William N. Violett House is individually listed in the National Register of Historic Places. Today it houses the Community Church of Waterford offices.

# Waterford Scattered Sites (54001-010)

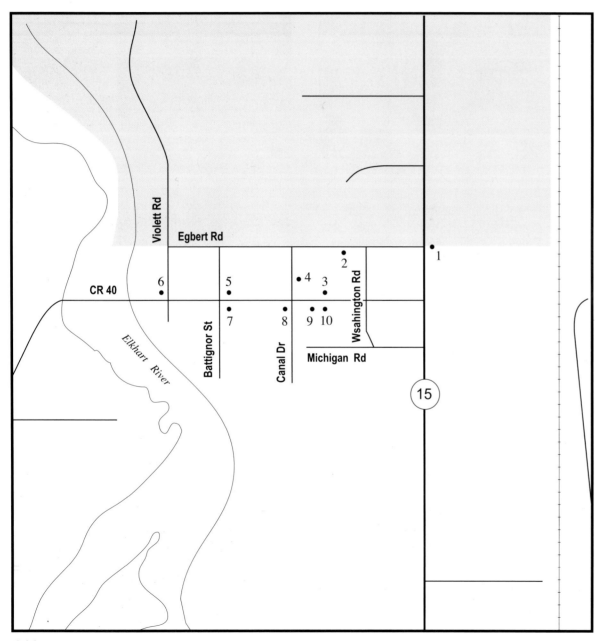

In 1833, William Layton Baker, one of the area's earliest settlers, built a grist mill on the eastern side of the Elkhart River in what is now Waterford, and a log house to the south (54006). Soon after, settlers constructed a dam across the river and a race along the river's eastern side. Another race was built on the western side of the river to serve new industries there. Cephas Hawks, who had come to the area with his family from Michigan, bought the grist mill in 1835. The following year, settlers built a school and a bridge over the Elkhart River at Elkhart Street (Egbert Road). Hawks, his son, and David Ballentine laid out Waterford in 1838 between the Elkhart River and the Logansport and White Pigeon Road (State Road 15).

The town, named after a ford across the Elkhart River, was a thriving community by the 1840s. There were several mills, businesses, and general stores. Several of the businesses, including a saw mill, distillery, woolen mill, and general store, were operated by the firm of Cephas Hawks and Sons. In 1847, the original grist mill was replaced with a larger mill.

The 1842 First Methodist Church was the first church in town. It was converted into a house in 1926 (54009). Members built the Waterford Christian Church in 1853 (54001). A covered bridge once spanned the river at Main Street (County Road 40), but was replaced by a metal truss bridge in 1901 that has also been replaced. Between 1854 and 1904, the town had a post office and was known as Waterford Mills. In 1868, upon the completion of the hydraulic canal in Goshen, Waterford's grist mill was dismantled and reassembled in Goshen where subsequent additions were made to it. Other businesses moved to Goshen and the dam at Waterford was dismantled.

The Warsaw, Goshen, and White Pigeon Railroad (later called the Cincinnati, Wabash, and Michigan Railroad), completed its line on the eastern side of Waterford in 1870 and built a depot. A waiting station was built along the Winona Interurban Railway, which ran along the western side of the railroad. However, there were no industries to serve and Waterford became a sort of early suburb to the county seat.

## WATERFORD SCATTERED SITES (54001-010)

**No. Rtg. Description**

**001  O   Waterford Christian Church;** 65532 SR 15; Gable-front/Greek Revival; 1853; *Architecture, Religion* (243)

**002  C   House;** 208 Egbert Rd.; Gable-front; c.1860; *Architecture* (243)

**003  C   House;** 19119 CR 40; Pyramidal-roof cottage; c.1900; Outbuildings: garage, workshop; *Architecture* (243)

**004  C   House;** 19147 CR 40; Western bungalow; c.1920; Outbuilding: carriage house; *Architecture* (424)

**005  C   Hawks House;** 19215 CR 40; Gable-front; c.1845; *Architecture* (243)

**006  O   William Layton Baker Log House;** 19307 CR 40; Single-pen; c.1834 (William Layton Baker, builder); *Architecture, Exploration/Settlement* (243)

**007  C   House;** 19220 CR 40; Gable-front; c.1870; Outbuilding: chicken house; *Architecture* (243)

**008  C   House;** 19164 CR 40; I-house; c.1870; Outbuildings: garages; *Architecture* (243)

**009  C   First Methodist Church;** 19132 CR 40; Gable-front/Greek Revival; 1842/1926; Outbuilding: garage; *Architecture, Religion* (243)

**010  C   House;** 19122 CR 40; California bungalow; c.1920; Outbuilding: garage; *Architecture* (243)

54003  This modest house is a good example of the pyramidal-roof cottage type.

54006  William Layton Baker built this log house south of his grist mill. Cephas Hawks bought the house in 1837.

54009  The former First Methodist Church dates to 1842 and was the first church in Waterford. In 1900 it was discontinued as a church; it sat vacant and was later used as a school before Ira Bechtel remodeled it into a house in 1926.

54001  The Waterford Christian Church's congregation dates to 1842 in Benton. This building dates to 1853 and once featured a belfry. Today it retains Greek Revival detailing, including its dentilated frieze with corner returns and original windows.

54005  The Hawks House dates to c.1845 and features brick walls with a wide, plain frieze band, a full-width porch with brick piers, and some original windows.

The First Methodist Church, shown with its steeple, date unknown. *Photo taken from* Waterford from Then to Now *by Lowell Bechtel*

167

# Harrison Township (55001-061)

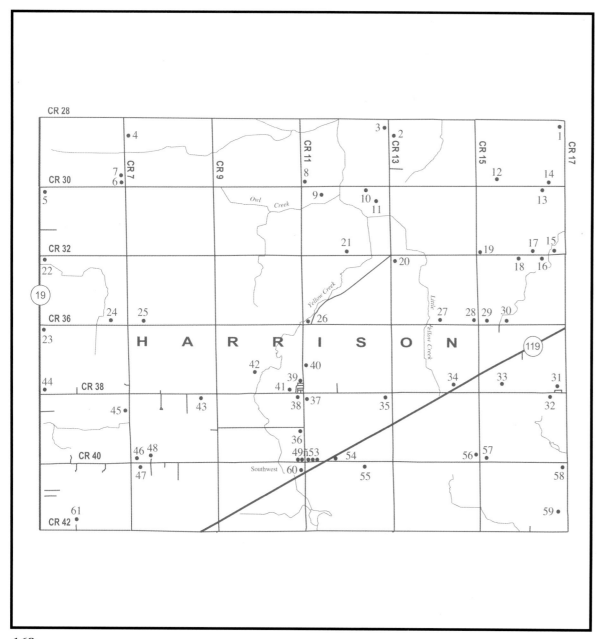

Harrison Township is located in the central part of Elkhart County. Daniel Stutsman arrived in 1831 and is the first reported settler in the area. By 1836, approximately ten families had settled in the area and every eligible voter voted for William Henry Harrison in that year's presidential election. Thus, when Harrison Township was divided out of Elkhart Township later that year, the county named it after Harrison.

Two small villages developed in the township. Harrison was located near the current intersection of County Roads 11 and 38. Little is known of the village and nothing of it remains there today. Two churches and three cemeteries are located at the intersection.

The second village, located at the intersection of County Roads 11 and 40, is now known as Southwest. Some sources claim that Southwest received its name for its location in relation to Goshen, but this cannot be verified. Today, Southwest consists of several houses and a cemetery.

A collection of small schoolhouses attest to the early importance of education in the township. There were once nine schools evenly distributed throughout the township, of which several still stand (60006, 60026, 60028). Today's educational needs are met by a modern elementary school, nearby high schools, and regional Old Order Mennonite schools. Harrison Township has a large Old Order Mennonite population who primarily cultivate the land. Several Old Order Mennonite churches are located in the area and horse-drawn buggies and bicycles are a common sight on roadways.

## HARRISON TOWNSHIP SCATTERED SITES (55001-061)

**No. Rtg. Description**

**001  C   House;** 61015 CR 17; Lazy-T; c.1880; *Architecture* (210)

**002  C   Moore Farm;** 61336 CR 13; Double-pile; c.1860; Outbuildings: Sweitzer farm, silo, wood shed; *Agriculture, Architecture* (210)

**003  C   Farm;** CR 13; Lazy-T; c.1870; Outbuilding: English barn; *Agriculture, Architecture* (210)

**004  C   Bemiller Farm;** CR 7; California bungalow; c.1935; Outbuildings: bank/basement barn, transverse-frame barn; *Agriculture, Architecture* (210)

**005  C   Farm;** 27919 CR 30; American foursquare; c.1908; Outbuilding: bank/basement barn; *Agriculture, Architecture* (656)

**006  N   Harrison Township District No. 3 School;** CR 7; T-plan; 1903 (Alpha B. Culp, builder); *Architecture, Education* (210)

**007  C   House;** 61907 CR 7; Dormer-front bungalow; c.1920; *Architecture* (210)

**008  C   House;** CR 30 & 11; Prairie; c.1925; *Architecture* (210)

**009  N   Murray Farm;** 24770 CR 30; Double-entry cube/Italianate; c.1872; Outbuilding: bank/basement barn; *Agriculture, Architecture* (210)

**010  N   Witmer Log House;** 24320 CR 30; Single-pen/log construction; 1842; *Architecture, Exploration/Settlement* (210)

55009  The Murray Farm includes this c.1872 double-entry Italianate cube house.

55015  The Gorsuch Farm features this c.1861 Italianate cube house.

**011  C   House;** 24100 CR 30; Italianate cube; c.1875; *Architecture* (210)

**012  N   Stutsman House & Cemetery;** 22731 CR 30; Double-pile; c.1872; Cemetery: c.1849-c.1936; *Architecture, Religion* (210)

**013  C   Farm;** 22284 CR 30; California bungalow/Craftsman; c.1920; Outbuildings: English barn, pumphouse; *Agriculture, Architecture* (210)

**014  C   Gunderman House;** 22187 CR 30; American foursquare; c.1915; *Architecture* (210)

**015  N   Gorsuch Farm;** 22121 CR 32; Italianate cube; c.1861; Outbuilding: transverse-frame barn; *Agriculture, Architecture* (210)

**016  N   Hayes House;** 22280 CR 32; Italianate cube; 1862; *Architecture* (210)

**017  C   Farm;** 22393 CR 32; Cape Cod; c.1925; Outbuilding: English barn; *Agriculture, Architecture* (210)

**018  C   Farm;** 22582 CR 32; Double-entry, double-pile; c.1870; Outbuilding: Sweitzer barn; *Agriculture, Architecture* (210)

**019  O   St. John's Lutheran Church & Cemetery;** CR 32; Greek Revival; 1853; Cemetery: c.1853-c.1990; *Architecture, Religion* (210) **NR**

**020  C   Farm;** 63060 CR 13; T-plan; c.1880; Outbuilding: bank/basement barn; *Agriculture, Architecture* (210)

**021  C   House;** 24427 CR 32; Minimal traditional; c.1954; *Architecture* (210)

**022  C   Farm;** 27888 CR 32; Lazy-T/Italianate; c.1890; Outbuildings: bank/basement barn, spring house; *Agriculture, Architecture* (656)

**023  C   Farm;** 27956 CR 36; Lazy-T; c.1880; Outbuilding: English barn; *Agriculture, Architecture* (656)

**024  C   Culp-Loucks Barn;** 27149 CR 36; Sweitzer barn; c.1877 (Henry Culp, builder); *Agriculture, Architecture* (210)

**025  C   Farm;** 27556 CR 36; American foursquare; c.1915; Outbuilding: dairy barn; *Agriculture, Architecture* (210)

**026  O   Harrison Township District No. 5 School;** CR 36 & CR 11; Bell tower front; 1911 (George B. Moyer, builder); *Architecture, Education* (210)

**027  O   House;** 23398 CR 36; Italianate cube; c.1860; *Architecture* (210)

**028  C   School;** 63983 CR 15; T-plan; c.1890/1963; *Architecture, Education* (210)

**029  O   Farm;** 22889 CR 36; Italianate; c.1850; Outbuilding: Sweitzer barn; *Agriculture, Architecture* (210)

**030  C   Barn;** 22659 CR 36; Sweitzer barn; c.1890; *Agriculture, Architecture* (210)

**031  C   Inbody Union Church & Cemetery;** 22111 CR 38; Gable-front; c.1860; Outbuilding: privy; Cemetery: c.1840-c.1999; *Architecture, Exploration/Settlement, Religion* (210)

55019  St. John's Lutheran Church was built in 1853 and is individually listed in the National Register of Historic Places.

**169**

55027 This house is an excellent, intact example of the Italianate cube type.

032 C **Farm;** 22164 CR 38; American foursquare; c.1925; Outbuilding: bank/basement barn; *Agriculture, Architecture* (210)

033 N **Baker Log House;** 22781 CR 38; Continental log house; 1836 (Elias Baker, builder); Outbuildings: guest house, privy, smokehouse, storage building, woodworking shop; *Architecture, Exploration/Settlement* (210)

034 C **Cabin Hill Farm;** SR 119; Lazy-T; c.1880; Outbuildings: bank/basement barn, shed, silo, transverse-frame barns; *Agriculture, Architecture* (210)

035 N **Farm;** CR 38; Italianate; c.1880; Outbuildings: bank/basement barn, silo; *Agriculture, Architecture* (210)

036 C **Yellow Creek Church of the Brethren;** 65575 CR 11; Gable-front; 1867/1969; *Architecture, Religion* (210)

037 C **Old Yellow Creek Cemetery;** CR 11; c.1845-c.1931; *Exploration/Settlement, Religion* (210)

038 C **Yellow Creek Frame Cemetery;** CR 38; c.1881-present; *Religion* (210)

039 C **Yellow Creek Mennonite Church & Cemetery;** 64901 CR 11; Colonial Revival; 1948; Cemetery: c.1884-present; *Architecture, Religion* (210)

040 C **Harrison Chapel Cemetery;** CR 11; c.1837-c.1981; *Exploration/Settlement, Religion* (210)

041 C **Yellow Creek Old Order Mennonite Church;** CR 38; Gable-front; c.1930; Outbuildings: hitching rails, privies, stables, water pump; *Architecture, Religion* (210)

042 C **Miller Cemetery;** CR 38 & CR 9; c.1856-c.1932; *Exploration/Settlement, Religion* (210)

043 C **Farm;** 26188 CR 38; Western bungalow; c.1914; Outbuildings: chicken house, corn crib, English barn; *Agriculture, Architecture* (210)

044 C **Farm;** 64954 SR 19; Lazy-T; c.1860; Outbuildings: house, Sweitzer barn; *Agriculture, Architecture* (656)

045 C **Farm;** 65311 CR 7; Italianate cube; c.1860; Outbuildings: corn cribs, pumphouse; *Agriculture, Architecture* (210)

046 C **German Church Cemetery;** CR 7 & CR 40, 1979-present; *Religion* (210)

047 C **Farm;** 26918 CR 40; 1 ½ I-house; c.1850; Outbuildings: English barn, privy, sheds; *Agriculture, Architecture* (210)

048 C **House;** 26735 CR 40; Colonial Revival; c.1950; Outbuilding: garage; *Architecture* (210)

049 C **House;** 25061 CR 40; California bungalow; c.1920; *Architecture* (210)

050 C **House;** 25013 CR 40; Minimal traditional; c.1940; *Architecture* (210)

051 C **House;** 24951 CR 40; California bungalow; c.1925; Outbuilding: garage; *Architecture* (210)

052 C **House;** 24919 CR 40; Upright-and-wing/ Italianate; c.1870; *Architecture* (210)

55029 This Italianate house is a large-scale example of the use of glacial stone in construction. The farm also features an impressive Sweitzer barn.

55055 The J.J. Rohrer House was built in 1854 and is individually listed in the National Register of Historic Places. The farm includes an original one-room stone house as well as a number of outbuildings.

053 C **Southwest Bible Church;** CR 40; Gable-front; c.1910; *Architecture, Religion* (210)

054 C **House;** 24683 CR 40; Lazy-T; c.1880; *Architecture* (210)

055 O **J.J. Rohrer Farm;** CR 40; Double-pile/ Greek Revival; 1854-1900; Outbuildings: chicken house, English barn, pioneer house, Sweitzer barn, sheds; *Agriculture, Architecture, Exploration/Settlement* (210) **NR**

056 N **Beitler/Wenger/Nunemaker Log House;** CR 15; Hall-and-parlor; 1836; Outbuilding: privy; *Architecture, Exploration/Settlement* (210)

057 N **Cross-Nunemaker Log House;** 22863 CR 40; Double-pen; c.1890; *Architecture* (210)

058 C **House;** CR 40 & CR 17; T-plan; c.1880; *Architecture* (210)

059 C **House;** 66717 CR 17; Lazy-T; c.1880; *Architecture* (210)

060 C **German Reformed Cemetery;** CR 11 & SR 119; c.1854-c.1998; *Exploration/Settlement, Religion* (210)

061 N **House;** 27601 CR 42; Double-entry, double-pile; c.1860; Outbuilding: milk house; *Architecture* (210)

# Olive Township (60001-047)

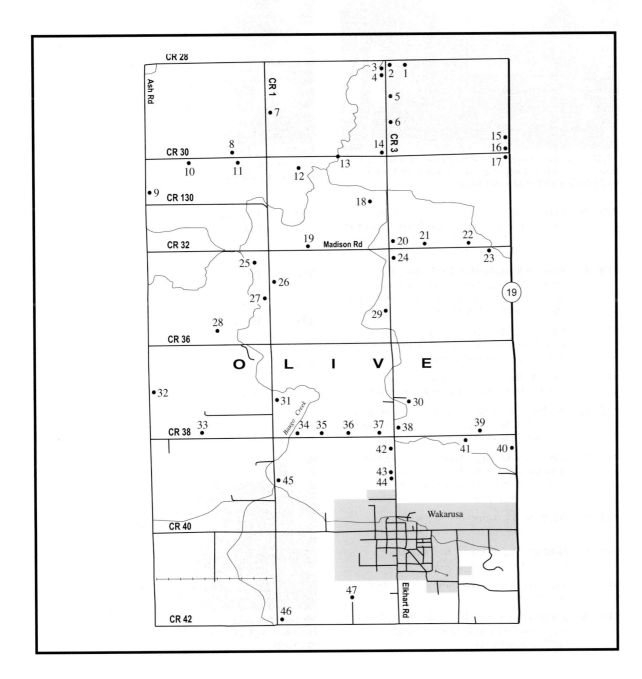

Agrarian Olive Township is located in the western part of Elkhart County and was officially formed in 1839, nine years after the establishment of the county. Only eighteen square miles, Olive Township is bordered to the west by St. Joseph County.

In 1833, Martin Sailor obtained the first Land Patent Deed for 80 acres in what would become Olive Township. By 1840, when the federal census was conducted, approximately 100 people resided in the township. Early settlers included the Martin, Sailor, Wilbert, Smeltzer, Pletcher, Holderman, Culp, Bell, Brown, and Lechlitner families. The settlers cleared land for farming, carved roads into the wilderness, and set up commercial enterprises.

The earliest recorded business in the township was Wilbert's Mill, located on County Road 32 half a mile east of the county line. Christian and Isaac Hunsberger and Andrew Clement owned Hunsberger's Brick and Sawmill, which provided bricks for many Olive Township houses. The mill no longer exists, but was located on land owned by Lowell Hunsberger.

Early communities in Olive Township included Salem, Olive Center, Tiletown, Winesburg, and Coonville. The only town still in existence is Wakarusa, which had its origin in the town of Salem. Salem was founded in 1852 when John Holderman, Jacob Pletcher, and John Smeltzer platted part of their farms. In 1860, Salem was renamed Wakarusa because another Salem already existed in Indiana. When the Wabash Railroad reached Olive Township in 1893, Wakarusa was relocated to its present location along the railroad about two miles south of the earlier village, which gradually disappeared.

In 1849, there were six school districts in the township: District No.1/Sailor School (60014), District No. 2/Mitchell School, District No. 3/Ehret

School, District No. 4/Olive Center School, District No. 5/Town School, and District No. 6/Holderman School. Many early church services were held in schools and other large buildings like barns. In 1852, the Methodist Episcopal congregation used the new log schoolhouse in Wakarusa. Other early congregations included the Holdeman Mennonites and Salem Baptists, among other denominations.

More recently, Olive Township became home to corporations including Nelson's, a company that specializes in barbeque chicken fundraisers, and a recreational vehicle production facility of the Monaco Coach Corporation. The railroad line residents once yearned for was dismantled in 1990. Agriculture remains important to the township's economy and family farms are still abundant throughout the township (60009, 60018, 60021).

## OLIVE TOWNSHIP SCATTERED SITES (60001-047)

**No. Rtg. Description**

**001 C House;** 28876 CR 28; T-plan; c.1890; Outbuildings: bank/basement barn, English barn; *Agriculture, Architecture* (656)

**002 C Olive Cemetery;** CR 3; c.1865-present; *Exploration/Settlement, Religion* (656)

**003 C Olive Mennonite Church;** 61081 CR 3; Gable-front; 1948; *Architecture, Religion* (656)

**004 C Olive West Cemetery;** CR 3; c.1889; *Religion* (656)

**005 C Laenbank Stock Farm;** CR 3; American foursquare; c.1890/c.1910; Outbuildings; corn cribs, dairy barn, garage, milk house; *Agriculture, Architecture* (656)

**006 C Farm;** CR 3; Gabled-ell; c.1890; Outbuilding: livestock barn; *Agriculture, Architecture* (656)

**007 C Farm;** 61524 CR 1; American foursquare; c.1920; Outbuildings: corn crib, English barn, machine shed, pumphouse; *Agriculture, Architecture* (656)

**008 C Farm;** 30351 CR 30; Lazy-T; c.1890; Outbuildings: English barn, livestock barns, machine shed; *Agriculture, Architecture* (656)

**60021** This Free Classic house retains clapboard and fishscale shingle siding, original windows, and a flat-roof porch with round wood columns.

**009 N Farm;** 62392 Ash Rd.; American foursquare; 1920; Outbuildings: bank/basement barn, drive-thru corn crib, garage; *Agriculture, Architecture* (656)

**010 C Samuel & Katherine Lechlitner Farm;** 30650 CR 30; Lazy-T; c.1890; Outbuildings: pumphouse, Sweitzer barn, windmill; *Agriculture, Architecture* (656)

**011 C Farm;** 30312 CR 30; California bungalow; c.1925; Outbuildings: barn, house, privy; *Agriculture, Architecture* (656)

**012 C Corn Crib;** 29732 CR 30; Drive-thru; c.1940; *Agriculture, Architecture* (656)

**013 C Bridge;** CR 30 over Baugo; Concrete girder; 1961 (C.W. Nicholson, engineer); *Engineering, Transportation* (656)

**014 C Olive Township District No. 1/Sailor School;** 29023 CR 30; American foursquare; 1910; Outbuilding: garage; *Architecture, Education* (656)

**015 C Barn;** SR 19; Transverse-frame barn; c.1890; *Agriculture, Architecture* (656)

**016 C House;** CR 30; American foursquare; c.1920; *Architecture* (656)

**017 C House;** CR 30; Gabled-ell; c.1900; *Architecture* (656)

**018 N Farm;** CR 3; Gabled-ell; c.1890; Outbuilding: bank/basement barn; *Agriculture, Architecture* (656)

**60022** This Free Classic house features orginial clapboard siding, windows, and doors, and a Craftsman-era porch with cobblestone piers.

**019 C Hunsberger House;** 29653 CR 32; Lazy-T/Italianate; 1832/c.1890; Outbuildings: garage, summer kitchen, windmill; *Architecture, Exploration/Settlement* (656)

**020 C Farm;** CR 3; Upright-and-wing/Italianate; c.1885; Outbuildings: bank/basement barn, milk house; *Agriculture, Architecture* (656)

**021 N Farm;** CR 32; Free Classic; c.1900; Outbuilding: English barn; *Agriculture, Architecture* (656)

**022 N Farm;** CR 32; Free Classic/Craftsman; c.1900; Outbuilding: English barn; *Agriculture, Architecture* (656)

**60026** This gabled-ell house has elements of the Italianate style, including tall, segmental-arched window openings.

**023 N Farm;** CR 32; Gabled-ell/Greek Revival; c.1870; Outbuildings: dairy barn, garage; *Agriculture, Architecture* (656)

**024 N Farm;** 63100 CR 3; Pennsylvania farmhouse; c.1880; Outbuildings: barn, summer kitchen, windmill; *Agriculture, Architecture* (656)

**025 C Christian Hunsberger Farm;** 63125 CR 1; I-house; c.1869; Outbuildings: bank/basement barn, chicken house, corn crib, livestock barn, milk house; *Agriculture, Architecture* (656)

**026 N Farm;** 66362 CR 1; Gabled-ell/Italianate; 1883; Outbuildings: bank/basement barn, corn crib, privy; *Agriculture, Architecture* (656)

**027 C Barn;** CR 1; English barn; c.1930; *Agriculture, Architecture* (656)

**028 C Farm;** CR 36; Outbuildings: chicken house, granary, hog house, milk house, pumphouse, sweitzer barn; *Agriculture, Architecture* (656)

**029 N Farm;** 63051 CR 3; American foursquare; c.1920; Outbuilding: grain bin; *Agriculture, Architecture* (656)

**030 C Barn;** 64564 CR 3; Rainbow-roof barn; *Agriculture, Architecture* (656)

**031 N Farm;** CR 1; Bank/basement barn; c.1890; Outbuildings: brooder house, corn crib, drive-thru corn crib, machine shed; *Agriculture, Architecture* (656)

60029 This American foursquare house displays decorative scored brick in a running bond pattern, a hipped porch with brick piers, and original windows with stone lintels and sills.

60031 This bank barn is one of several notable outbuildings on a County Road 1 farm.

**032 C House;** 64510 Ash Rd.; Italianate cube/American foursquare; c.1880/c.1920; *Architecture* (656)

**033 C Farm;** 30565 CR 38; Gabled-ell; c.1890/1924; Outbuildings: barn, corn cribs, machine shed, pumphouse; *Agriculture, Architecture* (656)

**034 C Shutz Cemetery;** CR 38; *Religion* (656)

**035 C House;** 29601 CR 38; Gabled-ell; c.1870; Outbuildings: garage, machine shed, milk house, pumphouse; *Architecture* (656)

**036 C Farm;** 29393 CR 38; Gabled-ell/Greek Revival; c.1870/1903; Outbuildings: English barn, shed; *Agriculture, Architecture* (656)

**037 C House;** 29105 CR 38; Ranch/International; c.1959; *Architecture* (656)

**038 N Farm;** 64878 CR 3; I-house/Greek Revival; c.1860; Outbuildings: garage, milk house, Sweitzer barn; *Agriculture, Architecture* (656)

**039 C House;** CR 38; I-house; c.1890; *Architecture* (656)

**040 C Farm;** 65109 SR 19; American foursquare; c.1920; Outbuildings: English barn, garage, transverse-frame barn; *Agriculture, Architecture* (656)

**041 C House;** CR 38; Gabled-ell cottage; c.1890; *Architecture* (656)

**042 N Farm;** CR 3; American foursquare; c.1915; Outbuildings: chicken house, corn crib, English barn; *Agriculture, Architecture* (656)

60038 This Greek Revival I-house boasts original clapboard siding with a thick cornice and corner boards, a portico with wood piers, and central entry flanked by carved wood panels.

**043 C House;** 65425 CR 3; American foursquare; c.1920; Architecture (656)

**044 C House;** CR 3; Gabled-ell; c.1900; *Architecture* (656)

**045 C Robert Lechtlitner Barn;** CR 1; Bank/basement barn; c.1902/1912; *Agriculture, Architecture* (656)

**046 C Letherman Grove;** CR 42; Gable-front; c.1950; *Architecture, Entertainment/Recreation* (656)

**047 C Radio Facility;** CR 42; 20th century functional; c.1955; *Architecture, Communications, Transportation* (656)

60042 This American foursquare has a full-width porch with wood and brick piers atop a stone wall.

# Wakarusa Downtown Historic District  (039-656-61001-041)

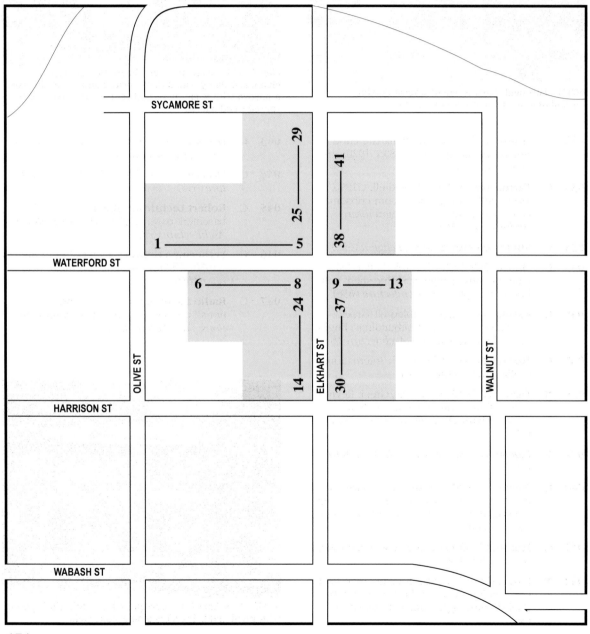

The Wakarusa Downtown Historic District is located downtown at the intersection of Elkhart and Waterford Streets. The district began in 1852, when the first three blocks of what became Wakarusa were platted. However, due to a devastating fire, most of the downtown buildings date to the turn of the 20th century.

Thomas Inks opened the district's first business when he moved his general store from the north side of town to the west side of North Elkhart Street. By the 1870s, A. W. Valentine operated a furniture store on South Waterford Street and performed the duties of undertaker, offering caskets and hearse services, and Adam Trisinger owned the City Meat Market on Elkhart Street. Other businesses included two hardware stores, shoe shops, barbers, a dentist, a drug store, and wagon and buggy dealers. Today, the area remains the mercantile center of Wakarusa, having a number of businesses.

A destructive fire struck downtown Wakarusa in 1899. It started in the Knisley & Burner Hardware Building, located on South Elkhart Street, and quickly consumed the rest of the block between East Waterford and Harrison Streets. At the time, Wakarusa had no fire-fighting equipment and the two telephone exchanges townspeople could have used to call for help were inside businesses already engulfed in flames. The Mary St. Claire House was the only building spared (61030).

By the early 1900s, business owners had rebuilt the block and there were two hardware stores, the furniture store/mortuary, and a drug store among other establishments. Those structures give the district its historic character today. A commercial building on South Elkhart Street still contains its original pressed-tin ceilings and is the only building in Wakarusa to retain its freight elevator, a 1910 Otis (61034). The building housed a hardware store until 1996. Today it houses an antique store and the publishing house of the *Wakarusa Tribune*. A second hardware store located within the block began as Yoder Bros. Hardware and is now Wakarusa Hardware (61036). It maintains a historic atmosphere, complete with a rolling wood ladder.

The Wakarusa Commercial Historic District experienced some decline as several long-time establishments went out of business. However, the Chamber of Commerce plans to beautify the downtown area to attract more businesses and customers. Despite some remodeling of storefronts, downtown Wakarusa retains a fine collection of historic structures, forming a cohesive historic district.

## WAKARUSA DOWNTOWN HISTORIC DISTRICT (039-656-61001-041)

| No. | Rtg. | Add. | Description |
|---|---|---|---|

**WEST WATERFORD STREET** *(north side)*

| 001 | C | 116 | **Garage;** Art Deco; c.1930 |
| 002 | C | NA | **Legion Memorial Building;** Arts and Crafts; 1949 |
| 003 | NC | 108 | **Commercial Building;** Parapet-front; c.1965 |
| 004 | N | NA | **Garage;** Art Deco; 1917 |
| 005 | NC | NA | **Government Building;** c.1980 |

**62056 The Wabash Railroad Depot in Wakarusa, c.1907.** *Photo courtesy of the Elkhart County Historical Museum*

**61004 The Art Deco Garage Building dates to 1917 and has a parapet roof with stone accents, a scored brick facade, and arched openings.**

**EAST WATERFORD STREET** *(north side)*

**No Sites**

**WEST WATERFORD STREET** *(south side)*

| 006 | C | NA | **Edward Lienhart Building;** Two-part commercial block; c.1915 |
| 007 | C | NA | **Commercial Building;** Two-part commercial block; c.1880 |
| 008 | NC | 109 | **Commercial Building;** Two-part commercial block; c.1880 |

**EAST WATERFORD STREET** *(south side)*

| 009 | NC | 101 | **Commercial Building;** c.1970 |
| 010 | C | 103 | **Commercial Building;** Italianate; c.1890 |
| 011 | C | NA | **Commercial Building;** Italianate; c.1890 |
| 012 | C | NA | **Commercial Building;** Two-part commercial block; c.1900 |
| 013 | C | 109 | **Commercial Building;** Parapet-front; 1907 |

**SOUTH ELKHART STREET** *(west side)*

| 014 | C | NA | **Commercial Building;** Arts and Crafts; 1917 |
| 015 | NC | 123 | **Commercial Building;** 1917 |
| 016 | C | NA | **House;** Queen Anne cottage; c.1890 |

| 017 | NC | NA | **House;** Upright-and-wing; c.1910 |
| 018 | NC | NA | **Parking Lot** |
| 019 | C | NA | **Post Office;** International; c.1960 |
| 020 | C | 109 | **Commercial Building;** 19th century functional; c.1890 |
| 021 | C | 109 | **Commercial Building;** Italianate; c.1890 |
| 022 | C | 105 | **Jacob Weldy Building;** 20th century functional; 1916 |
| 023 | C | 103 | **Weldy Block;** Two-part commercial block; c.1880 |
| 024 | C | NA | **Commercial Building;** Two-part commercial block; c.1880 |

**NORTH ELKHART STREET** *(west side)*

| 025 | N | NA | **Commercial Building;** Italianate; c.1905 |

**61025 This Italianate commercial building features cast iron elements on the second floor and a heavy bracketed cornice. Prism glass spans the transom area.**

61030 The Mary St. Claire House was the only structure on the block to survive a devastating fire in 1899.

| 026 | NC | NA | Vacant Lot |
| 027 | C | NA | **Commercial Building;** Parapet-front; c.1905 |
| 028 | C | NA | **Commercial Building;** Two-part commercial block; c.1905 |
| 029 | C | 115 | **Commercial Building;** Two-part commercial block; c.1905 |

## SOUTH ELKHART AVENUE (east side)

| 030 | N | 128 | **Mary St. Claire House;** T-plan; c.1880 |
| 031 | NC | NA | **Commercial Building;** c.1910 |
| 032 | C | NA | **Commercial Building;** Parapet-front; c.1905 |
| 033 | NC | NA | **Parking Lot** |
| 034 | N | 114 | **A.W. Gordon Building;** Romanesque Revival; 1910 |
| 035 | C | 110-14 | **Commercial Building;** Neoclassical; 1906 |
| 036 | N | NA | **E.J. Swartz Building;** Neoclassical; 1904 |
| 037 | C | NA | **Eshleman Building;** Italianate; 1904 |

61034 The A. W. Gordon Building dates to 1910 and displays decorative brick corbeling and a segmental-arch opening.

## NORTH ELKHART AVENUE (east side)

| 038 | C | NA | **Bank;** Neoclassical; c.1890 |
| 039 | NC | 100 | **Bank Addition;** One-part commercial block; c.1980 |
| 040 | NC | NA | **Parking Lot** |
| 041 | C | 112 | **Commercial Building;** Parapet-front; c.1920 |

61036 The E. J. Swartz Building dates to 1904 and boasts a fishscale/feather ironwork decoration and a cast iron facade made to resemble rusticated stone.

61038 This bank building features stone dentils and medallions beneath the cornice line and stone window and door surrounds.

# Wakarusa Scattered Sites (62001-058)

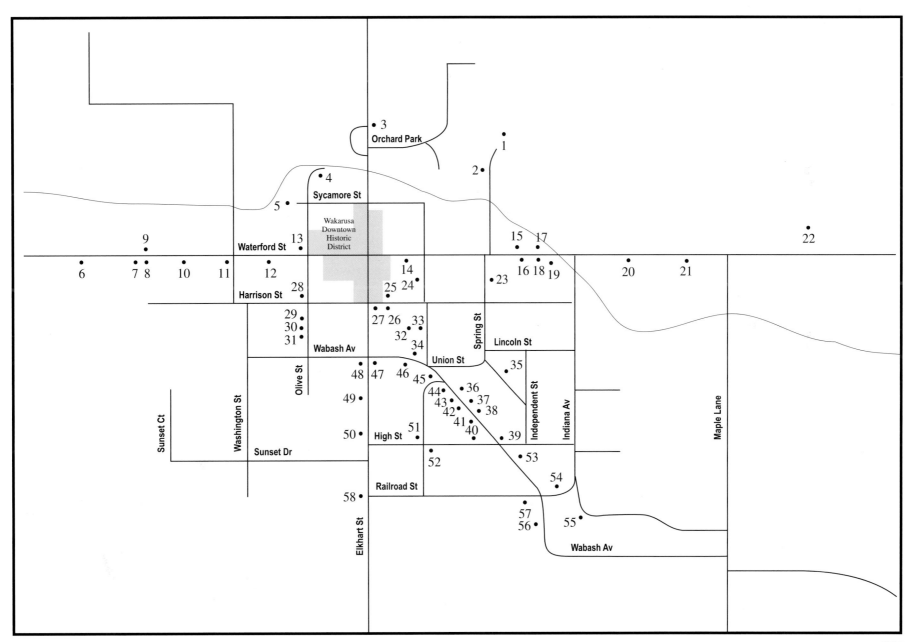

Wakarusa is located in the southeast part of Olive Township. In 1852, three neighboring farmers, John Holderman, John Smeltzer, and Jacob Pletcher, Jr., platted part of their land as the town of Salem. Later that day, the new town's first ten lots were sold, including one to Thomas Inks. Inks operated Wakarusa's first business, a general store. In 1854, Henry Myers platted a fourth block to the growing town. Another early, though short-lived business was the Salem Bank, established the same year. The bank moved from Wakarusa by 1863. In the 1860s, Wakarusa was home to many businesses including the Wakarusa General Store, the Olive House Hotel, the Wakarusa Flouring Mill, a farm implements store, a mercantile, four saloons, and boot, shoe, and harness makers.

Through the years, businesses changed hands and others emerged to serve evolving needs. Wakarusa grew steadily until 1899, when a devastating fire destroyed half of its commercial district. The T-plan Mary St. Claire House was spared from the flames and remains today (61030).

The Wabash Railroad came to Wakarusa in 1892 and the construction of a passenger depot began. The street running north from the depot was named Wabash Avenue and became home to many of Wakarusa's grand houses, including several notable American foursquares (62030, 62044, 62050). One was built from bricks salvaged from the dismantled Sailor School that was once located in the northern part of Olive Township (62053). Also in 1892, the railroad constructed a telegraph line. However, it was not until 1898 that business owners petitioned to run a telephone line from the depot to Wakarusa's commercial district.

Wakarusa's first school house was built in 1852-53. The log structure was located on South Elkhart. Church services, political meetings, and even funerals were also held in the building. Wakarusa's first brick school was constructed in 1867 on East Waterford Street, but in 1878 the two-story structure was dismantled because it was sinking. Its replacement, built the same year on the same site, was renovated in 1894 and again in the mid-1910s.

Maple Park played an important role in the development of Wakarusa. Between 1887 and 1915 there was a man-made pond at the park and Wakarusa residents used it as a place to fish, swim, perform baptisms, and harvest ice in the winter. Today Maple Park continues to be a popular recreation spot for the people of Wakarusa (62024).

## WAKARUSA SCATTERED SITES (62001-058)

| No. | Rtg. | Description |
|---|---|---|
| 001 | N | **Orchard Park Farm;** 208 E Waterford St.; Gable-front; c.1850; Outbuildings: bank/basement barn, barn, corn crib, garage, milk house, pumphouse, silo; *Agriculture, Architecture* (656) |
| 002 | C | **House;** E Waterford St.; Ranch; c.1950; Outbuilding: garage; *Architecture* (656) |
| 003 | C | **House;** 300 CR 3/Elkhart St.; Bungalow; c.1920; *Architecture* (656) |
| 004 | C | **House;** 204 Olive St.; Ranch; c.1950; *Architecture* (656) |
| 005 | C | **House;** Olive St.; Cape Cod; c.1945; Outbuilding: workshop; *Architecture* (656) |
| 006 | C | **House;** 413 W. Waterford St.; Dutch Colonial Revival; c.1925; Outbuilding: garage; *Architecture* (656) |
| 007 | N | **Larry Hahn House;** 403 W Waterford St.; Free Classic; c.1875/1925; Outbuilding: carriage house; *Architecture* (656) |
| 008 | C | **House;** 401 W Waterford St.; T-plan/Italianate; c.1870; *Architecture* (656) |

**62001  The Orchard Park Farm has a number of great outbuildings, including a milkhouse, corn crib, and grain bins.**

**62007  The Larry Hahn House's carriage house sheltered Wakarusa's first postal vehicle, a horse drawn carriage. The house was moved in 1925 so its owner could see downtown better. She later added the rounded portion of the porch for the same reason.**

| No. | Rtg. | Description |
|---|---|---|
| 009 | N | **House;** 400 W Waterford St.; Queen Anne; c.1875; Outbuilding: English barn; *Agriculture, Architecture* (656) |
| 010 | C | **House;** 307 W Waterford St.; American foursquare; c.1920; *Architecture* (656) |
| 011 | O | **House;** 301 W Waterford St.; T-plan/Italianate; c.1891; *Architecture* (656) |
| 012 | C | **House;** 207 W Waterford St.; Free Classic; c.1900; *Architecture* (656) |
| 013 | C | **House;** 200 W Waterford St.; Bungalow; c.1920; *Architecture* (656) |
| 014 | N | **House;** 117 E Waterford St.; Italian Renaissance Revival; c.1940; *Architecture* (656) |
| 015 | C | **House;** 304 E Waterford St.; T-plan; c.1890; *Architecture* (656) |
| 016 | C | **Industrial Building;** 313 E Waterford St.; 20th century functional; c.1930; *Architecture, Industry* (656) |
| 017 | C | **House;** 312 E Waterford St.; English cottage; c.1935; *Architecture* (656) |
| 018 | C | **House;** 307 E Waterford St.; Cape Cod; c.1940; Outbuilding: garage; *Architecture* (656) |
| 019 | C | **House;** 311 E Waterford St.; Minimal traditional; c.1945; Outbuilding: chicken house; *Architecture* (656) |
| 020 | C | **House;** 409 E Waterford St.; Cape Cod; c.1930; *Architecture* (656) |

**62009** This house is a good local example of the Queen Anne style. It features brick walls with fishscale shingles beneath the gable peak, a rounded wrap-around porch that is a nice example of early concrete work, and arched window openings.

**021  C  House;** 501 E Waterford St.; Ranch; c.1955; *Architecture* (656)

**022  C  Wakarusa Feed Center;** 704 E Waterford St.; Grain log/elevator; c.1935; *Agriculture, Architecture, Commerce* (656)

**023  C  House;** Spring St.; Queen Anne cottage/ Bungalow; c.1900; *Architecture* (656)

**024  C  Maple Park;** Harrison St. & Walnut St.; 1887; *Community Planning, Entertainment/ Recreation* (656)

**025  C  House;** 104 Harrison St.; Queen Anne; c.1900; *Architecture* (656)

**62011** This T-plan/Italianate house is outstanding because it is a rare example of a middle-class dwelling that retains its original porch.

**62014** This Italian Renaissance Revival house features a hipped roof with green barrel tiles, wide, overhanging eaves that emphasize the horizontal, and an exaggerated round hood over the entryway.

**026  C  House;** 105 E Harrison St.; Dormer-front bungalow; c.1920; Outbuilding: garage; *Architecture* (656)

**027  C  Odell's Auto Service;** 200 S Elkhart St.; 20th century functional; c.1950; *Architecture, Commerce* (656)

**028  C  House;** 111 S Olive St.; Gable-front; c.1900; Outbuilding: shed; *Architecture* (656)

**029  N  House;** 207 S Olive St.; Dormer-front bungalow/Craftsman; c.1910; *Architecture* (656)

**030  N  House;** 209 S Olive St.; American foursquare; c.1920; *Architecture* (656)

**031  C  House;** 211 S Olive St.; Western bungalow; c.1920; Outbuilding: garage; *Architecture* (656)

**62029** This dormer-front bungalow exhibits Craftsman style knee braces and ribbon windows.

**62030** This American foursquare house is in a nearly unaltered condition. It retains original siding, windows, and porch.

**032  C  Barn;** Walnut St.; English barn; c.1900; *Agriculture, Architecture* (656)

**033  C  Barn;** Walnut St.; English barn; c.1900; *Agriculture, Architecture* (656)

**034  C  House;** 108 E Wabash Ave.; Lazy-T; c.1890; Outbuilding: garage; *Architecture* (656)

**035  C  House;** 302 S Spring St.; Gable-front; c.1900; *Architecture* (656)

**036  C  House;** 206 E Wabash Ave.; Western bungalow; c.1920; *Architecture* (656)

**037  C  House;** 214 E Wabash Ave.; Dormer-front bungalow; c.1920; *Architecture* (656)

**62044** This American foursquare features dormers with ribbon windows, brick walls, and window openings accented by flat stone lintels and sills.

62045 This Dutch Colonial Revival house appears to be a variant of house No. 123 from the Sears Roebuck & Company catalog.

038  C  **House;** 216 E Wabash Ave.; Gable-front; c.1900; Outbuilding: garage; *Architecture* (656)

039  C  **House;** 224 E Wabash Ave.; American foursquare; c.1920; *Architecture* (656)

040  C  **House;** 210 High St.; Lazy-T; c.1880; *Architecture* (656)

041  C  **House;** 213 E Wabash Ave.; Dormer-front bungalow; c.1920; Outbuilding: garage; *Architecture* (656)

042  C  **House;** 207 E Wabash Ave.; American foursquare; c.1910; Outbuilding: garage; *Architecture* (656)

62049 This English cottage retains wood shingle siding and wood double-hung windows with wood trim.

62050 This American foursquare house is home to the Bird's Eye Museum, a venue that houses scale models of Wakarusa and Elkhart County properties, as well as National Register properties from around the state.

043  O  **House;** 205 E Wabash Ave.; American foursquare; c.1910; Outbuilding: garage; *Architecture* (656)

044  N  **House;** 203 E Wabash Ave.; American foursquare; c.1910; Outbuilding: garage; *Architecture* (656)

045  N  **House;** 111 E Wabash Ave.; Dutch Colonial Revival; c.1910; *Architecture* (656)

046  C  **House;** 107 E Wabash Ave.; Free Classic; c.1890; *Architecture* (656)

047  C  **House;** 300 S Elkhart St.; Free Classic; c.1890; *Architecture* (656)

048  C  **House;** 301 S Elkhart St.; Gable-front; c.1885; *Architecture* (656)

049  N  **House;** 313 S Elkhart St.; English cottage; c.1925; *Architecture* (656)

050  N  **House;** 325 S Elkhart St.; American foursquare; 1917; *Architecture* (656)

051  C  **House;** 106 High St.; Lazy-T; c.1860/c.1910; Outbuilding: garage; *Architecture* (656)

052  C  **House;** 400 Park St.; Lazy-T; c.1860; *Architecture* (656)

053  O  **House;** 300 E Wabash Ave.; Midwest box; c.1920; Outbuildings: carriage house, chicken house; *Architecture* (656)

054  C  **Barn;** Indiana Ave.; Transverse-frame barn; c.1900; *Agriculture, Architecture* (656)

62053 This Midwest box is a simplified version of an American foursquare, which would have a dormer window on its hipped roof and a larger porch. This nice example features original windows with stone lintels and sills.

055  C  **Wayne Feed Mill;** Railroad Ave.; 19th century functional; c.1850; *Agriculture, Architecture, Industry* (656)

056  N  **Wakarusa Depot;** Wabash Ave.; Stick; c.1890; Outbuilding: privy; *Architecture, Transportation* (656)

057  C  **Amoco Filling Station;** Wabash Ave.; 20th century functional; c.1950; *Architecture, Commerce* (656)

058  C  **Pletcher Cemetery;** S Elkhart St.; c.1850-c.1875; *Religion* (656)

Workers pose outside the Wakarusa Milling Co., c.1900. *Photo from* Images of America, Around Nappanee, Hometowns of the Heritage Trail *by Amy (Lant) Wenger.*

# Locke Township (65001-042)

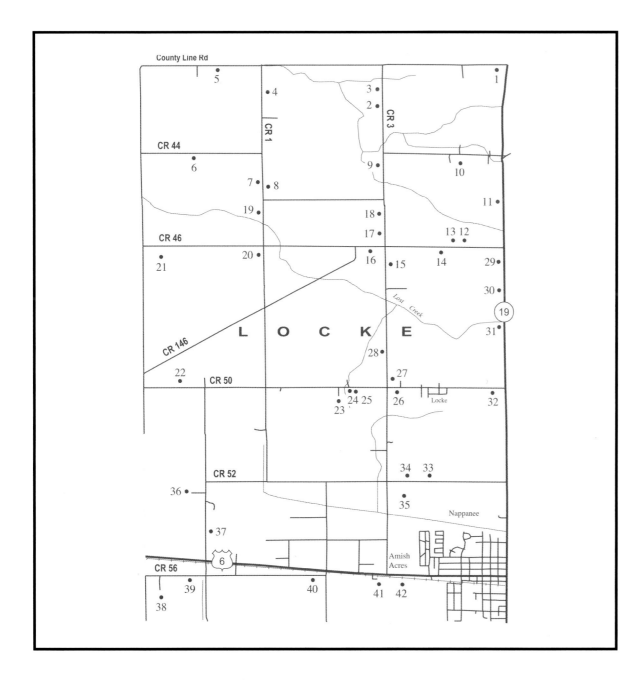

Locke Township is located in the southwest corner of Elkhart County, bordered by Kosciusko County to the south and Marshall and Saint Joseph Counties to the west. With the exception of a few cottage industries, Locke Township has always had an agricultural-based economy.

Before westward expansion reached the township, it was heavily forested and marshy. While rivers and streams were plentiful in northern Elkhart County, Locke Township had few and was among the county's last areas to be settled. The area's first settlers were Samuel Lockwood, his wife, and his six children, who arrived from Vermont in 1836. The township is believed to be named after the family. A short time later, they were followed by the families of Abner Hibray and John Pitts, both from New York. The three families chose land in the northern third of the township to settle.

In 1841, Locke Township was the last township in Elkhart County to be created, having previously been a part of Harrison, Union, and Olive Townships. There were only nine people eligible to vote in the 1841 election. Gradually, the population grew as people were drawn by the price of land, which was cheaper due to its forestation. It was not until 1846 that the township was settled in earnest as more land was cleared of trees. Many of the new settlers were either German immigrants or of German descent.

Union Church (later the South Union Church), was the township's first church. Its 1905 building remains today (65022). In 1881, the township had six schools: five framed and one of brick construction. As the population grew, Locke Town was laid out in 1867 to serve as the township's central community. The town developed in an area with no geographical advantages; there were no rivers, roads, or hills. At its peak, Locke had over forty houses, three doctors, a church, school, and hotel, among other businesses, and a population of more than 200 in 1873.

In the early 1870s, the Baltimore and Ohio Railroad's planned expansion of its lines to Chicago ran directly through the southern portion of Elkhart County. Had the railroad deemed Locke Town worthy of a five-mile detour, the town would have boomed. Instead, the line passed less than five miles south of the fledgling town through an area populated by a few scattered farms. Henry Eby, a prominent Locke Township resident, tried to save Locke Town by building a railroad depot and passenger house along the Locke-Union Township Line, naming it Locke Station. For a few months, trains stopped at Locke Station, but gradually other businesses developed around the depot and the village of Nappanee was created. The Locke Station Depot was moved and replaced by Nappanee on the B & O's schedule. Within a dozen years, nearly all the businesses in Locke Town had folded or moved to Nappanee, where the presence of the railroad boosted profitability. Today, a cluster of houses mark Locke Town.

In the late-19th and early-20th centuries, waves of Amish settlers from Wayne County, Ohio and Pennsylvania Dutch settlers from Berks County populated Locke Township. The two groups settled a few miles apart and, with the Amish communities in eastern Elkhart County and western LaGrange County, have grown to be the third largest Amish community in the world, with thirty-three Old Order Amish churches in the Nappanee area. Like other settlers in the township, the Amish chose the area in part because the cleared prairie land in the northern part of the county was too expensive. Many Amish farms in the township are still operated the traditional way.

## LOCKE TOWNSHIP SCATTERED SITES (65001-042)

**No. Rtg. Description**

**001 C Farm;** 28064 CR 42; Lazy-T; c.1880; Outbuildings: bank/basement barn, milk house, shed, silo; *Agriculture, Architecture* (656)

65006 This house retains a multi-colored slate roof and historic cedar shingles.

**002 C House;** 67421 CR 3; Dutch Colonial Revival; c.1930; *Architecture* (656)

**003 C J.I. Weldy Farm;** 67211 CR 3; Hall-and-parlor/Greek Revival; c.1860/c.1903; Outbuildings: machine shed, Sweitzer barn, shed; *Agriculture, Architecture* (656)

**004 C Farm;** 67282 CR 1; T-plan/Italianate; c.1870; Outbuildings: bank/basement barn, silo; *Agriculture, Architecture* (656)

**005 C North Union Cemetery;** CR 42; c.1859-c.1997; *Exploration/Settlement, Religion* (656)

**006 N Farm;** 30596 CR 44; Hall-and-parlor/I-house; c.1860; Outbuildings: bank/basement barn, chicken house, corn crib, machine shed, sheds, windmill; *Agriculture, Architecture* (656)

**007 C House;** 68335 CR 1; Gabled-ell; 1882; *Architecture* (656)

**008 C Weldy Farm;** 68362 CR 1; Gabled-ell/Italianate; 1893; Outbuildings: bank/basement barn, chicken house, corn crib, silo; *Agriculture, Architecture* (656)

**009 C Kent Farm;** 68133 CR 3; Central-passage/log construction; c.1860; Outbuildings: garage, Sweitzer barn, shed; *Agriculture, Architecture* (656)

**010 C Raimer House;** CR 44; T-plan; c.1870; *Architecture* (656)

**011 C Farm;** 68547 SR 19; L-plan; c.1930; Outbuildings: chicken house, garage, livestock barn, shed; *Agriculture, Architecture* (444)

**012 C Farm;** 28371 CR 46; Upright-and-wing; Outbuildings: chicken house, English barn, garage, machine shed, shed, silo; *Agriculture, Architecture* (444)

**013 N Locke Township District No. 4 School;** CR 46; Cross-plan; 1890; *Architecture, Education* (444)

**014 C Long Farm;** 28592 CR 46; American four-square; c.1920; Outbuildings: brooder house, livestock barn, machine shed; *Agriculture, Architecture* (444)

**015 C Farm;** 69206 CR 3; T-plan; c.1900; Outbuildings: drive-thru corn crib, English barn, milk house, silo; *Agriculture, Architecture* (444)

**016 C Fisher Farm;** 79084 CR 46; Colonial Revival; 1948; Outbuilding: Sweitzer barn; *Agriculture, Architecture* (444)

**017 C Farm;** 68859 CR 3; Double-pile; c.1900; Outbuildings: drive-thru corn crib, Sweitzer barn; *Agriculture, Architecture* (444)

**018 C Farm;** 68635 CR 3; Hall-and-parlor; c.1850; Outbuildings: chicken house, English barn, garage, machine shed, shed; *Agriculture, Architecture* (444)

65013 The Locke Township District No. 4 School dates to 1890 and was converted into a house in 1989. An identical school once stood at the intersection of CR 50 & CR 3.

**019 C House;** 68601 CR 1; Dutch Colonial Revival; c.1930; Outbuilding: shed; *Architecture* (444)

**020 C Farm;** CR 1; Gable-front; c.1880; Outbuildings: English barn, sheds; *Agriculture, Architecture* (444)

**021 C House;** 30814 CR 46; Upright-and-wing; c.1880; Outbuildings: windmills; *Architecture* (444)

**022 N South Union Chapel & Cemetery;** CR 50; Gable-front; c.1905; Outbuilding: privy; Cemetery: c.1880-present; *Architecture, Religion* (444)

**023 N Farm;** 29388 CR 50; Gabled-ell; c.1870; Outbuildings: corn crib, English barn, Sweitzer barn, sheds; *Agriculture, Architecture* (444)

**024 C Farm;** 29320 CR 50; Hall-and-parlor; c.1880; Outbuildings: chicken house, sheds; *Agriculture, Architecture* (444)

**025 C House;** 29250 CR 50; Upright-and-wing; c.1904; Outbuilding: garage; *Architecture* (444)

**026 C Farm;** 28900 CR 50; American foursquare/ Craftsman; c.1920; Outbuilding: livestock barn; *Agriculture, Architecture* (444)

65022 South Union Chapel retains its original slate roof and double-hung windows with stone lintels and sills and wood molding on the sides.

65023 This gabled-ell house has original clapboard siding and double-hung windows with wood molding.

**027 C Locke Township District No. 5 School;** 70438 CR 3; No style; 1890; *Architecture, Education* (444)

**028 C Farm;** 70071 CR 3; Upright-and-wing; c.1900; Outbuildings: chicken house, drive-thru corn crib, English barn, shed; *Agriculture, Architecture* (444)

**029 C Farm;** SR 19; Upright-and-wing; c.1910; Outbuildings: bank/basement barn, brooder house, corn crib, garage, machine shed, shed, silo; *Agriculture, Architecture* (444)

**030 C Farm;** 69507 SR 19; Upright-and-wing; c.1910; Outbuilding: livestock barn; *Agriculture, Architecture* (444)

**031 C Farm;** 69863 SR 19; Gabled-ell; c.1860; Outbuildings: bank/basement barn, garage, shed, windmill; *Agriculture, Architecture* (444)

**032 C Hess Farm;** 28156 CR 50; Upright-and-wing; c.1880; Outbuildings: chicken house, corn crib, livestock barn, privy, sheds, smokehouse, windmill; *Agriculture, Architecture* (444)

**033 C Farm;** 28645 CR 52; Lazy-T; c.1900; Outbuildings: chicken house, livestock barn; *Agriculture, Architecture* (444)

**034 C Barn;** 28813 CR 52; Sweitzer barn; c.1890; *Agriculture, Architecture* (444)

**035 O Farm;** CR 52; I-house/Federal; c.1860; Outbuildings: corn crib, garage, machine shed, Sweitzer barn, shed, smokehouse; *Agriculture, Architecture* (444)

**036 N Farm;** CR 100; Gabled-ell; Outbuilding: Sweitzer barn; *Agriculture, Architecture* (444)

**037 N Locke Township Cemetery;** CR 100; c.1886-present; *Religion* (444)

**038 C Farm;** 3082 CR 56; c.1890; Outbuilding: Sweitzer barn; *Agriculture, Architecture* (444)

**039 C Mullet Farm;** 30580 CR 56; Sweitzer barn; 1887/1913 (Benjamin Mullet, builder); Outbuildings: shed, silo, windmill, wood shed; *Agriculture, Architecture* (444)

**040 C Farm;** 29588 CR 56; T-plan; c.1890; Outbuildings: bank/basement barn, smokehouse, windmill; *Agriculture, Architecture* (444)

**041 N Clay Tile Factory;** US 6; 19th century functional; c.1880; *Architecture, Industry* (444)

**042 C Schmucker Farm;** US 6; Hall-and-parlor I-house; c.1865/c.1890; Outbuildings: bank/ basement barn, chicken house, drive-thru corn crib, garage, shed, windmill; *Agriculture, Architecture* (444)

65035 This house has had few alterations and retains its original porch, which is a rare find.

# Union Township (70001-073)

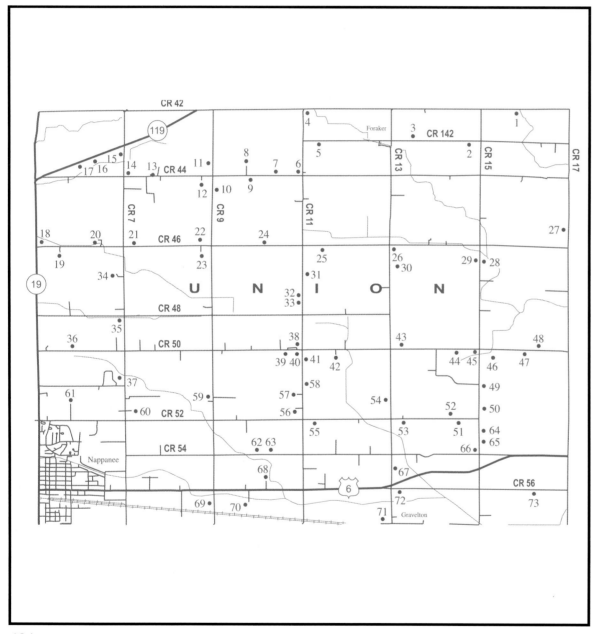

Union Township lies in southwestern Elkhart County and is bordered by Kosciusko County to the south. The B&O Railroad cut a path through the southern part of Union Township and the township contains a large portion of the city of Nappanee.

Swampy marshland once covered Union Township, but was drained to create arable land. Consequently, the land is rich, fertile, and excellent for farming. The area was also once heavily forested, but logging by early settlers quickly depleted that resource. Early pioneers in Union Township made a living by trapping the numerous beaver, fox, and deer in the area. They sold the sought-after furs and pelts in Goshen for generous profits.

A settler named Daniel Bainter is believed to be the first permanent white resident in the area. He built a cabin made of split logs in 1834. By the spring of 1837, enough settlers came to the area to induce the county to organize Union Township. Bainter's cabin was the site of the first elections, and according to lore, his sugar bowl served as the ballot box. The next year the township's first schoolhouse was built from logs.

The first ministers who came to Union Township were members of Baptist, German Baptist, Methodist, United Brethren, and Mennonite faiths. They traveled a circuit and usually held services in private residences or schools. Eventually a congregation from the Reformed faith built a church located east of Union Center, which they called "The Temple." By the 1880s, however, its members had all left the area and the abandoned church was torn down.

The coming of the railroad was the catalyst for the township's two towns. The smaller town, Foraker, was platted in 1892 after the Wabash Railroad came through the area. The larger town,

Nappanee, partially lies in Locke Township and was platted in 1874 near the Locke Station of the Baltimore and Ohio Railroad.

However, Union Township remains mostly rural and a number of significant farms attest to the importance of agriculture, including the Christian Stouder Farm (70024) and the Stump Homestead (70046).

## UNION TOWNSHIP SCATTERED SITES (70001-073)

**No. Rtg. Description**

**001  C  Bridge;** CR 42; Concrete girder; *Engineering, Transportation* (210)

**002  C  Farm;** 23240 CR 147; Gabled-ell; c.1890; Outbuildings: bank/basement barn, corn crib, garage, milk house, silo; *Agriculture, Architecture* (210)

**003  C  Ramer Farm;** CR 142; American foursquare; c.1918; Outbuilding: bank/basement barn; *Agriculture, Architecture* (210)

**004  C  Farm;** CR 11; American foursquare; c.1920; Outbuilding: English barn; *Agriculture, Architecture* (210)

**005  C  Farm;** 24820 CR 142; 1 ½ I-house; c.1890; Outbuildings: garage, livestock barn, windmill; *Agriculture, Architecture* (210)

**006  C  House;** 67951 CR 11; Minimal traditional; c.1940; Outbuilding: garage; *Architecture* (210)

**007  C  Farm;** 25347 CR 44; Gabled-ell; c.1880; Outbuildings: brooder house, English barn, garage; *Agriculture, Architecture* (210)

**008  C  Seidner Farm;** CR 44; Gabled-ell; c.1875; Outbuildings: bank/basement barn, garage, shed, silo; *Agriculture, Architecture* (210)

**009  C  House;** 25601 CR 44; American foursquare; c.1920; Outbuildings: garage, shed; *Architecture* (210)

**010  C  Metzler Farm;** 68148 CR 9; English cottage; c.1946; Outbuildings: corn cribs, garage, livestock barn; *Agriculture, Architecture* (210)

**70018  This Free Classic house is part of the Wisler Farm and retains its original slate roof.**

**011  C  Farm;** 67777 CR 9; L-plan; c.1880; Outbuildings: garage, livestock barn; *Agriculture, Architecture* (210)

**012  C  Farm;** CR 44; Gabled-ell; 1906; Outbuilding: bank/basement barn; *Agriculture, Architecture* (210)

**013  C  Bull Cemetery;** CR 44; c.1855-c.1880; *Exploration/Settlement, Religion* (210)

**014  N  Good School;** CR 44; Pyramidal-roof; 1900; *Architecture, Education* (210)

**015  C  House;** 67623 CR 7; Cape Cod; c.1930; Outbuilding: garage, sheds; *Architecture* (210)

**016  C  House;** 27388 SR 119; Gabled-ell; c.1890; *Architecture* (210)

**017  C  House;** 27622 SR 119; Gabled-ell; c.1925; Outbuildings: garage, shed; *Architecture* (210)

**018  N  Wisler Farm;** CR 46 & SR 19; Free Classic; 1907; Outbuilding: chicken house; *Agriculture, Architecture* (443)

**019  C  Farm;** CR 46 & SR 19; Gabled-ell; c.1900; Outbuildings: barns, shed, silo; *Agriculture, Architecture* (443)

**020  C  Providence Church Cemetery;** CR 46; c.1860-c.1945; *Religion* (443)

**021  C  House;** 26869 CR 46; Gabled-ell; c.1920; *Architecture* (443)

**022  C  House;** CR 46; Gabled-ell; c.1920; Outbuilding: garage; *Architecture* (443)

**023  C  Frederick Farm;** 26116 CR 46; Lazy-T; c.1880; Outbuildings: bank/basement barn, shed; *Agriculture, Architecture* (443)

**024  N  Christian Stouder Farm;** 25511 CR 46; Upright-and-wing; c.1840/c.1900; Outbuildings: barn/garage, log house; *Agriculture, Architecture, Exploration/Settlement* (443)

**025  C  House;** 24752 CR 46; Italianate; c.1870; Outbuildings: garage, shed; *Architecture* (443)

**026  C  Salem Mennonite Cemetery;** CR 13; c.1974-present; *Religion* (443)

**027  C  House;** CR 17; Central-passage; c.1870; Outbuilding: shed; *Architecture* (443)

**028  C  Farm;** 69256 CR 15; Upright-and-wing; c.1910; Outbuildings: English barn, machine shed, silos; *Agriculture, Architecture* (443)

**029  N  Log House;** CR 15; Single-pen; c.1840; *Architecture, Exploration/Settlement* (443)

**030  C  House;** 69280 CR 13; Gabled-ell/English cottage; c.1909/c.1920; Outbuilding: shed; *Architecture* (443)

**031  C  Farm;** 69384 CR 11; Gabled-ell; c.1870; Outbuildings: chicken house, garage, livestock barn, milk house, shed; *Agriculture, Architecture* (443)

**70024  Christian Stouder built this five room log house when he homesteaded his farm. In 1900 it was moved back from the street when the new upright and wing house was built.**

**70029** This single-pen log house is partially covered with tongue-and-groove and asphalt shingle siding. The early structure dates to c.1840.

**032 C Anglemeyer Farm;** 69619 CR 11; Gothic Revival; c.1862; Outbuildings: garage, house, livestock barn, machine shed, shed; *Agriculture, Architecture* (443)

**033 C John Anglemeyer Farm;** 69745 CR 11; Double-entry, double-pile; c.1860; Outbuildings: garage, privy, Sweitzer barn; *Agriculture, Architecture* (443)

**034 C Burkholder Farm;** 69415 CR 7; Gabled-ell; c.1886; Outbuildings: transverse-frame barn, summer kitchen, sheds, silo; *Agriculture, Architecture* (443)

**035 C Union Township District No. 4 School;** CR 7 & CR 48; T-plan; 1891; *Architecture, Education* (443)

**036 C Farm;** 21601 CR 50; Lazy-T; c.1900; Outbuildings: drive-thru corn crib; machine sheds, silo; *Agriculture, Architecture* (443)

**037 C Farm;** CR 7; T-plan; c.1900; Outbuilding: bank/basement barn; *Agriculture, Architecture* (443)

**038 C Union Center Cemetery;** CR 50 & CR 11; c.1860-present; *Religion* (443)

**039 C House;** 25210 CR 50; Hall-and-parlor/log construction; c.1850; *Architecture, Exploration/Settlement* (443)

**040 C Union Center Church of the Brethren;** CR 11 & CR 50; Gable-front; 1928; *Architecture, Religion* (443)

**041 C Anglemeyer Farm;** 70610 CR 11; Gable-front; c.1910; Outbuildings: bank/basement barn, sheds, *Agriculture, Architecture* (443)

**042 C Newcomer Farm;** CR 50; Gabled-ell; c.1870; Outbuilding: Sweitzer barn; *Agriculture, Architecture* (443)

**043 C Effert Farm;** 23877 CR 50; Upright-and-wing; c.1910; Outbuildings: corn crib, garage, silo; *Agriculture, Architecture* (443)

**044 C Farm;** 23244 CR 50; Central-passage; c.1870; Outbuildings: bank/basement barn, drive-thru corn crib, shed; *Agriculture, Architecture* (443)

**045 C House;** 23012 CR 11; Gable-front; c.1880; Outbuilding: garage; *Architecture* (443)

**046 O Stump Homestead;** CR 50; Log house; c.1840 (Daniel Stump, builder); Outbuildings: apple butter house, English barns, privy, shed, windmill; *Agriculture, Architecture, Exploration/Settlement* (443)

**047 C Farm;** 22468 CR 50; Minimal traditional; c.1930; Outbuildings: English barn, garage; *Agriculture, Architecture* (443)

**048 C Farm;** 22317 CR 50; Lazy-T; c.1900; Outbuildings: English barn, garage, privy, wood shed; *Agriculture, Architecture* (443)

**70046** Daniel Stump moved with his children from Canada in 1838. He was a minister and eventually bishop in the Brethren in Christ Church. This log house covered with wood siding was his home.

**70056** The gabled-ell Frenger House features wood clapboard and tongue-and-groove siding and historic double-hung windows with wood trim.

**049 C Farm;** 71052 CR 15; Lazy-T; c.1930; Outbuildings: chicken house, garage, machine shed, sheds, silo; *Agriculture, Architecture* (443)

**050 C Farm;** 71384 CR 15; Dormer-front bungalow; c.1930; Outbuildings: bank/basement barn, corn crib, garage; *Agriculture, Architecture* (443)

**051 C House;** 23288 CR 52; Lazy-T; c.1890; *Architecture* (443)

**052 N Solomon Stump House;** CR 52; Double-pen/log construction; c.1840 (Solomon Stump, builder); Outbuilding: windmill; *Architecture, Exploration/Settlement* (443)

**053 C Mint Still;** CR 52; Mint still; c.1880; *Architecture, Commerce* (443)

**054 C Freed House;** 71187 CR 13; 1 ½ New England cottage; c.1890; Outbuilding: shed; *Architecture* (443)

**055 C Anglemeyer House;** 24814 CR 52; American foursquare; c.1914; *Architecture* (443)

**056 N Frenger Farm;** 71347 CR 11; Gabled-ell; c.1880; Outbuildings: English barn, windmill; *Agriculture, Architecture* (443)

**057 C Farm;** 71138 CR 11; Double-entry I-house; c.1880; Outbuildings: barn, sheds; *Agriculture, Architecture* (443)

**058 C House;** CR 11; 1 ½ I-house; c.1900; Outbuilding: windmill; *Architecture* (443)

**059 C Farm;** 71249 CR 9; Lazy-T; c.1900; Outbuildings: garage, machine shed, Sweitzer barn, silos; *Agriculture, Architecture* (443)

70060 The gabled-ell Michael House exhibits Italianate details, including segmental-arched window openings and an original wrap around porch.

70067 This livestock barn is part of the Stuckman Farm. The family also raised potatoes.

70069 This house is the only example of the Prairie style in Union Township and is in nearly unaltered condition.

**060 N Michael Farm;** 71350 CR 7; Gabled-ell/ Italianate; c.1870; Outbuildings: English barn, garage, shed; *Agriculture, Architecture* (443)

**061 C Stahly Farm;** 27593 CR 52; I-house; 1860; Outbuildings: brooder house, machine shed, Sweitzer barn; *Agriculture, Architecture* (443)

**062 C Farm;** 25521 CR 54; Central-passage; c.1890; Outbuildings: chicken house, English barn, machine shed, milk house; *Agriculture, Architecture* (443)

**063 C Farm;** 25363 CR 54; Upright-and-wing; 1880; Outbuildings: drive-thru corn crib, English barn, garage, sheds; *Agriculture, Architecture* (443)

**064 C Farm;** CR 15; Gabled-ell; c.1900; Outbuildings: drive-thru corn crib, English barn, windmill; *Agriculture, Architecture* (443)

**065 C Brown Farm;** 71888 CR 15; Colonial Revival; c.1940; Outbuildings: chicken house, garage, machine shed, privy; *Agriculture, Architecture* (443)

**066 C Brown School;** 23023 CR 54; T-plan; 1888; *Architecture, Education* (443)

**067 N Stuckman Farm;** 72240 CR 13; Dutch Colonial Revival; 1936 (Stuckman, builder); Outbuildings: chicken house, corn crib, garage, livestock barn, machine shed, silo; *Agriculture, Architecture* (443)

**068 C Wysong Farm;** 25431 US 6; T-plan; c.1900; Outbuildings: bank/basement barn, garage; *Agriculture, Architecture* (443)

**069 N Farm;** 72729 CR 9; Prairie; c.1910; Outbuildings: Sweitzer barn, smokehouse, spring house; *Agriculture, Architecture* (443)

**070 C Miller Farm;** 25622 US 6; T-plan/Italianate; c.1870; Outbuilding: Sweitzer barn; *Agriculture, Architecture* (443)

**071 C Barn;** 72973 S County Line Rd.; English barn; c.1930; Outbuilding: shed; *Agriculture, Architecture* (443)

**072 C Farm;** CR 56; American foursquare; c.1920; Outbuildings: drive-thru corn crib, shed; *Agriculture, Architecture* (443)

**073 C House;** CR 56; Hall-and-parlor; c.1890; *Architecture* (443)

**Howard Dawson Farm, c.1920.** *Photo courtesy of the Elkhart County Historical Museum*

70069 This farm features a spring house and smoke house made from cobblestones.

# Downtown Nappanee Historic District  (039-444-71001-043)

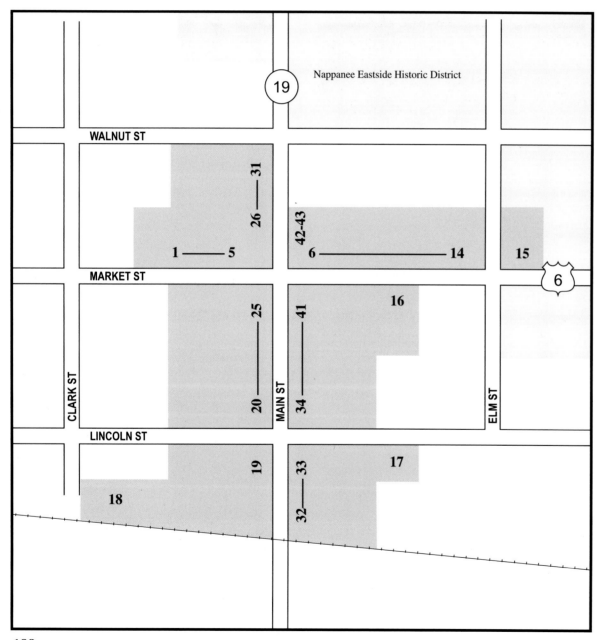

Nappanee Eastside Historic District

WALNUT ST

31
26
42-43
1 —— 5
6 —————— 14
15

MARKET ST

6

25
41
16

CLARK ST
20
MAIN ST
34
ELM ST

LINCOLN ST

19
33
17

18
32

The Downtown Nappanee Historic District lies almost entirely within the original 1874 plat of Daniel Metzler, John Culp Jr., and Henry Stahly. The only building outside the original town boundaries is the United States Post Office on East Market Street (71015). From its beginning, the district was a commercial area surrounded by residential neighborhoods; the size of the commercial area has remained relatively unchanged. Most new businesses have either moved into existing buildings or started further down East Market Street on the outskirts of town.

During its more than 130-year history, buildings in the district have been used for a number of purposes. One constant has been the presence of retail stores, which dominate the area today. Early businesses included the DeFreese Creamery, the first creamery in Indiana, established in 1882. The southern edge of the district is bordered by the Baltimore and Ohio Railroad's tracks. Hotels built to service railroad passengers included the Nappanee House and the Coppes Hotel, neither of which exists today. The proximity to the railroad and to the Nappanee Depot made the city a popular place for industries such as a carriage factory (71033) and the vacant Coppes Furniture Factory, in the Eastside Historic District (72110). The growth of commerce in Nappanee led to the need for banking institutions. Two buildings, the Farmers and Traders Bank (Nappanee's first bank) (71024) and the First National Bank (71037) remain, though neither is used as a bank. Stockyards, onion storage buildings, and other agricultural buildings once stood near the railroad tracks, but none survive today.

Different construction methods were employed in the district. The earliest downtown structures were wood-framed and constructed with local timber. As the town grew in the late 1890s, businesses needed more substantial structures. This resulted in a local building boom and many buildings in the district today date to that era. Those buildings were built with bricks, most manufactured in local kilns. During their construction, the original wood-framed structures were moved into the intersection of Main and Market Streets so business could continue, and the streets were closed at the intersection.

The result of the construction was a new, vibrant downtown that included the Hartman Brothers Store, lauded as the largest in Elkhart County. The building houses an antique store today (71022). During the first decade of the 20th century, the city paved its two major streets and installed brick sidewalks. Within a few years, they added streetlights, removed the town's original water pump from a sidewalk on South Main Street, and installed running water for indoor use.

## DOWNTOWN NAPPANEE HISTORIC DISTRICT (039-444-71001-043) NR

**No. Rtg. Add. Description**

**WEST MARKET STREET** *(north side)*

**001 C 152** **Wisler Building;** Parapet-front; 1925

**002 C 110** **Wisler Building;** Two-part commercial block; c.1915

**003 C 108** **Huffman Bakery;** Two-part commercial block; c.1900

**004 C 106** **Commercial Building;** Two-part commercial block; c.1915

**005 NC 102** **Office Building;** c.1990

**EAST MARKET STREET** *(north side)*

**006 NC NA** **Commercial Building;** c.1900

**007 C 104** **Commercial Building;** Parapet-front; c.1910

**008 C 106-08** **Wisler Building;** Craftsman; 1914

**71015 The 1935 United States Post Office is a good example of the Colonial Revival style, which was in fashion at the time due to the popularity of Colonial Williamsburg in Virginia.**

**009 C 110** **Commercial Building;** Art Deco; c.1930

**010 NC 112** **Commercial Building;** c.1870/ c.1970

**011 C 152** **Commercial Building;** Parapet-front; c.1875

**012 C 154-56** **Commercial Building;** Two-part commercial block; c.1915

**013 C 158** **Commercial Building;** One-part commercial block; 1955

**014 C 162** **Price Hospital;** Prairie; 1913

**015 N 202** **United States Post Office;** Colonial Revival; 1935

**EAST MARKET STREET** *(south side)*

**016 N 151** **Bechtel Building;** Italianate; 1888

**EAST LINCOLN STREET** *(south side)*

**017 C NA** **Nappanee City Hall;** Prairie; c.1917

**SOUTH MAIN STREET** *(west side)*

**018 N NA** **Baltimore & Ohio Railroad Depot;** Prairie; 1910

**019 NC 202** **Commercial Building;** c.1990

**South Main Street, c.1911.** *Photo courtesy of the Elkhart County Historical Museum*

**020 NC NA** **Parking Lot**

**021 C 158** **Commercial Building;** Two-part commercial block; 1935

**022 C 156** **Hartman Brothers Building;** Two-part commercial block; 1914

**023 C 106-12** **Commercial Building;** Two-part commercial block; c.1910

**024 N 104** **Justus Building/Farmers & Traders Bank;** Neoclassical; 1915

**025 C NA** **Kaufman's Department Store;** Italianate; 1902

**71016 The 1888 Bechtel Building is a good example of the Italianate style applied to a commercial building. It features a pressed metal cornice with decorative brackets and tall window openings with decorative pressed metal hoods.**

71018 The 1910 Baltimore and Ohio Railroad Depot was built in the Prairie style and features wide, slightly flared overhanging eaves, narrow horizontal wood siding, and a sandstone water table.

71024 The 1915 Neoclassical Farmers & Traders Bank Building is also known as the Justus Building. It boasts a grand entry flanked by large Ionic columns.

71041 The 1900 Dietrich Block is another good example of the Neoclassical style. Its most striking characteristics are the engaged second-story columns and its pressed metal parapet.

## NORTH MAIN STREET (west side)

| 026 | NC | 106 | Commercial Building; c.1965 |
| 027 | C | 110 | V.F.W. Building; One-part commercial block; c.1950 |
| 028 | C | 152 | Commercial Building; Craftsman; 1913 |
| 029 | C | 154 | Commercial Building; Craftsman; 1926 |
| 030 | C | 156-58 | Commercial Building; Craftsman; c.1915 |
| 031 | C | 160 | Yoder's Garage & Livery; Italianate; 1910 |

## SOUTH MAIN STREET (east side)

| 032 | NC | NA | Commercial Building; One-part commercial block; c.1930 |
| 033 | C | 201 | Nappanee Carriage Works; 20th century functional; 1900 |
| 034 | C | 159-61 | Commercial Building; Two-part commercial block; c.1900 |
| 035 | C | 155 | Commercial Building; Parapet-front; c.1930 |
| 036 | NC | 153 | Hotel; 1876/1986 |
| 037 | C | 151 | First National Bank; Neoclassical; 1908 |
| 038 | C | 111 | Metzler Shoe Company; One-part commercial block; 1929/c.1960 |

| 039 | NC | 109 | Jacob Walter's Drugstore; 1881 |
| 040 | C | 107 | Commercial Building; Craftsman; c.1910 |
| 041 | C | NA | Dietrich Block; Neoclassical; 1900 |

## NORTH MAIN STREET (east side)

| 042 | NC | 107 | Commercial Building; Two-part commercial block; c.1920 |
| 043 | C | 111 | Commercial Building; One-part commercial block; c.1920 |

71037 The 1908 Neoclassical First National Bank on Main Street has a limestone and brick facade.

# Nappanee Eastside Historic District (039-443-72001-198)

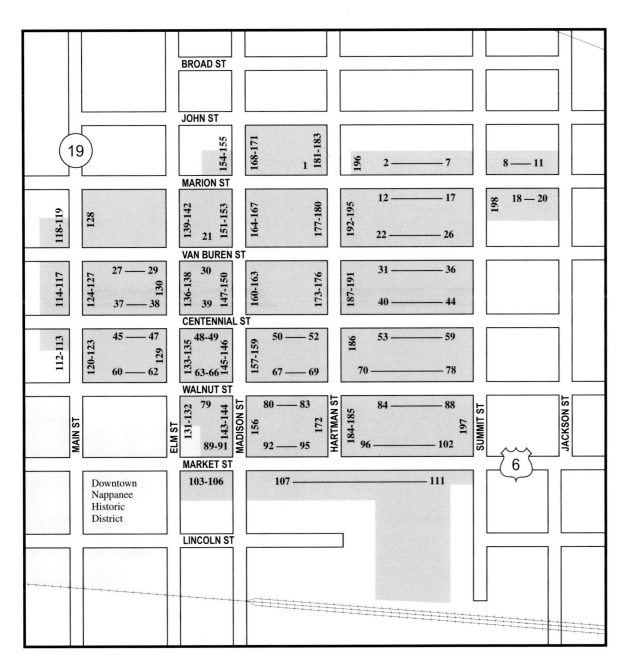

Nappanee's Eastside Historic District is located in the northeast corner of the original 1874 plat. It is bounded by Main Street to the west, Market Street to the south, Summit Street to the east, and Marion Street to the north. Because the streets were created in several different plats, the blocks are of different sizes, but all run either north and south or east and west. The district was listed in the National Register of Historic Places in 2003.

With few exceptions, the 140+ buildings in the district are single-family residences. The former elementary school sits on Main Street (72128), there are three churches located on Centennial and Market Streets (72038, 72103, 72107), an office building on Elm Street (72136), and the Coppes Cabinet Factory on Market Street (72110). The majority of construction took place during the early-20th century, although a few houses date from Nappanee's early years in the late-1800s. The district includes homes designed by local architects for some of the city's most prominent citizens as well as more humble, middle-class homes that are more vernacular in their architectural style. Some of the best examples of high-style architecture include Prairie-style houses on Madison and Market Streets (72094, 72152, 72168). There are also fine examples of Italianate, Queen Anne, Free Classic, Tudor Revival, Colonial Revival, and Mediterranean Revival houses. The Craftsman style is prevalent on both lavish houses and smaller bungalows and American Foursquares. Vernacular gable-fronts and gabled-ells are common house types in the district.

Since 1950, the neighborhood has undergone few major changes. Few houses have been constructed in the neighborhood since 1950 and there are few vacant lots. The east side of the 300 block of North Hartman Street is a good example of the changes houses in the district have undergone (72187-191). In 1905, Frank Coppes built the five identical Free Classic houses as speculative housing. While they all still contribute to the district, several have constructed new wings, replaced porches or siding, and made other alterations that reflect their age.

Revitalizing the historic character of the district is a high priority for many of the district's residents today. Several houses have been restored and the city of Nappanee replaced asphalt pavement with bricks on Madison Street and installed more appropriate street lights.

## NAPPANEE EASTSIDE HISTORIC DISTRICT (039-443-72001-198) NR

No. Rtg. Add. Description

### EAST MARION STREET (north side)

| | | | |
|---|---|---|---|
| 001 | N | 356 | **House;** Side-gable bungalow; c.1912 |
| 002 | C | 408 | **House;** Cape Cod; c.1930 |
| 003 | C | 452 | **House;** English cottage; c.1925 |
| 004 | C | 460 | **House;** Massed ranch; c.1950 |
| 005 | C | 466 | **House;** Free Classic; c.1915 |
| 006 | C | 470 | **House;** Side-gable bungalow/ Craftsman; c.1925 |
| 007 | C | 476 | **House;** Gable-front; c.1925 |
| 008 | N | 602 | **House;** Colonial Revival; c.1930 |
| 009 | C | 608 | **House;** Colonial Revival; c.1930 |
| 010 | N | 652 | **House;** English cottage; c.1930 |
| 011 | C | 658 | **House;** English cottage; c.1930 |

### EAST MARION STREET (south side)

| | | | |
|---|---|---|---|
| 012 | C | 451 | **House;** Minimal traditional; c.1938 |
| 013 | C | 453 | **House;** Colonial Revival; 1938 |
| 014 | C | 465 | **House;** Minimal traditional; c.1940 |
| 015 | C | 467 | **House;** Colonial Revival; c.1930 |
| 016 | C | 473 | **House;** Minimal traditional; c.1940 |
| 017 | NC | 475 | **House;** Pyramidal-roof; c.1935 |

**72019** This 1931 Tudor Revival house has brick walls with half-timbering, original windows, and a columned side patio.

| | | | |
|---|---|---|---|
| 018 | C | 607 | **House;** English cottage; c.1925 |
| 019 | N | 651 | **House;** Tudor Revival; 1931 |
| 020 | C | 657 | **House;** Colonial Revival; c.1938 |

### EAST VAN BUREN STREET (north side)

| | | | |
|---|---|---|---|
| 021 | C | 206 | **House;** Dormer-front bungalow/ Craftsman; c.1920 |
| 022 | C | 452 | **House;** Gable-front; 1915 |
| 023 | C | 454 | **House;** Gable-front; 1915 |
| 024 | N | 458 | **House;** Colonial Revival; 1937 |
| 025 | C | 502 | **House;** Gable-front; c.1910 |
| 026 | C | 508 | **House;** English cottage; c.1925 |

### EAST VAN BUREN STREET (south side)

| | | | |
|---|---|---|---|
| 027 | C | 107 | **House;** Dormer-front bungalow; c.1915 |
| 028 | NC | 151 | **House;** American foursquare; c.1915 |
| 029 | N | 157 | **House;** Western bungalow/Craftsman; c.1920 |
| 030 | C | 205 | **House;** Cape Cod; c.1940 |
| 031 | C | 451 | **House;** Pyramidal-roof; c.1920 |
| 032 | NC | 453 | **House;** Gabled-ell; c.1910 |
| 033 | C | 455 | **House;** Upright-and-wing; c.1910 |
| 034 | C | 503 | **House;** Upright-and-wing; c.1910 |
| 035 | NC | NA | **Vacant Lot** |
| 036 | C | 507 | **House;** Gable-front; c.1910 |

### EAST CENTENNIAL STREET (north side)

| | | | |
|---|---|---|---|
| 037 | C | 152 | **House;** T-plan; c.1885 |
| 038 | C | 158 | **Church of God;** 20th century functional; 1920 |
| 039 | C | 252 | **House;** English cottage; c.1920 |
| 040 | NC | 452 | **House;** Upright-and-wing; c.1910 |
| 041 | NC | 456 | **House;** Ranch; c.1960 |
| 042 | C | 458 | **House;** Gabled-ell; c.1895 |
| 043 | NC | 502 | **House;** Minimal ranch; c.1965 |
| 044 | NC | 508 | **House;** Gable-front; c.1950 |

### EAST CENTENNIAL STREET (south side)

| | | | |
|---|---|---|---|
| 045 | NC | 107 | **House;** L-plan; c.1900 |
| 046 | NC | 153 | **House;** Minimal ranch; c.1970 |
| 047 | NC | NA | **Vacant Lot** |
| 048 | NC | NA | **Vacant Lot** |
| 049 | C | 253 | **House;** Upright-and-wing; c.1870 |
| 050 | C | 307 | **House;** Gabled-ell; c.1880 |
| 051 | C | 351 | **House;** Gabled-ell; c.1880 |
| 052 | C | 357 | **House;** Gabled-ell; c.1895 |
| 053 | N | 403 | **House;** Gable-front; 1885 |
| 054 | C | 405 | **House;** Gabled-ell; c.1885 |
| 055 | C | 451 | **House;** Gable-front; c.1895 |
| 056 | NC | 455 | **House;** Traditional ranch; c.1965 |
| 057 | C | 457 | **House;** Gable-front; 1925 |

**72024** This 1937 Colonial Revival exhibits a symmetrical plan, side chimney, and slate roof.

**72066** This American foursquare features Colonial Revival details, including full-width front porch with tripled Corinthian columns.

**058  C  501    House;** Dormer-front bungalow; c.1910

**059  NC  507    House;** Upright-and-wing; c.1900

## EAST WALNUT STREET (*north side*)

**060  C  108    House;** American foursquare; c.1900

**061  C  152    House;** Free Classic; c.1890

**062  C  158    House;** Gable-front; c.1890

**063  C  202    House;** Central-passage; c.1900

**064  NC  208    House;** Upright-and-wing; c.1900

**065  N  252    House;** Mediterranean Revival; c.1925

**066  N  258    House;** American foursquare/ Colonial Revival; c.1910

**067  C  308    House;** Gable-front; c.1875

**068  C  352    House;** Gabled-ell; c.1890

**069  N  358    House;** Lazy-T; c.1880

**070  NC  402    House;** Gable-front; c.1910

**071  C  406    House;** Pyramidal-roof; c.1900

**072  NC  410    House;** Upright-and-wing; c.1900

**073  C  452    House;** Gabled-ell; c.1890

**074  C  456    House;** Gabled-ell; c.1890

**075  C  458    House;** L-plan; c.1910

**076  C  502    House;** California bungalow; c.1915

**077  NC  NA    House;** Gable-front; c.1910

**078  C  508    House;** Gabled-ell; c.1900

## EAST WALNUT STREET (*south side*)

**079  C  207    House;** American foursquare; 1915

**080  C  301    House;** Italianate cube; c.1890

**081  C  307    House;** Gable-front; c.1900

**082  N  351    House;** English cottage; 1935

**083  C  357    House;** Gabled-ell; c.1890

**084  C  451    House;** Upright-and-wing; c.1915

**085  NC  455    House;** Minimal traditional; c.1945

**086  C  457    House;** Gable-front; c.1890

**087  C  501    House;** Gabled-ell; c.1890

**088  C  507    House;** Gable-front; c.1885

## EAST MARKET STREET (*north side*)

**089  NC  208    House;** Queen Anne; c.1890

**090  NC  252    House;** Cross-gable square; c.1910

**091  C  258    Masonic Lodge;** Queen Anne; 1895

**092  O  302    Frank and Katharine Coppes House;** Queen Anne; c.1887 **NR**

**093  C  308    House;** Queen Anne; c.1895

**094  N  352    House;** American foursquare/ Prairie; c.1910

**095  C  356    House;** Dutch Colonial Revival; c.1900

**096  NC  402    House;** L-plan; c.1910

**72092** This 1893 Queen Anne style boasts a side turret with conical roof, wrap around porch, and various wall treatments.

**72094** This American foursquare has Prairie style details, including overhanging eaves and a full-width front porch with stone-faced columns.

**097  C  404    House;** Queen Anne; c.1895

**098  C  410    House;** T-plan; c.1885

**099  NC  452    House;** Gas Station; 20th century functional; c.1945

**100  C  462    House;** Gable-front; c.1895

**101  C  506    House;** Gable-front; c.1890

**102  N  508    House;** Italianate; c.1880

## EAST MARKET STREET (*south side*)

**103  N  201    Calvary Baptist Church;** Neoclassical; 1928

**104  NC  207    House/Office;** c.1990

**105  N  251    House;** Neoclassical; c.1925

**106  O  253    Arthur Miller House;** Colonial Revival; 1922 **NR**

**107  NC  301    Nappanee United Methodist Church;** c.1980

**108  NC  357    House/Office;** Minimal traditional; c.1945

**109  N  401    Coppes Office;** Queen Anne cottage; c.1900

**110  C  451    Coppes Factory;** 19th century functional; c.1885/c.1905

**111  C  507    House;** American foursquare; c.1915

## NORTH MAIN STREET *(west side)*

112　C　252　**House;** Free Classic; c.1915

113　NC　258　**House;** Gabled-ell; c.1910

114　N　302　**House;** Free Classic; 1902

115　C　306　**House;** Dormer-front bungalow; c.1905

116　NC　352　**House;** American foursquare; c.1915

117　N　358　**House;** Craftsman; c.1930

118　N　NA　**House;** Italianate; 1880

119　C　404　**House;** Gabled-ell; c.1915

## NORTH MAIN STREET *(east side)*

120　C　201　**House;** Gabled-ell; c.1899

121　C　207　**House;** American foursquare; 1900

122　NC　251　**House;** T-plan; c.1900

123　C　257　**House;** Gabled-ell; c.1900

124　NC　301　**Office Building;** c.1970

125　C　307　**House;** Gabled-ell; 1890

126　C　353　**House;** Colonial Revival; c.1930

127　C　357　**House;** Gabled-ell; c.1880

128　C　451　**School;** Art Deco; 1937

72106　This Colonial Revival house has three gabled dormers, double-hung wood windows, and a pedimented porch over the entry supported by Corinthian columns.

72114　This 1902 Free Classic house features wood shingle and clapboard siding. It currently houses a bed and breakfast.

## NORTH ELM STREET *(west side)*

129　C　252　**House;** Gable-front; c.1900

130　C　352　**House;** American foursquare; 1910

## NORTH ELM STREET *(east side)*

131　C　151　**House;** American foursquare; c.1915

132　C　157　**House;** Italianate; c.1885

133　NC　203　**House;** Minimal ranch; c.1945

134　C　253　**House;** Upright-and-wing; c.1900

135　N　257　**House;** Dormer-front bungalow; c.1915

136　C　301　**Office Building;** Art Moderne; 1925

137　C　351　**House;** Gabled-ell; c.1890

138　C　357　**House;** Gabled-ell; c.1900

139　C　401　**House;** Massed ranch; c.1965

140　NC　407　**House;** Gable-front; 1910

141　NC　451　**House;** Gable-front; c.1900

142　C　457　**House;** Gabled-ell; 1910

## NORTH MADISON STREET *(west side)*

143　C　152　**House;** Bungalow; 1905

72152　This Prairie style house exhibits a low-pitched, hipped roof with overhanging eaves, decorative bands that emphasize the horizontal, and stucco walls.

144　C　158　**House;** T-plan; c.1870

145　NC　252　**House;** Gable-front; c.1885

146　NC　256　**House;** Gabled-ell; c.1910

147　C　302　**House;** Gabled-ell; c.1900

148　C　308　**House;** Gable-front; 1915

149　C　352　**House;** Queen Anne; 1871

150　C　356　**House;** Gabled-ell; 1910

151　C　402　**House;** Free Classic; 1900

152　O　408　**House;** Prairie; c.1910

153　C　458　**House;** Gable-front; c.1860-1870

154　NC　502　**House;** Cross-gable square; c.1910

155　C　508　**House;** American foursquare; c.1910

## NORTH MADISON STREET *(east side)*

156　C　151　**House;** Upright-and-wing; c.1870

72157　This 1935 Tudor Revival house has stone walls, prominent chimneys, and gabled dormers.

**72185** This 1929 Tudor Revival house retains a slate roof, decorative brick work, and stone accents around the entry.

| 157 | N | 201 | **House;** Tudor Revival; 1935 |
| 158 | C | 251 | **House;** American foursquare; 1900 |
| 159 | NC | 257 | **House;** Gable-front; c.1915 |
| 160 | C | 301 | **House;** Gabled-ell; c.1900 |
| 161 | NC | 307 | **House;** Gabled-ell; c.1900 |
| 162 | C | 351 | **House;** Lazy-T; c.1900 |
| 163 | C | 355 | **House;** T-plan; c.1900 |
| 164 | NC | 401 | **House;** Gable-front; c.1995 |
| 165 | C | 405 | **House;** Colonial Revival; c.1925 |
| 166 | N | 451 | **House;** Lazy-T; 1879 |
| 167 | C | 455 | **House;** Gabled-ell; 1880 |
| 168 | C | 503 | **House;** Midwest box/Prairie; c.1920 |

**72189** This 1905 Free Classic house has a clipped front gable with extended cornice returns, original wood siding, and a wrap-around front porch supported by brick piers. This is one of five houses built by Frank Coppes that were originally identical.

**72191** This 1905 Free Classic house is another of the homes built by Frank Coppes as speculative housing. It has a side wing with ribbon windows and no porch.

| 169 | C | 507 | **House;** Dutch Colonial Revival; c.1915 |
| 170 | C | 553 | **House;** Gable-front; c.1915 |
| 171 | NC | 557 | **House;** Gabled-ell; c.1900 |

**NORTH HARTMAN STREET** *(west side)*

| 172 | NC | 152 | **House;** Gable-front; c.1900 |
| 173 | NC | 300 | **House;** Free Classic; c.1900 |
| 174 | C | 306 | **House;** American foursquare; 1922 |
| 175 | NC | 352 | **House;** T-plan; c.1900 |
| 176 | C | 350 | **House;** Gable-front/Craftsman; 1925 |
| 177 | C | 402 | **House;** Queen Anne; 1905 |
| 178 | C | 408 | **House;** English cottage; c.1935 |
| 179 | C | 452 | **House;** Upright-and-wing; c.1895 |
| 180 | C | 458 | **House;** Dormer-front bungalow; c.1930 |
| 181 | C | 508 | **House;** Gable-front/Craftsman; c.1900 |
| 182 | C | 552 | **House;** Gable-front; c.1915 |
| 183 | NC | 558 | **House;** Minimal traditional; c.1940 |

**NORTH HARTMAN STREET** *(east side)*

| 184 | C | 103 | **House;** Minimal traditional; 1937 |
| 185 | N | 153 | **House;** Tudor Revival; 1929 |
| 186 | C | 257 | **House;** Gabled-ell; c.1890 |
| 187 | N | 301 | **House;** Free Classic; 1905 (Frank Coppes, builder) |
| 188 | C | 303 | **House;** Free Classic; 1905 (Frank Coppes, builder) |
| 189 | N | 305 | **House;** Free Classic; 1905 (Frank Coppes, builder) |
| 190 | C | 351 | **House;** Free Classic; 1905 (Frank Coppes, builder) |
| 191 | N | 353 | **House;** Free Classic; 1905 (Frank Coppes, builder) |
| 192 | C | 401 | **House;** American foursquare; 1910 |
| 193 | C | 407 | **House;** Dormer-front bungalow/ Colonial Revival; 1924 |
| 194 | N | 451 | **House;** English cottage; 1925 |
| 195 | C | 457 | **House;** Dutch Colonial Revival; 1920 |
| 196 | C | 501 | **House;** Free Classic; c.1910 |

**SUMMIT STREET** *(west side)*

| 197 | NC | 152 | **House;** Minimal ranch; c.1965 |

**SUMMIT STREET** *(east side)*

| 198 | C | 457 | **House;** Prairie; c.1915 |

**72194** This 1925 English Cottage retains its original windows, including the front oriel.

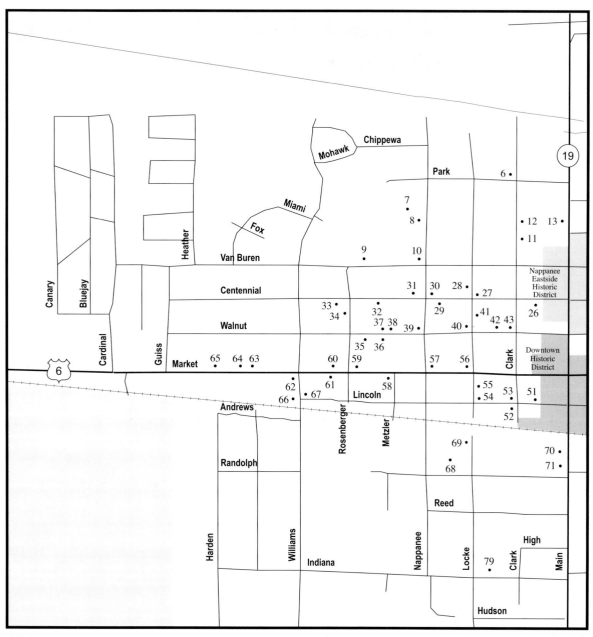

Elkhart County's youngest city is located on what was once the least desirable land in the county. The land was peppered with marshes and the few spots that were not saturated with water were densely covered with trees. The area's only geographic importance was that it was located on the lesser-known Continental Divide. Located approximately where Market Street lies, the boundary divides water that flows north through the Great Lakes and Saint Lawrence River to the Atlantic Ocean and water that flows south to the Ohio and Mississippi Rivers to the Gulf of Mexico.

Nappanee was created by people wishing to profit from its proximity to the railroad. In 1870, only one rail line existed connecting Chicago to the major cities of the East. The Baltimore and Ohio Railroad wanted to change that by extending their line westward to reach Chicago as quickly as possible. To do this, they laid their tracks in as straight a line as possible, making no effort to connect to any other cities or towns. As the tracks passed through southern Elkhart County, Locke Town, a growing city located just a couple miles north of the proposed line, was ignored. In order to have access to the railroad, Henry Eby, Locke's most prominent merchant, purchased a small amount of land and created Locke Station. Locke's other merchants soon followed. In 1874, the primary landowners, John Culp Jr., Henry Stahly, and Daniel Metzler, platted Nappanee around the station and sold lots at forty dollars each. Many of Locke's citizens and nearly all of its businesses moved to Nappanee, and by 1880, Nappanee had a population of 700 people.

Due to the amount of wood available in the area, the first major industries were related to forestry. In fact, the first sawmill predated the founding of the city. J.C. Mellinger and Frank Meyers started the mill, but it was soon bought by John and Frank Coppes, whose family quickly became

# Nappanee Scattered Sites-East Section (73001-079)

Nappanee's most prominent. Lumber from Coppes Mill was used in almost every building constructed in town before the turn of the 20th century; in addition, one of the largest ships on the Great Lakes, the steamer *Topeka,* was constructed of lumber from Coppes Mill in 1889. The Coppes and others in town soon moved into other wood-related industries, including furniture making and charcoal kiln construction.

As the marsh land and ponds around the village were drained, prosperous farms surrounding Nappanee used the town for storage and shipping. For a number of years onions were the most popular crop, but corn, hemp, and mint were also common. At one point, the area around Nappanee produced almost all of the hemp and mint grown in the United States.

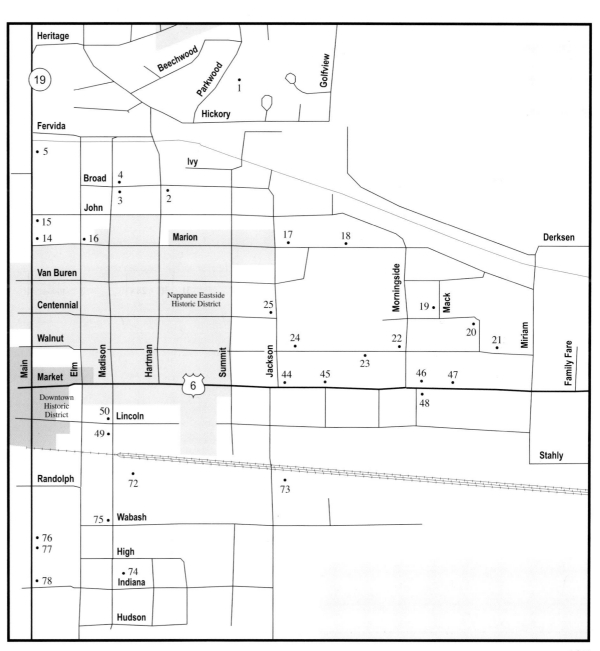

## NAPPANEE SCATTERED SITES (73001-079)

**No. Rtg. Description**

**001 C Stahly Farm;** 1061 Parkwood Dr.; Bank barn; Outbuildings: carriage house, windmill; *Agriculture, Architecture* (443)

**002 C House;** 403 Broad Ave.; English cottage; c.1930; Outbuilding: garage; *Architecture* (443)

**003 C House;** 301 Broad Ave.; Traditional ranch; c.1950; *Architecture* (443)

**004 C House;** 300 Broad Ave.; Colonial Revival; c.1940; *Architecture* (443)

**005 C House;** 755 N Main St.; Western bungalow/ Craftsman; c.1930; *Architecture* (444)

**006 C House;** 702 N Clark St.; Gable-front; c.1900; *Architecture* (444)

**007 N Schlabach Cabin;** West Park; Single-pen/ log construction; c.1852 (Schlabach, builder); *Architecture, Exploration/Settlement* (444)

**008 O Nappanee West Park & Pavilion;** Nappanee St. & Van Buren St.; 1923; *Architecture, Community Planning* (444) **NR**

**009 C House;** 556 W Van Buren St.; Dutch Colonial Revival; c.1920 (Heckman Homes, builder); *Architecture* (444)

**010 C House;** 402 N Nappanee St.; Gabled-ell; c.1910; *Architecture* (444)

**73007 The Schlabach Cabin is a single pen log house erected c.1852, and is one of Elkhart County's oldest buildings.**

**011 N House;** 453 N Clark St.; Gable-front; c.1900; Outbuilding: garage; *Architecture* (444)

**012 C House;** 551 N Clark St.; Gabled-ell; c.1900; *Architecture* (444)

**013 C North Main Street Mennonite Church;** N Main St.; Parapet-front; 1893/1952; *Architecture, Religion* (444)

**014 C House;** 501 N Main St.; Upright-and-wing; c.1915; *Architecture* (444)

**015 C House;** 557 N Main St.; Upright-and-wing; c.1895; *Architecture* (444)

**016 C House;** 501 N Elm St.; Gable-front; c.1910; *Architecture* (443)

**017 C House;** 706 E Marion St.; English cottage; c.1930; *Architecture* (443)

**018 C House;** 806 E Marion St.; Cape Cod; c.1940; *Architecture* (443)

**019 C Nappanee Church of the Brethren;** 301 Mack Dr.; Modern; 1959 (Alves O'Keefe, architect); *Architecture, Religion* (443)

**020 C House;** Highland St.; English cottage; c.1930; *Architecture* (443)

**021 C House;** Walnut St.; Dormer-front bungalow; c.1920; *Architecture* (443)

**022 C House;** 958 E Walnut St.; Craftsman; c.1930; *Architecture* (443)

**023 C House;** 857 E Walnut St.; Gable-front; c.1930; *Architecture* (443)

**024 C House;** 706 E Walnut St.; Gable-front; c.1940; *Architecture* (443)

**025 C House;** 658 E Centennial St.; Dutch Colonial Revival; c.1930; *Architecture* (443)

**026 C House;** 151 E Centennial St.; Ranch; c.1950; Outbuilding: garage; *Architecture* (444)

**027 C House;** 258 W Centennial St.; Upright-and-wing; c.1920; *Architecture* (444)

**028 C House;** 308 N Locke St.; Dormer-front bungalow/Craftsman; c.1920; *Architecture* (444)

**029 C House;** 351 W Centennial St.; English cottage; c.1920; *Architecture* (444)

**030 C House;** 301 Nappanee St.; T-plan/English cottage; c.1890/c.1920; *Architecture* (444)

**73004 A c.1940 Colonial Revival Style home that features thre gabled dormers.**

**73008 The 1923 Pavilion at Nappanee West Park was built as lodging for yearly chatauquas. It was listed on the National Register of Historic Places in 1994.**

**73032 This c.1910 Lazy T house retains its original clapboard siding and windows.**

73040 The 1946 First Brethren Church is a late example of the Art Moderne style having geometric-patterned ornament.

031 C **House;** 452 Centennial St.; Lazy-T; c.1925; Outbuilding: garage; *Architecture* (444)

032 C **House;** 507 W Centennial St.; Lazy-T; c.1910; *Architecture* (444)

033 C **House;** 605 W Centennial St.; Gable-front; 1880; *Architecture* (444)

034 C **House;** 252 Rosenberger St.; Free Classic; c.1900; *Architecture* (444)

035 C **House;** 551 W Walnut St.; Gabled-ell; c.1900; *Architecture* (444)

036 C **House;** 501 W Walnut St.; Gabled-ell; c.1910; *Architecture* (444)

037 C **Our Lady of Perpetual Help Roman Catholic Church;** 458 W Walnut St.; Side-steeple; c.1900; *Architecture, Religion* (444)

038 C **House;** 452 W Walnut St.; Gable-front; c.1935; *Architecture* (444)

039 C **House;** Nappanee St.; Cross-gable; c.1880; *Architecture* (444)

040 N **First Brethren Church;** Locke St. & Walnut St.; Art Moderne; 1946; *Architecture, Religion* (444)

041 C **House;** 207 Locke St.; Upright-and-wing; c.1930; *Architecture* (444)

042 C **House;** W Walnut St.; American four-square; c.1920; *Architecture* (444)

043 C **House;** 206 W Walnut St.; Lazy-T; c.1890; *Architecture* (444)

044 C **Nappanee Church of the Brethren;** 702 E Market St.; Romanesque Revival; 1884/1917; *Architecture, Religion* (443)

045 C **House;** 802 E Market St.; Upright-and-wing; c.1900; *Architecture* (443)

046 C **House;** E Market St.; Gabled-ell; c.1910; *Architecture* (443)

047 C **House;** 1056 E Market St.; Dormer-front bungalow/Craftsman; c.1920; *Architecture* (443)

048 C **House;** 1051 E Market St.; Gable-front; c.1910; *Architecture* (443)

049 C **House;** 252 S Madison St.; English cottage; c.1920; *Architecture* (443)

050 C **House;** 256 E Lincoln St.; Upright-and-wing; c.1930; *Architecture* (443)

051 C **House;** 152 W Lincoln St.; American four-square; c.1920; *Architecture* (444)

052 C **American Legion Hall;** W Lincoln St.; Depression modern; c.1930; *Architecture* (444)

053 C **House;** 156 S Clark St.; Prairie; 1920; *Architecture* (444)

054 C **House;** 155 S Locke St.; Gabled-ell; c.1910; Outbuilding: garage; *Architecture* (444)

055 C **Missionary Church;** 151 S Locke St.; Side-steeple/Gothic Revival; c.1890; *Architecture, Religion* (444)

73044 Built in 1884 with a 1917 update, the Nappanee Church of the Brethren is a fine example of the Romanesque Revival style.

73052 The Depression Modern style c.1930 American Legion Hall features a brick and sandstone facade and multi-paned windows.

056 N **John Hartman House;** W Market St.; Gabled-ell; c.1880; *Architecture* (444)

057 C **House;** W Market St.; Italianate; c.1880; *Architecture* (444)

058 C **House;** W Market St.; American four-square; c.1920; Outbuilding: garage; *Architecture* (444)

059 C **House;** 556 W Market St.; Gable-front; c.1900; *Architecture* (444)

060 C **House;** 606 W Market St.; Gabled-ell; c.1890; *Architecture* (444)

061 C **House;** 405 W Market St.; American four-square; c.1920; Outbuilding: garage; *Architecture* (444)

73053 This 1920 Prairie style house once served as a physician's office and residence.

73056 The gabled-ell John Hartman House retains original clapboard siding, windows, and doors.

062 C **House;** Market St. & Williams St.; Craftsman; c.1930; *Architecture* (444)

063 N **House;** 754 W Market St.; Upright-and-wing; c.1930; Outbuilding: garage; *Architecture* (444)

064 C **House;** 758 W Market St.; Dormer-front bungalow; c.1920; Outbuilding: garage; *Architecture* (444)

065 C **House;** 256 W Market St.; Gabled-ell; c.1900; *Architecture* (444)

066 C **House;** 156 S Williams St.; California bungalow; c.1930; *Architecture* (444)

067 C **House;** S Williams St.; Western bungalow; c.1920; *Architecture* (444)

068 C **House;** 302 S Nappanee St.; Cape Cod; c.1930; *Architecture* (444)

73070 This c.1900 grain elevator was once a flour mill.

**200**

73072 The c.1880 Mutschler Kitchen Company is an industrial complex built to be functional and attractive. The brick buildings have decorative inlays at the roofline.

069 C **House;** 306 E Locke St.; Gable-front; c.1900; *Architecture* (444)

070 C **Flour Mill;** S Main St.; Grain elevator; c.1900; *Agriculture, Architecture, Commerce* (444)

071 C **Commercial Building;** 356 S Main St.; Gable-front; c.1910; *Architecture, Commerce* (444)

072 N **Mutschler Kitchen Company;** S Madison St.; 19th century functional; c.1880; *Architecture, Industry* (443)

73078 This c.1910 Gothic Revival style church features a square steeple at the southwest corner.

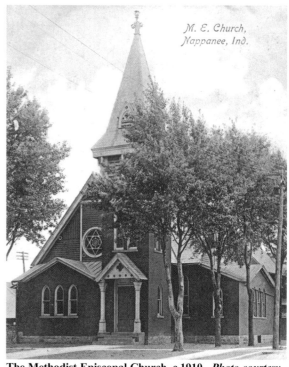

The Methodist Episcopal Church, c.1910. *Photo courtesy of the Elkhart County Historical Museum*

073 C **Lamb Brothers & Green/Cooper Brothers Building;** S Jackson St.; Italianate; 1909; *Architecture, Commerce, Industry* (443)

074 C **Michiana Hope Missionary Baptist Church;** S Madison St.; Gable-front/Gothic Revival; c.1900; *Architecture, Religion* (443)

075 C **Double House;** 456-458 S Madison St.; American foursquare; c.1920; *Architecture* (444)

076 C **Freese's Building;** S Main St.; 20th century functional; 1915; *Architecture, Commerce* (444)

077 C **George Freese's Sons Building;** 501 S Main St.; Parapet-front/Neoclassical; 1910; *Architecture, Commerce* (444)

078 C **Church;** S Main St. & Indiana Ave.; Gothic Revival; c.1910; *Architecture, Religion* (444)

079 C **House;** Indiana Ave.; Gabled-ell/Italianate; c.1890; *Architecture* (444)

# Amish Acres Scattered Sites (74001-010)

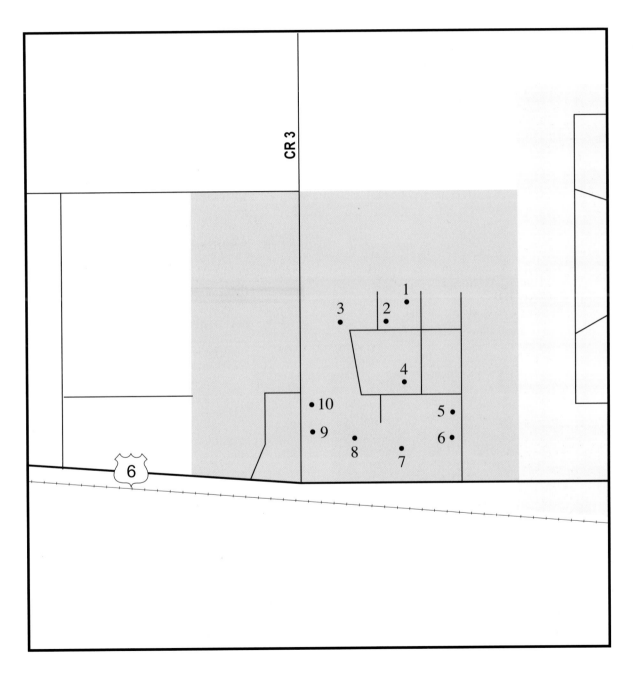

Amish Acres was the brainchild of Richard Pletcher. In 1968, he and local businessmen Gordon McCormick, Ivo "Pete" Heckaman, and Freeman Borkholder purchased the 80-acre Stahly-Manasses-Kuhns Farm for the express purpose of creating an outdoor living history museum of Amish farming life.

The farm's history began with Christian Stahly, a German immigrant, who came to America in 1835. In 1842, he settled in Elkhart County near what is today Nappanee and established his farm. The Stahlys were members of the Amish Mennonite Church. Mostly of German descent, the Mennonite immigrants sought refuge in communities in Lancaster County, Pennsylvania, northern Ohio, and Elkhart and LaGrange Counties in Indiana.

Life in the early years was difficult for the Stahlys. Christian and his pregnant wife had to live in their wagon while he built a log cabin. They also suffered the deaths of three of their seven children at a young age. However, their hard work and thrift paid off and the farm grew to encompass 187 acres.

In the 1870s, Christian Stahly gave 80 acres of his property to his son Moses. The farm switched hands over time until it was auctioned in 1968. Pletcher, whose family history dates back to the early Elkhart Mennonites, wanted to create an educational place that celebrated Amish history in the state and county.

Amish Acres has restored numerous historic structures, including a saw mill, blacksmith shop, ice house, and various barns. Additionally, new structures, such as a restaurant, theater, and gift shop, have been built. It remains an educational destination and draws tourists and students alike who want to glimpse Amish culture.

74004 The Chancy Thomas Blacksmith Shop, c.1870, was moved to Amish Acres from its original location six miles south.

**AMISH ACRES SCATTERED SITES (74001-010)**

| No. | Rtg. | Description |
|-----|------|-------------|

001 C **Pumphouse;** Gable-front; c.1890; *Architecture* (444)

002 C **House;** Upright-and-wing; c.1875; Outbuildings: broom shop, mint still, privy, saw mill; *Architecture* (444)

003 C **School;** Gable-front; c.1880; *Architecture, Education* (444)

004 N **Chancy Thomas Blacksmith Shop;** 19th century functional; c.1870; Outbuildings: carriage house, ice house, maple sugar camp; *Architecture, Commerce* (444)

74005 The double-pile Moses Stahly Farm remains in its near-original condition, with no modern conveniences added.

74006 The c.1890 Grosdaadi Haus was moved to the Amish Acres site around 1900.

005 O **Moses Stahly/Nissley/Kuhns Farm;** Double-pile; 1893; Outbuildings: brick bake oven, cold cellar, food drying house, hog house, house, milk house, privy, Sweitzer barn, smokehouse, windmill; *Agriculture, Architecture* (444) **NR**

006 O **Grosdaadi Haus;** Gable-front; c.1890; *Architecture* (444)

74008 This c.1860 single pen log house is made of squared logs joined with plaster, and was moved to its current site in 1973.

74009 This cider mill's original location was downtown Nappanee.

007 C **Frank Aker Round Barn;** 1600 W Market St.; Round barn; 1911; Outbuildings: Sweitzer barn; *Agriculture, Architecture* (444)

008 N **Log House;** Single-pen/log construction; c.1860; *Architecture, Exploration/Settlement* (444)

009 N **Cider Mill;** 19th century functional; c.1890; *Architecture, Commerce, Industry* (444)

010 N **Reverend R.J. Smid House;** Hall-and-parlor/log construction; 1853 (Joseph Smid, builder); *Architecture, Exploration/Settlement, Religion* (444)

74010 The 1853 Joseph Smid House belonged to the pastor of a Holland Mennonite congregation.

# Foraker Scattered Sites (75001-012)

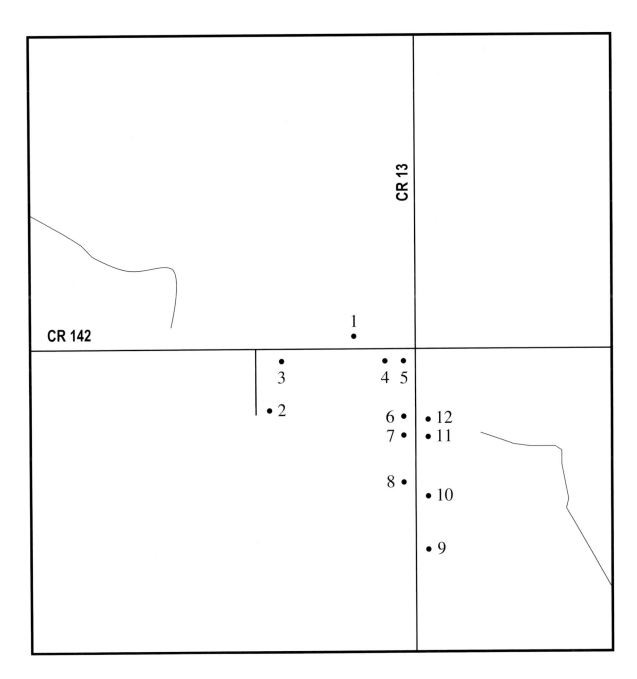

Located in the north-central part of Union Township is the small town of Foraker. The town was platted in 1892 from farmland that belonged to early resident Samuel Yoder and came into existence after the Wabash Railroad passed through the area.

The town was named after Republican Joseph B. Foraker. Foraker was popular throughout the nation for his strong stand against corruption and high debt in Ohio during his two terms as the state's governor in the 1880s. When the state elected Foraker to the U.S. Senate in 1896, he became a colorful firebrand and garnered the reputation of representing the interests of the Midwest, earning him the nickname "Fire Alarm Foraker."

Foraker grew steadily during the early-20th century thanks to the railroad. It eventually was large enough to support a grocery store, bank, lumber yard, garage, and church, which were all visible signs of the town's growing economic potential.

Most of Foraker's historic structures date to the 1920s through the 1950s, reflecting its short history. The town features many Craftsman bungalows (75006, 75008, 75009, 75012), which were popular during the 1920s.

**FORAKER SCATTERED SITES (75001-012)**

| No. | Rtg. | Description |
|---|---|---|

**001 C Foraker Fire Department;** 24025 CR 142; 20<sup>th</sup> century functional; 1950; *Architecture, Public Safety* (210)

**002 C House;** 24120 CR 142; 1 ½ I-house; c.1910; Outbuilding: garage; *Architecture* (210)

**003 C Commercial Building;** 24120 CR 142; Parapet-front; c.1940; Outbuilding: shed; *Architecture, Commerce* (210)

**004 N Bank Building;** CR 142; One-part commercial block; c.1920; *Architecture, Commerce, Economics* (210)

75004 Today it sits vacant, but this unassuming building used to serve the Foraker community as a bank.

75005 This is the only remaining Italianate building in Foraker. Built in 1920, it served as the Foraker General Store.

75009 The Culp House is another bungalow, built c.1915. It retains its original clapboard siding, knee braces, and front porch.

**005 C Foraker General Store;** CR 142; Italianate; c.1920; *Architecture, Commerce* (210)

**006 C House;** 67515 CR 13; Dormer-front bungalow/Craftsman; c.1920; Outbuilding: garage; *Architecture* (210)

**007 C House;** 67585 CR 13; Craftsman; c.1920; Outbuilding: garage; *Architecture* (210)

**008 C House;** 67605 CR 13; Dormer-front bungalow/Craftsman; c.1920; *Architecture* (210)

75006 Foraker abounds in bungalows. This example has a dormer front and Craftsman knee braces under the eaves.

**009 C Culp House;** 67674 CR 13; Dormer-front bungalow/Craftsman; c.1915 (Albert Culp, builder); Outbuilding: silo; *Architecture* (210)

**010 C House;** 67610 CR 13; California bungalow; c.1920; *Architecture* (210)

**011 C House;** 67596 CR 13; Dormer-front bungalow; c.1920; *Architecture* (210)

**012 C House;** 67586 CR 13; Dormer-front bungalow/Craftsman; c.1920; *Architecture* (210)

People pose in front of the Foraker General Store, c.1925. The store was owned by Henry S. Weaver. *Photo courtesy of the Elkhart County Historical Museum*

# Jackson Township (80001-046)

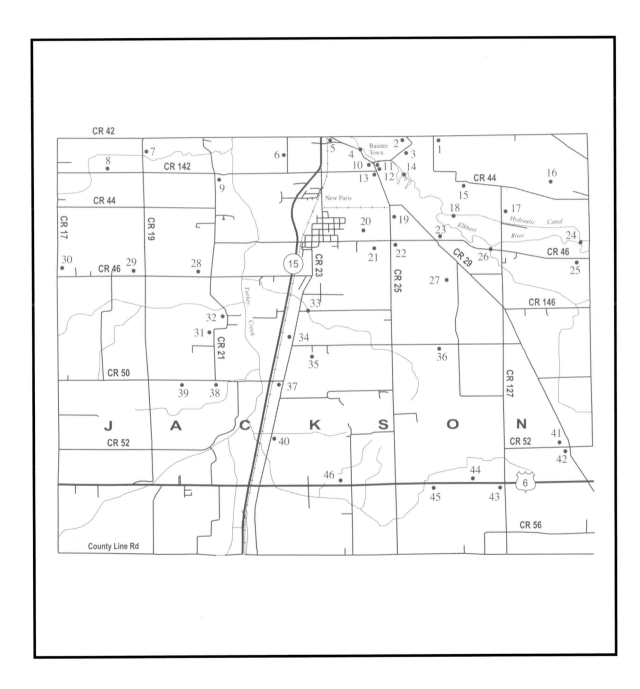

Bordered by Kosciuscko County on the south, Jackson Township lies in the south-central part of Elkhart County. The Elkhart River courses through the eastern part and Turkey Creek passes through the western part of the township. The township's first thoroughfare, Huntington Road, ran southwestwardly through the township's eastern part, intersecting the State Road. Additionally, the township claims the county's highest elevation located at Buzzards Hill, recently renamed Mt. Wawassee. Its larger communities include Baintertown and New Paris.

Organized in 1833 from a seceded part of Kosciusko County, Jackson Township's history is long and storied. For many years the area was home to a large Potawatomi village called O-nox-see or "The Five Medals." In 1812, General William Henry Harrison led troops to battle against the tribes and eventually burned the village. The tribe was forced to flee to Detroit and seek protection under the British stationed there.

The township was named for Colonel John Jackson, who in 1829 was the first white settler. He and his family settled in the township's eastern part. Col. Jackson was the first elected justice of the peace for the township.

Predominant early religious congregations included German Baptists and Methodist Episcopals. The township's first church was Solomon's Creek Church. Built in 1856, it no longer exists. In 1834, the township opened its first school in an existing log cabin about one-half mile north of New Paris. The first mill was built in 1831 near Benton. By the late-1800s, the township's greatest industry was the large woolen mills of Rodibaugh & Son.

Only two one-room schoolhouses exist in the township: School No. 2 at CR 29 and CR 142 (80013), and a school located at US 6 and CR 127

**205**

(80043). Both are boarded and in need of repairs, but they still retain some original features.

Jackson Township also boasts a number of extant Italianate farm houses built during the period roughly 1865-1880. Examples like the Rohrer-Swart Farm (80019), the Levi Arnold House (80034), and the William Ness House (80038) exhibit houses made of brick with classic Italianate features of decorative window hoods, bracketed cornices, tall and narrow windows, and front porches.

In the early 1900s the township began a system of dams and canals to harness energy. These include the Benton Hydro Spillway (80024), the Benton Hydro Dam (80018), the Baintertown Hydro Dam and Sluiceway (80014), and the Baintertown Hydro-electric Plant (80004) were all built around 1925. Most of these structures are now crumbling from neglect, but they represent early methods of creating power for rural areas.

## JACKSON TOWNSHIP SCATTERED SITES (80001-046)

**No. Rtg. Description**

**001** C **House;** 17654 CR 42; Italianate; c.1870; Architecture (243)

**002** C **Farm;** CR 42 & CR 142; T-plan; c.1870; Outbuildings: drive-thru corn crib, livestock barn, shed; *Agriculture, Architecture* (243)

**003** C **Bridge;** CR 142 over Little Elkhart River; Concrete slab; 1962; *Engineering, Transportation* (243)

**004** N **Baintertown Hydro-electric Plant;** CR 29; Neoclassical; 1925; *Architecture, Engineering, Industry, Science* (243)

**005** C **Baintertown Cemetery;** CR 29; c.1831-present; *Exploration/Settlement, Religion* (243)

**006** O **David Rodibaugh Farm;** 67261 CR 121; Lazy-T/Italianate; c.1865 (David Rodibaugh, builder); Outbuildings: drive-thru corn crib, livestock barn, machine shed; *Agriculture, Architecture* (243)

**80004** The 1925 Baintertown Hydro-electric Plant is a notable example of the Neoclassical style. Its machinery is still located inside the building.

**007** C **Farm;** 67180 CR 19; Western bungalow/ Craftsman; c.1915; Outbuilding: English barn; *Agriculture, Architecture* (243)

**008** C **House;** 21381 CR 142; American foursquare; c.1920; *Agriculture* (243)

**009** C **Farm;** 67520 CR 21; Gabled-ell/Greek Revival; c.1860; Outbuilding: English barn; *Agriculture, Architecture* (243)

**010** C **Farm;** CR 29; Upright-and-wing; c.1900; Outbuildings: shed, transverse-frame barn; *Agriculture, Architecture* (243)

**011** C **House;** CR 29; Gabled-ell; c.1890; Outbuildings: sheds; *Architecture* (243)

**012** N **House;** 67498 CR 29; Gable-front; c.1870; *Architecture* (243)

**013** C **Jackson Township District No. 2 School;** CR 29 & CR 142; Gable-front; c.1870; *Architecture, Education* (243)

**014** C **Baintertown Hydro Dam & Sluiceway;** Baintertown Park; 1925 (Interstate Hydro, builder); *Engineering, Industry, Science* (243)

**015** N **Thompson House;** 17142 CR 44; Gabled-ell; 1846; *Architecture, Exploration/Settlement* (243)

**016** C **Jackson Cemetery;** CR 44; c.1839-present; *Exploration/Settlement, Religion* (243)

**017** N **Farm;** 68096 CR 127; Craftsman; c.1915; Outbuilding: English barn; *Agriculture, Architecture* (243)

**018** C **Benton Hydro Dam;** Benton Hydro Park; 1925 (Interstate Hydro, builder); *Engineering* (243)

**019** O **Rohrer-Swart Farm;** 68146 CR 25; Gablefront/Italianate; c.1867; Outbuildings: English barn, sheds, silo; *Agriculture, Architecture* (243)

**020** C **Farm;** 18561 CR 46; Double-pile; c.1865; Outbuildings: drive-thru corn crib, English barn; *Agriculture, Architecture* (243)

**021** N **Harriman Farm;** 18480 CR 46; I-house/ Greek Revival; c.1835; Outbuildings: drive-thru corn crib, livestock barn, sheds; *Agriculture, Architecture, Exploration/Settlement* (243)

**022** N **Neff House;** 18238 CR 46; T-plan; c.1904 (Levi Neff, builder); Outbuildings: smokehouse; *Architecture* (243)

**023** C **Defries House;** 17477 CR 46; Gabled-ell; 1881; *Architecture* (243)

**024** C **Benton Hydro Spillway;** Benton Hydro Park; 1925 (Interstate Hydro, builder); *Engineering* (243)

**025** C **Farm;** 16173 CR 46; Greek Revival; c.1870; Outbuildings: bank/basement barn, corn crib; *Agriculture, Architecture* (411)

**026** C **Bridge;** CR 46 over Whelton Ditch; Concrete slab; c.1940; *Engineering, Transportation* (411)

**80006** Built on land purchased in the 1820s by early settler David Rodibaugh, this Italianate farmhouse is rated outstanding.

**80012** This c.1870 house is notable for its stone construction, one of the few in the area. This building used to serve as a store.

**027  C  House;** CR 27; Dormer-front bungalow; c.1930; *Architecture* (411)

**028  C  Whitehead Cemetery;** CR 46; c.1838-present; *Exploration/Settlement, Religion* (411)

**80019** Jackson Township boasts a number of Italianate farmsteads. The Rohrer-Swart Farm is an outstanding example that retains most of its original features.

**80034** With its ornate brackets under the eaves and tall, narrow windows, the 1879 Levi Arnold House is another fine Italianate farmhouse.

**029  C  Farm;** 21131 CR 46; T-plan; c.1870; Outbuildings: drive-thru corn crib, garage, sheds; *Agriculture, Architecture* (411)

**030  C  Roger House;** 21919 CR 46; Gable-front/ Craftsman; c.1940 (Henry Roger, builder); *Architecture* (443)

**031  C  Farm;** CR 21; Free Classic; c.1900; Outbuildings: bank/basement barn, machine shed; *Agriculture, Architecture* (411)

**032  N  House;** 69737 CR 21; Cross-gable; 1890; *Architecture* (411)

**033  C  Bridge;** CR 146 over ditch; Concrete slab; c.1940; *Engineering, Transportation* (411)

**034  N  Levi Arnold House;** 69835 CR 23; Italianate; 1879; Outbuilding: iron fence; *Architecture* (411)

**035  N  Farm;** 19156 CR 48; Italianate; c.1870; Outbuildings: drive-thru corn crib, Sweitzer barn, shed; *Agriculture, Architecture* (411)

**036  C  Farm;** 17728 CR 48; Italianate; c.1855; Outbuildings: English barn, garages, machine shed; *Agriculture, Architecture* (411)

**037  C  Water Tower;** CR 23 & CR 50; Water tower; c.1940; *Engineering* (411)

**038  N  William Neff House;** 20294 CR 50; Italianate; c.1880; *Architecture* (411)

**039  C  House;** CR 50; American foursquare; c.1915; *Architecture* (411)

**80046** The 1920 Bethany School is rated "notable" despite changes because it is the township's most intact historic school.

**040  N  Farm;** 71312 CR 23; Italianate; c.1875; Outbuilding: English barn; *Agriculture, Architecture* (411)

**041  C  Farm;** 64207 CR 52; Gabled-ell; c.1890; Outbuildings: bank/basement barn, shed; *Agriculture, Architecture* (411)

**042  C  Greenwood Cemetery;** CR 29 & CR 52; c.1849; *Exploration/Settlement, Religion* (243)

**043  C  School;** US 6 & CR 127; Gable-front; c.1870; *Architecture, Education* (411)

**044  C  House;** US 6; Upright-and-wing; c.1870; *Architecture* (411)

**045  O  E.O. Lutes Farm;** US 6, Lazy-T; 1892; Outbuildings: garages, Sweitzer barn; *Agriculture, Architecture* (411)

**046  N  Bethany School;** 18857 US 6; Craftsman; 1920 (C.B. Moyer, builder); *Architecture, Education* (411)

# New Paris Historic District (039-243-81001-066)

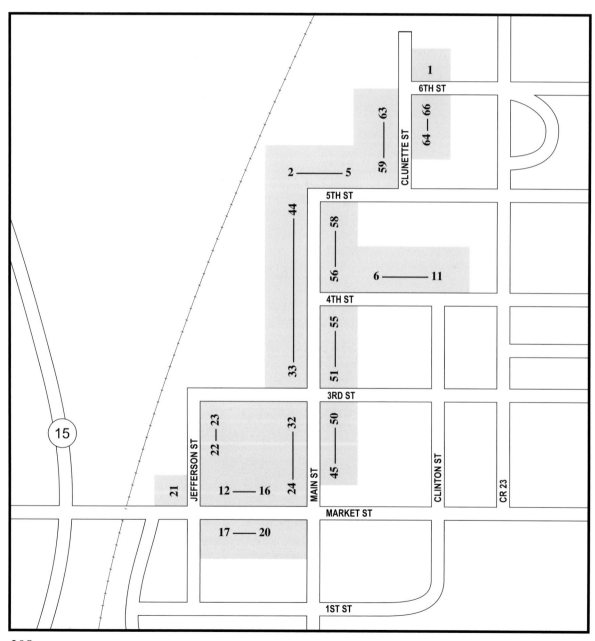

The New Paris Historic District stretches from 4th Street on the north to Market Street on the south and Clunette Street on the west to Jefferson Street on the east. The district comprises mostly residential buildings, with some commercial storefronts.

Significant for its architecture, the district boasts early-20th century styles including Craftsman bungalows (81001, 81011, 81041) and American foursquares (81006, 81010, 81033). The bungalows display Craftsman elements such as low-pitched roofs, wide eaves with knee braces, deep porches, and often feature central dormers. The foursquares are two-story houses with square footprints, featuring hipped roofs with central dormers and deep, full-width porches.

Other common residential styles in the district include the Colonial Revival (81009, 81044, 81054), traditional ranches (81064, 81065, 81066), and vernacular forms like gabled-ell (81002, 81037, 81051), gable-front (81012, 81021, 81023), and side-gabled (81013, 81047, 81050).

Commercial structures such as the I.O.O.F. Building (81028) and the drug store/barber shop (81024) on Main Street are also important examples of early-20th century commercial architecture.

## NEW PARIS HISTORIC DISTRICT (039-243-81001-066)

No. Rtg. Add. Description

### SIXTH STREET (north side)

001 N 19049 **House;** California bungalow/Craftsman; c.1925

### FIFTH STREET (north side)

002 C 19133 **House;** Gabled-ell; c.1900

003 C 19121 **House;** California bungalow; c.1920

004 C 19111 **House;** California bungalow; c.1915

005 C 19099 **House;** Minimal traditional; c.1945

### FOURTH STREET (north side)

006 C 19095 **House;** American foursquare; c.1915

007 N 19083 **House;** Bungalow/Craftsman; c.1915

008 C 19071 **House;** American foursquare; c.1910

009 C 19059 **House;** Colonial Revival; c.1930

010 C 19047 **House;** American foursquare; c.1905

011 N 19033 **House;** Dormer-front bungalow/Craftsman; 1927

81007 This bungalow exhibits Craftsman-style details, including knee braces that support overhanging eaves and exposed rafter tails.

81011 A good example of a dormer front bungalow, this 1927 house rests on a brick foundation.

### MARKET STREET (north side)

012 C 19191 **House;** Gable-front; c.1900

013 NC NA **House;** Side-gable; c.1920

014 C NA **Fire Hall;** 20th century functional; c.1940

015 C NA **Garage;** 20th century functional; c.1910

016 NC NA **House;** Upright-and-wing; c.1900

### MARKET STREET (south side)

017 C NA **Commercial Building;** Two-part commercial block; c.1910

018 C 19174 **Commercial Building;** One-part commercial block; c.1915

019 C NA **Commercial Building;** Two-part commercial block; 1914

020 C 19152 **Commercial Building;** Two-part commercial block; c.1910

### JEFFERSON STREET (west side)

021 C 68485 **House;** Gable-front; c.1900

### JEFFERSON STREET (east side)

022 C 68452 **House;** Dormer-front bungalow; c.1915

023 C 68438 **House;** Gable-front; c.1910

### MAIN STREET (west side)

024 N NA **Drug Store/Barber Shop;** Parapet-front; c.1900

025 NC NA **Commercial Building;** Two-part commercial block; c.1900

026 NC NA **Quonset Hut;** c.1950

027 NC NA **Commercial Building;** c.1970

028 C NA **I.O.O.F. Building;** Two-part commercial block; c.1915

029 C NA **Commercial Building;** Two-part commercial block; c.1910

030 C NA **New Paris Garage;** One-part commercial block; 1914

031 NC 68435 **House;** Gable-front; c.1900

032 N NA **Grace United Methodist Church;** Gothic Revival; 1896

033 C 68391 **House;** American foursquare; c.1910

034 C 68375 **House;** Gabled-ell; c.1900

035 C 68363 **House;** American foursquare; c.1910

036 NC 68353 **House;** T-plan; c.1900

037 N 68337 **House;** Gabled-ell; c.1900

81017 Though somewhat altered, this c.1910 commercial building retains an interesting oriel window.

209

**81020** This two-part commercial block features decorative pressed metal brackets.

**038 N 68327 House;** Dormer-front bungalow; c.1920

**039 C 68315 House;** American foursquare; c.1910

**040 N 68307 House;** American foursquare; c.1910

**041 N 68293 House;** Dormer-front bungalow/ Craftsman; c.1915

**042 C 68281 House;** Gable-front; c.1915

**043 C 68271 House;** L-plan; c.1900

**044 C 68249 House;** Dutch Colonial Revival; c.1930

## MAIN STREET (east side)

**045 C 68458 Commercial Building;** Two-part commercial block; c.1890

**046 NC 68452 House;** Gable-front; c.1915

**047 C 68434 House;** Side-gable; c.1920

**048 NC 68430 House;** Side-gable; c.1910

**81024** This drug store features pressed tin moldings.

**049 NC 68422 House;** Gable-front; c.1910

**050 NC 68412 House;** Side-gable; c.1900

**051 NC NA House;** Gabled-ell; c.1900

**052 C 68376 House;** Cross-gable; c.1910

**053 C 68634 House;** Gabled-ell; c.1900

**054 C 68352 House;** Colonial Revival; c.1930

**055 C 68334 House;** Hall-and-parlor; c.1900

**81032** This Gothic Revival style church has a square steeple topped by a slate roof.

**056 C NA House;** Gabled-ell; c.1900

**057 C 62276 House;** Gable-front; c.1910

**058 NC 68254 House;** California bungalow; c.1920

## CLUNETTE STREET (west side)

**059 C 68227 House;** California bungalow; c.1930

**060 C 68207 House;** Ranch; c.1955

**061 C 68197 House;** Craftsman; c.1930

**062 N 68183 House;** Craftsman; c.1930

**063 C 68167 House;** English cottage; 1929

## CLUNETTE STREET (east side)

**064 C 68212 House;** Traditional ranch; c.1950

**065 C 68196 House;** Traditional ranch; c.1955

**066 N NA House;** Traditional ranch; 1953

**81033** This American foursquare was built c.1910 and retains its sandstone lintels and columns.

# New Paris Scattered Sites (82001-034)

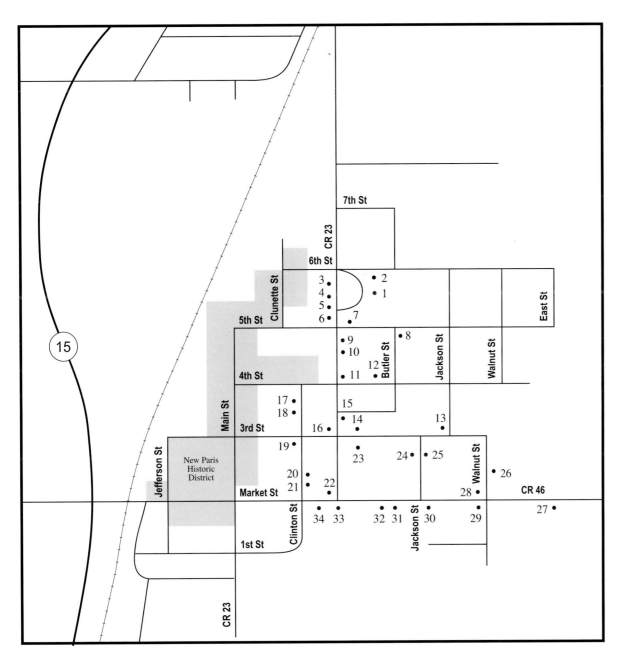

New Paris is situated in the north-central part of Jackson Township. The town came into existence when two local landowners, Isaac Abshire and Enoch Wright, decided to create a town from their property in 1838. They named it after New Paris, Ohio, where both men were born.

James R. McCord made the town's first official survey and plots of land were soon sold to prospective settlers. McCord went on to serve as Elkhart County's surveyor for the next twenty years.

The town's first settler was Frederick Harriman, the son-in-law of Enoch Wright. Harriman built a double log cabin and opened a wheelwright shop. He also served as the town's first constable. Eventually enough residents settled in the area to warrant a school house. John McGrew served as the town's first teacher in a log house he personally built.

The area's fertile farmland and its close proximity to Goshen, six miles to the north, allowed the town to thrive. At one point, local farmers supported a cooperative creamery. When New Paris became a stop on the railroad in 1870 the town's commerce prospered. By 1880, New Paris had become a major shipping point for grain, produce, and livestock. Grain elevators experienced economic boom years and funneled a lot of commerce through the small town. The largest such grain elevator in the town, Johnson & Son's, took in $500,000 in 1879, a phenomenal amount for the time.

Today, New Paris is a quiet town with a number of significant historic structures, including the high school (82001) and the community building (82002). Its historic district encompasses a number of residential and commercial structures.

## NEW PARIS SCATTERED SITES (82001-034)

**No. Rtg. Description**

**001 O New Paris High School;** 68080 Division St.; Neoclassical; 1927; *Architecture, Education* (243)

**002 O New Paris Community Building;** Division St. & Sixth St.; Art Deco; 1927; *Architecture, Education, Entertainment/Recreation* (243)

**003 C House;** 68607 Division St.; Western bungalow; c.1920; *Architecture* (243)

**004 C House;** Division St.; Dormer-front bungalow; c.1920; Outbuilding: garage; *Architecture* (243)

**005 C House;** 68087 Division St.; Minimal traditional; c.1954; *Architecture* (243)

**006 C House;** 68107 Division St.; Lazy-T; c.1880; *Architecture* (243)

**007 C House;** 68106 Division St.; Dormer-front bungalow; c.1920; Outbuilding: garage; *Architecture* (243)

**008 C House;** Butler St.; Upright-and-wing/Free Classic; c.1890; *Architecture* (243)

**009 C House;** 68126 Division St.; Dormer-front bungalow; c.1920; Outbuilding: garage; *Architecture* (243)

**010 N House;** 68136 Division St.; American foursquare; 1928; *Architecture* (243)

**011 N House;** 68158 Division St.; American foursquare; c.1920; Outbuilding: garage; *Architecture* (243)

**82002** Formerly the New Paris Community Building, today this remarkable Art Deco building is used as a school gym.

**012 C Commercial Building;** Fourth St.; 20th century utilitarian; c.1950; *Architecture, Commerce* (243)

**013 C House;** 18885 Third St.; Upright-and-wing; c.1900; *Architecture* (243)

**014 C House;** 18979 Third St.; American foursquare; c.1920; *Architecture* (243)

**015 C Commercial Building;** 68206 Division St.; Parapet-front; c.1900; *Architecture, Commerce* (243)

**016 C House;** Division St.; Central-passage; c.1880; *Architecture* (243)

**017 C House;** 68373 Clinton St.; Dutch Colonial Revival; c.1925; *Architecture* (243)

**018 C House;** 68389 Clinton St.; T-plan; c.1890; *Architecture* (243)

**019 C First Brethren Church;** Third St. & Clinton St.; Gothic Revival; 1958; *Architecture, Religion* (243)

**020 C House;** Clinton St.; Craftsman; c.1920; Outbuilding: garage; *Architecture* (243)

**021 C House;** 68472 Clinton St.; Colonial Revival; c.1950; *Architecture* (243)

**022 N New Paris Methodist Church;** Market St. & Division St.; Gothic Revival; 1885/1950; *Architecture, Religion* (243)

**023 C House;** 18974 Third St.; Gable-front; c.1880; *Architecture* (243)

**024 C House;** 68445 Jackson St.; Gable-front; c.1890; *Architecture* (243)

**025 C House;** 68434 Jackson St.; Upright-and-wing; c.1880; Outbuilding: shed; *Architecture* (243)

**026 C House;** 68462 Walnut St.; Gable-front bungalow; c.1920 (Ernest Mavzy, builder); *Architecture* (243)

**027 C New Paris Cemetery;** Market St.; c.1856-present; *Exploration/Settlement, Religion* (243)

**028 C House;** 18859 Market St.; Gable-front; c.1900; *Architecture* (243)

**029 C House;** 18864 Market St.; Cape Cod; c.1940; Outbuilding: garage; *Architecture* (243)

**030 C House;** 18912 Market St.; American foursquare; c.1910; *Architecture* (243)

**031 C House;** 18948 Market St.; Craftsman; c.1930; Outbuilding: garage; *Architecture* (243)

**032 C House;** 18964 Market St.; Hall-and-parlor; c.1880; *Architecture* (243)

**033 C House;** 19000 Market St.; American foursquare; c.1920; *Architecture* (243)

**034 C House;** 19026 Market St.; Double-pile; c.1880; *Architecture* (243)

**82010** This foursquare is unique in that is retains nearly all of its original features and is rare for its wooden clapboard siding.

**82001** New Paris High School is an outstanding example of the Neoclasscial style.

# Benton Township (85001-052)

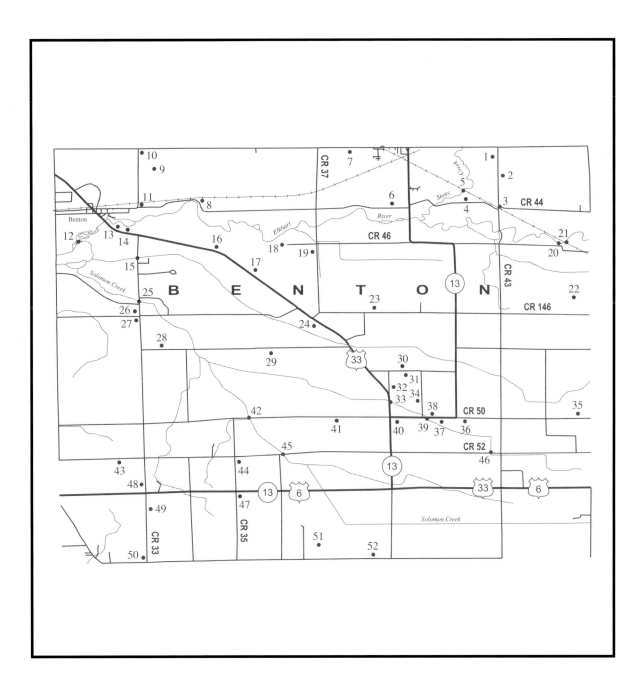

Benton Township is located in the southeastern corner of Elkhart County and is bordered to the east by Noble County and to the south by Kosciusko County. The township is relatively flat and the Elkhart River flows to the west in the northern part of the township, while Solomon Creek flows from the southeast to northwest. The canal of the Syracuse Power and Light Company begins at the Elkhart River in the northwestern part of the township and flows west. The former Lake Shore and Michigan Southern Railroad bisects the township's northeastern part, while the abandoned right-of-way of the Wabash Railroad cuts through the northwestern part. The town of Benton is located in the northwestern part of the township.

Benton Township was named after Thomas Hart Benton and was one of the earliest Elkhart County townships to be settled because it was on the Fort Wayne Road. Originally heavily forested, it was created from Elkhart Township in 1835. Matthew Boyd was Benton's earliest settler in 1828. Zacharius Butler and Martin Vance arrived the following year. Vance donated the land for Benton Lutheran Cemetery, where he is buried (85011). Several early mills were established along the Elkhart River. Other early settlers included John D. Elsea, who became one of the township's most prominent citizens, and George Simpson, whose farm stills stands (85002). Simpson is buried in the Brown Cemetery with many early Millersburg residents (85006). Many early Benton Township settlers were Amish.

In 1871, a fire devastated a large portion of the township. Due to dry conditions and sparks from passing locomotives, the fire destroyed over 1,000 acres of forest. Many people successfully fought the blaze to a save the town of Millersburg.

The Syracuse Power and Light Company was formed c.1900 and subsequently built a canal in

Benton and Jackson Townships. A hydroelectric power plant built on the canal in Jackson Township produced electricity for Syracuse in Kosciusko County. In 1910, a new spillway dam was built in Benton Township (85012). The Hawks Electric Light Company of Goshen took over operations c.1915, followed by the Interstate Power and Light Company of Kokomo in 1922.

## BENTON TOWNSHIP SCATTERED SITES (85001-052)

**No. Rtg. Description**

**001 C South Haven Cemetery;** CR 43; 1983-present; *Religion* (412)

**002 C George Simpson Farm;** 67490 CR 43; Central-passage; c.1850; Outbuildings: chicken house, dairy barn, English barn, shed; *Agriculture, Architecture* (412)

**003 C Lake Shore and Michigan Southern Railroad Bridge;** Metal girder; Railroad over CR 43; c.1900; *Engineering, Transportation* (412)

**004 C Farm;** 11393 CR 44; Upright-and-wing/Greek Revival; c.1850; Outbuildings: dairy barn, English barn, summer kitchen; *Agriculture, Architecture* (412)

**005 C Lake Shore and Michigan Southern Railroad Bridge;** Railroad over Stony Creek; c.1900; *Engineering, Transportation* (412)

**006 C Brown Cemetery;** CR 44; 1850-present; *Exploration/Settlement, Religion* (412)

**007 N Farm;** 12655 CR 42; Side-gable; c.1900; Outbuildings: chicken house, English barn, garage; *Agriculture, Architecture* (412)

**008 N Leacock Farm;** 14282 CR 44; Queen Anne; 1888; Outbuildings: dairy barn, drive-thru corn crib; *Agriculture, Architecture* (412)

**009 C Farm;** 67348 CR 33; Single-pen log house/Greek Revival; c.1850; Outbuildings: chicken house, English barn, granary, shed, summer kitchen; *Agriculture, Architecture* (412)

**010 N House;** 14966 CR 42; Lazy-T; c.1870; Outbuilding: machine shed; *Architecture* (243)

**011 C Benton Lutheran Cemetery;** CR 33 & CR 44; 1841-present; *Exploration/Settlement, Religion* (243)

**012 N Syracuse Power and Light Company Benton Spillway Dam;** On Elkhart River; Concrete dam; 1910; *Engineering* (243)

**013 N Lake Wawasee Baltimore and Ohio Railroad Depot;** 68226 US 33; Craftsman; c.1880; *Architecture, Transportation* (243)

**014 N Lee Cabin Inn;** 68306 US 33; Rustic; 1926; Outbuildings: cabins, shed; *Architecture, Commerce, Transportation* (243)

**015 C County Bridge No. 358;** Concrete girder; CR 53 over Dry Run Ditch; 1958; *Engineering, Transportation* (411)

**016 C House;** 68868 US 33; Dormer-front bungalow; c.1920; Outbuilding: shed; *Architecture* (412)

**017 C House;** 69060 US 33; Upright-and-wing; c.1870; *Architecture* (340)

**018 C Farm;** 68501 CR 37; L-plan; c.1870; Outbuildings: cold cellar, corn crib, privy, pumphouse, transverse-frame barn, windmill; *Agriculture, Architecture* (412)

**019 C Farm;** 68637 CR 37; T-plan; c.1890; Outbuildings: English barn, shed; *Agriculture, Architecture* (412)

**020 C Farm;** 10305 CR 46; Upright-and-wing; c.1900; Outbuildings: carriage house, chicken house, cold cellar, drive-thru corn crib, privy, pumphouse, shed, smokehouse, summer kitchen; *Agriculture, Architecture* (412)

**85008** The elegantly scroll-sawed bargeboard on the Leacock Farm adds to its notable rating.

**85013** Built c.1880, this depot originally served vacation-bound residents traveling to Lake Wawasee.

**021 C Lake Shore and Michigan Southern Railroad Bridge;** Plate girder; Railroad over Elkhart River; c.1900; *Engineering, Transportation* (412)

**022 C House;** 10167 CR 146; I-house; c.1860; Outbuildings: garage, shed; *Architecture* (340)

**023 N Thomas W. Roach House;** 12399 CR 146; Italianate; c.1880; Outbuildings: garage, machine shed, milk house; *Architecture* (340)

**024 C Farm;** 69727 US 33; T-plan; c.1880; Outbuildings: chicken house, garage, milk house, summer kitchen; *Agriculture, Architecture* (340)

**025 C County Bridge No. 357;** CR 33 over Solomon Creek; Concrete girder; 1952; *Engineering, Transportation* (411)

**026 N Solomon Creek E.U.B. Church and Cemetery;** 15051 CR 146; Gothic Revival; 1865/1889/1941; Cemetery: 1811-present; *Architecture, Exploration/Settlement, Religion* (411)

**027 N Solomon Creek School;** 15028 CR 146; T-plan/Romanesque Revival; 1889; *Architecture, Education* (411)

**028 N Farm;** 14797 CR 48; Lazy-T; c.1880; Outbuildings: chicken house, English barn, garage, milk house, silo; *Agriculture, Architecture* (340)

**029 C Farm;** 13540 CR 48; L-plan; c.1900; Outbuildings: English barn, machine shed, tool shed; *Agriculture, Architecture* (340)

**030 C Hire Cemetery;** CR 148; 1833-1996; *Exploration/Settlement, Religion* (340)

85014 This rustic cabin is one of few that remain from a roadside inn construction in the late 1920s-early 1930s.

**031 C House;** 12058 CR 148; Dormer-front bungalow; c.1920; *Architecture* (340)

**032 C William B. Hire Farm;** 70612 Old US 33; Gable-front; c.1860; Outbuildings: chicken house, corn crib, drive-thru corn crib, garage, silo, transverse-frame barn; *Agriculture, Architecture* (340)

**033 C Bridge;** US 33 over Hire Ditch; Concrete; c.1958; *Engineering, Transportation* (340)

**034 C John B. Hire House;** 70759 CR 39; Lazy-T/Italianate; 1865; Outbuilding: generator barn; *Architecture* (340)

**035 N Farm;** 10177 CR 50; L-plan; c.1870; Outbuildings: drive-thru corn crib, English barn, machine shed; *Agriculture, Architecture* (340)

**036 O Stephen F. Evans Farm;** 11382 CR 50; Lazy-T/Queen Anne; c.1885; Outbuildings: carriage house, English barn, house/garage, well; *Agriculture, Architecture* (340)

85023 Built c.1880, this Italianate style farm house was built by Thomas W. Roach.

**037 C House;** 11634 CR 50; Lazy-T; c.1880; Outbuilding: stable; *Architecture* (340)

**038 C House;** 11745 CR 50; Western bungalow; 1938; *Architecture* (340)

**039 C Bridge;** SR 13 over Hire Ditch; Concrete girder; c.1948; *Engineering, Transportation* (340)

**040 O Hire-Ott Farm;** 12092 CR 50; Dormer-front bungalow/Craftsman; c.1920; Outbuildings: English barn, machine shed, shed, windmill; *Agriculture, Architecture* (340)

**041 C Hiram Stetler Farm;** 12782 CR 50; Italianate; c.1865; *Architecture* (340)

**042 C County Bridge No. 340;** CR 50 over Solomon Creek; Concrete girder; 1960 (C.W. Nicholson, engineer); *Engineering, Transportation* (340)

**043 C Farm;** 15348 CR 52; Lazy-T; c.1870; Outbuildings: chicken house, drive-thru corn crib, garage; *Agriculture, Architecture* (411)

**044 N Benton Township District No. 3 School;** 71570 CR 35; c.1922; *Architecture, Education* (340)

**045 C County Bridge No. 342;** CR 53 over Solomon Creek; Concrete girder; 1961 (C.W. Nicholson, engineer); *Engineering, Transportation* (340)

**046 C Bridge;** CR 52 over Hire Ditch; Concrete girder; c.1940; *Engineering, Transportation* (340)

85027 Built in 1889 and closed in 1922, the Solomon Creek School is now a private residence.

85036 With its ornately decorated front porch, the c.1885 Stephen F. Evans farm is an outstanding example of the Queen Anne style.

**047 N Benton Township District No. 5 School/Hex School;** CR 35; T-plan/Romanesque Revival; 1895; *Architecture, Education* (340)

**048 C Albert Darr Farm;** 71860 CR 33; American foursquare; c.1900; Outbuildings: chicken house, garage, grain bin, milk house; *Agriculture, Architecture* (411)

**049 N Farm;** 72196 SR 13; American foursquare; c.1920; Outbuilding: transverse-frame barn; *Agriculture, Architecture* (411)

**050 C Farm;** 15012 S County Line Rd.; Hall-and-parlor; c.1850; Outbuilding: bank/basement barn; *Agriculture, Architecture* (411)

**051 C House;** CR 137; I-house; c.1870; Outbuilding: English barn; *Agriculture, Architecture* (340)

**052 C County Bridge No. 345;** Concrete girder; 1948; *Engineering, Transportation* (340)

# Benton Scattered Sites (86001-018)

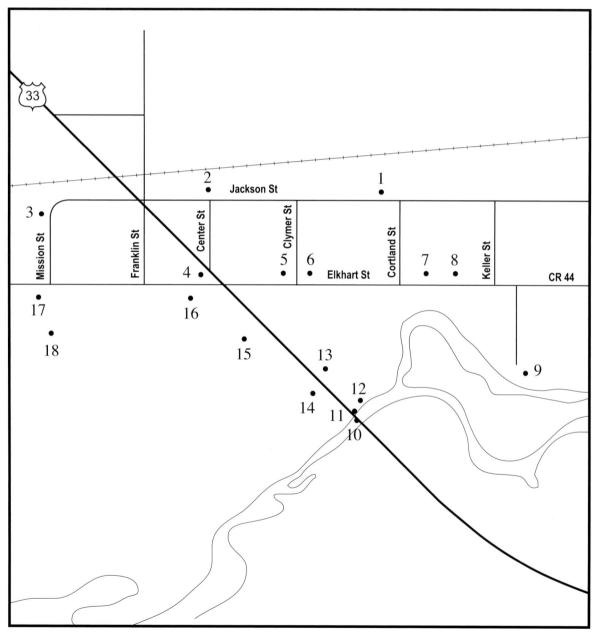

Matthew Boyd arrived in what became Benton in 1828, becoming the area's first settler. He operated a ferry across the ford on the Elkhart River when the water was high. The site was known for many years as Boyd's Landing and a boulder with a commemorative plaque marks the site (86011). His ferry was replaced by a bridge in the 1840s, and a concrete bridge now spans the river (86010). Boyd also operated a tavern on the south side of the river and his house still stands (86013). A c.1830 general store operated by James Banta and Jesse D. Vail served early settlers.

Captain Henry Beane laid out the town on the farm of John Longacre in 1832. The same year, the Fort Wayne Road came through town. Beane was an admirer of Senator Thomas Hart Benton of Missouri and he named the town in Benton's honor. The original plat included land west of Franklin and north of Elkhart Streets, and a portion east of Franklin and south of Elkhart Streets. Additions to the plat were subsequently made from the farms of Mathew Boyd and Samuel B. Clymer.

In 1836, a post office was moved from nearby Elkhart Prairie to Benton and Beane built a log school where he taught for many years. The Benton School (86018) was built in 1914, replacing an 1840s structure. Peter Darr built saw and grist mills on the Elkhart River, while other businesses located along the Fort Wayne Road, known at the time as Main Street (State Road 33). In 1838, a Baptist congregation built the first church in town.

It was anticipated that the Michigan Southern and Northern Indiana Railroad, (later called the Lake Shore and Michigan Southern Railroad), would build its line through Benton, but this did not happen. As a result, the town did not grow as quickly as other towns located along a railroad. The completion of the Wabash Railroad through the northern edge of town in 1892 occurred relatively late and had little effect on the town's growth. Benton, which had a depot for many years, became a shipping point for the railroad.

## BENTON SCATTERED SITES (86001-018)

**No   Rtg.   Description**

**001**   **C**   **House;** 15363 Jackson St.; I-house; c.1860; *Architecture* (243)

**002**   **C**   **House;** 15491 Jackson St.; Upright-and-wing; c.1870; Outbuildings: carriage house, garage; *Architecture* (243)

**003**   **C**   **Benton Methodist Church;** 61939 Mission St.; Greek Revival; 1845; *Architecture, Exploration/Settlement, Religion* (243)

**004**   **C**   **Community Building;** 68031 US 33; Parapet-front; c.1910; *Architecture* (243)

**005**   **N**   **House;** 15179 Elkhart St.; I-house; c.1850; *Architecture* (243)

**006**   **N**   **House;** 15175 Elkhart St.; Gable-front; c.1890; *Architecture* (243)

**007**   **O**   **Banta House;** 15161 Elkhart St.; Queen Anne/Romanesque Revival; 1908; *Architecture* (243)

**008**   **C**   **House;** 15159 Elkhart St.; Side-gable; 1921; Outbuilding: garage; *Architecture* (243)

**86009   This farm house was built c.1850, making it one of the earliest houses in the area.**

**009**   **N**   **Farm;** 15149 Elkhart St.; Side-gable/double-pile; c.1850; Outbuildings: bank/basement barn, chicken house, corn crib, privy; *Agriculture, Architecture* (243)

**010**   **N**   **Bridge;** US 33 over Elkhart River; Concrete arch; 1953; *Engineering, Transportation* (243)

**011**   **C**   **Benton Historical Marker;** US 33; 1923; *Exploration/Settlement, Transportation* (243)

**012**   **C**   **William Bunger House;** 68106 US 33; Side-gable bungalow/Craftsman; 1924; Outbuilding: garage; *Architecture* (243)

**013**   **C**   **Matthew Boyd Farm;** 68086 US 33; I-house; 1828; Outbuildings: chicken house, garage, privy, summer kitchen, well; *Agriculture, Architecture, Exploration/Settlement* (243)

**86013   This 1828 I-House belonged to Mathew Boyd, an early settler in Benton Township.**

**014**   **C**   **House;** 68093 US 33; Western bungalow; c.1920; *Architecture* (243)

**015**   **C**   **Commercial Building;** 68059 US 33; Parapet-front; c.1920; *Architecture, Commerce* (243)

**016**   **C**   **House;** 15536 Elkhart St.; Side-gable; c.1920; *Architecture* (243)

**017**   **C**   **House;** 15624 Elkhart St.; Gable-front; c.1900; Outbuilding: garage; *Architecture* (243)

**018**   **O**   **Benton School;** 15618 Elkhart St.; Craftsman; 1914 (A.H. Ellwood & Son, architect/David Holtzinger, builder); *Architecture, Education* (243)

**86007   Built in 1908, the Banta House is one of the most elaborate concrete block houses in Elkhart County.**

**86010   This concrete arch bridge built in 1953 spans the Elkhart River on US 33.**

**86018   The outstanding Benton School features a decorative belfry, slate roof, and ribbon windows.**

# Conclusion

# Historic Preservation in Elkhart County

## The Inventory as a Tool

The Indiana Historic Sites and Structures Inventory can serve as a starting place for encouraging historic preservation in Elkhart County. Individuals or organizations interested in nominating properties to the National Register of Historic Places can use the survey ratings as a guide in determining which properties should be nominated. Local governments and planning organizations can use the survey results as a planning tool, so that the county's unique cultural resources can be incorporated into long-range development planning. The survey can also awaken general awareness among citizens of the importance of protecting their heritage for the benefit of future generations.

## Forming Community Groups

Although preservation efforts on the part of the private individual may at times be successful, a group of citizens acting together can often achieve their preservation objectives more effectively.

Neighborhood associations and preservation committees can work with local and state agencies to encourage projects beneficial to preservation. They can also initiate projects on their own to increase awareness and appreciation of historic and architectural resources. Such activities can include walking tours, publications, exhibitions, site markings, lectures and programs, and lobbying for preservation legislation. Coverage by local newspapers of preservation-related issues or

events can also be a very effective means of increasing public awareness and support.

Legally incorporated, nonprofit organizations can become even more actively involved in the financial and technical aspects of preservation. Establishing such a group involves securing a charter, obtaining a 501(c)(3) Internal Revenue Service classification and defining an organizational structure. The group can then become directly involved with redevelopment through buying, marketing, and selling historic properties; establishing a revolving fund for making loans; seeking government or private grants; securing preservation covenants and facade easements; or actually restoring specific buildings. In many localities, existing organizations such as improvement associations or historical societies can conduct these programs.

# Private Organizations

There are numerous organizations already in existence that can assist with specific projects or in setting up the kinds of organizations discussed above. Membership in some of the private organizations can provide a way to learn about publications and programs that are available.

## Local Organizations

### The Elkhart County Historical Society and Museum

P.O. Box 434
304 West Vistula
Bristol, Ind. 46507
(574) 848-4322
www.elkhartcountyparks.org/

The Elkhart County Historical Society, Inc. was organized in 1896 and the original members began collecting artifacts soon after its inception. The mission of the society is to collect, preserve, and make accurate information pertaining to the county's history accessible to the public. The society owns a collection of over 20,000 artifacts, an archives, and a genealogy library—all of which are housed in the Elkhart County Historical Museum in Bristol. The museum building is owned and operated by the Elkhart County Parks and Recreation Department. The building, also known as the Rush Memmorial Center, was added to the National Register of Historic Places in 1991.

## Statewide Organizations

### Historic Landmarks Foundation of Indiana

340 West Michigan Street
Indianapolis, Ind. 46202-3204
(317) 639-4534 or (800) 450-4534
www.historiclandmarks.org

Historic Landmarks Foundation of Indiana (HLFI) is a statewide, private, nonprofit, membership-supported organization established to promote the preservation and restoration of Indiana's architectural and historic heritage. HLFI sponsors several programs on a statewide basis. The Indiana Historic Sites and Structures Inventory (county surveys), a program administered by the Indiana Division of Historic Preservation & Archaeology (DHPA), is undertaken by the DHPA in cooperation with HLFI. A revolving loan fund assists local non-profit organizations in saving, protecting, and reselling significant properties. HLFI also accepts facade easements and other property donations and arranges for covenants to protect buildings from undesirable change or

Opposite: **The Charles Isbell House in Elkhart (29014), c.1924.** *Photo courtesy of the Elkhart County Historical Museum*

demolition. In addition, the Foundation publishes a newsletter, *Indiana Preservationist*, and maintains a library of preservation publications available to members of HLFI. Regional offices in South Bend, Gary, Wabash, Jeffersonville, Aurora, Evansville, Cambridge City, Terre Haute, and Indianapolis provide consulting services for its members and coordinate activities on a statewide basis.

## Affiliate Council

Historic Landmarks Foundation of Indiana
340 West Michigan Street
Indianapolis, Ind. 46202-3204
(317) 639-4534 or (800) 450-4534
www.historiclandmarks.org

In 1978, Historic Landmarks Foundation of Indiana (HLFI) established an affiliate program to provide local preservation organizations around the state a close link with HLFI and each other. Historic Landmarks' affiliated organizations benefit from direct access to the professional expertise of Historic Landmarks' staff, priority for interest-free and low-interest loans from Historic Landmarks' statewide revolving fund, and supplemental funding assistance grants for organizational development. Each member of an affiliate group receives all of Historic Landmarks' publications. Through the Affiliate Council, composed of delegates from each affiliate organization, a forum facilitates the regular exchange of information and experience of Historic Landmarks' staff and affiliate members. The affiliates have also undertaken joint projects such as the sponsorship of annual statewide workshops.

## Indiana Alliance of Historic District Commissions

402 West Washington Street
South Bend, Ind. 46601
(574) 232-4534
north@historiclandmarks.org
http://pages.prodigy.net/hlfinro/

The Indiana Alliance of Historic District Commissions began in 1984, and membership is open to historic district commissions, preservation non-profits, and individuals. The Alliance sponsors regional workshops dealing with common problems of historic district commissions and how to form such a commission. The Alliance plans to initiate other services, including a quarterly newsletter, production of a training manual for commission members, establishment of a speakers' bureau, and a library of reference materials for use by members.

## Indiana Historical Society

450 West Ohio Street
Indianapolis, Ind. 46202
(317) 232-1882
www.indianahistory.org

The Indiana Historical Society is a private, non-profit membership organization chartered by the Indiana General Assembly. The Society provides several publications for its members, works with local historical groups, sponsors various historical and cultural programs and activities, and maintains a library at its Ohio Street address. It is also sponsor of the Indiana Junior Historical Society.

## *National Organizations*

## National Trust for Historic Preservation

1785 Massachusetts Avenue, N.W.
Washington, D.C. 20036
(202) 673-4000
www.nationaltrust.org

The National Trust for Historic Preservation is a private, nonprofit, nationwide organization chartered by Congress to encourage public participation in historic preservation. Dues from members, contributions from donors and matching grants from the National Park Service of the U.S. Department of the Interior support the programs of the National Trust. The Preservation Services Fund offers grants on a matching basis to nonprofit, membership-supported organizations to help pay for consultant services on preservation issues. A National Preservation Loan Fund provides low-interest loans to nonprofit organizations to establish revolving funds for improving significant properties. Maritime Preservation Grants provide 50-percent matching grants for a wide range of maritime projects. The Endangered Properties Fund is a $1-million fund to protect properties of national significance faced with serious threats.

## American Association for State and Local History (AASLH)

1717 Church Street
Nashville, Tenn. 37203
(615) 320-3203
www.aaslh.org

The AASLH is a nonprofit educational organization dedicated to advancing knowledge and appreciation of local history in the United States and Canada, providing help and materials on all aspects of local history. Membership benefits include the monthly *History News*, educational programs, job placement, audio-visual training programs, and discounts on books.

## Preservation Action

1054 31st Street N.W.
Suite 526
Washington, D.C. 20007
(202) 298-6180
www.preservationaction.org

A national nonprofit lobbying organization for preservation, Preservation Action carries out lobbying activity at the national level, monitors administrative and legislative action, disseminates information, and coordinates grass-roots lobbying activities through a system of statewide lobbying coordinators and preservation organizations. The organization regularly produces a series of "alerts" to maintain awareness of pending issues and motivate local lobbying efforts.

# Government Programs and Agencies

State and federal governments, as well as some local governments, have established programs that can be beneficial to historic properties. Some of these programs benefit properties included in the National Register of Historic Places or locally designated districts; others are generally available for any qualified properties, whether or not they are historic.

## Local Programs and Agencies

Since 1977, local governments in Indiana have been authorized by Indiana state law (I.C. 36-7-11) to enact ordinances creating historic district commissions, which may then designate historic districts and monitor changes affecting the districts' visual character. For further information, contact Historic Landmarks Foundation of Indiana or the Division of Historic Preservation and Archaeology.

The state also authorizes deductions or abatements in local property taxes if assessments have increased because of a rehabilitation (I.C.6-1.1-12). Property owners should contact their local township assessor for more information.

## State Programs and Agencies

### Division of Historic Preservation and Archaeology

402 W. Washington Street
Room W274
Indianapolis, Ind. 46204
(317) 232-1646
www.in.gov/dnr/historic

Indiana's State Historic Preservation Officer (SHPO) is the director of the Department of Natural Resources. Through the Division of Historic Preservation and Archaeology (DHPA), the SHPO administers state and federal government preservation programs. State programs include the Indiana Register of Historic Sites and Structures, which parallels the National Register program of the federal government, and the Indiana Historic Sites and Structures Inventory program, of which this *Elkhart County Interim Report* is a part.

**The Indiana Residential Historic Rehabilitation Tax Credit** is a program that allows owner-occupants to take a credit against state income tax liability equal to 20 percent of "qualified" preservation or rehab expenses. Interested property owners must receive approval from the DHPA prior to beginning work.

The DHPA also reviews state and federal government actions for their impacts on historic resources and administers the preservation programs offered by the National Park Service. These include the National Register, tax certification, and grants. The DHPA also provides technical assistance to the public and information on all aspects of historic preservation.

### Indiana Office of Rural Affairs

One North Capitol, Suite 600
Indianapolis, Ind. 46204
Community Economic Development:
(317) 232-1703
Indiana Main Street Program:
(317) 232-8912
www.state.in.us/

The Indiana Office of Rural Affairs assists rural communities in community development projects through its technical assistance and grant programs. The office also administers the **Indiana Main Street** program, a downtown economic revitalization program accomplished through merchant organization, economic restructuring, facade rehabilitation, and downtown promotion.

### Indiana Historical Bureau

140 North Senate Avenue
Indianapolis, Ind. 46204
(317) 232-2535
http://www.statelib.lib.in.us/www/ihb/ihb.html

The Indiana Library and Historical Department Act established and governs the Bureau as a state agency. Among its programs are aiding local historical organizations, providing free materials to teachers of Indiana history, and publishing the *Indiana Historian* and the *Indiana History Bulletin*. The Bureau is in charge of the Governors' Portraits Collection and the Indiana Historical Marker program.

### Indiana State Library

Indiana Division
140 North Senate Avenue
Indianapolis, Ind. 46204
(317) 232-3675
www.statelib.in.us

The Indiana Division of the State Library contains county and town histories, newspaper indices, historic photos, maps of Indiana, and special primary and secondary research resources dealing with Indiana's history and histories of most communities.

## Federal Programs and Agencies

### National Park Service

1100 L Street, N.W.
Washington, D.C. 20240
www.cr.nps.gov/nr

The National Park Service, U.S. Department of the Interior, administers the federal government's historic preservation programs. Foremost among these is the **National Register of Historic Places**, the nation's official list of its cultural resources worthy of preservation. The criteria for the National Register appear on page 10. Listing in the National Register provides recognition of a property's cultural significance and offers protection from the impact of state or federal projects by requiring review and comment by the State Historic Preservation Officer and the National Advisory Council on Historic Preservation. It does not, however, prevent a private owner from altering or disposing of the property as he or she wishes. The National Register is usually the first step in qualifying a property for the other federal programs encouraging preservation, such as the federal tax credit.

Substantial rehabilitation of income-producing buildings can qualify for an investment tax credit under the tax provisions of the Tax Act of 1986, which allows a 10-percent credit for structures at least 50 years old and 20-percent credit for certified historic structures. Structures must be listed in the National Register or located in a certified historic district to qualify for the 20-percent credit and must have the rehabilitation work reviewed for compliance with the Secretary of the Interior's Standards for Rehabilitation. The Park Service uses Historic Preservation Certification applications to identify eligible buildings and certify their rehabilitation.

The Park Service also administers Federal historic preservation grants-in-aid, which are available if appropriated by Congress. Amounts and eligibility requirements vary from year to year. In recent years, the Park Service has allotted funds for survey and planning projects, such as this Elkhart County Inventory, archaeological projects, and rehabilitation/acquisition projects.

**The Historic American Buildings Survey (HABS)** began in 1933 as a Civil Works Administration project. It provided funds for unemployed architects and draftsmen to record and document historic structures throughout the United States. The Library of Congress' Division of Prints and Photographs cares for this architectural data. A related program is the **Historic American Engineering Record (HAER)**, which records and documents structures significant in the history of American engineering and technology.

Please submit revisions or corrections to the information in this interim report to the Division of Historic Preservation and Archaeology, 402 W. Washington Street, Room W-274, Indianapolis, Ind. 46204.

Call (317) 232-1646 for more information.

Additional copies of this report may be available. Contact Historic Landmarks Foundation of Indiana, 340 W. Michigan Street, Indianapolis, Ind. 46202, (800) 450-4534, www.historiclandmarks.org for information.

The State Historic Preservation Offices administer the National Register, tax credit, and federal grants-in-aid programs. For information, application forms, or assistance, contact the Indiana Division of Historic Preservation and Archaeology at:

402 West Washington Street, Room W-274 Indianapolis, Ind. 46204 www.in.gov/dnr/historic (317) 232-1646

The Lake Shore & Michigan Southern Railroad Inspection Engine No. 24, c.1905. *Photo courtesy of the Elkhart County Historical Museum*

Left: The Elkhart County Courthouse (51024) as it appeared prior to its 1907 remodeling. *Photo courtesy of the Elkhart County Historical Museum*

## General References

Blumenson, John J. G. *Identifying American Architecture: A Pictorial Guide to Styles and Times 1600-1945*, 2nd ed. Nashville American Association for State and Local History, 1981.

Cooper, James L. *Artistry and Ingenuity in Artificial Stone*. Greencastle, IN: DePauw University, 1997.

_____. *Iron Monuments to Distant Posterity*. Greencastle, IN: DePauw University, 1997.

Derry, Anne et. al. *Guidelines for Local Surveys: A Basis for Preservation Planning*. Washington: National Register of Historic Places, 1985.

Fitch, James Marston. *Historic Preservation: Curatorial Management of the Built Environment*. Charlottesville: University Press of Virginia, 1990.

Glassie, Henry. *Vernacular Architecture*. Bloomington, IN: Indiana University Press, 2000.

Harris, Cyril M. *Historic Architecture Sourcebook*. NY: McGraw-Hill, 1977.

*Illustrated Historical Atlas of the State of Indiana*. Chicago: Baskin, Forster & Company, 1876. Reprinted, Indianapolis: Indiana Historical Society, 1968.

McAlester, Virginia & Lee. *A Field Guide to American Houses*. NY: Alfred A. Knopf, 1984.

McClelland, Linda. *National Register Bulletin: How to Complete the National Register Form*. Washington: National Park Service, 1997.

Noble, Allen. *Wood, Brick and Stone, The North American Settlement Landscape, Volumes I and II*. Amherst: University of Massachusetts Press, 1984.

Noble, Allen G. and Hubert G.H. Wilhelm, ed. *Barns of the Midwest*. Athens, OH: Ohio University Press, 1995.

Peat, Wilbur D. *Indiana Houses of the Nineteenth Century*. Indianapolis: Indiana Historical Society, 1962.

Poppeliers, John and S. Allen Chambers, Jr.. *What Style Is It?* Washington: John Wiley & Sons/The Preservation Press, 2003.

Roberts, Warren E. *Log Buildings of Southern Indiana*. Bloomington, IN: Trickster Press, 1996.

# Bibliography

Rifkind, Carole. *A Field Guide to American Architecture*. New York: New Library, 1980.

Schuler, Stanley. *American Barns, In a Class by Themselves*. Exton, PA: Schiffer, 1985.

Schweitzer, Robert, and Michael W.R. Davis. *America's Favorite Homes: Mail Order Catalogues as a Guide to Early 20th C. Houses*. Detroit: Wayne State Press, 1990.

Scully, Vincent. *American Architecture and Urbanism* (Revised Edition). New York: Henry Holt and Company, 1988.

Stevenson, Katherine Cole, and H. Ward Jandl. *Houses by Mail*. Washington, DC: The Preservation Press, 1986.

Walker, H. Jesse and Randall A. Detro. *Cultural Diffusion and Landscapes: Selections by Fred B. Kniffen*. Baton Rouge: Louisiana State University, 1990.

Whiffen, Marcus. *American Architecture Since 1790: A Guide to Styles*. Cambridge: The M.I.T. Press, 1969.

## Local References

Bartholomew, Henry S. K. *Pioneer History of Elkhart County Indiana with Sketches and Stories*. Goshen, Indiana: The Goshen Printery, 1930.

Bartholomew, H. S. K. *Stories and Sketches of Elkhart County*. Nappanee, Indiana: E. V. Publishing House, 1936.

Comstock, Vicki L. Brown. *Journey Into the Past: History of Olive Township, Elkhart County, Indiana*. n.p. 2001.

Deahl, Anthony. *A Twentieth Century History and Biographical Record of Elkhart County, Indiana*. Chicago: The Lewis Publishing Company, 1905.

*Elkhart County Interim Report: Indiana Historic Sites and Structures Report*. Indianapolis: Historic Landmarks Foundation of Indiana, 1978.

Garber, Dean G. *Elkhart County One Room Schools: the 3 Rs*. n.p. 1991.

*Goshen—The Next 10 Years, 1981-1991*. Goshen, IN: News Print Co., 1991.

*History of Elkhart County Indiana*. Chicago: Chas. C. Chapman & Co., 1881.

*History of Elkhart County Indiana., 2nd ed.* Chicago: Chas. C. Chapman and Co., 1971.

"History: Architecture." [web page] City of Elkhart. Available from http://www.elkhartindiana.org/content.php?id=28&c_id=148 Internet. Accessed 31 July 2005.

*An Illustrated Historical Atlas of Elkhart Co. Indiana*. Chicago: Higgins, Belden & Co., 1874.

"National New York Central Railroad Museum-Tour." [web page] National New York Central Railroad Museum. Available from http://www.nycrrmuseum.org/tour.html Internet. Accessed 6 July 2005.

"One Remarkable Year: 1903-1904." [web page] Goshen College. Available from http://www.goshen.edu/news/bulletin/03june/01_year.php Internet. Accessed 31 July 2005.

*Pictorial and Biographical Memoirs of Elkhart and St. Joseph Counties, 2nd ed.* Chicago: Goodspeed Brothers, 1982.

*Plat Book of Elkhart County Indiana*. Chicago: Geo. A. Ogle & Co., 1892.

Pletcher, Richard. "Coppes-Mutschler Historic District Heritage Conservation Area Preservation and Development Plan." [web page] Windmoyer Institute. Available from http://www.nappanee-indiana.com/coppes_historic_district.doc. Internet. Accessed 4 January 2005.

Pletcher, Richard, ed. "Notes about Coppes Bros. Kitchens." [web page] Amish Acres. Available from http://www.amishacres.com/aa_come_visit/miscellaneous/hoosier_cabinet_museum.htm. Internet. Accessed 4 January 2005.

*Standard Atlas of Elkhart County Indiana*. Chicago: Geo. A. Ogle & Co., 1915.

"Wakarusa, Indiana—History and Old Pictures." [web page] Biblical Viewpoints Publications. Available from www.wakarusa.org Internet. Accessed 31 July 2005.

This project received federal funds from the National Park Service. Regulations of the U.S. Department of the Interior strictly prohibit unlawful discrimination in the Department's federally assisted programs on the basis of race, color, national origin, age or handicap. Any person who believes he or she has been discriminated against in any program, activity, or facility operated by a recipient of federal assistance should write to: Director, Equal Opportunity Program, U.S. Department of the Interior, National Park Service, 1849 C Street NW, Washington, D.C. 20240.

Federal funds from the National Park Service, Department of the Interior, have partially financed this county interim report. However, the contents and opinions do not necessarily reflect the views and policies of the Department of the Interior, nor does the mention of trade names or commercial products constitute endorsement or recommendation by the Department of the Interior.

Weaver, Abraham E., ed. *A Standard History of Elkhart County Indiana, Volumes I & II*. Chicago: The American Historical Society, 1916.

Wenger, Amy. *Elkhart, Indiana*. Chicago: Arcadia Publications, 2002.

Weygand, James Lamar. *They Called It Nappanee*. Privately printed, 1945.

Young, Jean Ann. *Tales of a Hoosier Village: A History of Bristol, Indiana*. Bristol, IN: Wyndham Hall Press, 1988.

 **Printed on recycled paper.**

**Opposite: The Lake Shore & Michigan Southern Railroad Round House in Elkhart, date unknown.** *Photo courtesy of the Elkhart County Historical Museum*

# Index and Glossary

# Index of Places

28053  The Percival M. Cochran House in Elkhart's **Beardsley Avenue Historic District, c.1905.** *Photo courtesy of the Elkhart County Historical Museum*

**The Elliott House on South Elkhart Street (now CR 3) in downtown Wakarusa, c.1900.** *Photo from* **Images of America, Around, Nappanee, Hometowns of the Heritage Trail,** *by Amy (Lant) Wenger*

**The Presbyterian Church in Nappanee, c.1911.** *Photo courtesy of the Elkhart County Historical Museum*

**Drs. Crow's Osteopathic Home at 118 West Franklin Street in Elkhart, c.1905. The house was demolished in the early 1920s.** *Photo courtesy of the Elkhart County Historical Museum*

**Coppes House, downtown Nappanee, c.1914.** *Photo courtesy of the Elkhart County Historical Museum*

People stand in front of the Ozanne House on Main Street in Middlebury, c.1900. *Photo courtesy of the Elkhart County Historical Museum*

# T

# U

# V

# W

**53241  The gardens of the Major John W. Violett House in Goshen, c.1930.** *Photo courtesy of Tina Mellott*

# Y

**319 South Main Street in Middlebury, c.1895.** *Photo courtesy of the Elkhart County Historical Museum*

# Z

# Index of Streets with Inventoried Sites

| Street Name | Range | Twp(s)/SS(s)/HD(s) | Page No. |
|---|---|---|---|
| CR 2 | CR 35-CR39 | York Twp SS | 42-44 |
| | CR 19-CR 25 | Washington Twp SS | 45-47 |
| CR 3 | Indiana Ave-CR 28 | Baugo Twp SS | 58-60 |
| | CR 28-CR 42 | Olive Twp SS | 171-173 |
| | NA | Wakarusa SS | 177-180 |
| | County Line Rd-CR 56 | Locke Twp SS | 181-183 |
| CR 4 | CR 131-CR 1200W | York Twp SS | 42-44 |
| | NA | Osolo Twp SS | 51-53 |
| | NA | Cleveland Twp SS | 54-57 |
| CR 5 | NA | Osolo Twp SS | 51-53 |
| | NA | Cleveland Twp SS | 54-57 |
| CR 6 | CR 17-CR 21 | Washington Twp SS | 45-47 |
| | NA | Osolo Twp SS | 51-53 |
| | NA | Cleveland Twp SS | 54-57 |
| CR 7 | State Line Rd-SR 112 | Osolo Twp SS | 51-53 |
| | NA | Concord Twp SS | 61-64 |
| | CR 28-CR 42 | Harrison Twp SS | 168-170 |
| | NA | Union Twp SS | 184-187 |
| CR 8 | CR 131-CR 35 | York Twp SS | 42-44 |
| | NA | Washington Twp SS | 45-47 |
| | NA | Bristol SS | 48-50 |
| | NA | Middlebury Twp SS | 118-120 |
| CR 9 | NA | Osolo Twp SS | 51-53 |
| | NA | Concord Twp SS | 61-64 |
| | NA | Union Twp SS | 184-187 |

| Street Name | Range | Twp(s)/SS(s)/HD(s) | Page No. |
|---|---|---|---|
| CR 10 | SR 15-CR 31 | Washington Twp SS | 45-47 |
| | NA | Osolo Twp SS | 51-53 |
| | NA | Cleveland Twp SS | 54-57 |
| CR 10E | NA | Washington Twp SS | 45-47 |
| CR 11 | NA | Osolo Twp SS | 51-53 |
| | CR 22-CR 28 | Concord Twp SS | 61-64 |
| | | Elkhart SS | 89-112 |
| | CR 28-CR 42 | Harrison Twp SS | 168-170 |
| | NA | Union Twp SS | 184-187 |
| CR 12 | NA | York Twp SS | 42-44 |
| | SR 219-SR 112 | Cleveland Twp SS | 54-57 |
| | NA | Middlebury Twp SS | 118-120 |
| CR 13 | NA | Elkhart SS | 89-112 |
| | NA | Concord Twp SS | 61-64 |
| | NA | Dunlap SS | 113-114 |
| | CR 28-CR 42 | Harrison Twp SS | 168-170 |
| | CR 42-County Line Rd | Union Twp SS | 184-187 |
| | NA | Foraker SS | 203-204 |
| CR 14 | NA | Concord Twp SS | 61-64 |
| | NA | Jefferson Twp SS | 115-117 |
| | SR 13-CR 43 | Middlebury Twp SS | 118-120 |
| CR 15 | State Line Rd-St. Joe R | Osolo Twp SS | 51-53 |
| | NA | Concord Twp SS | 61-64 |
| | CR 28-CR 42 | Harrison Twp SS | 168-170 |
| | CR 42-County Line Rd | Union Twp SS | 184-187 |
| CR 16 | NA | Elkhart SS | 89-112 |
| | NA | Baugo Twp SS | 58-60 |
| | NA | Concord Twp SS | 61-64 |
| | CR 21-CR 23 | Jefferson Twp SS | 115-117 |
| | NA | Middlebury Twp SS | 118-120 |
| CR 17 | CR 42-Co. Line Rd | Union Twp SS | 184-187 |
| | CR 4-SR 120 | Washington Twp SS | 45-47 |
| | St. Joe R-CR 18 | Concord Twp SS | 61-64 |
| | SR 15-CR 27 | Jefferson Twp SS | 115-117 |
| | CR 28-CR 42 | Harrison Twp SS | 168-170 |
| CR 18 | SR 19-CR 17 | Concord Twp SS | 61-64 |
| | NA | Jefferson Twp SS | 115-117 |
| | NA | Middlebury Twp SS | 118-120 |
| CR 19 | State Line Rd-River Rd | Washington Twp SS | 45-47 |
| | NA | Jefferson Twp SS | 115-117 |
| | US 33-CR 42 | Elkhart Twp SS | 130-133 |
| | CR 42-County Line Rd | Jackson Twp SS | 205-207 |
| CR 20 | Co Line Rd-SR 19 | Baugo Twp SS | 58-60 |
| | CR 19-CR 31 | Jefferson Twp SS | 115-117 |
| | NA | Concord Twp SS | 61-64 |
| | CR 22-CR 43 | Middlebury Twp SS | 118-120 |

A stereopticon of the Elkhart County Jail in Goshen, c.1880. *Photo courtesy of the Elkhart County Historical Museum*

Elkhart Co. Jail, Goshen, Ind.

C.M.Brooks, Artist.

| Street Name | Range | Twp(s)/SS(s)/HD(s) | Page No. |
|---|---|---|---|
| CR 21 | NA | Baugo Twp SS | 58-60 |
| | CR 2-River Rd | Washington Twp SS | 45-47 |
| | NA | Jefferson Twp SS | 115-117 |
| | NA | Elkhart Twp SS | 130-133 |
| | CR 42-CR 50 | Jackson Twp SS | 205-207 |
| CR 22 | NA | Baugo Twp SS | 58-60 |
| | NA | Jefferson Twp SS | 115-117 |
| | NA | Middlebury Twp SS | 118-120 |
| | NA | Elkhart Twp SS | 130-133 |
| CR 23 | NA | Washington Twp SS | 45-47 |
| | NA | Jefferson Twp SS | 115-117 |
| | CR 42-County Line Rd | Jackson Twp SS | 205-207 |
| CR 24 | Co Line Rd-CR 3 | Baugo Twp SS | 58-60 |
| | CR 9-CR 13 | Concord Twp SS | 61-64 |
| | SR 15-CR 27 | Jefferson Twp SS | 115-117 |
| | NA | Middlebury Twp SS | 118-120 |
| CR 25 | CR 2-SR 15 | Washington Twp SS | 45-47 |
| | CR 42-County Line Rd | Jackson Twp SS | 205-207 |
| CR 26 | Co Line Rd-SR 19 | Baugo Twp SS | 58-60 |
| | CR 126-SR 15 | Jefferson Twp SS | 115-117 |
| | NA | Middlebury Twp SS | 118-120 |
| CR 27 | NA | Washington Twp SS | 45-47 |
| | NA | Jackson Twp SS | 205-207 |
| CR 28 | SR 219-SR 19 | Baugo Twp SS | 58-60 |
| | NA | Jefferson Twp SS | 115-117 |
| | NA | Elkhart Twp SS | 130-133 |
| | Ash Rd-SR 19 | Olive Twp SS | 171-173 |
| CR 29 | CR 14-CR 22 | Jefferson Twp SS | 115-117 |
| | NA | Elkhart Twp SS | 130-133 |
| | NA | Jackson Twp SS | 205-207 |
| CR 30 | NA | Clinton Twp SS | 125-127 |
| | SR 19-CR 17 | Harrison Twp SS | 168-170 |
| | Ash Rd-SR 19 | Olive Twp SS | 171-173 |
| CR 31 | CR 108-CR 10 | Washington Twp SS | 45-47 |
| | NA | Jefferson Twp SS | 115-117 |
| CR 32 | NA | Clinton Twp SS | 125-127 |
| | CR 17-CR 21 | Elkhart Twp SS | 130-133 |
| | SR 19-CR 17 | Harrison Twp SS | 168-170 |
| | Ash Rd-SR 19 | Olive Twp SS | 171-173 |
| CR 33 | NA | Middlebury Twp SS | 118-120 |
| | NA | Clinton Twp SS | 125-127 |
| | CR 34-CR 42 | Benton Twp SS | 213-215 |
| CR 34 | CR 31-County Line Rd | Clinton Twp SS | 125-127 |
| | US 33-CR 31 | Elkhart Twp SS | 130-133 |

| Street Name | Range | Twp(s)/SS(s)/HD(s) | Page No. |
|---|---|---|---|
| CR 35 | State Line Rd-CR 8 | York Twp SS | 42-44 |
| | NA | Middlebury Twp SS | 118-120 |
| | SR 4-CR 42 | Clinton Twp SS | 125-127 |
| | CR 50-County Line Rd | Benton Twp SS | 213-215 |
| CR 36 | NA | Clinton Twp SS | 125-127 |
| | NA | Elkhart Twp SS | 130-133 |
| | SR 19-CR 17 | Harrison Twp SS | 168-170 |
| | Ash Rd-SR 19 | Olive Twp SS | 171-173 |
| CR 37 | SR 12-CR 10 | York Twp SS | 42-44 |
| | NA | Middlebury Twp SS | 118-120 |
| | SR 4-CR 42 | Clinton Twp SS | 125-127 |
| | CR 42-CR 146 | Benton Twp SS | 213-215 |
| CR 38 | Ash Rd-SR 19 | Olive Twp SS | 171-173 |
| | CR 31-County Line Rd | Clinton Twp SS | 125-127 |
| | CR 17-CR 31 | Elkhart Twp SS | 130-133 |
| | NA | Goshen SS | 154-165 |
| | SR 19-CR 17 | Harrison Twp SS | 168-170 |
| CR 39 | SR 12-CR 10 | York Twp SS | 42-44 |
| | NA | Clinton Twp SS | 125-127 |
| | CR 148-CR 50 | Benton Twp SS | 213-215 |

**The New York Central Railroad Storehouse Office, c.1905. Catherine Bussard Christophel is seated in the foreground.** *Photo courtesy of the Elkhart County Historical Museum*

| Street Name | Range | Twp(s)/SS(s)/HD(s) | Page No. |
|---|---|---|---|
| CR 40 | CR 31-County Line Rd | Clinton Twp SS | 125-127 |
| | NA | Elkhart Twp SS | 130-133 |
| | Elkhart R-SR 15 | Waterford SS | 166-167 |
| | SR 19-CR 17 | Harrison Twp SS | 168-170 |
| CR 41 | NA | Middlebury Twp SS | 118-120 |
| | NA | Clinton Twp SS | 125-127 |
| CR 42 | CR 31-County Line Rd | Clinton Twp SS | 125-127 |
| | CR 17-CR 31 | Elkhart Twp SS | 130-133 |
| | SR 19-CR 17 | Harrison Twp SS | 168-170 |
| | Ash Rd-SR 19 | Olive Twp SS | 171-173 |
| | NA | Locke Twp SS | 181-183 |
| | SR 19-CR 17 | Union Twp SS | 184-187 |
| | NA | Jackson Twp SS | 205-207 |
| | NA | Benton Twp SS | 213-215 |
| CR 43 | CR 16-CR 24 | York Twp SS | 42-44 |
| | NA | Middlebury Twp SS | 118-120 |
| | SR 4-CR 42 | Clinton Twp SS | 125-127 |
| | CR 42-County Line Rd | Benton Twp SS | 213-215 |
| CR 44 | NA | Locke Twp SS | 181-183 |
| | SR 119-CR 17 | Union Twp SS | 184-187 |
| | CR 17-CR 21 | Jackson Twp SS | 205-207 |
| | NA | Benton Twp SS | 213-215 |
| CR 45 | NA | Concord Twp SS | 61-64 |
| CR 46 | NA | Locke Twp SS | 181-183 |
| | SR 19-CR 17 | Union Twp SS | 184-187 |
| | NA | Jackson Twp SS | 205-207 |
| | NA | Benton Twp SS | 213-215 |
| CR 48 | SR 19-CR 17 | Union Twp SS | 184-187 |
| | CR 23-CR 29 | Jackson Twp SS | 205-207 |
| | NA | Benton Twp SS | 213-215 |
| CR 50 | NA | Locke Twp SS | 181-183 |
| | SR 19-CR 17 | Union Twp SS | 184-187 |
| | CR 17-CR 23 | Jackson Twp SS | 205-207 |
| | NA | Benton Twp SS | 213-215 |
| CR 52 | CR 100-SR 19 | Locke Twp SS | 181-183 |
| | SR 19-CR 15 | Union Twp SS | 184-187 |
| | NA | Jackson Twp SS | 205-207 |
| | NA | Benton Twp SS | 213-215 |
| CR 53 | NA | Benton Twp SS | 213-215 |
| CR 54 | CR 7-CR 15 | Union Twp SS | 184-187 |
| CR 56 | NA | Locke Twp SS | 181-183 |
| | NA | Union Twp SS | 184-187 |
| CR 100 | CR 20-CR 22 | Baugo Twp SS | 58-60 |
| | CR 50-CR 56 | Locke Twp SS | 181-183 |
| CR 101 | CR 26-CR 28 | Baugo Twp SS | 58-60 |
| CR 104 | CR 17-CR 19 | Washington Twp SS | 45-47 |

| Street Name | Range | Twp(s)/SS(s)/HD(s) | Page No. |
|---|---|---|---|
| CR 105 | NA | Concord Twp SS | 61-64 |
| CR 113 | NA | Elkhart SS | 89-112 |
| | SR 120-CR 28 | Concord Twp SS | 61-64 |
| | NA | Dunlap SS | 113-114 |
| CR 115 | NA | Concord Twp SS | 61-64 |
| CR 118 | CR 1-CR 3 | Baugo Twp SS | 58-60 |
| | NA | Concord Twp SS | 61-64 |
| CR 121 | NA | Elkhart Twp SS | 130-133 |
| | CR 42-CR 142 | Jackson Twp SS | 205-207 |
| CR 123 | CR 2-CR 102 | Washington Twp SS | 45-47 |
| CR 126 | CR 9-CR 11 | Concord Twp SS | 61-64 |
| | NA | Jefferson Twp SS | 115-117 |
| | NA | Middlebury Twp SS | 118-120 |
| CR 127 | CR 44-County Line Rd | Jackson Twp SS | 205-207 |
| CR 129 | NA | Middlebury Twp SS | 118-120 |
| CR 131 | CR 4-CR 8 | York Twp SS | 42-44 |
| | NA | Middlebury Twp SS | 118-120 |
| CR 137 | NA | Benton Twp SS | 213-215 |
| CR 138 | NA | Elkhart Twp SS | 130-133 |
| CR 142 | CR 11-CR 17 | Union Twp SS | 184-187 |
| | NA | Foraker SS | 203-204 |
| | CR 17-CR 25 | Jackson Twp SS | 205-207 |
| CR 146 | NA | Jackson Twp SS | 205-207 |
| | NA | Benton Twp SS | 213-215 |
| CR 147 | NA | Union Twp SS | 184-187 |
| | NA | Foraker SS | 203-204 |
| CR 148 | US 33-SR 13 | Benton Twp SS | 213-215 |
| Crawford St | NA | Elkhart SS | 89-112 |
| Crescent St | NA | Elkhart SS | 89-112 |
| | NA | Goshen SS | 154-165 |
| Cross St | NA | Goshen SS | 154-165 |
| Cumberland Ave | NA | Osolo Twp SS | 51-53 |
| Dale St | NA | Elkhart SS | 89-112 |
| DeCamp Ave | NA | Elkhart SS | 89-112 |
| Dewey Ave | NA | Goshen SS | 154-165 |
| Dierdorf Rd | NA | Goshen SS | 154-165 |
| Division St | NA | Bristol SS | 48-50 |
| | NA | State-Division HD | 82-85 |
| | Riverside Blvd-Ind Ave | Goshen SS | 154-165 |
| | 7th-Market Sts | New Paris SS | 211-212 |
| Douglas St | NA | Goshen HD | 134-151 |
| | Hydraulic Canal-US 33 | Goshen SS | 154-165 |
| Dr. MLK Jr. Dr | NA | Elkhart SS | 89-112 |
| East Blvd | NA | Elkhart SS | 89-112 |
| East St | Waterfall Dr-State St | State-Division HD | 82-85 |
| Eden St | NA | Elkhart SS | 89-112 |

| Street Name | Range | Twp(s)/SS(s)/HD(s) | Page No. | Street Name | Range | Twp(s)/SS(s)/HD(s) | Page No. |
|---|---|---|---|---|---|---|---|
| Edgewater Dr | NA | Baugo Twp SS | 58-60 | Hively Ave | NA | Concord Twp SS | 61-64 |
| Edgewater Pl | NA | E.Jack./St.Joe Manor HD | 70-73 | | NA | Elkhart SS | 89-112 |
| Edwardsburg Rd | NA | Elkhart SS | 89-112 | Hubbard Ave | NA | Elkhart SS | 89-112 |
| Egbert Rd | Violett Rd-SR 15 | Waterford SS | 166-167 | Hudson St | NA | Elkhart SS | 89-112 |
| Elkhart St | NA | Bristol SS | 48-50 | Ideal Beach Rd | NA | Osolo Twp SS | 51-53 |
| | NA | Goshen SS | 154-165 | Illinois St | Depot St-SR 120 | Bristol SS | 48-50 |
| | NA | Wakarusa Downtown HD | 174-175 | Indiana Ave | NA | Morehouse HD | 86-88 |
| | NA | Wakarusa SS | 177-180 | | NA | Elkhart SS | 89-112 |
| | Mission-Keller Sts | Benton SS | 216-217 | | NA | Goshen SS | 154-165 |
| Elm St | Michigan St-SR 12 | Bristol SS | 48-50 | | NA | Wakarusa SS | 177-180 |
| | Broad-Lincoln Sts | Nappanee Eastside HD | 191-195 | | Harden-Jackson St | Nappanee SS | 196-200 |
| | Fervida-Indiana Ave | Nappanee SS | 196-200 | Interstate 80/90 | NA | York Twp SS | 42-44 |
| Emerson St | NA | Goshen SS | 154-165 | Island Park | NA | E.Jack./St.Joe Manor HD | 70-73 |
| Erwin St | NA | Elkhart SS | 89-112 | | NA | Elkhart SS | 89-112 |
| Foster Ave | NA | E.Jack./St.Joe Manor HD | 70-73 | Jackson St | NA | Elkhart Downtown HD | 65-69 |
| | NA | Elkhart SS | 89-112 | | NA | Goshen SS | 154-165 |
| Frailey Dr | NA | Cleveland Twp SS | 54-57 | | 6th-Market Sts | New Paris SS | 211-212 |
| Frances St | NA | Morehouse HD | 86-88 | | Mission-Keller Sts | Benton SS | 216-217 |
| Franklin St | NA | Elkhart Downtown HD | 65-69 | James St | NA | Elkhart SS | 89-112 |
| | NA | Elkhart SS | 89-112 | Jauriet Ct | NA | State-Division HD | 82-85 |
| Fremont St | NA | Elkhart SS | 89-112 | Jed Ln | NA | Goshen SS | 154-165 |
| Fulton St | NA | Elkhart SS | 89-112 | Jefferson St | NA | Elkhart SS | 89-112 |
| Gage Rd | NA | Elkhart SS | 89-112 | | Elm-Lincoln Sts | Millersburg SS | 128-129 |
| Garfield Ave | NA | Elkhart SS | 89-112 | | 3rd-9th Sts | Goshen HD | 134-151 |
| Glenmore St | NA | Dunlap SS | 113-114 | | 1st-3rd Sts | New Paris HD | 208-210 |
| Gordon Rd | NA | Elkhart SS | 89-112 | Kathryn Dr | NA | Cleveland Twp SS | 54-57 |
| Goshen Ave | NA | Elkhart SS | 89-112 | Kilbourn St | NA | Goshen SS | 154-165 |
| Grace Ave | NA | Elkhart SS | 89-112 | Lake Dr | NA | Osolo Twp SS | 51-53 |
| Grant St | NA | Elkhart SS | 89-112 | Lambert Ct | NA | Elkhart SS | 89-112 |
| Greene Rd | MA | Goshen SS | 154-165 | Lane Ave | NA | Elkhart SS | 89-112 |
| Greenleaf Blvd | NA | Osolo Twp SS | 51-53 | Laurel St | NA | Riverside/Prospect HD | 77-78 |
| | NA | Elkhart SS | 89-112 | | NA | Elkhart SS | 89-112 |
| Gra-Roy Dr | NA | Goshen SS | 154-165 | Lawndale Rd | NA | Elkhart SS | 89-112 |
| Grove St | NA | Elkhart SS | 89-112 | Lawrence St | NA | Elkhart SS | 89-112 |
| Hackett Rd | NA | Goshen SS | 154-165 | | NA | Middlebury SS | 121-124 |
| Hammond Ave | NA | Elkhart SS | 89-112 | Lexington Ave | NA | Cleveland Twp SS | 54-57 |
| Harrison St | NA | Elkhart SS | 89-112 | | NA | Elkhart Downtown HD | 65-69 |
| | NA | Wakarusa SS | 177-180 | | NA | Strong-Lexington HD | 79-81 |
| Hartman St | Broad-Market Sts | Nappanee Eastside HD | 191-195 | | NA | Elkhart SS | 89-112 |
| Hester St | NA | Elkhart SS | 89-112 | Liberty St | NA | Riverside/Prospect HD | 77-78 |
| Hickory St | R'side Blvd-Berkley Ave | Goshen SS | 154-165 | Lincoln St | NA | Millersburg SS | 128-129 |
| High St | NA | Elkhart Downtown HD | 65-69 | | 2nd-9th Sts | Goshen HD | 134-151 |
| | NA | Elkhart SS | 89-112 | | Clark-Elm Sts | Dwntwn Nappanee HD | 188-190 |
| | Elkhart St-Indiana Ave | Wakarusa SS | 177-180 | | Williams-Miriam | Nappanee SS | 196-200 |
| Highland Ave | NA | Elkhart SS | 89-112 | Lincoln Way E | NA | Goshen SS | 154-165 |
| Highland St | NA | Nappanee SS | 196-200 | Locke St | Park-Hudson | Nappanee SS | 196-200 |

| Street Name | Range | Twp(s)/SS(s)/HD(s) | Page No. |
|---|---|---|---|
| Longwood Ct | NA | E.Jack./St.Joe Manor HD | 70-73 |
| Mack Dr | NA | Nappanee SS | 196-200 |
| Madison St | Division-Charles Sts | State-Division HD | 82-85 |
| | NA | Goshen HD | 134-151 |
| | NA | Goshen SS | 154-165 |
| | Broad-Lincoln Sts | Nappanee Eastside HD | 191-195 |
| | Fervida-Hudson | Nappanee SS | 196-200 |
| Main St | NA | Concord Twp SS | 61-64 |
| | NA | Elkhart Downtown HD | 65-69 |
| | NA | Beardsley Ave HD | 74-76 |
| | NA | Elkhart SS | 89-112 |
| | NA | Middlebury Twp SS | 118-120 |
| | NA | Middlebury SS | 121-124 |
| | NA | Millersburg SS | 128-129 |
| | Pike-Plymouth Ave | Goshen HD | 134-151 |
| | NA | Goshen College SS | 152-153 |
| | NA | Goshen SS | 154-165 |
| | NA | Dwntwn Nappanee HD | 188-190 |
| | NA | Nappanee SS | 196-200 |
| | 1st-5th Sts | New Paris HD | 208-210 |
| Manor Ave | NA | Elkhart SS | 89-112 |
| Maple Row | NA | Elkhart SS | 89-112 |
| Marina Dr | NA | Osolo Twp SS | 51-53 |
| Marine Ave | NA | Elkhart SS | 89-112 |

| Street Name | Range | Twp(s)/SS(s)/HD(s) | Page No. |
|---|---|---|---|
| Marion St | NA | Elkhart SS | 89-112 |
| | Main-Jackson Sts | Nappanee Eastside HD | 191-195 |
| | Main St-Morningside | Nappanee SS | 196-200 |
| Market St | Clark-Elm sts | Dwntwn Nappanee HD | 188-190 |
| | Main-Jackson Sts | Nappanee Eastside HD | 191-195 |
| | NA | Nappanee SS | 196-200 |
| | NA | Amish Acres SS | 201-202 |
| | SR 15-CR 23 | New Paris HD | 208-210 |
| | SR 15-Walnut Sts | New Paris SS | 211-215 |
| Marshwood Rd | NA | Concord Twp SS | 61-64 |
| Mason St | NA | Elkhart SS | 89-112 |
| Mather Ave | NA | Elkhart SS | 89-112 |
| McDonald St | NA | Elkhart SS | 89-112 |
| Melrose Manor | NA | Elkhart SS | 89-112 |
| Michigan St | NA | Elkhart SS | 89-112 |
| Middlebury St | NA | Concord Twp SS | 61-64 |
| | NA | Elkhart SS | 89-112 |
| | NA | Goshen SS | 154-165 |
| MiddletonRun Rd | NA | Concord Twp SS | 61-64 |
| Mill St | Eugene Dr-CR 16 | Middlebury SS | 121-124 |
| | NA | Goshen SS | 154-165 |
| Miller St | NA | Osolo Twp SS | 51-53 |
| Mission St | Jackson-Elkhart Sts | Benton SS | 216-217 |
| Monroe St | NA | State-Division HD | 82-85 |
| | NA | Elkhart SS | 89-112 |
| | 3rd St-Cottage Ave | Goshen HD | 134-151 |
| | NA | Goshen SS | 154-165 |
| Morehouse Ave | NA | Morehouse HD | 86-88 |
| | NA | Elkhart SS | 89-112 |
| Morton St | NA | Elkhart SS | 89-112 |
| Mottville Rd | NA | Bristol SS | 48-50 |
| Moyer St | NA | Elkhart SS | 89-112 |
| Murray St | NA | Goshen SS | 154-165 |
| Myrtle St | NA | Elkhart SS | 89-112 |
| Nadel Ave | NA | Elkhart SS | 89-112 |
| Nappanee St | NA | Cleveland Twp SS | 54-57 |
| | Chippewa-Indiana Sts | Nappanee SS | 196-200 |
| Ne Ce Dah Ave | NA | Concord Twp SS | 61-64 |
| Newman St | NA | Concord Twp SS | 61-64 |
| North Shore Dr | SR 19-CR 11 | Osolo Twp SS | 51-53 |
| | NA | Cleveland Twp SS | 54-57 |
| North St | NA | Osolo Twp SS | 51-53 |
| Oakcrest Dr | NA | Cleveland Twp SS | 54-57 |
| Oak Grove Dr | NA | Cleveland Twp SS | 54-57 |
| Oak Leaf Pl | NA | Cleveland Twp SS | 54-57 |
| Oak Manor Pl | NA | Cleveland Twp SS | 54-57 |

**People gather in Middlebury to watch traveling men exhibit bears, c.1900.** *Photo courtesy of the Elkhart County Historical Museum*

243

| Street Name | Range | Twp(s)/SS(s)/HD(s) | Page No. |
|---|---|---|---|
| Oakland Ave | NA | Concord Twp SS | 61-64 |
| | NA | Elkhart SS | 89-112 |
| Oakridge | 1st-6th Sts | Goshen SS | 154-165 |
| Old SR 15 | NA | Jefferson Twp SS | 115-117 |
| Old US 20 | NA | Cleveland Twp SS | 54-57 |
| | SR 19-SR 120 | Concord Twp SS | 61-64 |
| Old US 33 | SR 219-SR 19 | Baugo Twp SS | 58-60 |
| | NA | Benton Twp SS | 213-215 |
| Olive St | NA | Wakarusa SS | 177-180 |
| Osborn Ave | NA | Cleveland Twp SS | 54-57 |
| Pacific St | NA | Elkhart SS | 89-112 |
| Park St | NA | Wakarusa SS | 177-180 |
| Parkwood Dr | NA | Nappanee SS | 196-200 |
| Pearl St | NA | Elkhart SS | 89-112 |
| Perkins Ave | NA | Concord Twp SS | 61-64 |
| Pike St | NA | Goshen HD | 134-151 |
| | NA | Goshen SS | 154-165 |
| Pl'sant Plain Ave | NA | Concord Twp SS | 61-64 |
| | NA | Elkhart SS | 89-112 |
| Plum St | NA | Elkhart SS | 89-112 |
| Plymouth Ave | NA | Goshen SS | 154-165 |
| Pottowatomi Dr | NA | Elkhart SS | 89-112 |
| Prairie St | NA | State-Division HD | 82-85 |
| | NA | Elkhart SS | 89-112 |
| Princeton St | NA | Elkhart SS | 89-112 |
| Prospect St | NA | Riverside/Prospect HD | 77-78 |
| | NA | Elkhart SS | 89-112 |
| Purl St | 3rd-9th Sts | Goshen HD | 134-151 |
| | 3rd-10th Sts | Goshen SS | 154-165 |
| Queen Ave | NA | Elkhart SS | 89-112 |
| | NA | Goshen SS | 154-165 |
| Railroad Ave | Elkhart St-Ind Ave | Wakarusa SS | 177-180 |
| Railroad St | Elm-Washington Sts | Millersburg SS | 128-129 |
| Rainbow Bend Blvd | NA | Cleveland Twp SS | 54-57 |
| | NA | Elkhart SS | 89-112 |
| Reynolds St | NA | Goshen SS | 154-165 |
| Rio Lindo Dr | NA | Cleveland Twp SS | 54-57 |
| Riverdale Dr | NA | Cleveland Twp SS | 54-57 |
| Riverside Blvd | Chicago-Berkey Aves | Goshen SS | 154-165 |
| Riverside Dr | NA | Beardsley Ave HD | 74-76 |
| | NA | Riverside/Prospect HD | 77-78 |
| R'view Manor Dr | NA | Cleveland Twp SS | 54-57 |
| Rosenberger St | Van Buren-Lincoln St | Nappanee SS | 196-200 |
| Roys Ave | NA | Elkhart SS | 89-112 |
| Scott St | Spring-Winslow Sts | Middlebury SS | 121-124 |
| Sherman St | NA | Elkhart SS | 89-112 |

| Street Name | Range | Twp(s)/SS(s)/HD(s) | Page No. |
|---|---|---|---|
| | Main-Lincoln Sts | Millersburg SS | 128-129 |
| Shore Lane Dr | NA | Osolo Twp SS | 51-53 |
| Simpson Ave | NA | Elkhart SS | 89-112 |
| Spring St | NA | Middlebury SS | 121-124 |
| | Waterford-Union Sts | Wakarusa SS | 177-180 |
| SR 4 | CR 31-Co Line Rd | Clinton Twp SS | 125-127 |
| | NA | Elkhart Twp SS | 130-133 |
| SR 13 | SR 4-CR 42 | Clinton Twp SS | 125-127 |
| | NA | York Twp SS | 42-43 |
| | NA | Middlebury Twp SS | 118-120 |
| | CR 42-US 33 | Benton Twp SS | 213-215 |
| SR 15 | NA | Washington Twp SS | 45-47 |
| | NA | Bristol SS | 48-50 |
| | NA | Jefferson Twp SS | 115-117 |
| | NA | Elkhart Twp SS | 130-133 |
| | NA | Waterford SS | 166-167 |
| SR 19 | NA | Osolo Twp SS | 51-53 |
| | St Joe R-CR 28 | Baugo Twp SS | 58-60 |
| | CR 28-CR 42 | Harrison Twp SS | 168-170 |
| | CR 28-CR 42 | Olive Twp SS | 171-173 |
| | Co Line Rd-US 6 | Locke Twp SS | 181-183 |
| | CR 42-US 6 | Union Twp SS | 184-187 |
| | NA | Elkhart SS | 89-112 |

**The Auditorium Building in Nappanee, c.1911.** *Photo courtesy of the Elkhart County Historical Museum*

# Glossary of Terms

**Applied ornamentation**    Any decorative feature added to a surface.

**Architrave**    The lower horizontal member of a classical *entablature* that also includes the *frieze* and *cornice*.

**Bay**    A repetitive division of a wall's surface, such as window and door openings.

**Board-and-batten** An exterior wall covering composed of vertical boards separated by gaps covered with thin boards called battens.

**Boxed eave**    An enclosed *eave*.

**Bracket**    An angled support member placed between a wall and an *eave*; mostly ornamental.

**Camelback truss**    A type of *Pratt truss* bridge having five slopes, with the top chord parallel to the bottom chord.

**Casement window**    A type of window whose hinge is located along its vertical edge and swings in or out.

**Character**    The distinctive qualities that make a building or structure what it is.

**Chevron**    An ornamental pattern shaped like a V. Also called a *zigzag*. Commonly found on Art Deco architecture.

**Chord**    An important component of a *truss bridge's* construction. Usually paired and horizontally-placed.

**Cohesive**    Describes the unity formed by the similarities of many distinct parts.

**Contextual**    A way of understanding a smaller segment by comparing it to a larger segment.

**Continuity**    An unbroken sequence, correlation, or bond.

**Corner post**    A vertical board that finishes a corner of a wood-sided building.

**Cornice**    A decorative *molding* that projects from the top of a wall where it meets the roofline. Also, the upper member of a classical *entablature* that also includes a *frieze* and *architrave*.

**Cornice return**    Found on a *gable* end where the *cornice* turns horizontally for a short segment. Common in Greek Revival architecture.

**Covenant**    A restrictive order attached to a property's deed that serves to protect the property from changes that would diminish its historical, architectural, or natural *character*.

**Crib**    Typically a small, wood-*frame* agricultural building used to store grain or corn.

**Cultural resources**    Human-made buildings, structures, works of art, memorials, etc., that a community has deemed significant for its age, beauty, innovation, or impact.

**Density**    The concentration of buildings within a certain area.

**Dormer window**    A window that protrudes from the *slope* of a roof that has side walls and a *hipped*, *gabled*, *shed*, or rounded roof.

**Double-hung window**    A type of window that has two vertically moving *sashes* that work independently and slide past each other.

**Drip molding**    Any *molding* that has the appearance of a drip. First designed to guide rainwater away from the structure.

**Easement**    A legal agreement that grants a partial interest in a historic property to a nonprofit organization in order to protect the property from changes that would compromise its historical, architectural, or natural *character*. An easement is permanently attached to a property's title and is binding on all future owners.

**Eave**    The portion of the roof that extends beyond the wall. Sometimes called an *overhang*.

**Economic restructuring**    A strategy of strengthening and encouraging business in downtown areas or historic commercial districts by identifying and meeting consumer demand.

**Elevation**    An exterior wall of a building.

**Ell**    A side wing of a building that is situated at a right angle to the main wing forming an "L" shape.

**Entablature**    A term derived from classical architecture to describe the *molding* that includes an *architrave*, *frieze*, and *cornice*, often spanning the expanse between columns.

**Extant**    Something that still exists.

**Fabric**    The materials that make up a community, place, or building.

**Façade**    The principal "face" or *elevation* of a building.

**Fenestration**    The arrangement of window openings in a building.

**Finial**    An ornamental object that tops architectural elements like *gables* or archways.

**Folk**    Designs derived from local building traditions that may or may not be executed by trained professionals.

**Footprint**    The shape of a building as seen from above.

**Frame construction**    A method of building in which the supporting structure is made of cut lumber.

**Frieze**    The middle member of a classical *entablature* that also includes an *architrave* and *cornice*.

**Frontage**    The portion of a building that faces the principal right-of-way, usually a street.

**Gable roof**    A roof having two *slopes* downward from a central ridge, forming a triangle on each end wall called a gable end. Common on gable-front structures.

**Gambrel roof**    A roof having a central ridge with a steeply-pitched slope paired with a low-pitched slope on each side of the ridge. Common in barns and Dutch Colonial Revival architecture.

**Workers pose in the entry of Metzler Shoe Company's former location in Nappanee, 1924.** *Photo courtesy of the Elkhart County Historical Museum*

**HABS**    An acronym for the Historic American Building Survey, a nationwide project that measures, draws, researches, and photographs historic buildings. Began in 1933 as a New Deal Project, the program was revived in 1966. HABS records are archived at the Library of Congress.

**HAER**    An acronym for Historic American Engineering Record, a nationwide project that measures, draws, researches, and photographs historic engineering structures such as bridges and dams. The program began in 1969. HAER records are archived at the Library of Congress.

**High-style**    Implies a design created by an architect or other trained professional and executed in an exemplary fashion.

**Hipped roof**    A roof having four slopes downward from a central ridge. Common on western bungalows.

**Historical resources**    A type of *cultural resource* that is significant for its age or contribution to local, state, or national history.

**Hood**    A molding that projects from the wall above a door or window opening used to deflect rainwater, but often decorative.

**Integral**    A portion of a building located beneath the roof line, such as a porch that does not extend beyond the roof line.

**Integrity**    The amount of authentic or original *fabric* that remains with a historic building or structure during its period of significance. Buildings with high integrity have few alterations.

**Knee brace**    A short piece of support lumber placed at an angle between a wall and an *eave*; usually decorative.

**Linear-plan**    A term used to describe a building having rooms or spaces laid out in a straight line. Such buildings have rectangular footprints.

**Macadam**    A type of early road invented by John Loudon McAdam that used broken stones laid in tight, symmetrical patterns and covered with small stones to create hard surfaces.

**Mansard roof**    A type of *hipped roof* having a steeply-pitched slope paired with a low-pitched or flat slope on each side of the building. Common in Second Empire architecture.

**Massed-plan**    A term used to describe a building that is more deep than wide. Such buildings usually have short *frontages* and extend deep into the lot.

**Molding**    A decorative element used to finish surfaces where two points meet, such as where a wall meets the roof or window and door openings.

**Mullion**    A *molding* that connects individual panes of glass within a window *sash*.

**National Register of Historic Places**    A list of properties maintained by the National Park Service that are significant at a local, state, or national level in areas of history, architecture, archeology, engineering, and/or culture.

**Non-contributing**    A property that is not historically significant based on National Register criteria.

**Overhang**    The portion of the roof that extends beyond the wall. Usually called an *eave*.

**Parapet**    A wall that extends above the roofline.

**Parker truss**    A type of *Pratt truss* bridge having an inclined top *chord* of more than five *slopes*.

**Pediment**    A triangular-shaped *molding* that sometimes caps doorways, windows, and *gable* ends. Common in Neoclassical and Colonial Revival architecture.

**Plan**    The shape of a building or structure as viewed from above; plans may be simple or complex depending on the building's shape and depth. Plan types include *linear, rectangular,* and *massed.*

**Portico**    A covered porch supported by a series of columns. Common in Neoclassical architecture.

**Pratt truss**    A metal *truss bridge* having horizontal and parallel *chords* whose strength relies on a series of interlocking triangles.

**Pressed metal**    Metal that is molded into shapes and used for *cornices,* window *hoods,* and other decorative *moldings.*

**Primary research**    Research that involves consulting information that has not been filtered through an interpretive source; examples include diaries, autobiographies, letters, newspaper articles, and census records.

**Prism glass**    A type of glass cut in small squares that deflect light and create prisms of color; commonly found in commercial building *transoms* and used as an additional light source.

**Rectangular plan**    A *plan* that is rectangular in shape; it may stand alone (simple) or be combined with other shapes to formed complex *plans.*

**Revolving loan fund**    A program by which an organization such as Historic Landmarks Foundation of Indiana loans money to a nonprofit organization to buy and/or rehabilitate endangered historic properties. Protective *covenants* are attached to the property's deed.

**Ribbon window**    A horizontal band of windows grouped together. Common in Prairie style architecture.

**Rubble stone**    Remnants of larger stones used for construction. Edges are not finished. May be used as a veneer or to construct fences or paths.

**Sash**    The moveable part of a window that holds the glass.

**Section 106**    A part of the National Historic Preservation Act of 1966 requiring federal agencies that fund any project that might affect *National Register*-eligible properties to evaluate that project's impact on said properties in conjunction with the State Historic Preservation Officer (SHPO), other interested individuals or organizations (called consulting parties), and occasionally with the Advisory Council on Historic Preservation. The agency must give the SHPO and the Advisory Council a reasonable opportunity to comment on the project in an effort to minimize any negative impacts on eligible properties. A type of environmental review.

**Secondary research**    Research that involves consulting information that has been filtered through an interpretive source; examples include textbooks, encyclopedias, biographies, and documentaries.

**Shed roof**    A roof having one *slope.*

**Slope**    A slanted roof surface.

**Surround**    A border, usually made of *molding,* that frames a panel, door, or window.

**Tracery**    Interlaced window *mullions* in the Gothic Revival style.

**Transom**    A short window located above a door or display window.

**Truss bridge**    A type of metal bridge that consists of parallel top and bottom *chords,* connected by a series of diagonal beams spanning the bridge's length that add strength.

**Vernacular**    A common way of building that is not designed by an architect. Often constructed by local carpenters who may or may not have consulted pattern books.

**Warren truss**    A type of *truss bridge* composed of parallel, flat top and bottom *chords,* with inclined end posts and diagonal interior posts.

**Zigzag**    Another term for *chevron.* Commonly found on Art Deco architecture.

**Carriages line Main Street in downtown Nappanee, c.1911.** *Photo courtesy of the Elkhart County Historical Museum*